# PSYCHOLOGY OF MEMORY

# PSYCHOLOGY OF EMOTIONS, MOTIVATIONS AND ACTIONS

Additional books in this series can be found on Nova's website
under the Series tab.

Additional E-books in this series can be found on Nova's website
under the E-book tab.

# NEUROSCIENCE RESEARCH PROGRESS

Additional books in this series can be found on Nova's website
under the Series tab.

Additional E-books in this series can be found on Nova's website
under the E-book tab.

# PSYCHOLOGY OF MEMORY

### DANNIE M. HENDRIX
### AND
### ORVAL HOLCOMB
### EDITORS

**Nova Science Publishers, Inc.**
*New York*

**Library of Congress Cataloging-in-Publication Data**

Psychology of memory / editors, Dannie M. Hendrix and Orval Holcomb.
    p. cm.
  Includes index.
  ISBN 978-1-61942-633-7 (hbk.)
  1. Memory.  I. Hendrix, Dannie M. II. Holcomb, Orval.
  BF371.P882 2011
  153.1'2--dc23
                          2011050475

*Published by Nova Science Publishers, Inc.* † *New York*

# CONTENTS

# PREFACE

In this book, the authors present current research in the study of the psychology of memory. Topics discussed include verbal association priming and episodic and semantic memory; working memory span tasks; capacity limits in visual short-term memory; processes of conscious and unconscious memory and prospective memory in children.

Chapter 1 - Two previously unrelated words (e.g., WINDOW-reason) can be episodically associated within a memory experiment. Several verbal new association priming paradigms have been developed to measure how the newly formed verbal associations modulate participants' performance in implicit memory tests; that is, when they are not aware their memories are being assessed. In this chapter, the authors review the literature and investigate whether this verbal new association priming can occur automatically is critically evaluated, with an emphasis on studies involving one or more than one of the following methodologies: test-awareness questionnaires, study intentionality manipulation, divided attention manipulation, functional dissociations, process dissociation procedure, amnesic research, neuroimaging techniques, and speeded implicit memory tests. The authors summarize the findings of these studies in tabular format, discuss the potential methodological concerns, elaborate the implication of verbal new association priming for the necessity to postulate a distinction between episodic memory and semantic memory, and suggest some future directions for this area of memory research.

Chapter 2 - Throughout the last century, numerous advances have been achieved in the field of memory research that have significantly increased our understanding of the brain structures and mechanisms underlying memory processes. Particularly, over the past few decades a great deal of attention has been devoted to the different ways by which memories can be modulated. For example, emotion is known to be a potent memory modulator, as emotionally arousing experiences have been shown to be better remembered than neutral ones. Moreover, stress and stress hormones have also been shown to modulate memory in complex ways. Given the relevance of emotions and stress in the development and maintenance of certain clinical conditions that involve at their core memory problems, such as post-traumatic stress disorder (PTSD) and depression, there is an impending need to further our current understanding of the roles these two aspects play on the memory problems behind these conditions. As a means to address these scientific inquiries, the present chapter aims to synthesize the current general literature about memory in relation to emotion and stress, in order to provide a perspective on how this body of knowledge could be translated to the clinical treatment for memory-affected conditions. The first section of this book chapter will cover the main memory categories, the stages underlying memory formation, the brain areas involved within each of those processes, as well as the modulating role of emotion on memory. In the second section, the chapter will detail the effects of stress and stress hormones on the modulation of memories. Finally, the last section will address potential new directions that could guide future memory studies, such as accounting for the role of sex differences, as well as through the development of novel, ecologically valid memory paradigms. As such, the authors suggest that by considering the previously described variables in innovative memory paradigms that closely match reality, future memory research will translate more effectively the knowledge generated through these methods into the development and improvement of therapeutic approaches for memory-related clinical conditions.

Chapter 3 - The importance of the medial temporal lobes (MTL) for declarative memory, i.e., the memory for events (episodic memory) and facts (semantic memory) was first highlighted by the case of the famous and well-studied patient H.M. He showed severe deficits in remembering his past and was unable to learn new facts and memorize events, that happened after undergoing brain surgery to remove most parts of his medial temporal lobes (MTL) in 1953. Semantic Facts (semantic memory) and autobiographical events (episodic memory) together comprise the declarative memory. Interestingly, his performance in procedural memory (where mainly motor skills are stored and working memory (a system that maintains and stores information in the short term) was not affected; i.e.,. H.M. could learn new motor skills but he could not remember that he had learned them. Decades of research have since revealed a network including the medial temporal lobes, in particular the hippocampus, but also the prefrontal cortex and medial and lateral parietal cortex to be involved in remembering events of one's past; i.e., episodic memory. Previously stored declarative information can be tested using different procedures. During *Free Recall* a subject would be asked to study a list of words and then, some time later, to recall as many words that they can remember. Free Recall strongly depends on an intact episodic memory. In *Recognition* tasks subjects are asked to decide whether a given item was previously presented at a list of items (old) or whether it was not presented in the original list (new). Surprisingly, H.M. had comparable recognition rates to healthy controls, when the procedures to assess recognition were adapted to his skills (for instance when he could view pictures longer before the recognition response, Freed and Corkin, 1988; Freed, Corkin, and Cohen, 1987). This raised the question if recognition is not only based on episodic memory, like free recall, but relies on an independent process involving other brain structures besides the MTL. Models of recognition memory that state two independent processes, recollection and familiarity, might give an explanation of the findings in H.M.s recognition performance. A person is able to judge whether the recognition of a previously learned item is based on a feeling of familiarity that the item was seen before, or because he or she remembers additional details about the study event, such as when or where it occurred (episodic memory). Recollection sometimes is referred to as contextual memory or relational based recognition, whereas familiarity is called non-contextual memory or item-based recognition (not to be confused with semantic memory). Thus, given this dissociation in recognition memory, patients with severe amnesia, as a result of selective brain damage in the MTL, might still have almost intact recognition memory, maintaining some of their quality of life. Extensive research has studied the nature of recollection and familiarity and revealed anatomical and functional substrates of recognition memory in the brain. This research basically developed two opposing views about the relationship between recollection and familiarity and about the association with hippocampal function.

In this chapter the authors will review this debate and the authors will present evidence, by others and their own research, in favor for the two process assumption.

Before the authors will introduce the two major opposing recognition memory models, the authors want to give an overview about different procedures to measure recognition memory, in the next section. This might be helpful in understanding how the models predict the empirical data.

Chapter 4 - The medial temporal lobe (MTL) of the brain is crucial for recognition memory, as shown by the severe memory deficits found in aging, and in patients with amnesia who have damage to this brain region. Recognition memory is thought to rely on two retrieval processes: the familiarity and the recollection processes, that are differentially affected in aging or following MTL damage (recollection is impaired while familiarity is relatively spared), and the characteristics of these processes have been discussed since the time of Aristotle. Familiarity is defined as a vague feeling of 'déjà-vu', for example when one recognizes a person but cannot identify this person by name. In contrast, recollection requires the integration of several features belonging to the event to be recognized, for example the identity of the person taking part to this event, and the spatial or temporal contexts of the event. Two major controversies currently fuel the debates in human recognition memory: 1) whether the familiarity and the recollection processes are truly qualitatively distinct processes, or whether they reflect different memory strengths of the same process; and 2) whether both processes share the same neural substrate: the hippocampus (HIP), or whether the HIP supports recollection only, and the cortex surrounding the HIP, the parahippocampal region (ParaHIP), supports familiarity. These conflicting findings are mainly based on the interpretation of Receiver Operating Characteristic (ROC) functions by the two leading models of recognition memory used to analyze memory performance in humans. Indeed, those models report either a selective recollection deficit following hippocampal damage (the dual process model), or an impairment of both the recollection and the familiarity processes (the one process model). This discrepancy is suggested to stem, at least in part, from the limited spatial resolution of standard human imaging techniques, which does not allow for a precise identification of the extent of the MTL damage in amnesic patients, and prevents a clear assessment of whether the damage is truly restricted to the HIP, or whether it also extends to the adjacent ParaHIP, which could in turn explain the additional familiarity deficits reported in some studies. In this chapter, after introducing those two main models of recognition memory, the author will first report how the authors developed new translational paradigms (human standard recognition memory tasks adapted to rats) using  rats to investigate whether the HIP supports only recollection, or both processes. Second, the author will report how the authors addressed the first controversy in this field: whether familiarity and recollection are distinct processes, by evaluating memory performance of control rats with those new translational paradigms. Then, the authors will show how they tackled the second major controversy in human recognition memory: whether the HIP supports selectively the recollection process, or both processes, by studying memory performance of rats with hippocampal damage with their new animal ROC paradigms across memory demands. Finally, the author will present recent data that extend beyond those controversies, and aim at elucidating whether the ParaHIP is functionally segregated in terms of its involvement in the familiarity and the recollection processes. In summary, studies mentioned in this chapter provide compelling evidence that the recollection and the familiarity processes are qualitatively distinct processes, that the HIP supports recollection (and not familiarity), and that the ParaHIP is functionally segregated in terms of familiarity and recollection.

Chapter 5 - Measures of working memory, requiring both the processing and storage of information, are widely used across a number of domains of psychology. This is in part because working memory scores serve as useful predictors of cognitive skills such as comprehension, problem solving and intelligence. However, there are no standard administration and scoring procedures for working memory tasks. For example, some researchers administer set sizes in ascending order, whilst others prefer a randomized order. Some investigators assign scores of the total number of stimuli in perfectly recalled trials, whilst others calculate the proportion of stimuli recalled correctly throughout the entire task. The current chapter begins with a brief overview of working memory span tasks, and then reviews a number of variations in task structure, administration and scoring procedures. The focus is on the effects of these variations on working memory scores and the predictive ability of working memory tasks. The practical implications of the findings are described, for instance working memory tasks are more predictive of higher order cognition if set sizes are presented in a randomized order and if proportion scoring is used. The findings are then discussed in relation to current theoretical accounts of working memory. It is suggested that the effects of many of the variations in administration and scoring reflect the degree which scores capture variance from active control or executive-attentional resources. More generally, it is suggested that researchers need to consider administration and scoring methods when employing working memory span tasks.

Chapter 6 - Visual short-term memory (VSTM) is the system that temporarily holds relevant visual information that is useful for a particular ongoing cognitive task. Most studies on VSTM have particularly focused on its storage capacity. Even though they have not yet resolved the fundamental question of why there is a capacity limit in the first place, those studies have converged to the conclusion that VSTM is extremely limited in capacity, holding only about three to four objects simultaneously. In this chapter, the author will review the different techniques that have been used to reveal the capacity limits in VSTM as well as the different factors that have been shown to influence this capacity. This review will consider both behavioural and neuroimaging work.

Chapter 7 - Conscious and unconscious forms of memory are explored based on results of the studies in which the two forms of memory within a test were separated by either the *process-dissociation* (for explicit tests) or the *metacognition-based dissociation* (for implicit tests) procedure.

The results across explicit and implicit tests suggest that conscious memory in a test is not only driven by the nature of the test but also driven conceptually, whereas its unconscious counterpart is driven strictly by the nature of the test itself.

Besides, the conscious memory benefits from a study condition to the extent that the memory driving process recapitulates the encoding process engaged in that study condition.

In contrast, its unconscious counterpart benefits to the extent that the cognitive environments, contents of preexisting association, or categorical structures at test and at study match to activate the same type of information (e.g., visual, lexical, or semantic) about a memory item.

Chapter 8 - Prospective memory refers to remembering to perform a delayed intention such as returning a library book. In this chapter, the authors focus on the role of motivation in prospective memory in children. The authors suggest two theses, specifically that motivation improves prospective memory performance in children and that it is particularly influential for younger children. A review of past research reveals support for both theses although research on motivation, and its relationship to age, in children's prospective memory is sparse. The authors report the results of a study of younger (age 7-8 years) and older (age 10-11 years) children in which parents were asked to complete diary reports for two weeks, describing their children's real-life prospective memory tasks on school days. The authors chose a naturalistic design because little is known about real prospective memory tasks children have and variables that affect their performance. The authors' results provide support for both of the central theses of this chapter. That is, prospective memory performance was better for tasks regarded as more important, and older children outperformed younger children on low importance tasks but not on high importance tasks. The authors conclude that motivational variables need to be considered in theoretical models of prospective memory in childhood, and the authors propose extending one motivational-cognitive model of prospective memory to explain prospective memory in children.

Chapter 9 - The research on prospective memory (ProM) has generated many controversies. Many of these controversies can be traced to conceptual and methodological issues including a failure to distinguish between ProM proper vs. vigilance/monitoring; use of poor, unreliable, and inefficient measurement methods (i.e., binary success/failure measures); ceiling effects; low sample sizes; and low statistical power. In this chapter, the authors examine the following questions: Does the delay between ProM instructions and the appearance of the first cue decrease performance on ProM tasks as predicted from the theoretical distinction between ProM proper and vigilance/monitoring? Does the instruction to ongoing task delay reduce ProM performance? Does larger numbers of ProM cues convert ostensibly ProM proper task into vigilance/monitoring task? Is the instruction to ongoing task (IO) delay more important than the ongoing task start to the appearance of the first cue (OC) delay? The results of three studies (two quantitative reviews of previous literature and one experimental study) indicate that delays decrease ProM performance and are important for flushing the previously formed plan from examinees' consciousness, that larger numbers of ProM cues convert ProM tasks to vigilance/monitoring tasks, and that the IO delay appears to be more or at least as important as the OC delay. The authors' third study also indicates that the continuous measures of ProM are superior to the binary measures of ProM in widespread use; the continuous measures are more efficient, reliable, valid, and less likely affected by ceiling effects. The binary success/fail measures of ProM should be abandoned in favor of the continuous measures of ProM and, to measure ProM proper rather than vigilance/monitoring, researchers should include IO and OC delays to flush the previously formed plan from consciousness.

In: Psychology of Memory
Editors: Dannie M. Hendrix and Orval Holcomb

ISBN: 978-1-61942-633-7
© 2012 Nova Science Publishers, Inc.

*Chapter 1*

# CAN NOVEL ASSOCIATIONS BE AUTOMATICALLY ACCESSED IN MEMORY? A REVIEW OF VERBAL NEW ASSOCIATION PRIMING STUDIES

## *Chi-Shing Tse and Xiaoping Pu*

The Chinese University of Hong Kong,
Hong Kong, China

## ABSTRACT

Two previously unrelated words (e.g., WINDOW-reason) can be episodically associated within a memory experiment. Several verbal new association priming paradigms have been developed to measure how the newly formed verbal associations modulate participants' performance in implicit memory tests; that is, when they are not aware their memories are being assessed. In this chapter, we review the literature and investigate whether this verbal new association priming can occur automatically is critically evaluated, with an emphasis on studies involving one or more than one of the following methodologies: test-awareness questionnaires, study intentionality manipulation, divided attention manipulation, functional dissociations, process dissociation procedure, amnesic research, neuroimaging techniques, and speeded implicit memory tests. We summarize the findings of these studies in tabular format, discuss the potential methodological concerns, elaborate the implication of verbal new association priming for the necessity to postulate a distinction between episodic memory and semantic memory, and suggest some future directions for this area of memory research.

**Keywords**: Associative Memory; Episodic Memory; Implicit Memory; New Association; Priming; Verbal Materials

# INTRODUCTION

An association in memory can be regarded as a relation between two stored concepts. When we meet a friend, we can remember her name via recognizing her face. When we learn a second language, we need to develop associations between the concepts or words in our first language and the words of this new language. The encoding, storage and retrieval of a novel association between two unrelated concepts, be they represented in words, pictures, objects or faces, are among the most basic mechanisms of knowledge acquisition. Two concepts are said to be associated if the presentation of one brings the second to the rememberer's awareness (Deese, 1965). For example, seeing a dog can lead us to think of a cat. However, for those associated concepts that are well-learned and stored in one's semantic memory (e.g., *dog-cat*), the activation from one concept to its related concepts does not always occur with the rememberer's awareness and intention. In this case, the activation is said to occur automatically (cf. Neely, 1977; Posner & Snyder, 1975). A question then emerges: is the rememberer necessarily aware of the retrieval of an association that is just freshly formed between two previously unrelated concepts, such as *dog* and *table* when they are presented close together spatially and temporally within the same memory episode? Can such a novel episodic association between two unrelated concepts be automatically accessed without the rememberer's intention? In this chapter, we evaluate the studies for the implicit retrieval of new associations and whether this retrieval is automatic and *truly* implicit (i.e., occurs without the rememberer's awareness).

# HISTORICAL NOTES ON THE CONCEPT OF A "NEW ASSOCIATION" IN HUMAN MEMORY

The concept of an "association" is almost as old as the human endeavor to understand how the mind works. Statements regarding the importance of associations and the manner in which they are acquired can be traced back to the Greek philosophers (Crowder, 1976). Aristotle formulated three laws governing the learning of new associations—similarity, contrast, and contiguity. The notion of associations was then taken up by the British Associationists (e.g., James Mill and David Hume) who regarded the association as a basic element of mental activities from which new concepts are formed. In accordance with their laws of association, all consciousness is presumed to originate from a combination of certain simple elements derived from our sensory experiences. When two sensations (e.g., the color word *blue* and digit *8*) are repeatedly encountered contiguously in time and/or space, an association can be developed between them in our memory. James (1890/1950) regarded this as the basis of association. In 1896, one of his students, Mary Whiton Calkins, introduced the paired-associate learning paradigm to empirically study memory for new associations. In this paradigm, people first learn color word and digit pairs (e.g., blue-8), with both members of each pair being simultaneously presented. In a subsequent cued recall test, they are given the color word (e.g., blue) and need to recall the associated digit (i.e., 8). Since then, this paired-associate learning procedure has been widely used to assess peoples' abilities to retrieve items or new associations in explicit and implicit memory tests. Explicit and implicit memory tests differ in the use of an instruction that does (i.e., explicit tests) or does not (i.e., implicit tests) require participants to intentionally retrieve the prior study episodes of the items or associations (Schacter, 1987). In an implicit memory test, participants are asked to identify, generate an answer, or make a judgment to a test item or pair that has or has not been presented in the study phase, when they are not explicitly told (and presumably do not notice) that their memories for the prior study episodes are being assessed. Although memory for new associations has traditionally been assessed in explicit memory tests, such as cued recall and episodic recognition over the past 30 years (see Crowder, 1976, Chapter 12; Murdock, 1982, for historical reviews), it has also been assessed by implicit memory tests, which are the focus of the current chapter.

Before evaluating whether previous studies on the implicit memory of new associations has successfully demonstrated automatic *new association priming*[1], we first provide the scope of the experiments that are to be reviewed in this chapter, define the terms used in a typical new association priming experiment, and point out the importance of assessing the automaticity of new association priming.

## SCOPE OF THE CURRENT REVIEW

Due to voluminous research on new association priming, we select the to-be-reviewed experiments based on the following criteria. (a) Because the central interest of the current review was *verbal* new association priming, we exclude studies concerning new associations for perceptual features (e.g., color and shape, DeSchepper & Treisman, 1996; face configuration, Bentin & Moscovitch, 1988; motor movement, Ellmore, Stouffer, & Nadel, 2008 ), letters (within non-words, Dorfman, 1994), text re-reading (e.g., Monti, Gabrieli, Wilson et al., 1997), response sequences (e.g., Stadler & Frensch, 1998), syntactic structures (e.g., Melinger & Dobel, 2005) and evaluative conditioning (e.g., de Houwer, Thomas, & Baeyens, 2001). (b) We exclude experiments that used explicit memory tests *unless* the researchers also tested the effect of novel verbal associations in implicit memory tests, because as discussed below, the functional dissociation in explicit vs. implicit memory performance can shed light on the automaticity of new association priming. (c) All of the new association priming studies to be reviewed involved the participants' first language. Although some priming studies (e.g., Jiang & Forster, 2001) have involved non-fluent bilinguals, none of them required monolinguals or bilinguals to *learn* a second language vocabulary within the experiment and then do an implicit memory test (e.g., translation priming) to test the priming of new association between words in their first and second languages.

---

[1] The new association priming in prior implicit memory research has been called associative repetition priming (e.g., Goshen-Gottstein & Moscovitch, 1995a), repetition priming for novel associations (e.g., Musen & Squire, 1993), or episodic priming (e.g., Neely & Durgunoglu, 1985). We prefer to use "new association priming" because the label "*episodic* priming" might pre-suppose that the mechanisms producing the new association priming differ from those producing semantic priming. The label "*associative* repetition priming" might refer to the repetition priming of the *new* association as well as the pre-existing associations (e.g., *dog-cat*), which is beyond the scope of our chapter. To distinguish the repetition priming produced by new episodic associations from those by new episodic plus old semantic associations, we label repetition priming for pre-existing associations as *old association priming*.

# DEFINITION OF CRITICAL TERMS

In this section, we define the critical terms (all in *italic*) used in the subsequent sections. An effect mediated by one's implicit memory, such as *item repetition priming*, must occur unintentionally. Participants are presumably unaware that (a) they are retrieving the previously acquired information and (b) their memories are being tested when they perform an implicit memory test. item repetition priming occurs when the study of an item results in faster reaction times (RTs) or fewer errors to the re-presentation of the studied, relative to non-studied, item in the test. The facilitation in RTs/accuracies can be attributed to the re-activation of the lexical or semantic representations of items that have once been exposed in the study phase (cf. Bower, 1996). Similarly, new association priming (i.e., priming of a *new verbal association*) occurs when the study of a novel association between two unrelated words leads in faster RTs or more accurate responses to the re-presentation of the studied, relative to non-studied, novel association in an implicit memory test. The facilitation in RTs/accuracies can be attributed to the re-activation of a novel association newly formed between the lexical/semantic representations of two items in the study phase (cf. Bower), although the detailed mechanism of how the new association can be re-activated has not been clearly specified in prior new association priming studies. Table 1 presents the implicit memory tests that have commonly been used in new association priming studies. Table 2 presents the conditions in a typical new association priming experiment. Consider the word-stem completion, the most commonly used implicit memory test in new association priming research. In this task, participants study word pairs in a study phase and then complete test stems (usually the first three letters of a 5- to 10-letter word) with the first word that comes to mind. The item repetition priming, new association priming, or old association priming is determined by the performance for the test stems when they are presented in different *test contexts* in an implicit memory test. After the unrelated word pair (REASON-house) is studied, new association priming is said to occur if the test stem (ho___) is more likely completed with the target (house) when the test stem appears with a studied *context word/prime* (REASON-ho___)[2], which has been studied together with the target (*intact pairs*), than when it appears with the studied context word (OBSERVE-ho___), which has not been studied together with the target (*UR-a recombined pairs,* see Table 2). (The appropriateness of using different types of extralist and intralist primes is discussed below.) Because both primes and targets in these intact and recombined pairs have been previously studied, the performance advantage for the intact pairs over the recombined pairs can only be explained by an implicit retrieval of the new association. Thus, the difference in performance between the intact and recombined pairs measures the priming of new episodic associations of the unrelated word pairs.[3] The item repetition priming occurs if the probability of correctly completing the studied target for a test stem for the recombined pair (OBSERVE-ho___) is higher than baseline performance of correctly completing a non-studied target in the test stem (REASON-ho___) when neither the target (house) nor its context word (REASON) has been

---

[2] The terms context word and prime are used interchangeably in this chapter.

[3] Strictly speaking, it is necessary to validate that these intact and recombined pairs had *equally weak (or no) pre-experimental associations* by having them be rated by naïve judges for their associative strength (cf. Nelson, McEvoy, & Schreiber, 1998). However, to our knowledge, only one study (Marsolek, Schacter, & Nicholas, 1996) has used this stringent criterion to prepare the stimuli.

studied. This kind of non-studied pair is called a *new pair*. For the sake of brevity, we refer to the typical repetition priming obtained in other non-new association priming studies as item repetition priming.[4] In addition to unrelated word pairs, some new association priming studies (e.g., Graf & Schacter, 1985) have included related word pairs. In these studies, after a related word pair (WINDOW-house) is studied, *old association priming* occurs if the test stem (ho___) is more likely completed with the target (house) when the test stem appears with the studied related context word (WINDOW-ho___) in intact pairs, than when the test stem appears with the studied related context word (DOOR-ho___) in *R-a* recombined pairs (see Table 2). Hence, this old association priming measures the priming of *episodic* associations of the related word pairs beyond their semantic relatedness.

In an implicit memory test, when participants (1) become aware of the relationship between the study phase and the test (e.g., recognizing that some of test items have been previously studied) *and then* (2) intentionally retrieve the items from study lists to boost their priming effects, *explicit contamination* (cf. McKone & Slee, 1997) is said to occur. According to Posner and Snyder's (1975, see also Neely, 1977; Neely & Kahan, 2001) definition of automaticity, if new association priming occurs automatically, it should be produced by fast-acting, capacity-free, and strategy-free activation spreading from the prime to its *episodically* related target. Similar to semantic priming research,[5] whether the new association priming occurs automatically might depend on how rapidly the activation spread across the novel associations. When the *stimulus-onset asynchrony* (SOA) between a context word (i.e., prime) and a target is shorter than 300 ms, participants might not have sufficient time to trigger the *explicit-memory retrieval strategy* (similar to intentional retrieval strategy—directly retrieving the studied targets to perform the implicit memory test, see *Speeded implicit memory test* section for more discussions). The effect observed under this circumstance should be relatively strategy-free and could be regarded as automatic. The relationship between automaticity and explicit contamination for the new association priming is asymmetrically complementary—if new association priming automatically occurs, it is no longer explicitly contaminated; but if new association priming is explicitly contaminated, it may or may not be automatic because it is the second step of explicit contamination (the use of an intentional retrieval strategy, cf. Tse & Neely, 2005) that violates the automaticity of new association priming. Based on this logic, participants' awareness of the study-test relationship might not always trigger them to use *strategies* when they do the implicit memory test. As to be discussed below, although several procedures (e.g., a speeded task) have been used to lessen explicit contamination or at least discourage the participants from using intentional retrieval strategies in the test, none of them is immune to methodological and theoretical criticisms.

---

[4] However, the item repetition priming obtained in the new association priming paradigm should not be compared with those in non-new association priming studies since most of new association priming studies rotate the targets, but not the studied context words, across all intact, recombined *and* new pairs. That is, they counterbalance the studied context words only across the intact and recombined pairs, but not the new pairs. Some earlier new association priming studies (e.g., Graf & Schacter, 1985) even used another group of participants to determine the *baseline* (the proportion of correct completion for new pairs) for measuring item repetition priming. To our knowledge, no study has examined whether and how the confound between the study status of context words and the test context (intact/recombined vs. new) affects item repetition priming.

[5] Semantic priming occurs when responses to a target (cat) are faster and/or more accurate in a lexical decision task or a naming task when that target is preceded by a related prime (MEOW) than by an unrelated prime (BUMP) (Meyer & Schvaneveldt, 1971).

# Table 1. New association priming paradigms

| Implicit Task | Study Item | Test Item | Participant's Task | Response Modality | Explicit Memory Test Satisfies RIC | Dependent Measure |
|---|---|---|---|---|---|---|
| Single-Item/ Double-Item Lexical Decision (Perceptual) | Unrelated word pair (WINDOW-reason) Presented in isolation or embedded in sentences/ Sim or Seq | Context Word (WINDOW) + Target (reason)/ Continuous/ Sim or Seq | Single-Item: To judge whether the target is a correctly spelled word/ Double-Item: To judge whether the context word and target are correctly spelled words | Identification | Speeded Associative Recognition | RTs and errors of lexical decisions to targets or context words + targets |
| Perceptual Identification (Perceptual) | Same as above | Forward Mask (######) + Context Word (WINDOW) + Target (reason) + Backward Mask (######)/ Sim or Seq | Read aloud the context word and/or target | Production | No | Proportion of correctly identified targets or context words + targets |
| Word-Stem Completion (Perceptual) | Same as above | Context Word (WINDOW) + Test-Stem (rea___)/ Sim or Seq | Read silently the context word and complete the test stem with the first word that comes to mind | Production | Stem-Cued Recall | Proportion of correctly completed test stems |
| Word-Fragment Completion (Perceptual) | Same as above | Context Word (WINDOW) + Test-Fragment (r_ a_o_)/ Sim or Seq | Read silently the context word and complete the test fragment with the first word that comes to mind | Production | Fragment-Cued Recall | Proportion of correctly completed test fragments |
| Picture-Label Same/Different Judgment [a] (Perceptual) | Same Pair: A picture of a grape + label *grape*/ Different Pair: A picture of a potato + label *cow*/ Sim | Continuous (see Note a)/ Sim | Decide whether the picture and the label refer to the same concept (i.e., same-pair) or different concepts (i.e., different-pair) | Identification | Speeded Associative Recognition | RTs and errors of same/different judgment (based on "different" response) |
| Re-reading/ Naming (unrelated word pairs) (Perceptual) | Unrelated word pairs (WINDOW-reason)/ Seq | Context Word (WINDOW) + Target (reason)/ Continuous/ Seq | Read aloud the context word and/or target | Identification | Speeded Associative Recognition | RTs to correctly read a short list of context words + targets |

| Implicit Task | Study Item | Test Item | Participant's Task | Response Modality | Explicit Memory Test Satisfies RIC | Dependent Measure |
|---|---|---|---|---|---|---|
| Re-reading/ Naming (compound nonword)[b] (Perceptual) | Unrelated words combined to form nonwords (fishdust, bookwrist)/ Sim | Continuous (see Note b)/ Sim | Read aloud compound non-words | Identification | Speeded Associative Recognition | RTs to correctly read a short list of context words + targets |
| Category Exemplar Generation (Conceptual) | Unrelated word pairs presented in isolation (MOSS-newspaper)/ Sim | Context Word + Question e.g., MOSS, first 4 exemplars of reading materials?/ Sim | Read silently context word and produce (or a couple) exemplars that come to mind | Production | Cued Recall | Proportion of correctly generated targets |
| Free Association (Conceptual) | Unrelated word pairs presented in isolation (WINDOW-reason)/Sim | Context Word Old Context (WINDOW) + New Context (JUMP) | Read silently context word and generate the first (or a couple) word come to mind | Production | Cued Recall | Proportion of correctly generated targets |
| Synonym Judgment[c] (Conceptual) | Unrelated word pairs presented in isolation (WINDOW-reason)/ Sim or Seq | Context Word (WINDOW) + Target (reason)/ Sim | Decide whether the context word and target refer to the same meaning | Identification | Speeded Associative Recognition | RTs and errors of synonym judgment to context word-target (based on "no" responses) |
| Animacy Decision (Conceptual) | Same as above | Context Word (WINDOW) + Target (reason)/ Sim | Decide whether the target refers to a living or non-living object | Identification | Speeded Associative Recognition | RTs and errors of animacy decision to context word-target |
| Relatedness Judgment[c] (Conceptual) | Same as above | Context Word (WINDOW) + Target (reason)/ Sim | Decide whether the context word and target are semantically related | Identification | Speeded Associative Recognition | RTs and errors of relatedness judgment to context word-target (based on "no" responses) |

# Table 1. (Continued)

| Implicit Task | Study Item | Test Item | Participant's Task | Response Modality | Explicit Memory Test Satisfies RIC | Dependent Measure |
|---|---|---|---|---|---|---|
| Picture-Label Same/Different Category Judgment [a] (Conceptual) | Same Pair: A picture of a grape + label *orange*/ Different Pair: A picture of a potato + label *cow* | Continuous (see Note a)/ Sim | Decide whether the picture and label refer to concepts in the same (i.e., same-pair) or different categories (i.e., different-pair) | Identification | Speeded Associative Recognition | RTs and errors of same/different category judgment (based on "no" response) |

*Note:* In the Study Item column, Seq = the context word and target are presented sequentially (one at a time on the screen), Sim = the context word and target are presented simultaneously (at the same time on the screen). In the Test Item column, see Table 2 for different types of test pairs, except see the following Notes a-b. "Continuous" means that in some experiments using the labeled tasks, participants make responses to all study and test trials with the same response requirement (e.g., lexical decision). Trials in the study and test blocks are continuously presented (i.e., without a break in between), such that participants cannot distinguish the structure of study and test lists. See text for the definition of identification vs. production response modalities. In the Explicit Memory Test Satisfies RIC column, all of the test items in the explicit memory tests that satisfy the retrieval intentionality criterion (see text) are displayed in the same way as those in the corresponding implicit memory tests; in speeded associative recognition participants are presented a test pair and decide whether the two words in this pair have been studied together in the study phase. In the Dependent Measure column, the findings in some tasks such as lexical decision were reported for two dependent measures, reactions times (RTs) and % errors. Because many % error measures produce ceiling effects, unless a speed-accuracy tradeoff occurred, we only discuss and tabulate the RT data for these tasks in this chapter.

[a] In a picture-label same-different judgment task, the types of test pairs include intact same-pairs (a picture of a grape + label *grape*), new same-pairs (a picture of a dog + label *dog*), intact different-pairs (a picture of a potato + label *cow*), recombined different-pairs (a picture of a pencil + label *cow*), new different-pairs (a picture of a dish + label *coffee*). In both the picture-label same-different judgment task and the picture-label same-different category judgment task, the typical finding is *negative* new association priming (i.e., RTs to intact different-pairs were *slower* than those to recombined different-pairs), which indicates that participants' *familiarity* with the new association in previously judged different pairs interfered with their producing "different" responses to the repeated intact different-pairs, relative to the recombined different-pairs.

[b] The types of test pairs include intact compound non-word (fishdust), recombined compound non-word (fishwrist), and new compound non-word (coffeelamp).

[c] In a synonym judgment or a relatedness judgment task, the typical finding is *negative* new association priming (i.e., RTs to intact pairs were *slower* than those to recombined pairs), which indicates that the participants' *familiarity* with the new association in previously judged unrelated pairs interfered with their producing "unrelated" responses to the repeated intact unrelated pairs, relative to the recombined unrelated pairs.

In an implicit memory test, when participants (1) become aware of the relationship between the study phase and the test (e.g., recognizing that some of test items have been previously studied) *and then* (2) intentionally retrieve the items from study lists to boost their priming effects, *explicit contamination* (cf. McKone & Slee, 1997) is said to occur. According to Posner and Snyder's (1975, see also Neely, 1977; Neely & Kahan, 2001) definition of automaticity, if new association priming occurs automatically, it should be produced by fast-acting, capacity-free, and strategy-free activation spreading from the prime to its *episodically* related target. Similar to semantic priming research,[6] whether the new association priming occurs automatically might depend on how rapidly the activation spread across the novel associations. When the *stimulus-onset asynchrony* (SOA) between a context word (i.e., prime) and a target is shorter than 300 ms, participants might not have sufficient time to trigger the *explicit-memory retrieval strategy* (similar to intentional retrieval strategy—directly retrieving the studied targets to perform the implicit memory test, see *Speeded implicit memory test* section for more discussions). The effect observed under this circumstance should be relatively strategy-free and could be regarded as automatic. The relationship between automaticity and explicit contamination for the new association priming is asymmetrically complementary—if new association priming automatically occurs, it is no longer explicitly contaminated; but if new association priming is explicitly contaminated, it may or may not be automatic because it is the second step of explicit contamination (the use of an intentional retrieval strategy, cf. Tse & Neely, 2005) that violates the automaticity of new association priming. Based on this logic, participants' awareness of the study-test relationship might not always trigger them to use *strategies* when they do the implicit memory test. As to be discussed below, although several procedures (e.g., a speeded task) have been used to lessen explicit contamination or at least discourage the participants from using intentional retrieval strategies in the test, none of them is immune to methodological and theoretical criticisms.

## Categories of Implicit Memory Tests

An implicit memory test can be relatively more perceptually- or conceptually-driven (e.g., Jacoby, 1983). Hence, the distinction between "perceptual" and "conceptual" tests is graded, not all-or-none. Criteria to determine whether an implicit memory test is predominantly perceptually- or conceptually-driven were proposed by Roediger, Weldon, and Challis (1989, see also Roediger, Marsh, & Lee, 2002). In *perceptual implicit memory tests* (see Table 1), participants typically identify degraded, fragmented, or short-duration test items. Perceptual processing is most beneficial when the physical features between the study items or pairs and the test items or pairs are maximally overlapping. Priming on such a test is facilitated by their physical similarity but diminished, if not eliminated, by a change in their physical characteristics (e.g., a switch in presentation modality, as in Pilotti, Bergman, Gallo et al., 2000). However, perceptual tests are insensitive to the meaning-related manipulations that have been found to greatly affect explicit memory performance (e.g., levels of processing, as

---

[6] Semantic priming occurs when responses to a target (cat) are faster and/or more accurate in a lexical decision task or a naming task when that target is preceded by a related prime (MEOW) than by an unrelated prime (BUMP) (Meyer & Schvaneveldt, 1971).

in Jacoby & Dallas, 1981). In contrast to perceptual tests, *conceptual implicit memory tests* (see Table 1) require participants to semantically process the test items or cues when they make the judgments or produce the answers. These tests are sensitive to meaning-related manipulations (e.g., levels of processing, as in Mulligan, Guyer, & Beland, 1999; semantic relatedness, as in Barry, 2007) but not perceptual-related manipulations (e.g., a switch in presentation modality, as in Vaidya, Gabrieli, Keane et al., 1997). Semantic processing is more beneficial when the conceptual analyses for the study items or pairs and test items or pairs are more similar. Compared to perceptual implicit memory tests, relatively fewer new association priming studies have used conceptual implicit memory tests.

Apart from the distinction between perceptual vs. conceptual implicit memory tests, Fleischman and Gabrieli (1998) categorized implicit memory tests by their response modalities: *production vs. identification*. In a production test (e.g., word-stem completion), participants need to generate possible candidates and produce an answer to fill out a test cue (e.g., for STE___, they are STEEP, STEAM, STEAL, STEAK, STEEL...). Because only one answer at a time can be given in this task, the production process must be followed by a (potentially competitive) selection process via which a single entry is chosen for a response. Studying a word lays down a memory trace, increasing the chance that a lexical entry matched to the trace will be selected from among the generated candidates. Since the direct retrieval of studied items could facilitate this matching process, the production component of these tests might more easily trigger the participants to use an explicit-memory retrieval strategy (see Tse & Neely, 2005 for a further discussion). [7] On the contrary, in an identification test (e.g., lexical decision), participants need to judge the lexicality or other dimensions for test items that are presented intact. Once the cue is accurately matched with an entry in a mental lexicon and a participant makes a response based on that entry, then the response is correct. Since participants do not need to generate any items to identify the test items, they have less incentive to use the explicit-memory retrieval strategy to do the test. This is even more likely the case when the task is speeded because intentionally retrieving the study items might be less effective than directly producing the answers to the test items in this task (see *Speeded implicit memory test* section for more discussions).

## Theories of Implicit Memory

Because the current review focuses on an evaluation of the automaticity of new association priming, we do not discuss any specific theories of implicit memory for explaining new association priming and indeed very few, if any, of the new association priming studies used implicit memory theories to account for their findings. However, because some of these theories are tangentially mentioned in the following sections, we briefly introduce the relevant ones here. Whether implicit memory is regarded as a memory *system* (e.g., Schacter, 1990) or a memory *process* (e.g., Roediger, 1990, 2003) has been one

---

[7] Although the perceptual identification task was treated as an identification task in prior research (e.g., Gabrieli, Keane, Zarella et al., 1997), it could also be regarded as a self-paced production task because when responding to a degraded and rapidly presented test item (e.g., the word face) participants need to generate several candidates that are orthographically or phonologically similar to it (e.g., lace and fade) and choose the most likely one. This process is analogous to those used in word-stem completion or word-fragment completion tasks (cf. Kinoshita, 2001).

of the most debated topics in the implicit memory literature (see Nairne, 2005, for a recent discussion). The representative theories of system and process views are multiple memory systems (Tulving & Schacter, 1990) and transfer appropriate processing (Roediger et al., 1989), respectively. The proponents of the memory system view consider explicit and implicit memory as separate systems. They identify several subsystems (i.e., the perceptual representation system) that mediate performance on perceptual implicit memory tests (Squire, 1992) by using experimental procedures designed to dissociate explicit vs. implicit memory performance (see the *Functional dissociation* section) or by examining the performance of patients with deficits in certain brain areas. The perceptual representation system consists of separate, domain-specific processing units responsible for deriving and storing a structural, presemantic representation of stimulus input (Schacter, 1994). The study-phase processing of an item may create a representation of its particular visual-perceptual features called a perceptual record. At test, this record facilitates the re-processing of the studied items and produces repetition priming, indicating the level of implicit memory. In contrast, the proponents of the memory processing consider explicit and implicit memory as two distinct processes. They assert that item repetition priming or new association priming becomes greater as the overlap in cognitive operations at study and at test becomes larger—transfer appropriate processing. Incongruent perceptual characteristics at study and at test (e.g., match in fonts between study and test) likely affect performance on perceptual tests such as word-stem completion (e.g., J. S. Brown & Carr, 1993), but not conceptual tests. The enhancement of conceptual processing at study (e.g., by requiring pleasantness ratings) tends to increase performance on conceptual tests such as the category exemplar generation task (e.g., McDermott & Roediger, 1996), but not on perceptual tests. The debate regarding the processing vs. system views has partially subsided because it is now agreed that there is no single "implicit memory system/process" or "explicit memory system/process": the performance on any given memory test draws on multiple memory systems or processes. This leads some researchers to postulate an intermediate position that both separate systems and processes are involved in their memory models (e.g., Moscovitch, 1994).

## PURPOSE OF THE CURRENT REVIEW

Whether or not item repetition priming occurs automatically has been one of the intensively investigated topics in the implicit memory literature (e.g., Schacter, Bowers, & Booker, 1989; Jacoby, 1991, 1998). This topic is important because the implicit (unintentional) retrieval of acquired information is one of the essential characteristics of implicit memory. Similar to item repetition priming, new association priming has often been assumed to occur without participants' intentionally retrieving the study episodes. However, while item repetition priming is produced by a repeated exposure of a word that participants are familiar with and have encountered prior to the experiment, new association priming is produced by repeated exposure of a novel association that participants presumably have not encountered before. Hence, it may be premature to assume that the new association priming also occurs automatically. Indeed, as discussed below, the automaticity of new association priming has, in fact, not been convincingly supported in prior new association priming studies. If new association priming is found not to occur automatically, whether it should still be regarded as an implicit memory phenomenon must be reconsidered. Despite the importance of testing the automaticity of new association priming, most prior reviews of implicit memory have focused on item repetition priming, such as Roediger and McDermott (1993), Fleischman and Gabrieli (1998) and Bowers and Schacter (1993). Even though a few of them (e.g., Bowers & Schacter; Dew, Bayen, & Giovanello, 2007) did review new association priming studies, almost none of them place the automaticity of new association priming as their foci. To our knowledge, there were only two exceptions to this. The first one was Zeelenberg, Pecher and Raaijmakers (2003), who evaluated a small number of new association priming studies and concluded that new association priming occurs automatically. However, their arguments need to be re-evaluated for two reasons. First, they based their conclusion on only 14 new association priming studies, all of which involved implicit memory tests that required participants to make rapid responses (e.g., lexical decision) or to identify degraded targets (e.g., perceptual identification). Zeelenberg et al. did this because they assumed that the findings in non-speeded, *production* tests (e.g., word-stem completion) are *always* contaminated by participants' explicit memory strategies. This assumption, however, might not be correct in light of the functional dissociations that have been reported for the performance on non-speeded implicit word-stem completion tasks and explicit stem-cued recall tasks. Thus, in the current review, we assess the automaticity of new association priming based on the findings of both non-production and production tasks. Second, Zeelenberg et al. evaluated the automaticity of new association priming based only on studies involving healthy young adults. However, more than 20 new association priming studies involving both normal and clinical populations have also been reported. Thus, in the current review, we survey the findings from both healthy young adults and amnesic patients, the most investigated clinical population, for revealing a more complete picture regarding the automaticity of new association priming. Another review that assessed the automaticity of new association priming was Dew, Bayen, and Giovanello (2007). By reviewing *only* new association priming studies that involved young and older adults, these authors examined the effect of older adults' associative deficit on their implicit memory performance. Relevant to the current review, Dew et al. concluded that the magnitude of new association priming could be modulated by participants' attention and encoding strategies (e.g., elaboration) in the tasks. As these factors have long been regarded as factors that affected young adults' explicit memory, Dew et al.'s conclusion seems to support that the new association priming is *not* automatic in nature. As elaborated below, our in-depth evaluation of previous new association priming studies also suggests that due to various methodological and theoretical concerns, automatic new association priming has not been convincingly demonstrated.

Having defined the terms that are frequently used in this chapter and highlighted why a more extensive literature review is needed for assessing the automaticity of new association priming, we now analyze previous findings to test whether new association priming *can* automatically occur and highlight under what circumstance this "automatic" new association priming may be susceptible to explicit contamination in implicit memory tests.

# AUTOMATICITY AND EXPLICIT CONTAMINATION OF NEW ASSOCIATION PRIMING

As noted earlier, explicit contamination (cf. McKone & Slee, 1997) occurs in implicit memory tests when participants (a) are aware of the relationship between the study phase and the test *and then* (b) use an explicit-memory retrieval strategy (i.e., directly retrieving the studied items) to perform the test. If the performance on an implicit memory test can (at least partially) be attributed to participants' using an explicit-memory retrieval strategy, item repetition priming and new association priming should not be regarded as automatic. To minimize explicit contamination, researchers have employed eight different research methodologies in their studies. They include test-awareness questionnaires, study intentionality manipulations, divided attention manipulations, functional dissociations, the process dissociation procedure, amnesic research, neuroimaging research, and speeded implicit memory tests, and are discussed to evaluate whether prior research has successfully demonstrated automatic new association priming.

## Test-Awareness Questionnaire

If participants are able to use an explicit-memory retrieval strategy in an implicit memory test, they should first be aware of the relationship between the study and the test. To assess their *retrospective* awareness of the study-test relationship, some researchers have asked participants to fill out a test-awareness questionnaire at the end of the experiments. Consider Bowers and Schacter (1990) as an example. Their questionnaire consisted of four questions that probed participants' test awareness during their performance on a word-stem completion task. The first two were open-ended questions ("What did you think was the purpose of the word-stem completion task you just finished?"; "What was your general strategy in completing the word stems?") and the latter two were more pointed ("Did you notice any relation between the words we showed you earlier and the words produced on the word-stem completion task?"; "While doing the word-stem completion task, did you notice whether you completed some of the stems with the words studied in the earlier list?"). Participants who spontaneously mentioned the study episodes in response to the first two questions *or* responded "yes" to one of the latter questions were classified as "test aware". Those who responded "no" to *all* four questions were categorized as "test unaware". Based on this classification, researchers separately analyzed performance of test-aware vs. test-unaware participants.

Bowers and Schacter (1990) showed that only the test-aware, but not the test-unaware, participants showed significant new association priming and concluded that the effects were probably mediated by participants' explicit memory strategies (which were triggered *after* the participants had become aware of the study-test relationship). Subsequent studies including this questionnaire obtained similar findings[8] (e.g., McKone & Slee, 1997, see Table 3

---

[8] In addition to the studies shown in Table 3, O'Hanlon, Wilcox, and Kemper (2001) and Van der Linden, Bruyer, and Dave (1992) also used the test-awareness questionnaire in their experiments. O'Hanlon et al. did not find any test-aware participants. Van der Linden et al. found more than 80% of their participants to be aware of the study-test relationship. However, because none of these participants admitted to having used the explicit-

*Difference* column). Rybash (1994) examined young and older adults' new association priming in a word-fragment completion task and found that regardless of age, both test-aware and test-unaware participants showed significant item repetition priming. However, only the test-aware young and older adults showed significant new association priming. The test-aware participants showed significant age differences in item repetition priming (i.e., young adults demonstrated stronger item repetition priming than older adults), but not so in new association priming. The latter result is puzzling because if older adults trigger the explicit-memory retrieval strategy as effectively as their younger counterparts (since they showed as strong new association priming as did the young adults), there should be no age difference in item repetition priming as well. In addition, Howard, Fry, and Brune (1991) did find significant age differences in new association priming for their test-aware participants across three experiments, contradicting Rybash's results. While Howard et al. found that their test-unaware participants also showed significant new association priming in one experiment, this finding was not replicated in their other experiments. Gooding, Mayes, van Eijk et al. (1999) used a multiple-level scale to assess participants' test awareness and found that the new association priming was positively correlated with test awareness.

In summary, the new association priming studies using a test-awareness questionnaire showed that the effect only occurred (or was at least much stronger) when participants were aware of the relationship between the study phase and the implicit memory test. This was qualified by the findings of one-sample *t* tests that were performed on the test-aware vs. test-unaware difference for new association priming, $t(20)=5.23$, shown in Table 3. [However, the test-aware vs. test-unaware difference was not significant in item repetition priming, $t(12)=1.29$.]

However, the *post-hoc* analyses of new association priming for test-aware vs. test-unaware participants may not always reveal the influence of explicit contamination in an implicit memory test due to the following reasons. First, because the test-awareness questionnaire was always given after the participants had finished the implicit memory test, the greater priming (probably via *truly implicit* retrieval) in the test might lead them to be, despite *retrospectively*, more aware of the study-test relationship. The priming effect might then be the cause but not the effect of test awareness because the test-awareness questionnaire captures only the *correlation*, but not the *causal relationship*, between participants' test awareness and their implicit memory performance.

Second, researchers often identified more test-aware participants than test-unaware participants in most, if not all, of the previous studies using a test-awareness questionnaire. The findings that test-aware, but not test-unaware, participants showed significant priming might be due to their insufficient statistical power to detect the attenuated priming effects for the test-unaware participants. Some researchers tried to avoid this by using a longer retention interval, such that more participants became test-unaware (Rybash, 1994). However, this might confound participants' test awareness with study-test retention interval. Rybash (Experiment 2) did not find any new association priming for his test-unaware participants in a delayed word-stem completion task (see Table 3), but this null new association priming could be attributed to the delay of the word-stem completion task, rather than participants' being unaware of the study-test relationship.

---

memory retrieval strategy, Van der Linden et al. did not consider the test awareness as a factor in their data analyses.

## Table 3. New association priming studies involving a test-awareness questionnaire

| Year | Study (Experiment) | Implicit Task | Manipulated Condition | Test-aware Participants | | | | | Test-unaware Participants | | | | | Difference | |
|---|---|---|---|---|---|---|---|---|---|---|---|---|---|---|---|
| | | | | Intact | Recb | New | IRP | NAP | Intact | Recb | New | IRP | NAP | IRP | NAP |
| 1990 | Bowers & Schacter (2a) | Word-Stem Completion | -- | 0.26 | 0.12 | 0.08 | 0.04[b] | 0.14*[b] | 0.13 | 0.13 | 0.08 | 0.05[b] | 0[b] | -0.01*[a] | 0.14*[a] |
| 1990 | Bowers & Schacter (2b) | | -- | 0.28 | 0.15 | 0.08 | 0.07[b] | 0.13*[b] | 0.10 | 0.11 | 0.08 | 0.03[b] | -0.01[b] | 0.04[a] | 0.14*[a] |
| 1990 | Bowers & Schacter (2c) | | | 0.30 | 0.13 | 0.08 | 0.05[b] | 0.17*[b] | 0.15 | 0.14 | 0.08 | 0.06[b] | 0.01[b] | -0.01[a] | 0.16*[a] |
| 1990 | Bowers & Schacter (3) | | Test Informed | 0.25 | 0.15 | 0.08 | 0.07*[b] | 0.10*[b] | 0.13 | 0.14 | 0.08 | 0.06[b] | -0.01[b] | 0.01[a] | 0.11*[a] |
| | | | Test Uninformed | 0.20 | 0.16 | 0.08 | 0.08*[b] | 0.04[b] | 0.10 | 0.13 | 0.08 | 0.05[b] | -0.03[b] | 0.03[a] | 0.07[a] |
| 1991 | Howard et al. (1) | Word-Stem Completion | Young | -- | -- | -- | -- | 0.19*[a] | -- | -- | -- | -- | 0.19*[a] | -- | 0.00[a] |
| | | | Old | -- | -- | -- | -- | -0.01[a] | -- | -- | -- | -- | -0.04[a] | -- | 0.03[a] |
| 1991 | Howard et al. (2) | Word-Stem Completion | Young | -- | -- | -- | -- | 0.14*[a] | -- | -- | -- | -- | 0.04[a] | -- | 0.10*[a] |
| | | | Old | -- | -- | -- | -- | 0.07*[a] | -- | -- | -- | -- | 0.22*[a] | -- | -0.15[a] |
| 1991 | Howard et al. (3) | Word-Stem Completion | Young | -- | -- | -- | -- | 0.16*[a] | -- | -- | -- | -- | 0.08[a] | -- | 0.08[a] |
| | | | Old | -- | -- | -- | -- | 0.07[a] | -- | -- | -- | -- | 0.04[a] | -- | 0.03[a] |
| 1994 | Rybash (1) | Word-Fragment Completion | Young-Immediate | 0.85 | 0.76 | 0.32 | 0.44*[b] | 0.09*[b] | -- | -- | -- | -- | -- | -- | -- |
| | | | Young-Delay | 0.68 | 0.54 | 0.33 | 0.21*[b] | 0.14*[b] | 0.58 | 0.54 | 0.32 | 0.22[b] | 0.04[b] | -0.01[a] | 0.10*[a] |
| | | | Old-Immediate | 0.61 | 0.46 | 0.23 | 0.23*[b] | 0.15*[b] | -- | -- | -- | -- | -- | -- | -- |
| | | | Old-Delay | 0.39 | 0.31 | 0.20 | 0.11[b] | 0.08[b] | 0.32 | 0.32 | 0.21 | 0.11[b] | 0.00[b] | 0.00[a] | 0.08[a] |
| 1994 | Rybash (2) | Word-Fragment Completion | Young-Immediate | 0.68 | 0.46 | 0.12 | 0.34*[b] | 0.22*[b] | 0.35 | 0.20 | 0.13 | 0.07[b] | 0.15[b] | 0.27*[a] | 0.07*[a] |
| | | | Young-Delay | 0.48 | 0.35 | 0.15 | 0.20*[b] | 0.13*[b] | 0.34 | 0.40 | 0.13 | 0.27*[b] | -0.06[b] | -0.07[a] | 0.19*[a] |
| | | | Old-Immediate | 0.42 | 0.26 | 0.03 | 0.23*[b] | 0.16*[b] | 0.13 | 0.12 | 0.01 | 0.11*[b] | 0.01[b] | 0.12*[a] | 0.15*[a] |
| | | | Old-Delay | 0.39 | 0.12 | 0.03 | 0.09*[b] | 0.27*[b] | 0.15 | 0.13 | 0.03 | 0.10*[b] | 0.02[b] | -0.01[a] | 0.25*[a] |
| 1997 | McKone & Slee (2) | Word-Stem Completion | Less elaborative encoding | 0.26 | 0.22 | 0.22 | -- | 0.04*[c] | 0.17 | 0.19 | 0.13 | -- | -0.02[c] | -- | 0.06[a] |
| | | | More elaborative encoding | 0.31 | 0.22 | 0.22 | -- | 0.09*[c] | 0.12 | 0.19 | 0.13 | -- | -0.06[c] | -- | 0.15*[a] |
| 1999 | Gooding et al. (1) | Word-Stem Completion | Full attention at study | 0.17 | 0.07 | 0.11 | -0.04[b] | 0.10*[b] | 0.08 | 0.05 | 0.11 | -0.06[b] | 0.03[b] | 0.02[a] | 0.07*[a] |
| | | | Divided attention at study | 0.17 | 0.06 | 0.10 | -0.04[b] | 0.11*[b] | 0.07 | 0.05 | 0.10 | -0.05[b] | 0.02[b] | 0.01[a] | 0.09*[a] |

# Table 3. (Continued)

| Year | Study (Experiment) | Implicit Task | Manipulated Condition | Test-aware Participants | | | | | Test-unaware Participants | | | | | Difference | |
|---|---|---|---|---|---|---|---|---|---|---|---|---|---|---|---|
| | | | | Intact | Recb | New | IRP | NAP | Intact | Recb | New | IRP | NAP | IRP | NAP |
| 2010 | Dew & Giovanello (1) | Speeded size judgment | Young | 967 | 1043 | 1152 | 109[b] | 76[b] | 970 | 1037 | 1086 | 49[b] | 67[b] | 60[a] | 9[a] |
| | | | Old | 1405 | 1489 | 1580 | 91[b] | 84[b] | 1277 | 1402 | 1506 | 104[b] | 125[b] | -13[a] | -41[a] |
| 2010 | Dew & Giovanello (2) | Inside/outside classification | Young | 898 | 966 | 1134 | 168[b] | 68[b] | 856 | 898 | 1022 | 124*[b] | 42[b] | 44[a] | -26[a] |
| | | | Old | 1164 | 1254 | 1423 | 169[b] | 90[b] | 1346 | 1436 | 1716 | 280*[b] | 90[b] | -111[a] | 0[a] |

*Note*— * $p < .05$ (two-tailed), ^ $p < .05$ (one-tailed). Intact = intact pair condition, Recb = recombined pair condition, New = new pair condition. IRP = item repetition priming, NAP = new association priming, the values in the intact, recb, new, IRP and NAP columns are either RTs or proportions, depending on the implicit task. (See Table 1 dependent measure column.). Difference = priming effect yielded by test-aware participants – priming effect yielded by test-unaware participants. The letter-label next to IRP and NAP indicates the procedure for assessing statistical significance: a – directly reported by the authors; b – *t*s computed based on the standard errors; c – *t*s computed based on the main effect of manipulated variables. Test-Informed participants were told that some of the test stems could be completed as study words, whereas the test-uninformed participants were not told about that. Because Howard et al. (1991) only reported the NAP for their test-aware participants and their full set of participants, we used this information to compute the NAP for their test-unaware participants and reported them (as well as those of test-aware participants) here.

Third, even if participants' responses in a test-awareness questionnaire indeed reflect their true mental state during the implicit memory test, the interpretation of this data is still problematic because participants might only become aware of the relation *after* they produce a response. This involuntary aware memory (Kinoshita, 2001; Richardson-Klavehn, Gardiner, & Java, 1994; Schacter et al., 1989) occurs when the target is retrieved automatically but then participants recognize (or are involuntarily aware of) it as having been studied before. That is, the participants' answers to the test stems might *involuntarily* trigger their explicit memory of a previously studied item. However, new association priming (or item repetition priming) that is mediated by this involuntary aware memory may not necessarily be produced by the *intentional* retrieval of studied items as participants might still *not* have used the explicit-memory retrieval strategy before and after their explicit memory of the studied items had been involuntarily triggered. In other words, test awareness is merely a necessary, but not sufficient, condition for the participants' initiation of an explicit-memory retrieval strategy. Participants could continue to obey the instruction and respond with the first word that came to mind even after they are aware of the study-test relationship. Some researchers (McKone & Slee, 1997; Rybash, 1994; Van der Linden, Bruyer, & Dave, 1992) addressed this by adding extra questions in their test-awareness questionnaire. In particular, their test-aware participants were asked whether they had changed their strategy *after* they became aware of the study-test relationship. In some item repetition priming studies (e.g., Richardson-Klavehn, Gardiner, & Java, 1996), only the test-aware participants who admitted to having used an explicit-memory retrieval strategy showed no explicit vs. implicit functional dissociation of some variables (e.g., levels of processing). In contrast, the test-aware participants who denied having used the explicit-memory retrieval strategy did show the typical dissociation for their implicit and explicit memory performance under the same experimental manipulation. This indicates that not all test-aware participants use an explicit-memory retrieval strategy. Other studies (e.g., Fay, Isingrini, & Pouthas, 2005; Mace, 2003, 2005; Dew & Giovanello, 2010) used RT measures to evaluate the relationship between test awareness and the use of an explicit-memory retrieval strategy. These researchers assumed that test-aware participants who use an explicit-memory retrieval strategy should respond more slowly to test stems (cf. Hintzman & Curran, 1997) than those who do not use such strategy in a word-stem completion task. However, they showed that both test-aware and test-unaware participants did not differ in their RTs in the word-stem completion task, suggesting that the test-aware participants do not necessarily use the explicit-memory retrieval strategy. Even though the test-aware participants showed significantly stronger item repetition priming than test-unaware participants, Mace found that test-aware and test-unaware participants did not differ in their RTs for producing answers in a word-stem completion task. While this finding awaits further replication for the new association priming, this at least shows that the relationship between one's conscious awareness and one's intention to retrieve is not straightforward. Because it is not certain whether test-aware participants by default showed explicit memory contamination—they did not necessarily use an explicit retrieval strategy even when they were aware of the study-test relationship, it may be more appropriate to compare the performance of participants who claimed to be *unaware* of the connection between the study and test with those who claimed to have used the explicit retrieval strategy during the test.

In summary, the interpretations of test-awareness questionnaire data are far from clear. Although previous studies (see Table 3 *Difference* column) generally showed that only test-aware, but not test-unaware, participants produced significant new association priming, it is necessary (a) to verify whether the questionnaire can genuinely capture the participants' test awareness and (b) to clarify the relationship between test awareness and the explicit-memory retrieval strategy if one wants to use this data to assess the automaticity of new association priming. Before ending this section, it is worth pointing out the *proportion of studied test items*, a variable that has not been manipulated in any new association priming studies using test-awareness questionnaires.

Previous studies showed that item repetition priming was stronger when the proportion of studied test items was high than when it was low (Allen & Jacoby, 1990; Jacoby, 1983, but see Challis & Roediger, 1993). According to Tse and Neely (2005), the more often the correct answers of test trials are previously studied items in a test, the more likely participants are to become aware of the study-test relationship, and in turn, the more opportunities they would have to use an explicit-memory retrieval strategy to enhance their performance on the test. In contrast, a low proportion of studied test items might make the participants less likely to recognize the study-test relationship. Even if some participants might recognize that, they would have less incentive to use the explicit-memory retrieval strategy due to the rare occasion that this strategy could be helpful. The performance on the production tests (e.g., word-stem completion) may be even more likely influenced by the proportion of studied test items. In these tests, participants need to generate and produce the answers to the test cues, so they might have a higher chance of generating the studied words when the proportion of studied test items is high. By noticing the frequency of the studied words being generated, participants would be more aware of a study-test relationship and in turn more likely to adopt the explicit-memory retrieval strategy. Future research should manipulate the proportion of studied test items, with the use of a test-awareness questionnaire, to investigate the influence of test awareness on new association priming and item repetition priming. If greater new association priming occurs when the proportion of studied test items is high, this would provide indirect evidence that the participants are using an explicit-memory retrieval strategy in the implicit memory tests.[9]

---

[9] Some previous findings apparently provided evidence against the role of the proportion of studied test items in inducing the participants' awareness of the study-test relationship. Bowers and Schacter (1990) found that nearly half of their participants were aware of the study-test relationship even when their word-stem completion task had a very low proportion of studied test items (15%). They found no item repetition priming for their test-aware or test-unaware participants but significant new association priming only for their test-aware, but not test-unaware, participants. Richardson-Klavehn, Lee, Joubran et al. (1994) found that more than 90% of their participants were test-aware even when their perceptual identification task had a low proportion of studied test items (25%). They found item repetition priming for their test-aware participants. (They did not report the data of their test-unaware participants due to too few observations.) However, these findings might not sufficiently undermine the hypothesis that the proportion of studied test items could affect the occurrence of explicit contamination. First, no systematic analysis has been done on the relationship between participants' test awareness and the proportion of studied test items, so these two cases might only be exceptions, but not the norm. Second, the fact that many participants were test-aware in experiments with a low proportion of studied test items does not necessarily contradict the claim that the high proportion of studied test items could boost the participants' test awareness. Third, even though the proportion of studied test items and the self-reported test awareness were indeed unrelated, the interpretation of this null correlation may still be complicated by the questionable validity of the test-awareness questionnaire. Thus, using the proportion of studied test items to directly *manipulate* participants' test awareness seems to avoid the problems arisen from the interpretation of the data yielded by the test-awareness questionnaire only.

## Study Intentionality and Divided Attention

Instead of using a test-awareness questionnaire to detect the participants' awareness of the study-test relationship, some new association priming studies tried to reduce participants' test awareness by using the incidental study instruction (study intentionality manipulation) or to prevent participants from using an explicit-memory retrieval strategy by having them performed a secondary task during the implicit memory test (divided attention manipulation).

Regarding the study intentionality manipulation, participants who receive an intentional study instruction are told that they will be given a (typically unspecified) memory test at the end of the experiment, whereas those who receive incidental study instructions are not told anything about the test. The latter participants do not anticipate a memory test and *might* not be even aware that the purpose of the experiment is to assess their memory performance. Hence, they might be less likely to use the explicit-memory retrieval strategy when they do the implicit memory test, which is even less likely to be regarded as a part of a *memory* experiment due to the use of incidental study instruction. This study intentionality manipulation has often been found *not* to modulate the item repetition priming (e.g., word-stem and word-fragment completion tasks in Neill, Beck, Bottalico et al., 1990). To our knowledge, only three new association priming studies have directly manipulated study intentionality (Bowers & Schacter, 1990; Cermak, Bleich, & Blackford, 1988b; White, Abrams, & Byrd, 2009). Cermak et al. had their participants study word pairs in a deep study task (sentence generation) with either intentional or incidental study instructions. The participants were then given either a word-stem completion task (that was described as a distractor task) or an explicit stem-cued recall task. The intentional study group showed greater new association priming and better stem-cued recall performance than the incidental study group. In fact, the new association priming yielded by Cermak et al.'s incidental study group did not even approach significance. On the contrary, Bowers and Schacter found only a non-significant positive effect of study intentionality on new association priming (intentional: 17% vs. incidental: 14%). As Bowers and Schacter had more participants receiving intentional (24) and incidental study instructions (60) than Cermak et al. had (8 in each study intentionality group), their null difference was unlikely due to inadequate statistical power. (Power analyses could not be performed because neither Bowers & Schacter nor Cermak et al. reported sufficient statistical information in their papers.). White et al. had young and older adults acquire word pairs under either incidental or intentional study instructions and do an implicit or explicit memory test. They found significant new association priming whether participants received incidental or intentional study instruction. Neither participants (young vs. older adults) nor study intentionality (intentional vs. incidental) showed a functional dissociation in the explicit/implicit memory test. However, White et al. did not measure the new association priming by using the conventional recombined word pairs as the baseline (see Table 2). Rather, they merely cued participants with new unrelated words, so the interpretation of their results may be clouded by the confound between item repetition priming and new association priming. To shed more light on the effect of study intentionality on item repetition priming and new association priming, we analyzed new association priming and item repetition priming in 67 previous new association priming studies that used either incidental or intentional study instruction in the study phase (yet none of them directly manipulated the study intentionality).[10] Given a limited number of observations for the other types of implicit memory tests, we focused on the studies using a word-stem completion task. We evaluated the effect of study intentionality by performing independent-sample $t$ tests for new association priming and for item repetition priming. Study intentionality had a small but significant effect on new association priming [17% vs. 13%, $t (65) = 2.59$] but had no effect on item repetition priming [12% vs. 11%, $t (51) = .50$], consistent with previous item repetition priming studies (e.g., Neill et al., 1990). In summary, unlike with item repetition priming, participants who intentionally study the word pairs with the anticipation of a memory test tend to show greater new association priming than those who do not have this anticipation. Because study intentionality produces a similar effect on participants' new association priming (but not item repetition priming) and on their explicit memory performance (see Cermak, Blackford, O'Connor, & Bleich, 1988a), new association priming may be partially produced by participants' using the explicit-memory retrieval strategy.

Two new association priming studies (Gooding et al., 1999; Kinoshita, 1999) using the divided attention manipulation *at test* have been reported (see Light, Kennison, Prull et al., 1996, for experiments that manipulated the participants' attention, full vs. divided, *in the study task*). These authors reasoned that if new association priming could be attenuated when participants' attention was disrupted at test (e.g., by doing a secondary task), such effects would likely be mediated by a memory controlled process that demands attentional resources (see Footnote 11). Unfortunately, the findings of these two studies were contradictory.

Kinoshita (1999) obtained a significant reduction in new association priming when participants performed the word-stem completion task and monitored the digit sequence for "consecutive three odd-digits" (i.e., the secondary task) simultaneously. This was the case whether the divided attention was manipulated within or between participants. Kinoshita, however, found that item repetition priming was stronger when participants' attention was divided than when it was not. Although the author did not explicitly explain how this counter-intuitive finding happens, we consider that to be evidence for the participants' having used the explicit-memory retrieval strategy in the implicit memory tests (which would argue against the automaticity of new association priming). Those whose attention was divided might do better to alleviate the demand of the word-stem completion task by focusing on the test stems, rather than the context words. They did so because they considered themselves not to have sufficient capacity processing the context words and generating possible answers to the test stems. This explains why the divided-attention participants' proportion of correct completion did not differ for the intact (27%) and recombined pairs (31%) and produced significant item repetition priming but not new association priming, relative to new pairs (10%). The participants traded off item repetition priming at the expense of new association priming, such that the magnitudes of item repetition priming and new association priming were negatively correlated.[11]

---

[10] White et al.'s (2009) findings were not included in this analysis due to the confound in their experimental design.

[11] There are also some circumstances in which the positive correlation between the item repetition priming and new association priming is expected. For example, when the study pairs were either clearly or degradedly presented at study, the degraded study pairs likely yield smaller magnitude of item repetition priming and new association priming, though, to our knowledge, this has not yet been tested in any new association priming studies.

**Table 2. Typical conditions in a new association priming paradigm**

| Test Context | Example of Study Pairs (Context Word-Target) | Example of Test Pairs (Context Word-Target) in a word-stem completion task |
|---|---|---|
| Unrelated (UR) Intact Pair | REASON-house, OBSERVE-wolf | REASON-ho___ |
| Unrelated Neutral Pair | REASON-house, OBSERVE-wolf | XXX-ho___ or BLANK-ho___ |
| Unrelated Pair with Extralist Prime (UR-e) | REASON-house, OBSERVE-wolf | DAMP-ho___ |
| Unrelated Recombined Pair with Appropriate Intralist Prime (UR-a) | REASON-house, OBSERVE-wolf | OBSERVE-ho___ |
| Unrelated Recombined Pair with Inappropriate Intralist Prime (UR-i) | REASON-logic, BUILDING-house | REASON-ho___ |
| New Pair (i.e., Nonstudied Baseline) | -- | REASON-ho___ or WINDOW-ho___ |
| Related (R) Intact Pair | WINDOW-house, DOOR-knob | WINDOW-ho___ |
| Related Neutral Pairs | WINDOW-house, DOOR-knob | XXX-ho___ or BLANK-ho___ |
| Related Pair with Extralist Prime (R-e) | WINDOW-house, DOOR-knob | BUILDING-ho___ |
| Related Recombined Pair with Appropriate Intralist Prime (R-a) | WINDOW-house, DOOR-knob | DOOR-ho___ |
| Related Recombined Pair with Inappropriate Intralist Prime (R-i) | WINDOW-dog, BONE-house | WINDOW-ho___ |

Item repetition priming = RT/percent correct difference between Unrelated Recombined Condition and Nonstudied Baseline Condition

New association priming = RT /percent correct difference between Unrelated Intact Condition and Unrelated Recombined Condition

Old association priming = RT /percent correct difference between Related Intact Condition and Related Recombined Condition

Note—See the text of *Speeded implicit memory tests* section for the definitions of appropriate (*UR-a*, *R-a*) and inappropriate (*UR-i*, *R-i*) recombined pairs.

However, the above "tradeoff" explanation apparently fails to account for the finding of full-attention participants. Because those who paid full attention to the word-stem completion task should focus more on the context words, they were supposed to show significant new association priming *and* item repetition priming that was *at least* at the same level as the one demonstrated by divided-attention participants. As reported by Kinoshita (1999), the full-attention participants did show significant new association priming (12%; 31% in intact pairs vs. 19% in recombined pairs), but their item repetition priming (9%; 19% in recombined pairs vs. 10% in new pairs) was significantly weaker than that shown by divided-attention participants (21%). Hence, the full-attention instruction produced new association priming by lowering participants' performance for the recombined pairs (from 31% to 19%), but not boosting their performance for the intact pairs (from 27% to 31%). How could new association priming be significant when item repetition priming did not even approach significance? This apparently counter-intuitive data might be parsimoniously explained if one considers that full-attention participants were more likely to use the explicit-memory retrieval strategy than divided-attention participants when they performed the word-stem completion task.[12] When the full-attention participants attempted to intentionally *retrieve* the studied pairmates cued by context words, they might be successful for the intact pairs. However, for the recombined pairs, since the retrieved pairmate corresponding to the context word did not fit into the test stem, the wrong answer might then *block* the participants from generating answers to the test stems in those trials and, in turn, reduce their proportion of correct completion for these recombined pairs. Thus, this *retrieval blocking* strengthened the new association priming and weakened the item repetition priming by lowering full-attention participants' performance for the recombined pairs. In contrast, because the divided-attention participants did not even process the context words, they were less likely to use them to *retrieve* the studied pairmates in the word-stem completion task. Hence, the divided-attention task might have made it less likely for the participants to use an explicit-memory retrieval strategy and *paradoxically* preserve their item repetition priming. In short, Kinoshita's counter-intuitive findings of full- and divided-attention participants could be accounted for by assuming the explicit-memory retrieval strategy to be involved in her word-stem completion task.

Contrary to Kinoshita (1999), Gooding et al. (1999) found virtually equivalent new association priming (and item repetition priming) whether their participants performed the word-stem completion task alone or simultaneously with an arithmetic task for flanking digits. Since their divided-attention manipulation did reduce explicit stem-cued recall performance, these authors argued that their null difference in the word-stem completion task could not be due to a weak attentional manipulation and concluded that new association priming occurs automatically. Unlike Kinoshita, the performance for Gooding et al.'s intact and recombined pairs was not affected by the divided attention manipulation, indicating that some subtle manipulations in Kinoshita but not in Gooding et al. might have triggered the

---

[12] Kinoshita (1999) argued that even though participants showed impaired new association priming when their attention was divided, it does not entail that they intentionally retrieved the study items when their attention was not divided because the task demanding attentional resource does not necessarily demand the participants to perform with intentional, willed action (cf. Norman & Shallice, 1986). The present analyses, however, suggested that Kinoshita's new association priming was mediated not only by the "unintentional" attentional resource, but probably also by an intentional retrieval process that was triggered by participants' use of explicit-memory retrieval strategy.

participants' use of strategies. For instance, as in the study task, Kinoshita's participants studied fewer study pairs (35) with a deeper processing task (sentence generation) than Gooding et al.'s did (117, relatedness rating), the stronger association they formed for the unrelated word pairs might make them more likely to use an explicit-memory retrieval strategy in the word-stem completion task. Future research should use the same set of study materials and orthogonally manipulate the level-of-processing and attentional demand at test to resolve the conflict in the findings between these two studies.

Before ending this section, the tradeoff (negative correlation) between the item repetition priming and new association priming, as mentioned in our explanation for Kinoshita's (1999) findings, deserves more discussion. The tradeoff could occur in production implicit memory tests when participants have divided attention, but it could also occur at study when participants encode the item vs. association. Despite not being directly relevant to the automaticity of new association priming, the *encoding tradeoff* of the item information, at the expense of associative information, during the study phase could weaken new association priming in the implicit memory test and blur the interpretation of this effect. When the participants study the unrelated word pairs, they might strategically focus on the item information for the context words and/or targets, rather than the associative information. (This is more likely to occur when participants have divided attention at study and/or when the intentional study instruction was used.) If they adapt this "tradeoff" strategy, they may show strong item repetition priming but a weak new association priming because they do not encode the novel associations as they should have.[13] Such a reduction in new association priming could thus be due entirely to the poor encoding of the novel associations. However, this finding (i.e., a reduction in new association priming when the participants have divided attention at study) might be (wrongly) interpreted as evidence against the automaticity of new association priming. To unambiguously interpret the findings of new association priming reduction in future new association priming studies, participants should be directly instructed to encode the associative information during the study phase (e.g., self-generated new associations). This should ensure that the participants do not encode the novel associations at the expense of item information, such that the new association priming reduction could be used as clearer evidence for or against the automaticity of new association priming.

---

[13] An alternative explanation to explain the weakened new association priming but intact item repetition priming is that participants form the association between two words as a new Gestalt at study. However, in some implicit memory tests (e.g., word-stem completion), because participants receive only the context words and need to generate the targets and the context words might less likely reactivate the whole Gestalt they formed during the study phase, participants might have difficulty producing the target even when they were given a context word in the intact pairs. Thus, their new association priming might then be weakened. This explanation can be tested by comparing new association priming for implicit memory tests that present the context word with a *deformed test cue* (e.g., word-stem/fragment completion—Gestalt-incongruent test) with those that present the context word with an *intact target* (e.g., double-item lexical decision—Gestalt-congruent test). Given that participants who receive different implicit memory tests have learned unrelated word pairs by the same study procedure, those who receive the Gestalt-congruent test should demonstrate stronger new association priming than those who received the Gestalt-incongruent test. (The proportion gain can be used as an index of new association priming to avoid the scaling difference.) A further manipulation for study instruction (i.e., emphasizing item or associative encoding) could also be used to tear apart this "Gestalt re-activation hypothesis" with the item/associative encoding tradeoff hypothesis. To our knowledge, no experiment has tested this idea.

## Functional Dissociation

In implicit memory research, it is common to compare the effects of various independent variables on participants' performance on explicit and implicit memory tests. The goal of these studies is to test a functional dissociation between explicit and implicit memory tests. A functional dissociation is observed when a variable has different effects on the explicit and implicit memory performance (Neely, 1989; Reingold, 2003; but see Dunn & Kirsner, 1988, for a critique of the logic of functional dissociation). For example, while amnesia almost always reduces explicit memory performance, it rarely affects the magnitude of item repetition priming in implicit memory tests (e.g., Graf & Schacter, 1985). In contrast, a mismatch in the font types of study items and test items weakens item repetition priming in perceptual implicit memory tests, but normally does not affect explicit memory performance (e.g., Fleischman, Vaidya, Lange et al., 1997). When the functional dissociation of a variable is found in the performance in explicit vs. implicit memory tests, this suggests that the two measures of memory tap functionally distinct memory systems or processes (e.g., Roediger, 1990; Roediger & McDermott, 1993). If a variable significantly affects explicit memory performance, but not implicit memory performance, one might infer that an explicit-memory retrieval strategy is not, at least not significantly, at play during implicit memory tests. This latter claim, however, is true only when the retrieved information involved in the two kinds of memory tests is *assumed* to be identical. (That is, both implicit and explicit memory tests measure the same kind of *information*, which is retrieved via two different processes in implicit and explicit memory tests.) Otherwise, one could not determine whether an experimental manipulation affects the same processing mechanism for retrieving the explicit vs. implicit information in a memory test, the explicit vs. implicit memory processing for retrieving the similar kinds of information, or both. In short, whether new association priming occurs automatically should be inferred from the functional dissociation on the explicit vs. implicit memory processing, but not on the processing of the information involved in explicit vs. implicit memory tests.

Despite the commonly obtained finding of function dissociations between explicit and implicit memory performance found for item repetition priming, such dissociations have not been consistently reported in new association priming studies. The findings in all previous new association priming studies that included both implicit and explicit memory tests in their experiments are summarized in Table 4. Collapsed across all test types and manipulated conditions, only 44 (42%) of 106 Test Type (Explicit vs. Implicit) × Manipulated Condition comparisons showed a dissociation in new association priming (see Table 4 *Dissociation NAP* column) and 54 of 78 (69%) comparisons showed a dissociation in item repetition priming (see Table 4 *Dissociation IRP* column). However, these dissociations do not always reflect different retrieval processes. As Dunn and Kirsner (1988) argued, explicit and implicit memory tests might not tap distinct memory systems or different retrieval processes (i.e., the relationship between memory tests and memory systems may not necessarily be "transparent"). Merikle and Reingold (1991) also pointed out that one problem in interpreting the functional dissociations stems from the fact that the testing procedure of explicit and implicit memory tests can be quite different, such as the presentation format of test pairs.

## Table 4. New association priming studies testing for a functional dissociation in explicit vs. implicit memory performance

| Year | Study (Experiment) | # of P | Satisfy RIC? | Manipulated Condition | Implicit Memory Test Task | Intact | Recb | New | IRP | NAP | Explicit Memory Test Task | Intact Hit | Recb FA | New FA | I-R | Dissociation Critical Manipulation | IRP | NAP |
|---|---|---|---|---|---|---|---|---|---|---|---|---|---|---|---|---|---|---|
| 1985 | Graf & Schacter (1) | 1 | No | Generate sentences | Word-Stem Completion | 0.50 | 0.23 | 0.12 | 0.11*[a] | 0.27*[b] | Cued-Recall | 0.35 | -- | -- | -- | Levels of Processing | yes | no |
|  |  |  |  | Judge number of vowels |  | 0.22 | 0.20 | 0.12 | 0.08*[a] | 0.02[b] |  | 0 | -- | -- | -- |  |  |  |
| 1985 | Graf & Schacter (2) | 1 | No | Young-Generate sentences | Word-Stem Completion | 0.34 | 0.22 | 0.13 | 0.09*[d] | 0.12*[b] | Cued-Recall | 0.64 | -- | -- | -- | Participant | yes | yes |
|  |  |  |  | Amnesic-Generate sentences |  | 0.32 | 0.18 | 0.13 | 0.05*[d] | 0.13*[b] |  | 0.02 | -- | -- | -- |  |  |  |
|  |  |  |  | Control-Generate sentences |  | 0.32 | 0.21 | 0.13 | 0.08*[d] | 0.11*[b] |  | 0.35 | -- | -- | -- |  |  |  |
| 1985 | Neely & Durgunoglu (1) | 2 | No | 150-ms SOA | Lexical Decision | 822 | 836 | -- | -- | 14[a] | Item Recognition RT | 873 | 935 | -- | 62*[a] | SOA | no | no |
|  |  |  |  | 950-ms SOA |  | 792 | 832 | -- | -- | 40*[a] |  | 818 | 934 | -- | 116*[a] |  |  |  |
| 1985 | Neely & Durgunoglu (2) | 2 | No | 150-ms SOA | Lexical Decision | 790 | 780 | -- | -- | -10[a] | Item Recognition RT | 896 | 972 | -- | 76*[a] | SOA | no |  |
|  |  |  |  | 950-ms SOA |  | 735 | 749 | -- | -- | 14[a] |  | 836 | 953 | -- | 117*[a] |  |  |  |
| 1986 | McKoon & Ratcliff (1) | 1 | No | 50-ms SOA | Lexical Decision | 482 | 491 | 476 | -15[b] | 9[b] | Cued-Recall | 0.40 | -- | -- | -- | SOA | no | yes |
|  |  |  |  | 150-ms SOA |  | 447 | 487 | 475 | -12[b] | 40*[b] |  | 0.40 | -- | -- | -- |  |  |  |
| 1986 | Moscovitch et al. (2) | 1 | No | Young | Rereading | 1180 | 1320 | 1310 | -10 | 140*[c] | Associative Recognition | 0.79 | 0.21 | 0.24 | 0.58*[c] | Participant | yes | yes |
|  |  |  |  | Old |  | 1980 | 2385 | 2420 | 35 | 405*[c] |  | 0.73 | 0.35 | 0.36 | 0.38*[c] |  |  |  |
|  |  |  |  | Memory disordered |  | 1990 | 2350 | 2320 | -30 | 360*[c] |  | 0.59 | 0.56 | 0.54 | 0.02 |  |  |  |
| 1986 | Moscovitch et al. (3) | 1 | No | Young | Rereading | 1100 | 1220 | 1360 | 260[c] | 120*[c] | Associative Recognition | 0.95 | 0.50 | 0.04 | 0.45*[a] | Participant | yes | no |
|  |  |  |  | Old |  | 1810 | 1980 | 2230 | 250*[c] | 170*[c] |  | 0.78 | 0.51 | 0.11 | 0.27*[a] |  |  |  |
|  |  |  |  | Alzheimer disease |  | 1980 | 2060 | 2220 | 240*[c] | 80*[c] |  | 0.63 | 0.61 | 0.49 | 0.02[a] |  |  |  |
| 1986a | Schacter & Graf (1) | 1 | Yes | Generate words | Word-Stem Completion | 0.42 | 0.22 | 0.09 | 0.13*[a] | 0.20*[c] | Stem-Cued Recall | 0.62 | 0.37 | -- | 0.25*[c] | Levels of Elaboration | no | yes |
|  |  |  |  | Generate sentences |  | 0.41 | 0.25 | 0.09 | 0.16*[a] | 0.16*[c] |  | 0.72 | 0.41 | -- | 0.31*[c] |  |  |  |

# Table 4. (Continued)

| Year | Study (Experiment) | # of P | Satisfy RIC? | Manipulated Condition | Implicit Memory Test | | | | | Explicit Memory Test | | | | | Dissociation (yes or no?) | | |
|---|---|---|---|---|---|---|---|---|---|---|---|---|---|---|---|---|---|
| | | | | | Task | Intact | Recb | New | IRP | NAP | Task | Intact Hit | Recb FA | New FA | I-R | Critical Manipulation | IRP | NAP |
| 1986a | Schacter & Graf (2) | 1 | Yes | Immediate-Generate sentences | Word-Stem Completion | 0.35 | 0.19 | 0.11 | 0.08*[b] | 0.16*[c] | Stem-Cued Recall | 0.60 | 0.35 | -- | 0.25*[c] | Levels of Elaboration | yes | yes |
| | | | | Immediate-Rate relatedness | | 0.31 | 0.16 | 0.11 | 0.05[b] | 0.15*[c] | | 0.34 | 0.32 | -- | 0.02[c] | | | |
| | | | | Delay-Generate sentences | | 0.26 | 0.15 | 0.11 | 0.04[b] | 0.11*[c] | | 0.48 | 0.18 | -- | 0.30*[c] | Levels of Elaboration | yes | yes |
| | | | | Delay-Rate relatedness | | 0.24 | 0.12 | 0.11 | 0.01[b] | 0.12*[c] | | 0.27 | 0.20 | -- | 0.07[c] | Retention Interval | yes | yes |
| 1987 | Graf & Schacter (1) | 1 | Yes | Proactive Interference | Word-Stem Completion | 0.35 | 0.21 | 0.10 | 0.11^[d] | 0.14*[b] | Stem-Cued Recall | 0.45 | 0.26 | -- | 0.19*[b] | Interference | yes | yes |
| | | | | Control | | 0.32 | 0.18 | 0.10 | 0.08*[d] | 0.14*[b] | | 0.67 | 0.31 | -- | 0.36*[b] | | | |
| | | | | Retroactive Interference | | 0.32 | 0.21 | 0.10 | 0.11^[d] | 0.11*[b] | | 0.40 | 0.28 | -- | 0.12*[b] | Interference | yes | no |
| | | | | Control | | 0.34 | 0.17 | 0.10 | 0.07^[d] | 0.17*[b] | | 0.55 | 0.35 | -- | 0.20*[b] | | | |
| 1987 | Graf & Schacter (2) | 1 | No | Retroactive Interference | Word-Stem Completion | 0.36 | 0.20 | 0.09 | 0.11*[d] | 0.16*[b] | Pair Matching | 0.36 | 0.07 | -- | 0.29*[b] | Interference | yes | yes |
| | | | | Control | | 0.39 | 0.24 | 0.09 | 0.15*[d] | 0.15*[b] | | 0.54 | 0.07 | -- | 0.47*[b] | | | |
| 1988b | Cermak et al. (1) | 1 | Yes | Korsakoff disease | Word-Stem Completion | 0.35 | 0.36 | -- | -- | -0.01[b] | Stem-Cued Recall | 0.22 | -- | -- | -- | Participant | | yes |
| | | | | Alcoholic intoxicated | | 0.15 | 0.24 | -- | -- | -0.09[b] | | 0.53 | -- | -- | -- | | | |
| 1988b | Cermak et al. (2) | 1 | Yes | Incidental | Word-Stem Completion | 0.18 | 0.20 | -- | -- | -0.02[a] | Stem-Cued Recall | 0.71 | -- | -- | -- | Study Intentionality | | no |
| | | | | Intentional | | 0.53 | 0.29 | -- | -- | 0.24*[a] | | 0.85 | -- | -- | -- | | | |
| 1988b | Cermak et al. (3) | 1 | Yes | Normal | Word-Stem Completion | 0.06 | 0.13 | -- | -- | -0.08[b] | Stem-Cued Recall | 0.40 | -- | -- | -- | Participant | | no |
| | | | | Korsakoff disease | | 0.26 | 0.29 | -- | -- | -0.03[b] | | 0.31 | -- | -- | -- | | | |
| | | | | Alcoholic intoxicated | | 0.09 | 0.20 | -- | -- | -0.11[b] | | 0.48 | -- | -- | -- | | | |
| 1989 | Graf & Schacter (1) | 1 | Yes | Generate sentences | Word-Stem Completion | 0.46 | 0.25 | 0.10 | 0.15*[b] | 0.21*[b] | Stem-Cued Recall | 0.86 | 0.39 | -- | 0.47*[b] | Levels of Elaboration | yes | yes |
| | | | | Generate story | | 0.46 | 0.27 | 0.10 | 0.17*[b] | 0.19*[b] | | 0.69 | 0.35 | -- | 0.34*[b] | Levels of Elaboration | yes | yes |
| 1989 | Graf & Schacter (2) | 2 | Yes | Sort sentences by topic | Word-Stem Completion | 0.28 | 0.18 | 0.08 | 0.10*[b] | 0.10[b] | Stem-Cued Recall | 0.72 | 0.29 | -- | 0.43*[b] | Levels of Elaboration | yes | yes |

| Year | Study (Experiment) | # of P | Satisfy RIC? | Manipulated Condition | Implicit Memory Test | | | | | | Explicit Memory Test | | | | | Dissociation (yes or no?) | | |
|---|---|---|---|---|---|---|---|---|---|---|---|---|---|---|---|---|---|---|
| | | | | | Task | Intact | Recb | New | IRP | NAP | Task | Intact Hit | Recb FA | New FA | I-R | Critical Manipulation | IRP | NAP |
| | | | | Sort sentences by length | | 0.26 | 0.17 | 0.08 | 0.09[b] | 0.09[b] | | 0.44 | 0.28 | – | 0.16[b] | | | |
| 1989 | Graf & Schacter (3) | 1 | No | Concrete word pairs | Word-Stem Completion | 0.40 | 0.22 | 0.11 | 0.11*[b] | 0.18*[b] | Cued Recall | 0.64 | 0.91 | – | 0.37[b] | Word Concreteness | yes | no |
| | | | | Abstract word pairs | | 0.26 | 0.22 | 0.11 | 0.11*[b] | 0.04[b] | | 0.39 | 0.69 | – | 0.24[b] | | | |
| 1989 | Graf & Schacter (4) | 1 | Yes | Concrete word pairs | Word-Stem Completion | 0.47 | 0.24 | 0.09 | 0.15*[b] | 0.23*[b] | Stem-Cued Recall | 0.58 | 0.28 | – | 0.30*[b] | Word Concreteness | yes | no |
| | | | | Abstract word pairs | | 0.29 | 0.20 | 0.09 | 0.11*[b] | 0.09*[b] | | 0.42 | 0.26 | – | 0.16*[b] | | | |
| 1989 | Mayes & Gooding (1) | 1 | Yes | Normal | Word-Stem Completion | 0.67 | 0.39 | 0.15 | 0.24*[b] | 0.29*[b] | Stem-Cued Recall | 0.87 | | | – | Participant | no | no |
| | | | | Control | | 0.53 | 0.31 | 0.15 | 0.16*[b] | 0.22*[b] | | 0.62 | | | – | | | |
| | | | | Amnesic | | 0.35 | 0.32 | 0.15 | 0.17*[b] | 0.03[b] | | 0.31 | | | – | | | |
| 1989 | Nilsson et al. (1) | 1 | No | Young | Lexical Decision | – | – | – | – | 26*[b] | Cued Recall | 0.73 | – | – | – | Participant | yes | yes |
| | | | | Old | | – | – | – | – | 65[b] | | 0.18 | – | – | – | | | |
| | | | | Alcoholic intoxicated | | – | – | – | – | 6[b] | | 0.36 | – | – | – | | | |
| | | | | Sleep Deprived | | – | – | – | – | 25[b] | | 0.46 | – | – | – | | | |
| 1989 | Schacter & Graf (1) | 1 | Yes | Visual Study | Word-Stem Completion | 0.35 | 0.20 | 0.10 | 0.10*[a] | 0.15*[a] | Stem-Cued Recall | 0.56 | 0.33 | – | 0.23*[c] | Study Modality | yes | yes |
| | | | | Auditory Study | | 0.24 | 0.21 | 0.14 | 0.07*[a] | 0.03[d] | | 0.54 | 0.25 | – | 0.29*[c] | | | |
| 1989 | Schacter & Graf (2) | 1 | Yes | Visual Study | Word-Stem Completion | 0.39 | 0.19 | 0.11 | 0.08*[d] | 0.20*[a] | Stem-Cued Recall | 0.74 | 0.44 | – | 0.30*[c] | Study Modality | no | yes |
| | | | | Auditory Study | | 0.29 | 0.22 | 0.11 | 0.11*[d] | 0.07*[a] | | 0.69 | 0.42 | – | 0.27*[c] | | | |
| 1989 | Schacter & Graf (3) | 1 | Yes | Visual-Pre-expose-Visual-Study | Word-Stem Completion | 0.40 | 0.23 | 0.12 | 0.11*[d] | 0.17*[c] | Stem-Cued Recall | 0.56 | 0.34 | – | 0.22*[c] | Study Modality | yes | yes |
| | | | | Visual-Pre-expose-Auditory-Study | | 0.39 | 0.26 | 0.12 | 0.14*[b] | 0.13*[b] | | 0.66 | 0.26 | – | 0.40*[c] | Study Modality | | |
| | | | | Auditory-Pre-expose-Visual-Study | | 0.33 | 0.20 | 0.12 | 0.08*[d] | 0.13*[b] | | 0.58 | 0.26 | – | 0.32*[c] | Study Modality | no | yes |
| | | | | Auditory-Pre-expose-Auditory-Study | | 0.24 | 0.17 | 0.12 | 0.05*[a] | 0.07[a] | | 0.57 | 0.25 | – | 0.32*[c] | Modality Pre-exposure | yes | yes |

# Table 4. (Continued)

| Year | Study (Experiment) | # of P | Satisfy RIC? | Manipulated Condition | Implicit Memory Test Task | Intact | Recb | New | IRP | NAP | Explicit Memory Test Task | Intact Hit | Recb FA | New FA | I-R | Dissociation (yes or no?) Critical Manipulation | IRP | NAP |
|---|---|---|---|---|---|---|---|---|---|---|---|---|---|---|---|---|---|---|
| 1989 | Schacter & Graf (4) | 1 | Yes | Visual Study | Word-Stem Completion | 0.31 | 0.22 | 0.13 | 0.09*[b] | 0.09*[c] | Stem-Cued Recall | 0.56 | 0.30 | – | 0.26*[c] | Study Modality | no | yes |
| | | | | Auditory Study | | 0.36 | 0.20 | 0.13 | 0.07[b] | 0.16*[c] | | 0.57 | 0.32 | – | 0.25*[c] | | | |
| 1989 | Schacter & McGlynn (1) | 1 | Yes | Read idiom definition | Free Association | 0.06 | – | 0.00 | – | 0.06^[c] | Cued Recall | 0.24 | – | – | – | Levels of Processing | | yes |
| | | | | Read idiom in sentence | | 0.03 | – | 0.00 | – | 0.03[b] | | 0.28 | – | – | – | | | |
| | | | | Read idiom and its synonym | | 0.02 | – | 0.00 | – | 0.02[b] | | 0.08 | – | – | – | | | |
| | | | | Judge number of letters | | 0.01 | – | 0.00 | – | 0.01[b] | | 0.02 | – | – | – | | | |
| 1989 | Schacter & McGlynn (2) | 2 | Yes | Read idiom definition | Free Association | 0.14 | – | 0.00 | – | 0.14*[d] | Cued Recall | 0.45 | – | – | – | Levels of Processing | | no |
| | | | | Read idiom in sentence | | 0.21 | – | 0.00 | – | 0.21*[d] | | 0.53 | – | – | – | | | |
| | | | | Read idiom and its synonym | | 0.08 | – | 0.00 | – | 0.08*[d] | | 0.22 | – | – | – | | | |
| | | | | Judge number of letters | | 0.02 | – | 0.00 | – | 0.02[b] | | 0.09 | – | – | – | | | |
| | | 4 | | Read idiom definition | Free Association | 0.16 | – | 0.00 | – | 0.16*[d] | Cued Recall | 0.66 | – | – | – | Levels of Processing | | no |
| | | | | Read idiom in sentence | | 0.21 | – | 0.00 | – | 0.21*[d] | | 0.62 | – | – | – | | | |
| 1989 | Schacter & McGlynn (2) | 4 | Yes | Read idiom and its synonym | Free Association | 0.10 | – | 0.00 | – | 0.10*[d] | Cued Recall | 0.35 | – | – | – | | | |
| | | | | Judge number of letters | | 0.04 | – | 0.00 | – | 0.04[d] | | 0.15 | – | – | – | | | |
| | | 8 | Yes | Read idiom definition | Free Association | 0.25 | – | 0.00 | – | 0.25*[d] | Cued Recall | 0.79 | – | – | – | Levels of Processing | | no |
| | | | | Read idiom in sentence | | 0.25 | – | 0.00 | – | 0.25*[d] | | 0.71 | – | – | – | # of P | | no |

| Year | Study (Experiment) | # of P | Satisfy RIC? | Manipulated Condition | Implicit Memory Test | | | | | | Explicit Memory Test | | | | | Dissociation (yes or no?) | | |
|---|---|---|---|---|---|---|---|---|---|---|---|---|---|---|---|---|---|---|
| | | | | | Task | Intact | Recb | New | IRP | NAP | Task | Intact Hit | Recb FA | New FA | I-R | Critical Manipulation | IRP | NAP |
| | | | | Read idiom and its synonym | | 0.17 | -- | 0.00 | -- | 0.17*[d] | | 0.56 | -- | -- | -- | | | |
| | | | | Judge number of letters | | 0.05 | -- | 0.00 | -- | 0.05[d] | | 0.19 | -- | -- | -- | | | |
| 1989 | Schacter & McGlynn (3) | 1 | Yes | Read idiom in sentence | Free Association | 0.59 | -- | 0.39 | -- | 0.20*[a] | Cued Recall | 0.71 | -- | -- | -- | Levels of Processing | | yes |
| | | | | Judge number of letters | | 0.60 | -- | 0.44 | -- | 0.16*[a] | | 0.60 | -- | -- | -- | | | |
| 1989 | Schacter & McGlynn (4) | 2 | Yes | Read idiom in sentence | Free Association | 0.27 | -- | 0.00 | -- | 0.27*[c] | Cued Recall | 0.71 | -- | -- | -- | Levels of Processing | | no |
| | | | | Judge number of letters | | 0.01 | -- | 0.00 | -- | 0.01[b] | | 0.04 | -- | -- | -- | | | |
| 1989 | Schacter & McGlynn (4) | 4 | Yes | Read idiom in sentence | Free Association | 0.29 | -- | 0.00 | -- | 0.29[c] | Cued Recall | 0.82 | -- | -- | -- | Levels of Processing | | no |
| | | | | Judge number of letters | | 0.01 | -- | 0.00 | -- | 0.01[b] | | 0.08 | -- | -- | -- | | | |
| | | 8 | | Read idiom in sentence | Free Association | 0.32 | -- | 0.00 | -- | 0.32*[c] | Cued Recall | 0.88 | -- | -- | -- | Levels of Processing | | no |
| | | | | Judge number of letters | | 0.01 | -- | 0.00 | -- | 0.01[b] | | 0.18 | -- | -- | -- | # of P | | no |
| 1989 | Smith et al. (1) | 1 | No | Judge number of vowels in both words | Lexical Decision | 542 | 553 | 572 | 19*[c] | 11[b] | Item Recognition (RGN)/Pair-Matching (PM) | 0.68 (RGN) | 0.06 (PM) | -- | -- | Levels of Processing | yes | yes |
| | | | | Judge pleasantness | | 519 | 522 | 547 | 25*[c] | 3[b] | | 0.85 (RGN) | 0.18 (PM) | -- | -- | | | |
| | | | | Memorize pairs by rote | | 535 | 545 | 569 | 24*[c] | 10[b] | | 0.76 (RGN) | 0.24 (PM) | -- | -- | | | |
| | | | | Generate sentences | | 580 | 572 | 611 | 39*[c] | -8[b] | | 0.84 (RGN) | 0.91 (PM) | -- | -- | | | |
| 1989 | Smith et al. (2) | 1 | No | 250-ms SOA | Lexical Decision | 525 | 522 | 547 | 25*[a] | -3[b] | Item Recognition/Pair-Matching | 0.80 (RGN) | 0.52 (PM) | -- | -- | SOA | no | no |
| | | | | 1000-ms SOA | | 561 | 569 | 563 | -6[b] | 8[b] | | 0.75 (RGN) | 0.43 (PM) | -- | -- | | | |
| 1990 | Bowers & Schacter (2a) | 1 | Yes | Test Aware | Word-Stem Completion | 0.26 | 0.12 | 0.08 | 0.04[b] | 0.14*[b] | Stem-Cued Recall | 0.43 | 0.12 | -- | 0.31*[a] | Test Awareness | yes | no |

## Table 4. (Continued)

| Year | Study (Experiment) | # of P | Satisfy RIC? | Manipulated Condition | Implicit Memory Test | | | | | Explicit Memory Test | | | | | Dissociation (yes or no?) | | |
|---|---|---|---|---|---|---|---|---|---|---|---|---|---|---|---|---|---|
| | | | | | Task | Intact | Recb | New | IRP | NAP | Task | Intact Hit | Recb FA | New FA | I-R | Critical Manipulation | IRP | NAP |
| 1990 | Bowers & Schacter (2b) | 1 | Yes | Test Unaware | Word-Stem Completion | 0.13 | 0.13 | 0.08 | 0.05[b] | 0[b] | Stem-Cued Recall | 0.20 | 0.06 | -- | 0.14*[a] | | -- | -- |
| | | | | Test Aware | | 0.28 | 0.15 | 0.08 | 0.07^[b] | 0.13*[b] | | 0.52 | 0.18 | -- | 0.34*[a] | Test Awareness | yes | no |
| 1990 | Bowers & Schacter (2c) | 1 | Yes | Test Unaware | Word-Stem Completion | 0.10 | 0.11 | 0.08 | 0.03[b] | -0.01[b] | Stem-Cued Recall | 0.17 | 0.06 | -- | 0.11*[a] | | -- | -- |
| | | | | Test Aware | | 0.30 | 0.13 | 0.08 | 0.05[b] | 0.17*[b] | | 0.66 | 0.18 | -- | 0.48*[a] | Test Awareness | yes | no |
| 1990 | Bowers & Schacter (3) | 1 | Yes | Test Unaware | Word-Stem Completion | 0.15 | 0.14 | 0.08 | 0.06[b] | 0.01[b] | Stem-Cued Recall | 0.27 | 0.07 | -- | 0.20*[a] | | -- | -- |
| | | | | Informed-Aware | | 0.25 | 0.15 | 0.08 | 0.07*[b] | 0.10*[b] | | 0.50 | 0.07 | -- | 0.43*[a] | Test Awareness | yes | no |
| | | | | Informed-Unaware | | 0.13 | 0.14 | 0.08 | 0.06[b] | -0.01[b] | | 0.42 | 0.09 | -- | 0.33*[a] | Test Awareness | no | no |
| | | | | Uninformed-Aware | | 0.20 | 0.16 | 0.08 | 0.08*[b] | 0.04[b] | | 0.54 | 0.19 | -- | 0.35*[a] | Test Awareness | yes | no |
| | | | | Uninformed-Unaware | | 0.10 | 0.13 | 0.08 | 0.05[b] | -0.03[b] | | 0.46 | 0.16 | -- | 0.30*[a] | Test Informedness | yes | no |
| 1990 | Mutter et al. (1) | 1 | No | Closed head injury | Word-Stem Completion | 0.37 | 0.27 | 0.10 | 0.17*[b] | 0.10[b] | Cued Recall | 0.25 | -- | -- | -- | Participant | yes | yes |
| | | | | Control | | 0.31 | 0.19 | 0.13 | 0.06[b] | 0.12^[b] | | 0.47 | -- | -- | -- | | | |
| | | | | Young | | 0.38 | 0.23 | 0.13 | 0.10*[b] | 0.15*[b] | | 0.59 | -- | -- | -- | | | |
| | | | Yes | Closed head injury | | 0.37 | 0.27 | 0.10 | 0.17*[b] | 0.10[b] | Stem-Cued Recall | 0.57 | -- | -- | -- | | | |
| | | | | Control | | 0.31 | 0.19 | 0.13 | 0.06^[b] | 0.12^[b] | | 0.65 | -- | -- | -- | | | |
| | | | | Young | | 0.38 | 0.23 | 0.13 | 0.10*[b] | 0.15*[b] | | 0.70 | -- | -- | -- | | | |
| 1991 | Chen & Yang (2) | 1 | Yes | Proactive interference | Word-Stem Completion | 0.47 | 0.49 | -- | -- | 0.03[a] | Stem-Cued Recall | 0.48 | 0.73 | -- | 0.26*[a] | Interference | yes | no |
| | | | | Retroactive interference | | 0.45 | 0.46 | -- | -- | 0.01[a] | | 0.50 | 0.76 | -- | 0.26*[a] | | | |
| 1991 | Christensen & Birrell (2) | 1 | No | Alzheimer disease | Word-Stem Completion | 0.46 | 0.23 | 0.23 | 0[b] | 0.22*[b] | Cued-Recall | 6.2 | -- | -- | -- | Participant | yes | yes |
| | | | | Old | | 0.37 | 0.23 | 0.25 | -0.02[b] | 0.14*[b] | | 11 | -- | -- | -- | | | |
| | | | | Control | | 0.50 | 0.27 | 0.15 | 0.12[b] | 0.23*[b] | | 14 | -- | -- | -- | | | |
| | | | | Young | | 0.44 | 0.20 | 0.16 | 0.04[b] | 0.24*[b] | | 16.2 | -- | -- | -- | | | |
| 1991 | Howard et al. (1) | 1 | Yes | Young | Word-Stem Completion | 0.33 | 0.14 | 0.14 | 0[b] | 0.19*[b] | Stem-Cued Recall | 0.49 | 0.34 | -- | 0.15*[a] | Participant | yes | no |
| | | | | Old | | 0.18 | 0.14 | 0.11 | 0.03[b] | -0.03[a] | | 0.13 | 0.14 | -- | -0.01[a] | | | |

| Year | Study (Experiment) | # of P | Satisfy RIC? | Manipulated Condition | Implicit Memory Test | | | | | Explicit Memory Test | | | | | Dissociation (yes or no?) | | |
|---|---|---|---|---|---|---|---|---|---|---|---|---|---|---|---|---|---|
| | | | | | Task | Intact | Recb | New | IRP | NAP | Task | Intact Hit | Recb FA | New FA | I-R | Critical Manipulation | IRP | NAP |
| 1991 | Howard et al. (2) | 1 | Yes | Young | Word-Stem Completion | 0.34 | 0.17 | 0.12 | 0.05[b] | 0.13[^,a] | Stem-Cued Recall | 0.84 | 0.80 | -- | 0.04[a] | Participant | yes | yes |
| | | | | Old | | 0.30 | 0.16 | 0.11 | 0.05[b] | 0.10*[a] | | 0.48 | 0.38 | -- | 0.10*[a] | | | |
| 1991 | Howard et al. (3) | 1 | Yes | Young | Word-Stem Completion | 0.35 | 0.20 | 0.10 | 0.10*[b] | 0.15*[a] | Stem-Cued Recall | 0.66 | 0.27 | 0.10 | 0.39*[a] | Participant | yes | no |
| | | | | Old | | 0.20 | 0.13 | 0.09 | 0.04[b] | 0.07[a] | | 0.36 | 0.24 | 0.09 | 0.12*[a] | | | |
| 1991 | Micco & Masson (1) | 1 | Yes | Copy word pairs | Word-Stem Completion | 0.28 | 0.24 | 0.21 | 0.03[a] | 0.04[a] | Stem-Cued Recall | 0.24 | 0.24 | -- | 0[a] | Levels of Processing | yes | yes |
| | | | | Generate sentences | | 0.30 | 0.23 | 0.23 | 0[a] | 0.07*[c] | | 0.44 | 0.28 | -- | 0.16*[a] | | | |
| 1992 | Van der Linden et al. (1) | 1 | Yes | Young-Rate relatedness | Word-Stem Completion | 0.25 | 0.17 | 0.04 | 0.13*[b] | 0.08[b] | Stem-Cued Recall | 0.64 | -- | -- | -- | Levels of Elaboration | yes | yes |
| | | | | Old-Rate relatedness | | -- | 0.18 | 0.04 | 0.14*[b] | -- | | 0.35 | -- | -- | -- | | | |
| | | | | Young-Generate sentence | | 0.44 | 0.19 | 0.04 | 0.15*[b] | 0.25*[b] | | 0.42 | -- | -- | -- | | | |
| | | | | Old-Generate-sentence | | -- | 0.18 | 0.04 | 0.14*[b] | -- | | 0.29 | -- | -- | -- | | | |
| 1993 | Musen & Squire (1) | 1 | No | Normal | Rereading | 16.30 | 17 | 18 | 1*[d] | 0.70[b] | Three-alternative choice recognition | 82.50 | 67.50 | 83.30 | 15*[b] | Participant | no | no |
| | | | | Amnesia | | 14.20 | 14.80 | 16.30 | 1.50*[d] | 0.60[b] | | 51.20 | 41.20 | 45 | 10*[b] | | | |
| 1994 | Paller & Mayes (3) | 1 | No | Normal | Perceptual Identification | 0.77 | 0.63 | 0.29 | 0.34*[c] | 0.14*[a] | Item Recognition | 0.92 | -- | -- | -- | Participant | yes | no |
| | | | | Amnesia | | 0.71 | 0.68 | 0.40 | 0.28*[c] | 0.03[a] | | 0.49 | -- | -- | -- | | | |
| 1995a | Goshen-Gottstein & Moscovitch (1) | 1 | No | High frequency-Shallow encoding | Double-item Lexical Decision | 885 | 874 | 912 | 38[b] | -11[b] | Pair Recognition | 0.63 | 0.59 | 0.55 | 0.04[a] | Levels of Processing | yes | no |
| | | | | High frequency-Deep encoding | | 868 | 909 | 953 | 44[b] | 41[b] | | 0.85 | 0.69 | 0.87 | 0.16*[a] | | | |
| | | | | Low frequency-Shallow encoding | | 974 | 1028 | 1103 | 75*[b] | 54[b] | | 0.58 | 0.54 | 0.65 | 0.04[a] | Levels of Processing | no | no |
| | | | | Low frequency-Deep encoding | | 968 | 1035 | 1174 | 139*[b] | 67*[b] | | 0.90 | 0.78 | 0.92 | 0.13*[a] | Word Frequency | yes | yes |
| 1995a | Goshen-Gottstein & Moscovitch (2) | 1 | No | High frequency-Deep encoding | Double-item Lexical Decision | 537 | 533 | 539 | 6[b] | -4[b] | Pair Recognition | 0.90 | 0.72 | 0.86 | 0.18*[c] | Word Frequency | yes | yes |
| | | | | Low frequency-Deep encoding | | 567 | 587 | 626 | 39*[b] | 20[b] | | 0.94 | 0.83 | 0.92 | 0.11*[c] | | | |

# Table 4. (Continued)

| Year | Study (Experiment) | # of P | Satisfy RIC? | Manipulated Condition | Implicit Memory Test | | | | | Explicit Memory Test | | | | | Dissociation (yes or no?) | | |
|---|---|---|---|---|---|---|---|---|---|---|---|---|---|---|---|---|---|
| | | | | | Task | Intact | Recb | New | IRP | NAP | Task | Intact Hit | Recb FA | New FA | I-R | Critical Manipulation | IRP | NAP |
| 1996 | Light et al. (2) | 1 | No | Young full attention at test | Naming | 672 | 681 | 698 | 17*[a] | 9^[c] | Associative Recognition | 0.49 | 0.25 | 0.09 | 0.24*[a] | Participant | yes | yes |
| | | | | Old full attention at test | | 735 | 746 | 761 | 15*[a] | 11^[c] | | 0.35 | 0.25 | 0.08 | 0.11*[a] | | | |
| | | | | Young divided attention at test | | 681 | 687 | 698 | 11^[a] | 6[c] | | 0.18 | 0.13 | 0.09 | 0.04^[a] | Participant | no | no |
| | | | | Old divided attention at test | | 759 | 754 | 761 | 7[a] | -5[c] | | 0.14 | 0.14 | 0.08 | 0.01[a] | Attention | no | no |
| 1996 | Marsolek et al. (1A/1B) | 2 | Yes | Left hemi-same font in study & test | Word-Stem Completion | 0.17 | 0.16 | 0.08 | 0.08*[b] | 0.01[b] | Stem-Cued Recall | 29.10 | 17.80 | 9.80 | 11.30[d] | Match in Font Type | no | yes |
| | | | | Left hemi-diff font in study & test | | 0.14 | 0.11 | 0.08 | 0.03[b] | 0.03[b] | | 15.60 | 14.80 | 9.80 | 0.80[d] | | | |
| | | | | Right hemi-same font in study & test | | 0.25 | 0.17 | 0.09 | 0.08*[b] | 0.08*[b] | | 28.90 | 20.90 | 9.90 | 8[d] | Match in Font Type | no | no |
| | | | | Right hemi-diff font in study & test | | 0.11 | 0.15 | 0.09 | 0.06*[b] | -0.05*[b] | | 22.40 | 18.40 | 9.90 | 4[d] | Presented Hemisphere | no | no |
| 1996 | Marsolek et al. (2A/2B) | 2 | Yes | Left hemi-same font in study & test | Word-Stem Completion | 0.22 | 0.20 | 0.08 | 0.12*[b] | 0.02[b] | Stem-Cued Recall | 24.90 | 25.30 | 10.10 | -0.40[d] | Match in Font Type | yes | no |
| | | | | Left hemi-diff font in study & test | | 0.23 | 0.17 | 0.08 | 0.10*[b] | 0.06*[b] | | 22.60 | 19.90 | 10.10 | 2.70[d] | | | |
| | | | | Right hemi-same font in study & test | | 0.25 | 0.20 | 0.08 | 0.12*[b] | 0.05*[b] | | 30.40 | 23.40 | 10.40 | 7[d] | Match in Font Type | yes | no |
| | | | | Right hemi-diff font in study & test | | 0.11 | 0.18 | 0.08 | 0.09*[b] | -0.07*[b] | | 25.20 | 20.40 | 10.40 | 4.80[d] | Presented Hemisphere | yes | yes |
| 1996 | Nicolas & Carbonnel (1) | 1 | Yes | Judge number of right angle | Word-Stem Completion | 0.46 | 0.43 | 0.18 | 0.25*[a] | 0.03[b] | Stem-Cued Recall | 0.31 | 0.22 | -- | 0.09*[c] | Levels of Processing | no | no |
| | | | | Generate sentence | | 0.47 | 0.45 | 0.18 | 0.27*[a] | 0.02[b] | | 0.62 | 0.51 | -- | 0.11*[c] | | | |
| 1996 | Nicolas & Carbonnel (3) | 1 | Yes | Word context at study | Word-Stem Completion | 0.44 | 0.43 | 0.18 | 0.25*[a] | 0.01[b] | Stem-Cued Recall | 0.68 | 0.56 | 0.43 | 0.12*[c] | Word/Picture Context | yes | yes |
| | | | | Picture context at study | | 0.31 | 0.19 | 0.18 | 0.01[b] | 0.12*[c] | | 0.58 | 0.46 | 0.45 | 0.12*[c] | | | |

| Year | Study (Experiment) | # of P | Satisfy RIC? | Manipulated Condition | Implicit Memory Test | | | | | | Explicit Memory Test | | | | | Dissociation (yes or no?) | | |
|---|---|---|---|---|---|---|---|---|---|---|---|---|---|---|---|---|---|---|
| | | | | | Task | Intact | Recb | New | IRP | NAP | Task | Intact Hit | Recb FA | New FA | I-R | Critical Manipulation | IRP | NAP |
| 1996 | Spieler & Balota (2) | 3 | No | Young Massed Immediate | Naming (only target) | 502 | 542 | 562 | -- | 40*[b] | Cued Recall | 0.78 | 0.55 | -- | -- | Massed/Spaced | yes | yes |
| | | | | Young Spaced Immediate | | 528 | 550 | 568 | -- | 22*[b] | | 0.74 | 0.61 | -- | -- | | | |
| | | | | Old Massed Immediate | Naming (only target) | 672 | 672 | 700 | -- | 0[a] | Cued Recall | 0.56 | 0.33 | -- | -- | Massed/Spaced | no | no |
| | | | | Old Spaced Immediate | | 671 | 671 | 700 | -- | 0[a] | | 0.49 | 0.36 | -- | -- | Participant | yes | yes |
| 1997 | Gabrieli et al. (1) | 2 | No | Normal | Perceptual Identification | 0.56 | 0.47 | 0.25 | 0.22*[b] | 0.09[b] | Three-alternative choice recognition | 0.62 | 0.26 | 0.08 | 0.36*[a] | Participant | yes | yes |
| | | | | Amnesia | | 0.55 | 0.43 | 0.24 | 0.19*[a] | 0.12*[a] | | 0.42 | 0.33 | 0.21 | 0.09[b] | | | |
| 1997 | McKone & Slee (1) | 1 | No | Related word pair | Double-item Lexical Decision | 704 | 812 | 823 | -- | 108*[a] | Cued Recall | 95.10 | -- | -- | -- | Study-pair Relatedness | no | no |
| | | | | Unrelated word pair | | 836 | 844 | 836 | -- | 8[a] | | 52.10 | -- | -- | -- | | | |
| 1997 | McKone & Slee (2) | 1 | Yes | Less elaborative encoding | Word-Stem Completion | 0.26 | 0.22 | 0.22 | -- | 0.04[c] | Stem-Cued Recall | 0.46 | 0.14 | 0.47 | 0.32*[a] | Levels of Elaboration | no | no |
| | | | | More elaborative encoding | | 0.31 | 0.22 | 0.22 | -- | 0.09[c] | | 0.72 | 0.14 | 0.47 | 0.58*[a] | | | |
| 1998 | Ergis et al. (1) | 1 | Yes | Alzheimer Disease | Word-Stem Completion | 0.16 | 0.19 | 0.06 | 0.13*[a] | -0.03[c] | Stem-Cued Recall | 0.16 | 0.76 | -- | -- | Participant | yes | yes |
| | | | | Old | | 0.21 | 0.20 | 0.09 | 0.11*[a] | 0.02[a] | | 0.83 | 0.05 | -- | -- | | | |
| | | | | Young | | 0.34 | 0.21 | 0.10 | 0.11*[b] | 0.14*[a] | | 0.89 | 0.04 | -- | -- | | | |
| 1999 | Brooks (2) | 1 | Yes | Related word pair | Free Association | 0.61 | -- | 0.17 | -- | 0.44*[a] | Cued Recall | 0.67 | 0.05 | -- | 0.62*[a] | Study-pair Relatedness | no | no |
| | | | | Unrelated word pair | | 0.42 | -- | 0.01 | -- | 0.41*[a] | | 0.61 | 0.04 | -- | 0.57*[a] | | | |
| 1999 | Gooding et al. (1) | 1 | Yes | Full attention at study | Word-Stem Completion | 0.24 | 0.18 | 0.11 | 0.07*[b] | 0.06^[a] | Stem-Cued Recall | 0.47 | 0.28 | 0.14 | 0.19*[a] | Attention | yes | yes |
| | | | | Divided attention at study | | 0.22 | 0.17 | 0.11 | 0.06*[b] | 0.05^[a] | | 0.26 | 0.22 | 0.09 | 0.04*[a] | | | |
| 1999 | Gooding et al. (1) | 1 | No | Full attention at study | Word-Stem Completion | 0.25 | 0.17 | 0.11 | 0.06[b] | 0.08*[a] | Item Recognition | 0.86 | 0.73 | 0.13 | 0.13*[b] | Attention | no | no |
| | | | | Divided attention at study | | 0.23 | 0.16 | 0.10 | 0.06*[b] | 0.07*[a] | | 0.80 | 0.68 | 0.20 | 0.12*[b] | | | |
| 1999 | Yang Weng, Guan et al. (2) | 1 | No | Deep encoding-Concrete word pair | Word-Stem Completion | 0.80 | 0.48 | 0.28 | 0.20*[b] | 0.32*[b] | Item Recognition | -- | -- | -- | 4.93 (d') | Word Concreteness | yes | no |

**Table 4. (Continued)**

| Year | Study (Experiment) | # of P | Satisfy RIC? | Manipulated Condition | Implicit Memory Test | | | | | | Explicit Memory Test | | | | | | Dissociation (yes or no?) | | |
|---|---|---|---|---|---|---|---|---|---|---|---|---|---|---|---|---|---|---|---|
| | | | | | Task | Intact | Recb | New | IRP | NAP | Task | Intact Hit | Recb FA | New FA | I-R | Critical Manipulation | IRP | NAP |
| | | | | Deep encoding-Abstract word pair | | 0.70 | 0.47 | 0.27 | 0.20*$^b$ | 0.23*$^b$ | | — | — | — | 3.31 (d') | | | |
| 1999 | Yang Weng, Guan et al. (2) | 1 | No | Shallow encoding-Concrete word pair | Word-Stem Completion | 0.57 | 0.44 | 0.30 | 0.14*$^b$ | 0.13*$^b$ | Item Recognition | — | — | — | 0.40 (d') | Word Concreteness | yes | yes |
| | | | | Shallow encoding-Abstract word pair | | 0.44 | 0.53 | 0.26 | 0.27*$^b$ | -0.09^$b$ | | — | — | — | 0.50 (d') | | | |
| 2000 | Goshen-Gottstein et al. (1) | 1 | No | Normal | Double-item Lexical Decision | 715 | 738 | 815 | 77*$^c$ | 23*$^a$ | Pair Recognition | 0.84 | 0.47 | — | 0.38*$^a$ | Participant | yes | yes |
| | | | | Amnesic | | 1213 | 1322 | 1420 | 98*$^c$ | 109*$^a$ | | 0.53 | 0.46 | — | 0.07^$a$ | | | |
| 2000 | Srinivas et al. (1) | 1 | No | Congruous context | Category Verification | 1699 | 1684 | — | — | 15^$b$ | Item Recognition | 0.71 | 0.78 | — | -0.07^$a$ | Context Congruity | no | no |
| | | | | Incongruous context | | 1984 | 1829 | — | — | 155*$^a$ | | 0.72 | 0.98 | — | -0.26*$^a$ | | | |
| 2001 | O'Hanlon et al. (1/2) | 1 | Yes | Young-Judge number of syllable | Word-Stem Completion | 0.21 | 0.17 | 0.08 | 0.09*$^b$ | 0.04^$b$ | Stem-Cued Recall | 0.18 | 0.20 | 0.10 | 0.10^$a$ | Participant | no | no |
| | | | | Old-Judge number of syllable | | 0.14 | 0.14 | 0.07 | 0.07*$^b$ | 0^$b$ | | 0.12 | 0.09 | 0.09 | 0^$a$ | | | |
| | | | | Young-Generate sentence | | 0.31 | 0.18 | 0.08 | 0.10*$^b$ | 0.13^$b$ | | 0.65 | 0.32 | 0.11 | 0.21*$^a$ | Participant | yes | |
| | | | | Old-Generate sentence | | 0.17 | 0.14 | 0.08 | 0.06*$^b$ | 0.03^$b$ | | 0.31 | 0.16 | 0.07 | 0.09^$a$ | Levels of Processing | yes | |
| 2002 | Yang et al. (1) | 1 | No | Normal | Perceptual Identification | 0.66 | 0.48 | 0.23 | 0.25*$^b$ | 0.18*$^b$ | Associative Recognition | — | — | — | 2.88 (d') | Participant | yes | no |
| | | | | Frontal lobe lesion | | 0.60 | 0.51 | 0.22 | 0.29*$^b$ | 0.09^$b$ | | — | — | — | 2.09 (d') | | | |
| 2003 | Uttl et al. (1) | 1 | No | Immediate-Word pair | Perceptual Identification | 0.71 | 0.62 | 0.51 | 0.11^$b$ | 0.09^$b$ | Item Recognition | 0.79 | 0.69 | 0.08 | 0.10*$^b$ | Word/Picture Context | no | no |
| | | | | Immediate-Picture pair | | 0.72 | 0.61 | 0.50 | 0.11^$a$ | 0.11^$a$ | | 0.82 | 0.70 | 0.09 | 0.12*$^b$ | | | |
| | | | | Delay-Word pair | | 0.61 | 0.59 | 0.51 | 0.08*$^b$ | 0.02^$b$ | | 0.61 | 0.58 | 0.30 | 0.03^$b$ | Word/Picture Context | yes | no |
| | | | | Delay-Picture pair | | 0.59 | 0.59 | 0.48 | 0.11*$^b$ | 0^$b$ | | 0.72 | 0.61 | 0.28 | 0.11*$^b$ | Retention Interval | no | no |

| Year | Study (Experiment) | # of P | Satisfy RIC? | Manipulated Condition | Implicit Memory Test — Task | Intact | Recb | New | IRP | NAP | Explicit Memory Test — Task | Intact Hit | Recb FA | New FA | I-R | Dissociation — Critical Manipulation | IRP | NAP |
|---|---|---|---|---|---|---|---|---|---|---|---|---|---|---|---|---|---|---|
| 2003 | Uttl et al. (2) | 1 | No | Young-Word pair | Perceptual Identification | 0.62 | 0.56 | 0.43 | 0.13*[b] | 0.06*[a] | Item Recognition | 0.88 | 0.79 | 0.19 | 0.09[b] | Word/Picture Context | no | no |
| | | | | Young-Picture pair | | 0.64 | 0.55 | 0.44 | 0.11*[b] | 0.09*[a] | | 0.86 | 0.75 | 0.18 | 0.11*[b] | | | |
| | | | | Old-Word pair | | 0.48 | 0.38 | 0.36 | 0.02[b] | 0.10*[a] | | 0.74 | 0.71 | 0.22 | 0.03[b] | Word/Picture Context | no | yes |
| | | | | Old-Picture pair | | 0.49 | 0.48 | 0.41 | 0.07^[b] | 0.01[b] | | 0.76 | 0.65 | 0.21 | 0.11*[b] | Retention Interval | no | no |
| 2003 | Vakil & Oded (1) | 1 | No | Normal | Word-Stem Completion | 0.75 | 0.34 | 0.17 | 0.17*[b] | 0.41*[b] | Cued-Recall | 0.56 | – | – | – | Participant | yes | no |
| | | | | Closed head injury | | 0.59 | 0.30 | 0.17 | 0.13*[b] | 0.29*[b] | | 0.44 | | | | | | |
| 2003 | Yang et al. (1) | 1 | No | Normal | Perceptual Identification | 0.66 | 0.48 | 0.23 | 0.25*[a] | 0.18*[a] | Associative Recognition | 0.87 | 0.34 | – | 2.88 (d') | Participant | yes | no |
| | | | | Amnesic | | 0.49 | 0.52 | 0.23 | 0.29*[a] | -0.03[b] | | 0.79 | 0.46 | – | 1.30 (d') | | | |
| 2005 | Carlesimo et al. (1) | 6 | No | Normal | Lexical Decision | 650 | 678 | 673 | -5[b] | 28*[c] | Cued-Recall | 0.28 | – | – | – | Participant | yes | no |
| | | | | Amnesic | | 785 | 804 | 799 | -5[b] | 19*[c] | | 0.06 | – | – | – | | | |
| 2005 | Silberman et al. (1) | 20 | Yes | Related word pairs | Free Association | 0.08 | – | – | – | 0.08*[a] | Cued-Recall | 0.39 | – | – | – | Study-pair Relatedness | | no |
| | | | | Unrelated word pairs | | 0.01 | – | – | – | 0.01[a] | | 0.19 | – | – | – | | | |
| 2006 | Verfaellie et al. (1A) | 1 | Yes | Normal | Category Generation | 0.69 | 0.55 | 0.46 | 0.09*[c] | 0.14*[a] | Cued-Recall | 0.58 | 0.33 | 0 | 0.25*[c] | Participant | yes | no |
| | | | | Amnesic | | 0.53 | 0.50 | 0.40 | 0.10*[c] | 0.03[a] | | 0.24 | 0.12 | 0.02 | 0.12*[c] | | | |
| 2006 | Verfaellie et al. (1B) | 1 | Yes | Rate relatedness | Category Generation | 0.58 | 0.49 | 0.48 | 0.01[b] | 0.09[a] | Cued-Recall | 0.78 | 0.51 | 0.01 | 0.27*[a] | Levels of Elaboration | yes | no |
| | | | | Generate sentence | | 0.70 | 0.59 | 0.53 | 0.06*[c] | 0.11*[c] | | 0.58 | 0.38 | 0 | 0.20*[c] | | | |
| 2009 | Laver (2) | 1 | No | Young | Rereading | 0.54 | 0.48 | | | 0.06[b] | Item recognition | | | | 2.18(d') | Participant | no | no |
| | | | | Middle-aged | | 0.47 | 0.41 | | | 0.06[b] | | | | | | | | |
| | | | | Old | | 0.4 | 0.38 | | | 0.02[b] | | | | | 2.00(d') | | | |
| | | | | Young | | 459 | 480 | | | -21[b] | | | | | 1.78(d') | | | |
| | | | | Middle-aged | | 457 | 458 | | | -1[b] | | | | | | | | |
| | | | | old | | 460 | 452 | | | 8[b] | | | | | | | | |
| 2009 | White et al. | 1 | Yes | Young-incidental encoding | Word-Stem Completion | 0.38 | 0.33 | | | 0.05[b] | Stem-Cued Recall | 0.55 | 0.51 | | 0.04[b] | Participant | | no |

# Table 4. (Continued)

| Year | Study (Experiment) | # of P | Satisfy RIC? | Manipulated Condition | Implicit Memory Test | | | | | | Explicit Memory Test | | | | | Dissociation (yes or no?) | | |
|---|---|---|---|---|---|---|---|---|---|---|---|---|---|---|---|---|---|---|
| | | | | | Task | Intact | Recb | New | IRP | NAP | Task | Intact Hit | Recb FA | New FA | I-R | Critical Manipulation | IRP | NAP |
| | | | | Old-incidental encoding | | 0.44 | 0.39 | | | $0.05^b$ | | 0.53 | 0.44 | | $0.09*^b$ | Levels of Processing | | no |
| | | 1 | Yes | Young-intentional encoding | | 0.44 | 0.40 | | | $0.04^b$ | | 0.55 | 0.46 | | $0.09*^b$ | | | |
| | | | | Old-intentional encoding | | 0.37 | 0.34 | | | $0.03^b$ | | 0.52 | 0.43 | | $0.09*^b$ | | | |

Note — $* p < .05$ (two-tailed), $^\wedge p < .05$ (one-tailed). The highlighted rows are the experiments involving amnesic patients. RIC = retrieval intentionality criterion, # of P = number of study-pair presentations, RT = reaction time, SOA = stimulus-onset asychrony in msec. Intact = intact pair condition, Recb = recombined pair condition, New = new pair condition. IRP = item repetition priming, NAP = new association priming, the values in the intact, recb, new, IRP and NAP columns are either RTs or proportions, depending on the implicit task. (See Table 1 *dependent measure* column.) The values in the intact hit (proportion of correctly recalling/recognizing the studied items/pairs), recb FA (proportion of incorrectly recalling/recognizing the non-studied items/pairs), and new FA columns are all proportions. In "Dissociation?" column, yes = dissociation occurs between implicit and explicit memory performance, no = the effect of the manipulated variables is in the same direction for explicit and implicit memory performance. The letter-label next to IRP and NAP indicates the procedure for assessing statistical significance: a – directly reported by the authors; b – $ts$ computed based on the standard errors; c – $ts$ computed based on the main effect of manipulated variables; d – the largest or smallest $ts$ reported by the authors.

When a word pair (e.g., WINDOW-reason) appears at study, the pair can be re-presented (a) intact and clearly in an episodic item recognition test, (b) intact but degraded in a perceptual identification task, (c) with a context word and only the first three letters of its target in a word-stem completion task, (d) with a context word and its target being several-letters-deleted in a word-fragment completion task, or (e) with only context word but not its target in a cued recall task. If the explicit and implicit memory tests used in an experiment present the test pairs differently, it is possible that the observed dissociation is only due to such a difference, but not the implicit vs. explicit retrieval processes.

To resolve this problem, Schacter et al. (1989, see also Neely, 1989) proposed the *retrieval intentionality criterion*. Experiments that fulfill this criterion hold constant all task demands (e.g., presentation format of test items) and the experimental manipulations of implicit and explicit memory tests *except* for their instructions, which either tells the participants to refer to the study list to perform the task (an explicit instruction) or makes no mention of the study phase at all (an implicit instruction). For example, in Graf and Schacter's (1987) test phase, they gave the same displays of test items (context word + test stem, e.g., WINDOW-rea___) to all participants, with half of them receiving the explicit instruction (i.e., stem-cued recall task) and half, the implicit instruction (i.e., word-stem completion task). They found that their interference manipulation significantly hurt explicit stem-cued recall performance, but not new association priming in the implicit word-stem completion. Because the processing requirements (producing an answer to a stem) were held constant for explicit and implicit memory tests except the reference to the study episodes, a dissociation produced by the interference manipulation could be interpreted as evidence that this manipulation affected the explicit, but not implicit, memory system (or retrieval processes).[14] (See Table 1 *"Explicit Memory Test Satisfies RIC"* column for the implicit memory tests and their corresponding explicit memory tests that satisfy the retrieval intentionality criterion.) To assess explicit vs. implicit functional dissociations for previous new association priming studies by taking retrieval intentionality criterion into consideration, we screen out the experiments that did not satisfy the retrieval intentionality criterion (see in Table 1 *"Satisfy RIC?"* column), leaving 61 of 106 (57%) comparisons in prior new association priming experiments that fulfilled the retrieval intentionality criterion. The retrieval intentionality criterion was fulfilled when the implicit word-stem completion task was paired up with the explicit stem cued-recall task, the implicit free association task was paired up with the explicit cued recall task, or the implicit category exemplar generation task was paired up with the explicit cued recall task. Of these 61 comparisons, only 25 (41%) reported an explicit vs. implicit functional dissociation in new association priming. For the item repetition priming, 43 (55%) of 78 comparisons fulfilled the retrieval intentionality criterion and of these 43 comparisons, 32 (74%) showed the explicit vs. implicit functional dissociation in new association priming.[15] Hence, whereas about 75% of new association

---

[14] However, sometimes it is difficult to pair up an implicit memory test with an explicit memory test for satisfying the retrieval intentionality criterion. For example, for the perceptual identification task in which test items/pairs are presented very rapidly (< 100 ms), even the speeded episodic recognition memory test seems not to be its explicit counterpart as in this test,3 the test items are not rapidly presented and participants' speeded recognition decisions still last for at least 400 ms, much longer than the presentation duration of test items in the perceptual identification task.

[15] The explicit vs. implicit functional dissociation in new association priming was more likely found in perceptual implicit memory tests (19 of 41, 46%) than in conceptual implicit memory tests (2 of 14, 14%). However, this finding should be interpreted with caution because relatively few studies used conceptual memory tests in their

priming experiments satisfying the retrieval intentionality criterion showed functional dissociations in item repetition priming, fewer than half of new association priming experiments satisfying the retrieval intentionality criterion showed functional dissociations in new association priming. The $\chi^2$ test confirmed that the item repetition priming was more likely to show a functional dissociation than the new association priming in prior new association priming experiments, $\chi^2(1, N=106)=11.37, p<.05$. Moreover, as shown in Table 5, none of the manipulated variables except study modality showed a consistent dissociation in new association priming. Some variables such as levels of processing/elaboration, which typically affect explicit memory performance, sometimes modulated new association priming, but some variables such as participants, which usually dissociate the item repetition priming and explicit memory performance, did not always affect the new association priming. Hence, new association priming might be more likely contaminated by the participants' using the explicit-memory retrieval strategy than item repetition priming.[16]

In summary, because previous new association priming experiments did reveal explicit vs. implicit functional dissociations under *some* circumstances (e.g., study modality manipulation), one could argue that new association priming might *occasionally* occur automatically. Nonetheless, it should be noted that the explicit and implicit memory tests may not be *pure* indicators for measuring explicit and implicit memory processes, respectively, because the participants might recruit both memory processes when they perform either test. Prior research did show that the explicit vs. implicit functional dissociations can be simulated by single-process (rather than explicit/implicit two-process) memory models (e.g., Dunn & Kirsner, 1988; Ratcliff, Van Zandt, & McKoon, 1995). Hence, even though the performance in explicit and implicit memory tests could sometimes be functionally dissociated, the performance on implicit memory tests might *just* be "relatively" automatic because they rely *less* on the participants' explicit-memory retrieval strategy, contrary to the explicit memory tests in which participants depend *more* on explicit recollection. To further validate the automaticity of new association priming, some researchers used the process dissociation procedure, a more direct technique that does not hinge on an association between tasks (implicit and explicit) and processes (more automatic and less automatic), in their new association priming studies, which are to be reviewed as follows.

---

experiments and the types of perceptual and conceptual implicit memory tests were very limited—only the word-stem completion, category exemplar generation and free association tests were used in prior new association priming experiments that did not violate the retrieval intentionality criterion.

[16] On the one hand, the comparisons of item repetition priming and new association priming imply that new association priming was more likely explicitly contaminated than item repetition priming because the functional dissociation was found less frequently for new association priming than for item repetition priming. On the other hand, the null explicit vs. implicit functional dissociation *per se* might not provide definitive evidence for explicit contamination in new association priming because a null finding can be attributed to reasons other than the commonality of processing for new association priming and for explicit memory (see also Neely, 1989). For example, insufficient statistical power to detect a functional dissociation and the experimental manipulations that affect the *encoding*, rather than the *retrieval*, of study-pairs could also lead to the finding that both explicit and implicit memory performance were affected by a variable in the same direction.

**Table 5. Summary of the occurrence of functional dissociation as a function of independent-variable manipulation in explicit vs. implicit memory performance (Only the experiments satisfying the retrieval intentionality criterion and the independent variables having manipulated in more than 1 experiment are included)**

| Critical Manipulation | Item repetition priming | | New association priming | |
|---|---|---|---|---|
| Dissociation? | Yes | No | Yes | No |
| Number of study-pair presentations | 0 (0%) | 0 (0%) | 0 (0%) | 2 (100%) |
| Interference | 2 (100%) | 0 (0%) | 1 (33%) | 2 (67%) |
| Levels of Processing/Elaboration | 8 (80%) | 2 (20%) | 9 (45%) | 11 (55%) |
| Match in Font Type | 2 (50%) | 2 (50%) | 1 (25%) | 3 (75%) |
| Participant | 7 (78%) | 2 (22%) | 4 (33%) | 8 (67%) |
| Presented Hemisphere | 1 (50%) | 1 (50%) | 1 (50%) | 1 (50%) |
| Study Modality | 2 (40%) | 3 (60%) | 5 (100%) | 0 (0%) |
| Study-pair Relatedness | 0 (0%) | 0 (0%) | 0 (0%) | 2 (100%) |
| Test Awareness | 4 (80%) | 1 (20%) | 0 (0%) | 5 (100%) |

## Process Dissociation Procedure

In implicit memory literatures, researchers have used the process dissociation procedure (e.g., Jacoby, 1991, 1998; Jacoby, Toth, & Yonelinas, 1993) to tear apart the contributions of automatic, unintentional retrieval processes and controlled, intentional retrieval processes to the occurrence of item repetition priming (see below for an elaboration of this logic). They found that these two processes *co-determine* item repetition priming in implicit memory tests. For example, Toth, Reingold and Jacoby (1994) used the process dissociation procedure to estimate the extent that automatic and controlled processing contribute on the level-of-processing effect of the item repetition priming in the word-stem completion task. [The item repetition priming is stronger after the study items have been deeply encoded (e.g., pleasantness ratings) than shallowly encoded (e.g., vowel counting).] Their estimates showed the level-of-processing effect on item repetition priming was largely, if not entirely, produced by controlled processing, rather than by automatic processing, suggesting that such an effect could be due to the participants' use of a conscious, retrieval strategy in a word-stem completion task. As displayed in Table 6, three new association priming studies used the process dissociation procedure in their experiments. To illustrate how this procedure is used in the new association priming paradigm, we use Reingold and Goshen-Gottstein (1996b) as an example. Similar to Toth et al.'s level-of-processing manipulation, these authors evaluated the contribution of automatic vs. controlled processes to new association priming after the word pairs had been incidentally studied in a shallow (word pair copy) or a deep (sentence generation) study task. In their word-stem completion task, although participants still needed to produce an answer to the test pairs, each of which consisted of a context word and a test stem, the originally implicit instruction (i.e., complete the stem with the first word come to mind, see Table 1) was replaced by either an inclusion or an exclusion instruction. Half of their participants were given the inclusion instruction and the other half, exclusion. Those who received the inclusion instruction were told to complete stems with words they had seen in the study phase, and if they could not retrieve such words, to complete stems with the first word that came to mind. Those who received the exclusion instruction were told *not* to complete stems with any studied words but instead to complete them with new non-studied words. The logic of process dissociation procedure relies on the opposition process participants trigger when they perform this exclusion task, in which they pit the automatic and controlled processes against each other. They use the controlled process to successfully *exclude* the studied words. At the same time, the automatic process leads them to produce the studied words to complete the stems. Hence, in the exclusion task, a studied word is incorrectly produced as a completion only if it automatically comes to mind (the process labeled as $A$) *and* when participants fail to intentionally recollect (and then reject) it (the process labeled as $1 - C$). Assuming that $A$ and $C$ operate independently, the probability of completing a stem with a studied word in the exclusion task, $p$ (exclusion), is $A (1 - C)$. In the inclusion task a studied word is correctly completed when participants intentionally recollect it ($C$) *or* if they fail to recollect the word ($1 - C$) *but* it comes to mind automatically ($A$), so the probability of completing a stem with a studied word in the inclusion task, $p$ (inclusion), is $C + A (1 - C)$.

## Table 6. New association priming studies involving a process dissociation procedure

| Year | Study (Experiment) (All used word-stem completion task) | Manipulated Condition | Inclusion Task | | | | | Exclusion Task | | | | | Process Dissociation Estimates | | | | | |
|---|---|---|---|---|---|---|---|---|---|---|---|---|---|---|---|---|---|---|
| | | | Intact | Recb | New | IRP | NAP | Intact | Recb | New | IRP | NAP | Intact-Auto | Recb-Auto | NAP-Auto | Intact-Control | Recb-Control | NAP-Control |
| 1996a | Reingold & Goshen-Gottstein (2) | Word pair | 0.51 | 0.39 | 0.22 | 0.17*[b] | 0.12*[a] | 0.30 | 0.29 | 0.23 | 0.06*[b] | 0.01[b] | 0.19 | 0.08 | 0.11*[b] | 0.21 | 0.10 | 0.11*[b] |
| | | Picture prime + Word target | 0.49 | 0.36 | 0.22 | 0.14*[b] | 0.13*[a] | 0.30 | 0.28 | 0.22 | 0.06*[b] | 0.02[a] | 0.37 | 0.29 | 0.08*[b] | 0.37 | 0.32 | 0.05*[b] |
| 1996b | Reingold & Goshen-Gottstein (2) | Generate sentence | 0.55 | 0.37 | 0.22 | 0.15*[b] | 0.18*[a] | 0.25 | 0.26 | 0.20 | 0.06*[b] | -0.01[b] | 0.32 | 0.29 | 0.03*[b] | 0.30 | 0.10 | 0.20*[b] |
| 1996b | Reingold & Goshen-Gottstein (3) | Copy sentence | 0.41 | 0.39 | 0.22 | 0.17*[b] | 0.02[b] | 0.32 | 0.28 | 0.22 | 0.06*[b] | 0.04*[b] | 0.35 | 0.31 | 0.04*[b] | 0.10 | 0.10 | 0.00 |
| 1998 | Rybash et al. (1) | Young | 0.69 | 0.53 | 0.09 | 0.44*[b] | 0.16*[b] | 0.10 | 0.11 | 0.12 | -0.01[b] | -0.01[b] | 0.14 | 0.12 | 0.02 | 0.59 | 0.42 | 0.17*[b] |
| | | Old | 0.43 | 0.33 | 0.09 | 0.24*[b] | 0.10*[b] | 0.15 | 0.20 | 0.11 | 0.09*[b] | -0.05[b] | 0.20 | 0.20 | 0.00 | 0.27 | 0.13 | 0.14*[b] |
| 1998 | Rybash et al. (2) | Young | 0.69 | 0.41 | 0.07 | 0.34*[b] | 0.28*[b] | 0.24 | 0.29 | 0.12 | 0.17*[b] | -0.05[b] | 0.36 | 0.31 | 0.05 | 0.43 | 0.12 | 0.31*[b] |
| | | Old | 0.40 | 0.32 | 0.08 | 0.24*[b] | 0.08[b] | 0.20 | 0.25 | 0.10 | 0.15*[b] | -0.05[b] | 0.26 | 0.26 | 0.00 | 0.20 | 0.07 | 0.13*[b] |
| 1999 | Yang et al. (1) | Shallow Encoding | 0.24 | 0.21 | 0.11 | 0.10^[b] | 0.03[b] | 0.13 | 0.11 | 0.10 | 0.01[b] | 0.02[b] | 0.16 | 0.15 | 0.01 | 0.10 | 0.10 | 0.00*[b] |
| | | Deep Encoding | 0.71 | 0.51 | 0.14 | 0.37*[b] | 0.20*[b] | 0.06 | 0.10 | 0.11 | -0.01[b] | -0.04[b] | 0.30 | 0.24 | 0.06*[b] | 0.49 | 0.21 | 0.28*[b] |

Note — * $p < .05$ (two-tailed), ^ $p < .05$ (one-tailed). Auto = estimated contribution of the automatic process, Control = estimated contribution of the controlled process. Intact = intact pair condition, Recb = recombined pair condition, New = new pair condition. IRP = item repetition priming, NAP = new association priming, the values in the intact, recb, new, IRP and NAP columns are proportions. The letter-label next to IRP and NAP indicates the procedure for assessing statistical significance: a – directly reported by the authors; b – $ts$ computed based on the standard errors

By solving arithmetic equations for $p$ (inclusion) and $p$ (exclusion), researchers use the proportion of correct completion for intact and recombined pairs in the inclusion and exclusion tasks, respectively, to estimate, for each participant, the contribution of the automatic processes, $A = \dfrac{p \text{ (exclusion )}}{1 - p \text{ (inclusion )} + p \text{ (exclusion )}}$, and controlled processes, $C = p$ (inclusion) - $p$ (exclusion), for their new association priming.

Using the process dissociation procedure, Reingold and Goshen-Gottstein (1996b) showed that the controlled process (.20), but not the automatic process (.03), significantly contributed to the new association priming produced by sentence generation (deep study task), consistent with previous item repetition priming studies (e.g., Toth et al., 1994). Rybash, Santoro and Hoyer (1998) had their young and older adults deeply encode the study pairs and receive both inclusion and exclusion tasks (in different blocks) in the word-stem completion task. Replicating Reingold and Goshen-Gottstein's results, they found that young and older adults' word-stem completion performance were significantly mediated by the controlled processes, but not by the automatic processes (see Table 6 *Process Dissociation Estimates* column[17]). Reingold and Goshen-Gottstein argued that as new association priming produced by a deep study task is mediated only by controlled, intentional retrieval of new associations, it is not surprising that new association priming has rarely been demonstrated by densely amnesic patients who are profoundly impaired in their ability to retrieve the study episodes (see also *Amnesic research* section), or by test-unaware participants who report not having intentionally retrieved the study episodes. In another experiment (1996a) using the process dissociation procedure, Reingold and Goshen-Gottstein found that *both* automatic and controlled processes contributed to new association priming when a *distinctive* context (i.e., context words presented verbally and pictorially) at study was reinstated in the subsequent word-stem completion task. This was the case even though a shallow study task (i.e., reading aloud) was used in this experiment. Hence, the reinstatement of distinctive contexts was sufficient to provide vivid episodic details that support the automatic and controlled retrieval of associative information in a word-stem completion task.

Apart from the deep encoding or the reinstatement of distinctive contexts, Reingold and Goshen-Gottstein also found small yet significant new association priming when the word pairs were studied via copying (i.e., shallow study, see also Micco & Masson, 1991). Their process dissociation estimates showed that this priming was *only* mediated by the automatic processes (.04) but not by the controlled processes (.00).[18] The authors concluded that this finding "may prove an important marker for automatic retrieval processing" (p. 404) and they predicted that the densely amnesic patients and test-unaware participants should show similar results. However, these predictions might not be easily tested. Because the new association

---

[17] The overall automatic estimate for the new association priming shown in Table 6 was significant, $t(9)=3.52$, so was the overall controlled estimate for the new association priming, $t(9)=4.14$. However, as mentioned below, the problems associated with the validity of process dissociation procedure might blur the interpretation of this seemingly strong evidence for the automaticity of new association priming.

[18] Unlike Reingold and Goshen-Gottstein (1996b), Yang et al. (1999) did not show any new association priming after Chinese character pairs were studied in a shallow study task. However, their shallow study task (i.e., judging the orthography of Chinese two-character words) was different from the one used in Reingold and Goshen-Gottstein (i.e., copying the word pairs). While Yang et al.'s participants attended to specific features of individual characters on a word pair, Reingold and Goshen-Gottstein's participants processed each word pair as a unitized whole when they copied them. This unitized vs. separate encoding distinction may explain the discrepancy between the two studies.

priming produced by a shallow study task was fairly small (< 5%), at least 50 *densely* amnesic patients should be recruited to have sufficient statistical power (i.e., 0.8, $p=.05$, two-tailed) for detecting the effect. (This is estimated by J. Cohen's, 1988, *d* of .49 based on *t* of 2.08 and *N* of 36 in Reingold & Goshen-Gottstein, 1996b.) Such a large number of densely amnesic patients might be difficult to recruit (see *Amnesic Research* for a possible solution— drug-induced "amnesic" healthy young adults). Also, it is logically impossible to have participants undergo the process dissociation procedure without having them be aware, at least to a certain extent, that their memories are being assessed by inclusion/exclusion word-stem completion tasks. Yet even when we could assume Reingold and Goshen-Gottstein's "automatic" new association priming to be replicable, this effect should still be interpreted with caution due the following reasons.

First, previous studies using the process dissociation procedure often assumed that participants fully understood the inclusion/exclusion instructions and responded to them in the same manner. Graf and Komatsu (1994) noted that the data yielded by the process dissociation procedure might be confounded with differences in memory for and understanding of the instructions. For instance, Jennings and Jacoby (1993, see also Rybash et al., 1998) reported that 23% of their older adults' data was discarded because they failed to follow the instructions. If the failure to follow the process dissociation procedure instructions was due to the participants' forgetting the inclusion and exclusion instructions or to their failure to monitor the source memory of studied items, the remaining samples would have better memory or source monitoring skills than the discarded ones. As the participants with poorer source monitoring abilities were eliminated in these studies, the process dissociation estimates of automatic and controlled processes may no longer reflect a genuine picture of their contributions to new association priming or item repetition priming.

Second, some researchers (e.g., Curran & Hintzman, 1995, 1997) questioned the assumption of process dissociation procedure that the contributions of automatic vs. controlled processes are independent. For example, Curran and Hintzman showed that the lengthened study time increases the estimate of controlled process but decreases the estimate of automatic process that contributes to item repetition priming. This negative, participant-based correlation between estimates of automatic and controlled processes was contrary to the strong positive, item-based correlation between estimates of automatic and controlled processes, suggesting that participants could trade off the automatic and controlled processes, inconsistent with the critical assumption for the process dissociation procedure—automatic and controlled processes are independent. This controversy has not been resolved (see also Hirshman, 2004, for a recent discussion of this topic).

In summary, studies using the process dissociation procedure showed that new association priming produced by elaborative encoding can be attributed to controlled processing and new association priming produced by shallow encoding can be attributed to automatic processing. Because the process dissociation procedure has only been applied to experiments using word-stem completion task in new association priming studies, it is important to modify and apply the process dissociation procedure to other perceptual and conceptual implicit memory tests so as to validate the generalizability of these findings. More germane to the automaticity of new association priming, future researchers should replicate Reingold and Goshen-Gottstein's (1996b) shallow-study-induced new association priming as well as its process dissociation estimates so as to verify if new association priming is mediated by automatic processing. Yet the interpretation of this *automatic* new association priming might still be clouded by the questionable validity and assumption of process dissociation procedure. Hence, even though Jacoby's (1991, 1998) method of opposition might resolve the "process purity" problem in implicit memory tests, the process dissociation estimates for automatic and controlled processes should be interpreted with caution due to the potentially problematic assumption (i.e., the independence of automatic vs. controlled processes during the test). While the use and interpretation of process dissociation procedure depends on whether automatic (implicit) and controlled (explicit) memory processes operate independently, it is possible to directly address the explicit contamination problem by using the participants who *cannot* employ an explicit-memory retrieval strategy during an implicit memory test. One clinical population that fits this criterion is patients who suffer from global amnesia.[19]

## Amnesic Research

Global amnesia is characterized by the failure to encode and/or retrieve new episodes and facts accompanied by intact performance on other cognitive domains, such as procedural skills (e.g., typing) (Squire, 1992). Since the medial temporal lobe that is responsible for the formation and retrieval of new memory traces is often damaged in amnesic patients, their explicit memory performance is often heavily deteriorated. However, contrary to their poor performance on explicit memory tests, previous studies have often reported intact item repetition priming for amnesic patients (e.g., Diamond & Rozin, 1984; Graf, Squire, & Mandler, 1984). Among the earliest item repetition priming studies, Warrington and Weiskrantz (1968, 1970, 1974) showed that after studying a list of words, in a word-stem completion task, amnesic patients completed test stems (REA___) more often with studied words (REASON) than with non-studied words (READER), although they failed to identify the identical studied words in an episodic item recognition test. This explicit vs. implicit functional dissociation in amnesic patients has been replicated in later item repetition priming studies that satisfied the retrieval intentionality criterion (e.g., using the same presentation format of test items in implicit word-stem completion task and explicit stem-cued recall task in Graf et al., 1984). Intact item repetition priming in amnesic patients has been reported in other perceptual (e.g., picture naming task in Cave & Squire, 1992; word-fragment completion task in Vaidya, Gabrieli, Keane et al., 1995), and conceptual implicit memory tests (e.g., free association task in Shimamura & Squire, 1984; category exemplar generation task in Graf, Shimamura, & Squire, 1985). Recent neuroimaging research revealed that amnesic patients are able to show intact item repetition priming because unlike explicit

---

[19] Previous new association priming research also involved other populations, such as older adults (e.g., Moscovitch, Winocur, & McLachlan, 1986; Spieler & Balota, 1996; Uttl, Graf, & Cosentino, 2003), frontal lobe patients (e.g., Yang, Weng, Guan et al., 2002), Alzheimer's disease patients (e.g., Ergis, Van der Linden, & Deweer, 1998), patients with a closed head injury (e.g., Mutter, Howard, Howard et al., 1990; Vakil & Oded, 2003), Korsakoff disease patients (e.g., Cermak et al., 1988a), and even healthy young adults who were deprived of sleep (Nilsson, Backman, & Karlsson, 1989). Here, we focus only on amnesic research because this population has been the most intensively investigated in previous new association priming studies and their substantial impairment in explicit memory performance is one of the benchmarks for diagnosing amnesia (Aggleton & Saunders, 1997). Because these patients are presumably not able to use any explicit-memory retrieval strategy to perform the implicit memory tests (but see below), if they could show intact new association priming, this suggests that the retrieval of new association might occur without the involvement of an explicit-memory retrieval strategy.

memory that is mediated by the medial temporal lobe, implicit memory is mediated by posterior neocortical regions (occipital and frontal cortices, e.g., Schacter & Buckner, 1998) that are often preserved in amnesic patients.

Do amnesic patients show intact new association priming? What does this tell us about the automaticity of new association priming as well as the general memory processing of amnesic patients? First, the findings that amnesic patients who have *zero* explicit memory ability showed new association priming as strong as that of their healthy controls would suggest that new association priming occurs even when the performance in implicit memory tests can no longer be explicitly contaminated (Moscovitch, Goshen-Gottstein, & Vriezen, 1994). Second, such priming could also inform whether the locus of memory deficit is at the encoding stage or at the retrieval stage. According to the *encoding-deficit hypothesis*, the memory deficit for amnesic patients is due to their failure to "relate or bind together into a compositional representation any set of perceptually distinct objects or events" (N. J. Cohen, Poldrack, & Eichenbaum, 1997, p. 135). Because amnesic patients have damaged medial temporal lobes, they fail to bind together disparate pieces of information, form complex associations and integrate memory traces (Curran & Schacter, 1997; Johnson & Chalfonte, 1994). Thus, amnesic patients typically cannot *acquire* a new association between two items. This encoding-deficit hypothesis has been supported by explicit memory research—amnesic patients perform much more poorly on tasks requiring memory for the *associations* between items than on tasks requiring memory for *individual items* (e.g., N. J. Cohen & Eichenbaum, 1993; Turriziani, Fadda, Caltagirone et al., 2004). In contrast, the *retrieval-deficit hypothesis* (e.g., Goshen-Gottstein, Moscovitch, & Melo, 2000) suggests that amnesic patients' poor explicit memory performance might be due to their inability to retrieve, rather than form, novel episodic associations. It is the failure to *intentionally* retrieve, rather than acquire, new associations that undermines amnesic patients' performance on explicit memory tests. Whether or not amnesic patients demonstrate an intact new association priming would be informative as to whether their deficits were due to the encoding vs. retrieval deficits. On the one hand, if amnesic patients fail to form any *new* associations due to their damaged medial temporal lobe, they would necessarily fail to show new association priming in implicit memory tests. If amnesic patients' implicit memory is only preserved for item-specific, non-relational information (due to their intact neocortical structures), but not for association-specific, relational information (Schacter, 1994; Schacter & Tulving, 1994), this may provide support to the encoding-deficit hypothesis. However, if performing the implicit memory tests does not require intentional retrieval, the retrieval-deficit hypothesis predicts that amnesic patients would show new association priming comparable to that of their matched controls. This would then suggest that their memory deficit is not in the formation, but in the retrieval, of novel episodic associations. In other words, the episodic association well-learned by amnesic patients is only inaccessible but not unavailable when they perform the explicit memory tests.

# Table 7. New association priming studies involving amnesic patients and their matched controls

| Year | Study (Experiment) | Implicit Task | Manipulated Condition | Matched Control | | | | | | | | Amnesic Patients | | | | | | | | Priming Difference | |
|---|---|---|---|---|---|---|---|---|---|---|---|---|---|---|---|---|---|---|---|---|---|
| | | | | N | Age | YE | Intact | Recb | New | IRP | NAP | N | Age | YE | Intact | Recb | New | IRP | NAP | IRP | NAP |
| 1985 | Graf & Schacter (2) | Word-Stem Completion | Generate sentence | 12 | 47.2 | -- | 0.32 | 0.21 | 0.13 | 0.08*[d] | 0.11*[b] | 12 | 42.3 | 12.3 | 0.32 | 0.18 | 0.13 | 0.05*[d] | 0.13*[b] | 0.03[a] | -0.03[a] |
| 1986 | Moscovitch et al. (2) | Re-reading | Study pairs in isolation | 12 | 71.4 | -- | 1280 | 1850 | 1720 | -130[c] | 570*[c] | 8 | 50.6 | -- | 1290 | 1700 | 1530 | -170[c] | 410*[c] | 40[a] | 160[a] |
| | | | Study-pairs in sentence | 12 | 71.4 | 11.9 | 2680 | 2920 | 3120 | 200[c] | 240*[c] | 8 | 50.6 | 12.6 | 2690 | 3000 | 3110 | 110[c] | 310*[c] | 90[a] | -70[a] |
| 1988b | Cermak et al. (1) | Word-Stem Completion | -- | 8 | 57.0 | -- | 0.15 | 0.24 | -- | -- | -0.09[b] | 8 | 60.0 | -- | 0.35 | 0.36 | -- | -- | -0.01[b] | -- | -0.08[a] |
| 1988b | Cermak et al. (3) | Word-Stem Completion | -- | 7 | 58.0 | -- | 0.09 | 0.20 | -- | -- | -0.11[b] | 7 | 60.0 | -- | 0.26 | 0.29 | -- | -- | -0.03[b] | -- | -0.08[a] |
| 1989 | Shimamura & Squire (1) | Word-Stem Completion | -- | 12 | 48.9 | 13.9 | 0.35 | 0.23 | 0.15 | 0.09*[d] | 0.12*[a] | 12 | 54.1 | 13.3 | 0.28 | 0.27 | 0.11 | 0.16*[d] | 0.01[a] | -0.08[a] | 0.12*[a] |
| 1989 | Shimamura & Squire (2) | | -- | 16 | 54.0 | 13.9 | 0.23 | 0.15 | 0.11 | 0.04[a] | 0.09*[a] | 12 | 54.1 | 13.3 | 0.20 | 0.21 | 0.13 | 0.09*[a] | -0.01[a] | -0.04[a] | 0.10[a] |
| 1989 | Mayes & Gooding (1) | Word-Stem Completion | Rate relatedness | 12 | 46.6 | -- | 0.53 | 0.31 | 0.15 | 0.16*[b] | 0.22*[b] | 12 | 45.6 | -- | 0.35 | 0.32 | 0.15 | 0.17*[b] | 0.03[b] | -0.01[a] | 0.19*[a] |
| 1993 | Musen & Squire (1) | Re-reading | Presented once | 12 | 61.8 | 14.2 | 16.30 | 17 | 18 | 1*[d] | 0.70[c] | 10 | 60.9 | 12.2 | 14.20 | 14.80 | 16.30 | 1.50*[d] | 0.60[c] | -0.5[a] | 0.10[a] |
| 1993 | Musen & Squire (2a) | | Presented once, Immediate Test | 12 | 63.0 | 13.2 | 9.80 | 10 | 10.60 | 0.60^[a] | 0.20[d] | 8 | 63.0 | 12.2 | 9.20 | 9.90 | 10.30 | 0.40[a] | 0.70[d] | 0.2[a] | -0.50[a] |
| | | | Presented once, Delay Test | 12 | 63.0 | 13.2 | 9.65 | 10.30 | 10.10 | -0.20[b] | 0.65[d] | 8 | 63.0 | 12.2 | 9.75 | 10.40 | 9.78 | -0.62[b] | 0.65[d] | 0.42[a] | 0[a] |
| 1993 | Musen & Squire (2b) | | Presented eight times, Immediate Test | 12 | 62.8 | 13.8 | 8.50 | 10 | 11.20 | 1.20*[d] | 1.50*[d] | 9 | 62.8 | 12.2 | 7.90 | 10.20 | 12 | 1.80*[d] | 2.30*[d] | -0.60[a] | -0.80[a] |
| 1993 | Musen & Squire (3) | Perceptual Identification | Study pairs in isolation | 24 | 61.8 | -- | 0.74 | 0.65 | 0.45 | 0.20*[a] | 0.09^[a] | 8 | 60.9 | 12.2 | 0.72 | 0.58 | 0.49 | 0.09[a] | 0.14*[a] | 0.11*[a] | -0.05*[a] |
| | | | Study pairs as compound non-words | 24 | 61.8 | -- | 0.68 | 0.60 | 0.36 | 0.24*[b] | 0.08*[b] | 8 | 60.9 | 14.9 | 0.60 | 0.58 | 0.39 | 0.19*[b] | 0.02[b] | 0.05[a] | 0.06*[a] |
| 1994 | Paller & Mayes (3) | Perceptual Identification | -- | 12 | 42.0 | -- | 0.77 | 0.63 | 0.29 | 0.34*[c] | 0.14*[a] | 12 | 47.0 | -- | 0.71 | 0.68 | 0.40 | 0.28*[c] | 0.03[a] | 0.06[a] | 0.11*[a] |

| Year | Study (Experiment) | Implicit Task | Manipulated Condition | Matched Control | | | | | | | | Amnesic Patients | | | | | | | | Priming Difference | |
|---|---|---|---|---|---|---|---|---|---|---|---|---|---|---|---|---|---|---|---|---|---|
| | | | | N | Age | YE | Intact | Recb | New | IRP | NAP | N | Age | YE | Intact | Recb | New | IRP | NAP | IRP | NAP |
| 1997 | Gabrieli et al. (1) | Perceptual Identification | -- | 48 | 56.1 | 14.1 | 0.56 | 0.47 | 0.25 | 0.22*[b] | 0.09[b] | 24 | 55.9 | 12.9 | 0.55 | 0.43 | 0.24 | 0.19*[a] | 0.12*[a] | 0.03[a] | -0.03[a] |
| 2000 | Goshen-Gottstein et al. (1) | Double-item Lexical Decision | -- | 12 | 55.5 | 13.6 | 715 | 738 | 815 | 77*[c] | 23*[a] | 15 | 50.7 | 13.6 | 1213 | 1322 | 1420 | 98*[c] | 109*[a] | 21[a] | -86*[a] |
| 2003 | Yang et al. (1) | Perceptual Identification | -- | 18 | 35.7 | 11.5 | 0.66 | 0.48 | 0.23 | 0.25*[a] | 0.18*[a] | 18 | 34.9 | 11.7 | 0.49 | 0.52 | 0.23 | 0.29*[a] | -0.03[b] | -0.04[a] | 0.21*[a] |
| 2005 | Carlesimo et al. (1) | Lexical Decision | -- | 10 | 39.7 | 14.1 | 650 | 678 | 673 | -5[b] | 28*[c] | 10 | 44.7 | 12.9 | 785 | 804 | 799 | -5[b] | 19*[c] | 0[a] | 9[a] |
| 2006 | Verfaellie et al. (1A) | Category Generation | -- | 20 | 58.0 | 14.2 | 0.69 | 0.55 | 0.46 | 0.09*[c] | 0.14*[a] | 21 | 57.0 | 14.3 | 0.53 | 0.50 | 0.40 | 0.10*[c] | 0.03[a] | -0.01[c] | 0.11[a] |
| 2006 | Verfaellie et al. (2A/2B) | Relatedness Judgment | -- | 25 | 56.6 | 14.5 | 1650 | 1550 | 1550 | 0[b] | -100*[c] | 17 | 58.3 | 14.2 | 2750 | 2400 | 2500 | 100*[a] | -350*[c] | -100[a] | -250[a] |

Note.— * $p < .05$ (two-tailed), ^ $p < .05$ (one-tailed). N = number of participants, Age = mean age, YE = mean years of education, Intact = intact pair condition, Recb = recombined pair condition, New = new pair condition. IRP = item repetition priming, NAP = new association priming, the values in the intact, recb, new, IRP and NAP columns are either RTs or proportions, depending on the implicit task. (See Table 1 *dependent measure* column.) Priming difference = priming effect yielded by matched control group − priming effect yielded by amnesic patients. The letter-label next to IRP and NAP indicates the procedure for assessing statistical significance: a − directly reported by the authors; b − *t*s computed based on the main effect of manipulated variables; d − the largest or smallest *t*s reported by the authors. The WAIS-R (intelligence test) scores of amnesic patients were 99 in Cermak, Bleich, and Blackford (1988b), 101 in Gabrieli et al. (1997), 96 in Goshen-Gottstein et al. (2000), 96 in Graf and Schacter (1985), 100 in Mayes and Gooding (1989), 108 in Musen and Squire (1993), 101 in Paller and Mayes (1994), 103 in Shimamura and Squire (1989), and 100 in Verfaellie et al. (2006). The WMS (explicit memory) scores of amnesic patients were 112 in Carlesimo et al. (2005), 103 in Gabrieli et al. (1997), 81 in Graf and Schacter (1985), and 96 in Verfaellie et al. (2006).

Although the new association priming studies for amnesic patients shed light on the automaticity of new association priming and the dissociation between the encoding vs. retrieval deficit hypotheses, it is still unclear, despite more than 20 years of research, whether amnesic patients consistently show significant new association priming or explicit vs. implicit functional dissociations in new association priming (i.e., they show intact new association priming yet greatly reduced, if not eliminated, explicit memory performance). Table 7 shows the findings of previous new association priming studies that involved amnesic patients (see also the highlighted rows in Table 4 for the explicit vs. implicit functional dissociation in amnesic studies).

To our knowledge, Graf and Schacter (1985) reported the first study that examined the new association priming in amnesia. Having studied unrelated word pairs in an elaborative, albeit incidental, study task (i.e., relatedness rating) and then performed a word-stem completion task, their amnesic patients showed as high new association priming as their matched controls.[20] As amnesic patients' performance on explicit cued recall tasks was much poorer than their matched controls', the dissociation in explicit vs. implicit memory performance indicated that the amnesic patients' intact new association priming may unlikely be contaminated by the use of an explicit-memory retrieval strategy. This finding was later replicated in new association priming studies using a perceptual identification task (Gabrieli, Keane, Zarella et al., 1997; Musen & Squire, 1993, Experiment 4), a re-reading task (Moscovitch, Winocur, & McLachlan, 1986, Musen & Squire, Experiment 3), a single-item lexical decision task (Carlesimo, Perri, Costa et al., 2005), a double-item lexical decision task (Goshen-Gottstein et al., 2000) and a category exemplar generation task (Verfaellie, Martin, Page et al., 2006), although not all of them find a functional dissociation in amnesic patients' explicit vs. implicit memory performance (e.g., Carlesimo et al., 2005; Mayes & Gooding, 1989; Musen & Squire, 1993; Paller & Mayes, 1994; Verfaellie et al., 2006; Yang, Weng, Guan et al., 2003). The absence of a functional dissociation could suggest that the amnesic patients in these studies had residual explicit memory—that is, they could still employ an explicit-memory retrieval strategy to perform implicit memory tests.

However, other studies had difficulty finding even a significant new association priming (e.g., Cermak et al., 1988b; Musen & Squire, 1993, Experiments 1-2; Paller & Mayes, 1994; Shimamura & Squire, 1989; Yang et al., 2003; see single-case studies in Hayman, MacDonald, & Tulving, 1993; Rajaram & Coslett, 2000a, 2000b; Tulving, Hayman, & MacDonald, 1991). This is puzzling because the procedures used in some of these studies were almost identical to those used in studies yielding significant new association priming for amnesic patients. For instance, using a re-reading paradigm with unrelated word pairs presented in isolation or embedded in sentences (see Table 1), Moscovitch et al. (1986, Experiment 2) found an equivalent level of new association priming for memory-disordered patients and their matched controls even though they only read aloud the stimuli at study and at test (i.e., shallow study task). Musen and Squire (1993, Experiment 1) failed to find any new association priming for their *pure amnesic* patients[21] and matched controls when they

---

[20] The amnesic patients and their matched controls in all of amnesic new association priming studies were equated by their ages and years of education. These studies also screened out those amnesic patients who had problems in motoric execution. Hence, the baseline difference (e.g., in the proportion of correct completions for non-studied targets or in RTs) should presumably be roughly equivalent for amnesic patients and matched controls.

[21] Moscovitch et al. (1986, Experiment 2) used participants in different clinical populations (e.g., amnesic and Alzheimer's disease patients) in their memory-disordered group and did not separately report their data

studied the unrelated word pairs only once with a deep, elaborative study strategy.[22] They (Experiment 2b) found significant and equivalent effects for both groups only when they used a shallow, read-aloud strategy to study the compound non-words (see Table 1) nine times, with all compound non-words on the test list being either *intact* or *recombined*. However, because Musen and Squire did not have their amnesic patients perform the explicit memory test, there was no way to assess whether these patients had used an explicit-memory retrieval strategy. If the amnesic patients have residual explicit memory ability, they might still use the explicit-memory retrieval strategy to perform implicit memory tests and show significant new association priming, especially after they had encountered the studied compound non-words nine times. Hence, the significant amnesic patients' new association priming found in Musen and Squire's re-reading tasks might not necessarily support the automaticity of new association priming or the retrieval-deficit hypothesis because it was not clear whether their amnesic patients in fact had zero explicit memory ability.

Using a perceptual identification task, Musen and Squire (1993, Experiment 3) found comparable new association priming for amnesic patients and their matched controls. Although Gabrieli et al. (1997) later replicated the intact new association priming for amnesic patients, subsequent studies (e.g., Paller & Mayes, 1994; Yang et al., 2003) failed to find significant new association priming for their amnesic patients. Although Gabrieli et al. and Yang et al. differed in their stimulus types (unrelated English word pair vs. unrelated Chinese two-character word pair) and their numbers of study-pair presentation (2 vs. 1), it is unknown how these differences could modulate the amnesic patients' ability to show new association priming. Paller and Mayes and Gabrieli et al. differed in the number of study-pair presentation (2 vs. 1) and in the presentation format at test—the test pairs were presented simultaneously in Gabrieli et al., but sequentially in Paller and Mayes. In both studies, their word pairs were presented simultaneously at study. While the mismatch in the study-test presentation format (cf. Goshen-Gottstein & Moscovitch, 1995a) can apparently explain why Paller and Mayes' amnesic patients failed to show new association priming, it does not explain why their matched controls *did* show significant new association priming. Also, even though Yang et al. simultaneously presented the word pairs at study and at test in their perceptual identification task, they failed to obtain any new association priming for their amnesic patients (see also Yang, Weng, Guan et al., 2002, for a similar finding for frontal lobe patients). Thus, it is unclear whether the absence of amnesic patients' new association priming in Paller and Mayes was due to their failure to form episodic associations at study (consistent with the encoding-deficit hypothesis) or their failure to show the new association priming when the presentation format of word pairs was incongruent at study and at test (consistent with the retrieval-deficit hypothesis).

Similar to the evidence provided by re-reading tasks, it is also ambiguous whether Musen and Squire's (1993) and Gabrieli et al.'s (1997) findings were contaminated by their amnesic patients' using the explicit-memory retrieval strategy in a perceptual identification task. The rapidly presented targets and unlimited response deadline might have encouraged their

---

whereas Musen and Squire (1993) and other studies discussed below used groups of relatively pure amnesic patients.

[22] However, Moscovitch et al. (1986) and some of the experiments in Musen & Squire (1993) failed to obtain even significant item repetition priming for both memory disordered/amnesic patients and matched controls, inconsistent with prior item repetition priming studies that used word-stem completion and perceptual identification tasks.

participants to base their identifications on explicit memory retrieval. Musen and Squire did not include an explicit memory test to assess their amnesic patients' explicit memory ability, so there was no way to validate their patients' explicit memory performance. Although Gabrieli et al.'s amnesic patients did perform much more poorly than their matched controls in a three-alternative forced choice recognition test, the processing demands for their perceptual identification task and recognition test were very different, thus violating the retrieval intentionality criterion. While the perceptual identification task requires a perceptual reanalysis of the studied pairs for producing them, the recognition test demands more conceptual processing—participants need to retrieve the new association to pair up the context word with one of the three items. The two tasks also differ in their processing speeds: the test pairs are presented very rapidly (e.g., 30 ms) in the perceptual identification task, whereas they stay on the screen after the presentation onset in the recognition test. The violation of retrieval intentionality criterion blurs the interpretation of Gabrieli et al.'s functional dissociation on the amnesic patients' implicit vs. explicit memory performance and renders this to be too weak to support the automaticity of new association priming.

Apart from the contradictory evidence in new association priming studies using perceptual identification and re-reading tasks, even the finding of seminal word-stem completion experiment (i.e., Graf & Schacter, 1985) could not always be replicated in subsequent studies. Mayes and Gooding (1989) obtained intact new association priming only for matched controls but not amnesic patients when they used an incidental learning task involving slightly shallower processing than the task used by Graf and Schacter. Mayes and Gooding's participants studied the unrelated word pairs embedded in sentences (vs. in isolation) and rated their imageability (vs. generating sentences in Graf & Schacter). While the impaired new association priming for Mayes and Gooding's amnesic patients might reasonably be attributed to their using a shallower study task than Graf and Schacter's, their matched controls actually showed an new association priming twice as strong (.22) as Graf and Schacter's (.11). Thus, Maye and Gooding's amnesic patients were more sensitive than matched controls to the level-of-processing manipulation in new association priming, a finding that is inconsistent with prior item repetition priming findings that amnesic patients are equally (e.g., Keane, Gabrieli, Monti et al., 1997), if not less, sensitive (e.g., Jenkins, Russo, & Parkin, 1998) to the level-of-processing manipulation than matched controls. As to be elaborated below, Graf and Schacter's findings might be even further complicated by their post-hoc analyses (Schacter & Graf, 1986b).

While almost all new association priming amnesic studies here used perceptual implicit memory tests, to date only one has used a conceptual implicit memory test. Verfaellie et al. (2006, Experiment 2) found significant and equivalent new association priming for their amnesic patients and matched controls in a relatedness judgment task (see Table 1); however, in their Experiment 1, only matched controls, but not amnesic patients, showed new association priming in a category exemplar generation task (see Table 1). To account for this discrepancy, Verfaellie et al. proposed a "relational vs. fused" dichotomy in the representation of new associations (cf. Eichenbaum & N. J. Cohen, 2001), akin to the production vs. identification response modality in implicit memory tests (Fleischman & Gabrieli, 1998). Because participants need to identify the studied words (in a pair) when they do the relatedness judgment task, this identification process relies on a rigidly bound representation of study configuration (as a Gestalt) without preserving the individual status of the constituent elements (fused representation). (See also Footnote 12 for a similar idea in the discussion of an item/associative encoding tradeoff hypothesis.) In contrast, because participants need to produce the targets to test stems when they perform the category exemplar generation task, it depends on whether they can flexibly link the separate elements into a representation that preserves the integrity of constituent elements (relational representation). Since the medial temporal lobe is critical for the creation of relational representations (e.g., N. J. Cohen et al., 1997), amnesic patients' impaired new association priming in a category exemplar generation task reflects their inability to create and access a flexible, relational representation. The amnesic patients show new association priming when the task requires them to implicitly access/identify the fused, holistic representation of unrelated pairs, but not so when the task requires them to implicitly retrieve/produce the targets that are freshly associated with context words (i.e., from the relational representation of a new association; see also Johnson's, 1992, MEM model, for a similar idea). While Verfaellie et al.'s findings apparently fit nicely with this fused vs. relational dichotomy, this dichotomy cannot always explain the findings in perceptual implicit memory tests. On the one hand, it explains why amnesic patients' new association priming occurs in lexical decision tasks (Goshen-Gottstein et al., 2000) that require only the identification of fused representations, but not in word-stem completion tasks (e.g., Shimamura & Squire, 1989, but see Graf & Schacter, 1985) that require the patients to "reconstruct the stimulus configuration on the basis of partial information" (Verfaellie et al., p. 97). On the other hand, the fused vs. relational dichotomy fails to explain the absence of new association priming for amnesic patients in some studies using a perceptual identification task (e.g., Yang et al., 2003) in which participants only identify the rapidly and simultaneously presented word pairs (see also Footnote 6 for a possible explanation), or a re-reading task (e.g., Musen & Squire, 1993) in which participants only read aloud the unrelated word pairs. Had the amnesic patients been able to identify/access the fused representation of the new association, they would have produced new association priming in these two tasks, which require only the identification (or access) of new associations. Hence, it is important to test the generalizability of Verfaellie et al.'s fused vs. relational dichotomy by having amnesic patients and matched controls performed production and/or identification perceptual implicit memory tests within a single experiment.

The aforementioned ambiguous pattern of data from amnesic patients does not provide much support for the automaticity of new association priming. This data fails to show new association priming in some cases (e.g., Mayes & Gooding, 1989). Even when they showed significant new association priming, the absence of a functional dissociation in amnesic patients' explicit vs. implicit memory performance (e.g., Musen & Squire, 1993, Experiment 1) suggested that their new association priming might in part be due to their residual explicit memory, as reflected by their above chance performance in explicit memory tests.

Indeed, the absence of a functional dissociation has not been the only evidence showing that the amnesic patients' new association priming was explicitly contaminated. Schacter and Graf (1986b) reported post-hoc analyses for their amnesic patients' priming effects in their 1985 paper and found that their new association priming was predominantly produced by a few milder amnesic patients who showed relatively better explicit cued recall performance. That is, the new association priming was, in fact, virtually non-existent for their densely amnesic patients who had zero explicit memory ability (see also Verfaellie, Croce, & Milberg, 1995, for evidence from a single-case study). If the new association priming depends on the severity of amnesia, it suggests that a certain level of explicit memory may be necessary to produce new association priming.[23] This has indeed been supported by post-hoc correlation analyses performed in subsequent studies. (To our knowledge, no new association priming studies have filtered out amnesic patients' scores in some standardized test batteries that reflect their explicit memory ability by treating the scores as a covariate in their analyses.) Although Shimamura and Squire (1989) failed to obtain overall new association priming for amnesic patients in a word-stem completion task, their amnesic patients' new association priming (+.56) but not item repetition priming (+.17) was significantly correlated with their scores on the Wechsler Memory Scale (WMS), a standardized test for explicit memory.[24] Similar findings were reported for Mayes and Gooding's (1989) word-stem completion task (+.46) and Paller and Mayes' (1994) perceptual identification task (+.20), even though these correlations were not significant due to their small sample sizes (12 each). Mayes and Gooding also found a reliable positive correlation between the new association priming and cued recall performance for amnesic patients who did not show any new association priming or associative memory in their cued recall. In Yang et al.'s (2003) perceptual identification task, new association priming was significantly correlated with WMS scores (+.63) and the d' in their explicit memory task (+.40), but not with item repetition priming (+.17) (see also Yang et al., 2002, for similar correlation findings yielded by their frontal lobe patients). To examine the role of residual explicit memory in the occurrence of new association priming, Carlesimo et al. (2005) divided their amnesic patients into two groups based on a median split of their cued recall performance: high vs. low performer. They re-analyzed new association priming for each group and found that only high (47 ms) but not low performers (0 ms) showed significant new association priming despite their very small sample sizes (4 and 6, respectively). This suggests that new association priming might likely be modulated by an explicit-memory retrieval strategy that relatively mild amnesic patients used in the implicit memory test. Thus, the findings yielded by these correlation/median-split analyses corroborated Schacter and Graf's post-hoc observation that amnesic patients with residual explicit memory show greater new association priming.[25]

However, we do not consider that the moderate correlation between amnesic patients' WMS scores and new association priming could conclusively show that new association priming at test must be caused by participants' using an explicit-memory retrieval strategy. First, amnesic patients' explicit memory performance can be independent of how likely they are to use the explicit-memory retrieval strategy in implicit memory tests. Second, even though standardized memory tests show that amnesic patients are able to form and intentionally retrieve the new association, it is still possible that in the new association priming paradigms, they establish the associations at study and then implicitly (i.e., without the involvement of explicit memory) access them during the implicit memory test. In other

---

[23] Though Cermak et al. (1988a) reported a severely amnesic encephalitic patient (SS) who showed significant new association priming in a word-stem completion task, in their experiment they failed to find any effect for their matched controls, showing that their experimental design may not be sensitive enough to detect the effect for healthy participants. Also, it might indicate that the effect was spurious for the single dense amnesic patient.

[24] As suggested by Yang et al. (2003), terms like mild, moderate and severe amnesia are imprecise descriptions for memory impairment that might be defined very differently by various researchers. Hence, it is necessary to use the standardized test batteries, for example, WMS, to provide a systematic pre-experimental assessment of the patients' degree of memory deficit, which could then be correlated with their priming performance.

[25] To date, all correlation analyses were reported from studies using perceptual implicit memory tests; no study has tested whether the correlation between residual explicit memory and new association priming holds in the experiments using conceptual implicit memory tests.

words, the third factor that mediates the correlation between WMS scores and new association priming could be one's ability to form new associations at study. When amnesic patients are more capable of constructing new associations at study, they are more likely to (a) have better explicit memory performance and (b) show stronger new association priming. Therefore, the apparent correlation between (a) and (b) might not necessarily show that the new association priming must be modulated by explicit memory, as reflected by WMS scores or other explicit memory tasks. Thus, the amnesic patients' intact new association priming might not necessarily provide any evidence against the automaticity of new association priming. But as this logical argument could not rule out the possibility that a certain degree of amnesic patients' intact new association priming could be attributed to their residual explicit memory, the findings of amnesic patients' intact new association priming does not necessarily support the automaticity of new association priming either.

In addition to the ambiguity of amnesic patients' intact new association priming, the reliability of this finding is also questionable. Shimamura and Squire (1989) reported a low test-retest reliability of amnesic patients' new association priming. In the first session, their mild amnesic patients' showed non-significant yet numerically large new association priming (8.7% vs. 10.5% for matched controls). This numeric effect, however, disappeared one week later in the second session when the same group of amnesic patients studied the same set of study pairs and received the same word-stem completion task as the first one. Paller and Mayes (1994) also found a virtually non-existent test-retest reliability ($r=.05$) of new association priming when their amnesic patients were re-tested (with the same materials and procedures) in the second session after 9 weeks. (Because in these studies, the amnesic patients were instructed to study the same set of word pairs again in the second session, the absence of new association priming was not due to the decay of new association priming over the interval between the first and second sessions.) Thus, even though some of previous studies did report amnesic patients' showing intact new association priming and/or functional dissociation for their implicit vs. explicit memory performance, it is still unknown whether these findings could even be replicated by using the same group of amnesic patients, same set of study and test materials and procedures.

In summary, even though some amnesic patents did show significant new association priming (e.g., Graf & Schacter, 1985), the effects were mediated by residual explicit memory (e.g., Schacter & Graf, 1986b) or in some cases, not even reliable, as reflected by the absence of test-retest reliability (e.g., Shimamura & Squire, 1989). Even though a few studies did report intact new association priming for the amnesic patients who did not possess any explicit memory ability (e.g., Goshen-Gottstein et al., 2000), the reliability of these findings awaits further verification. Hence, it may be safe to conclude that, to date, amnesic patients do not reliably demonstrate new association priming, in a sharp contrast to their ability to show intact item repetition priming (e.g., Squire, 1992). This conclusion suggests that the occasional findings of intact new association priming for amnesic patients might not be used to support the automaticity of new association priming or the retrieval-deficit hypothesis, which predicts that the amnesic patients with zero explicit memory ability should always show new association priming. In contrast, the encoding-deficit hypothesis seems to be more plausible than the retrieval-deficit hypothesis. Because the amnesic patients cannot form new episodic associations between two unrelated items, they fail to perform in the subsequent memory test whether it taps explicit or implicit retrieval of these associations. If this latter case is true, even whether amnesic new association priming studies are informative to verify the automaticity of new association priming should be questioned because it could be the deficit in the encoding stage, rather than in the retrieval stage, that modulates the occurrence of the effect. The null new association priming of amnesic patients might only be due to their failure to encode the unrelated word pairs at first. This possibility was actually supported by a dissociation of amnesic patients' item repetition priming and new association priming in neuroimaging research (e.g., Chun & Phelps, 1999). The item repetition priming occurs in the posterior neocortical structures, but the occurrence of new association priming seems to involve the medial temporal lobe. Since the damage in the medial temporal lobe is the signature for identifying amnesic patients, it is not surprising that they fail to show any new association priming, provided that they do not have any explicit memory ability.[26]

Another implication of the above literature review is that densely amnesic patients who have zero explicit memory ability (provided that the findings are replicable) must be used in order to unambiguously test the automaticity of new association priming. However, the recruitment of these patients is very costly and time-consuming. It is also difficult to arrange the same group of densely amnesic patients to do replication experiments. This raises the issue of whether an alternative participant pool can be used to study the automaticity of new association priming. A drug-induced amnesia in healthy young adults seems to be a more promising approach for future "amnesic" new association priming studies. Hirshman and his colleagues (e.g., Hirshman, Passannante, & Arndt, 2001) reported some implicit (item repetition priming) and explicit memory studies, in which Midazolam, a drug that is used to reduce anxiety and to produce amnesia for surgical procedures, was administered to healthy young adults. The purpose of this drug administration is to temporarily induce dense anterograde amnesia to the participants at the beginning of the experiment. As Midazolam might disrupt the ability to intentionally encode and retrieve the information even when participants remain alert enough to perform tasks normally, the explicit-memory retrieval strategy should be completely eliminated for these drug-administered young adults. Midazolam has been found to produce larger impairments on explicit memory tests such as free recall and recognition memory than on implicit memory tests such as perceptual identification and free association tasks (e.g., Hirshman et al.; see also Polster, McCarthy, O'Sullivan et al., 1993, for the first implicit memory study using this drug). Because the administration of Midazolam is economical and can induce young adults to be densely amnesic within a short period, it could be used (with the permission of Institutional Review Board) in future research to investigate the automaticity of new association priming. If an explicit-memory retrieval strategy is necessary for producing new association priming, the effect should be significantly reduced, if not completely eliminated, by the administration of

---

[26] Gooding, Mayes, and van Eijk (2000) reported a meta-analysis for amnesic patients' new association priming. In addition to new *verbal* associations, which we focus on in the current chapter, they also included studies with nonword, novel patterns, color-word association, word-voice association, non-familiar faces, geometric object drawings, and even unfamiliar Korean melodies. They found that amnesic patients had overall poorer implicit memory performance than the matched controls and this was the case regardless of the number of study-pair presentations, type of response modality (production vs. identification), and the compatibility of participants' responses at study and at test. Similar to us, Gooding et al. concluded that amnesic patients failed to acquire and store the new associations. Two cautionary notes, however, should be taken into account. (a) Gooding et al. did not separately analyze previous data by stimulus type. This might mask some of the inconsistencies of new association priming of amnesic patients for specific kinds of stimuli. (b) Gooding et al. did not identify the severity of amnesia across studies. As listed in their Table 1 (p. 668), they included studies using *mild* amnesic patients (e.g., Graf & Schacter, 1985; Shimamura & Squire, 1989). It is unclear to what extent this might have clouded their conclusion.

Midazolam, as is so for the explicit memory performance. To our knowledge, no verbal new association priming study has been reported that involves the administration of Midazolam. Chun (2005, see also Park, Quinlan, Thornton et al., 2004) reported a non-verbal new association priming study with the administration of Midazolam, in which healthy young adults were tested on an implicit-learning visual search task, once after the administration of Midazolam and once after the administration of a placebo. The participants who took Midazolam before the task did not show facilitation in their visual search RTs for the repeated configurations, but those in both Midazolam and placebo conditions demonstrated a general speed-up in their visual search performance across blocks. In other words, the drug-induced amnesia affected the priming of repeated novel spatial associations, but not the practice effect. Thus, without any influence of an explicit-memory retrieval strategy, the repetitions of new spatial associations did not enhance the drug-induced amnesic participants' implicit memory performance, casting doubt on the automaticity of new association priming for novel spatial associations. Because this is the only new association priming experiment that employed the drug-induced amnesia procedure, future researchers need to replicate the finding and test if it can be generalized to verbal materials. It is also important to administer Midazolam before and after the study of new associations in order to examine the role of the explicit-memory retrieval strategy in the encoding and retrieval of new association priming. Should drug-induced amnesia eliminate verbal new association priming, this would serve as strong evidence against the automaticity of verbal new association priming.

## Neuroimaging Evidence

By observing brain activity when participants perform implicit memory tests (see Henson, 2003, for a review), researchers can directly reveal the involvement of an explicit-memory retrieval strategy in producing new association priming. To our knowledge, only two neuroimaging new association priming studies (Badgaiyan, Schacter, & Alpert, 2003; Yang, Meckingler, Xu et al., 2008) has been reported. As in the standard new association priming paradigm, Badgaiyan et al.'s participants studied a list of unrelated word pairs. When they performed the word-stem completion task, they were scanned and recorded by positron emission tomography for the change in their cerebral blood flow. Badgaiyan et al. obtained the typical new association priming in their behavioral measures (i.e., the proportion of correctly completed test stems was higher for intact pairs than for recombined pairs). From their neuroimaging data, they observed reduced cerebral blood flow in the extrastriate cortex when participants filled out the test stems in intact and recombined pairs, relative to new pairs, showing the pattern of implicit memory similar to those found in previous neuroimaging item repetition priming studies (e.g., Schacter & Badgaiyan, 2001). However, when participants completed the test stems in intact and recombined pairs, they also found an increased cerebral blood flow in the left inferior frontal gyrus, which has been associated with explicit memory (e.g., Rugg, Fletcher, Chua et al., 1999; Thompson-Schill, D'Esposito, Aguirre et al., 1997), but not with implicit memory because this region was found to have reduced, rather than increased, activation in item repetition priming (e.g., Badgaiyan, Schacter, & Alpert, 1999). More importantly, cerebral blood flow was increased only in the right medial temporal lobe when participants completed the test stems in intact pairs, but not in recombined pairs, showing that activation of the medial temporal lobe should be critical for the production of new association priming. As the latter pattern of activation is typically associated with explicit memory, but not implicit memory (e.g., Schacter, Alpert, Savage et al., 1996), Badgaiyan et al.'s neuroimaging data clearly revealed an involvement of explicit memory retrieval in new association priming, at least when it was found in the word-stem completion task. Yang et al. used another method to control for the explicit memory contamination problem in the new association priming paradigm. In the study phase, participants were required to read aloud the word pairs appeared on the screen as quickly and accurately as possible (encoding task), with the presentation duration of the word pairs being changed by researchers according to participants' reading performance. Specifically, the duration would be reduced if the percentage of the correct reading response was higher than 30%, but lengthened if the percentage of correct reading response was lower than 30%. This procedure induced participants' final explicit memory performance at the chance level (i.e., d' did not significantly differ from 0) in the associative recognition test, such that Yang et al. argued that the influence of explicit memory on new association priming tasks (i.e., a perceptual identification task) could be successfully excluded. Indeed, participants showed significant new association priming in the implicit perceptual identification task but a null difference between intact and recombined word pairs in the associative recognition test, indicating a functional dissociation. Yang et al.'s neuroimaging findings confirmed previous findings that new association priming is different from item repetition priming in that it is related to activation in the medial temporal lobe (i.e., associated with explicit memory, but not implicit memory). They further reported a functional dissociation within the medial temporal lobe in that the parahippocampal cortex, but not the hippocampus, was involved in the new association priming. However, these findings should be interpreted with caution. Specifically, Yang et al.'s interpretation of neuroimaging data might have confounded the new association priming with the item repetition priming because they defined new association priming by a conjunction of activated brain regions being observed in both intact pairs vs. new pairs and in both intact pairs vs. recombined pairs. Furthermore, even though one could replicate the finding that the medial temporal lobe is involved in producing new association priming, thereby providing the most direct evidence for explicit contamination in new association priming, it is noteworthy that using neuroimaging data to make inferences about underlying cognitive processes may not always be straightforward (see Henson, 2005, for a detailed discussion). Nonetheless, future neuroimaging studies should gather evidence from different populations (e.g., densely amnesic patients) as well as from experiments manipulating variables that modulate the susceptibility of explicit contamination. By validating data from neuroimaging measures with data from traditional behavioral measures, one could not only reveal the neuroanatomical locus of implicit/explicit memory involvement in new association priming, but also shed light on the automaticity of new association priming.

## Speeded Implicit Memory Tests

To largely reduce, if not eliminate, any potential explicit contamination in new association priming, some researchers (e.g., Pecher & Raaijmakers, 1999; Zeelenberg et al., 2003) have used only identification implicit memory tests that require speeded responses (e.g., lexical decision). They argue that production implicit memory tests are more likely to trigger the explicit-memory retrieval strategy than identification implicit memory tests because such a strategy is more likely to benefit production test performance (e.g., word-stem completion). Participants can complete a test stem more quickly and accurately by directly retrieving a studied pairmate for the context word and test stem than by, at first, generating some possible answers for it. In contrast, the use of this strategy may hurt speeded identification test performance (e.g., lexical decision) as participants can judge the lexicality of a test pair more quickly by directly accessing the words in their lexicon than by retrieving them. The differential susceptibility to explicit contamination in production vs. identification implicit memory tests is qualified by the facts that: (a) automatic retrieval is assumed to be executed more quickly than conscious retrieval (Reingold & Toth, 1996; Richardson-Klavehn & Gardiner, 1998; Yonelinas & Jacoby, 1994) and (b) the intentionally retrieved information only becomes available about 500 ms after the onset of the test item (Gronlund & Ratcliff, 1989; Hintzman & Curran, 1995, 1997). However, to our knowledge, no new association priming studies have directly tested whether a long response deadline encourages participants to use the explicit-memory retrieval strategy in implicit memory tests (cf. McKone & Murphy, 2000; Tse & Neely, 2005). This idea could be tested by varying the response deadlines or signal delays (e.g., 500 ms, 2 s, or 5 s) on each test trial or measuring the participants' RTs in new association priming studies (see Fay et al., 2005; Horton, Wilson, Vonk et al., 2005; Mace, 2005 for item repetition priming word-stem completion studies with RT measures). Provided that the use of explicit-memory retrieval strategy is time consuming and given that the proportion of studied test items is high, if new association priming is in fact mediated by an explicit-memory retrieval strategy, it should be stronger when the response signal delay is long than when it is short and should also be positively correlated with participants' RTs. Apart from the untested assumption that the explicit-memory retrieval strategy must be involved when implicit memory tests yield long RTs (or are performed without a response deadline), as we elaborate below, even the nature of a speeded implicit memory test does not guarantee the occurrence of new association priming to be strategy-free—the priming could still be modulated by some subtle factors in the experiment. As the lexical decision task is the most frequently used speeded task in the new association priming literature, we focus the following discussion on the studies using this task. The logic, however, can be applied to other speeded tasks (e.g., category verification and picture-label same/different judgment).

In a typical trial of a lexical decision task used in new association priming research, participants are presented the context word and target either simultaneously or sequentially (see Table 2 for the type of test items). They need to press a key to respond whether or not the presented word(s) is (or are) correctly spelled in single-item (or double-item) lexical decision tasks. In some cases, when the context word and target are presented sequentially, participants are to read the context word silently and respond to the target (e.g., Neely & Durgunoglu, 1985). Though not conceptualized as implicit memory, McKoon and Ratcliff (1979) were the first to show new association priming in a lexical decision task. In their first experiment, participants studied, with an anticipation of a memory test at the end of the experiment, 6-7 related (e.g., DOOR-knob) or unrelated pairs (e.g., REASON-house). They were then presented the items of these pairs (with other filler "non-studied" words and non-words) sequentially in a continuous lexical decision task. As in other new association priming paradigms, some test pairs were intact pairs (the target was preceded by the same context word as it was studied, e.g., REASON-house), and some were recombined pairs (the target was not preceded by the same context word as it was studied, e.g., OBSERVE-house). The participants made a lexical decision to every test item without being notified of the structure of the sequence or the purpose of the task. McKoon and Ratcliff found significant and equivalent new association priming and old association priming. They (1986) later replicated new association priming when they required participants to respond only to targets and when the SOA between context word and target was set to be as short as 150 ms. Also, this effect was not modulated by the proportion of intact pairs in the lexical decision task, so McKoon and Ratcliff considered it not likely affected by participants' use of strategy, as shown in previous short-term semantic priming studies (cf. Neely, Keefe, & Ross, 1989) and concluded that the new verbal associations participants learned could trigger automatic priming.

However, the generality of this effect is in question using a design highly similar to McKoon and Ratcliff (1979, 1986) with a few very subtle procedural differences, Durgunoglu and Neely (1987, see also Carroll & Kirsner, 1982; Neely & Durgunoglu, 1985; Smith, MacLeod, Bain et al., 1989) replicated the new association priming only when they used a specific set of parameters that was exactly the same as the one McKoon and Ratcliff used. Durgunoglu and Neely manipulated (a) the list composition of short (150-ms) and long (950-ms) SOAs—that is, whether in the lexical decision task participants received a block of trials with only long-SOA prime-target pairs or a block of trials with short- and long-SOA prime-target pairs intermixed, (b) whether or not the primes of related test pairs were studied, and (c) whether or not the targets of non-word test pairs were studied. Durgunoglu and Neely replicated McKoon and Ratcliff's new association priming in the long-SOA trials when (a) they were not intermixed with short-SOA trials, (b) the primes of related test pairs were not studied, and (c) non-word test items had not been studied. Because the new association priming occurred at a long SOA of 950 ms, it was susceptible to the participants' use of strategies. However, Durgunoglu and Neely obtained new association priming at a short-SOA (i.e., 150 ms) only when (a) all word test items were studied and all non-word test items were not studied and (b) the primes of related test pairs were not studied. While it is not clear why old association priming did not occur for the related target that was presented with a studied prime on Durgunoglu and Neely's test lists, the complete confound between the lexical status and the study status of test items might have induced their participants to use what Tse and Neely (2005) have called the predictive lexicality strategy for producing new association priming. That is, the participants could use target's study status to predict its lexical status in the lexical decision task because the test items must be words when they have been studied and non-words when they have not. Thus, even using the speeded lexical decision task in which the participants are assumed not to use any strategies when making their responses, new association priming might still occur only when the experimental manipulation serves to make episodic information (i.e., study status of the test item) available and useful for making lexical decisions.[27] This occurred whether the prime-target SOA was short or long, indicating that a short SOA might not always prevent the participants from using strategies in new association priming studies. Thus, Durgunoglu and Neely's findings suggest that new

---

[27] Although Smith, MacLeod, Bain et al. (1989) did not find new association priming when they also confounded the study status and test status of their non-words, their use of an *incidental* study task might have made it less likely for their participants to be aware of the study-test relationship and in turn, less likely to use the explicit-memory retrieval strategy in the subsequent lexical decision task.

association priming may not occur without at least some involvement of the explicit-memory retrieval strategy.[28]

Apart from McKoon and Ratcliff (1979, 1986) and Neely and Durgunoglu (1985, 1987), subsequent new association priming studies using the lexical decision task were also not immune to explicit contamination. Using a short-term semantic priming paradigm, den Heyer (1986) repeated by blocking the identical related, unrelated, and neutral (BLANK) prime-target pairs (and also word-nonword pairs) six times. Although this study was not conducted to investigate new association priming, the repetition of unrelated prime-target pairs might be regarded as a demonstration of new association priming. Regardless of short (100 ms) or long (550 ms) SOA, den Heyer obtained significant and robust (75-112 ms) new association priming (when comparing the RTs for unrelated pairs in the first vs. sixth block). This was in contrast to the other studies in which the new association priming did not occur even when the unrelated pairs were intentionally studied (e.g., Durgunoglu & Neely, 1987), rather than processed in a shallow task as in den Heyer (i.e., merely making lexical decisions to the target after silently reading the prime). Nevertheless, after taking the practice effect into account by subtracting the *boost* in RTs for the trials with neutral primes (in the first vs. sixth block) from new association priming, the 51 ms effect was significant only at a long SOA, but the 33 ms effect at a short SOA was not, indicating that den Heyer's new association priming may have occurred only when his participants had enough time to use an explicit-memory retrieval strategy.

In contrast to den Heyer (1986) who found new association priming (at least at a long SOA) when the unrelated prime-target pairs were shallowly processed, in some studies, new association priming did not occur even when the unrelated pairs had been extensively studied. Dagenbach, Horst, and Carr (1990, see also Silberman, Miikkulainen, & Bentin, 2005) had their participants learn pairs of unrelated words in an hour-long study-test procedure that produced a nearly perfect recall of the target cued by its prime. This kind of session was repeated for 8-10 times over five weeks. In each of these sessions, participants were also given a continuous lexical decision task (see Table 1) before the cued recall task. After these multiple study-test sessions, they were given a lexical decision task with a 200 ms prime-target SOA. On each trial, participants silently read the prime and made a lexical decision to the subsequently presented target. Dagenbach et al. obtained small yet significant new association priming despite their small sample size (12-14). Because Dagenbach et al. included studied non-words in their lexical decision task, it is unlikely that their participants could rely on the predictive lexicality strategy. Hence, they argued that their new association priming was automatic. However, the automaticity of these new association priming should be interpreted with caution. Dagenbach et al. (see also Graf & Schacter, 1985; Schrijnemakers & Raaijmakers, 1997, for a similar problem) used extralist primes in their "recombined" pairs to measure new association priming (see UR-e pairs in Table 2). Hence, their intact pairs

---

[28] One could argue that Neely and Durgunoglu (1985, 1987) failed to obtain the standard semantic priming in all but one of their conditions (Durgunoglu & Neely, Experiment 2). This was contrary to McKoon and Ratcliff (1979) who did reliably find this effect for their *studied* related pairs. Thus, certain unknown aspects of Neely and Durgunoglu's procedures may have interfered with the processes that normally give rise to new association priming (e.g., the proportion of studied test items was lower in Neely & Durgunoglu, .20-.33, than in McKoon & Ratcliff, .50-.89—yet how this factor might affect the *semantic* priming awaits future investigation.) However, even though McKoon and Ratcliff's semantic priming occur for their *studied* related pairs, these effects might have also been due to participants' strategies (e.g., they would expect to see a *related* target after they made lexical decisions to the prime).

consisted of a studied context word and a studied target but their "recombined" pairs consisted of a non-studied context word and a studied target.[29] Thus, the amount of study for the context word was confounded with the intact vs. recombined test context. The unfamiliarity of the context word in the recombined pairs might consume more cognitive resources for the participants and make them less prepared to recognize (and, in turn, make a decision to) the subsequent target. Because Dagenbach et al. gave their participants multiple study-test sessions, the difference in familiarity of the studied vs. non-studied context words should be quite large. This factor might have thus slowed down participants' RTs to the targets of the recombined pairs and, in turn, overestimated the new association priming. As the size of Dagenbach et al.'s new association priming was already small, it is possible that after removing this extraneous factor, the effect would become non-significant. Hence, Dagenbach et al.'s data does not convincingly demonstrate the automaticity of new association priming.

In another series of experiments using a double-item lexical decision task (see Table 1), Goshen-Gottstein and Moscovitch (1995a, 1995b, see also Goshen-Gottstein et al., 2000) also obtained overall significant new association priming. Again, their experiments might also be susceptible to explicit contamination. Because the overall RTs were about 900-1000 ms (450-500 ms for each test item) in their simultaneous double-item lexical decision task, their participants might use a single item to cue their lexical decisions via using the available episodic information (Hintzman & Curran, 1997). This was more likely the case in Goshen-Gottstein and Moscovitch because the authors explicitly mentioned that "...some of the letter-string pairs had appeared at study." (1995a, p. 1234, see also McKone & Slee, 1997, for a similar manipulation). Even though their participants were asked to "disregard [the studied letter-string pairs], as it was purely due to convenience of setting up the experiment", previous research (Bowers & Schacter, 1990, Experiment 3) showed that participants who received this kind of "explicit" instruction showed stronger new association priming than those who did not. Hence, the new association priming reported in Goshen-Gottstein and Moscovitch might also be explicitly contaminated.

One could argue against the influence of explicit contamination in Goshen-Gottstein and Moscovitch's (1995a, 1995b) double-item lexical decision task by showing that the reported RTs in this task were 400 ms faster than those in their explicit pair recognition test. If the explicit-memory retrieval strategy did play a role in the lexical decision task, the RTs in this task would have been similar to those in episodic recognition. However, as argued by Neely (1989, Footnote 6), longer RTs in episodic recognition do not necessarily mean that the "time" required for episodic information to become available is long because the RTs in episodic recognition are likely much longer than the time it takes for the episodic information, which is sufficient to discriminate studied from non-studied items, to become available in memory. That is, after episodic information becomes sufficiently activated, considerably more time might also be consumed by an effortful decision as to which response is indicated by this activated episodic information and response selection and execution. Because these latter two processes need not be done when participants use the episodic information to make their lexical decisions, the RTs in this "implicit" memory task should still be much faster than

---

[29] A better way to create the recombined pairs is to re-pair the studied unrelated pairs to form an unrelated yet newly combined pair (see *UR-a* pairs in Table 2), such that context words should receive same amount of study in both intact and recombined pairs (see below for more discussions).

those in episodic recognition even when participants do, in fact, use the explicit-memory retrieval strategy to make their responses.

One could also use the functional dissociation logic to argue against possible explicit contamination in Goshen-Gottstein and Moscovitch (1995a) because while their overall new association priming was of similar magnitude after shallow and deep study tasks, their explicit pair recognition performance was significantly better after deep study task than after shallow study task (i.e., the level-of-processing effect). However, a closer inspection on Goshen-Gottstein and Moscovitch's data revealed that the null level-of-processing effect in new association priming occurred only for low-frequency words (13 ms) but not for high-frequency words (52 ms). Because the Frequency × New Association Priming × Level-of-Processing interaction did not approach significance, the authors did not report the significance of the level-of-processing effect for their high-frequency words (or other statistics, e.g., standard deviation, which allow one to compute its significance). However, this numerically large, probably even statistically significant, level-of-processing effect for high-frequency words beclouds the interpretation of this "functional dissociation" in Goshen-Gottstein and Moscovitch's new association priming vs. pair recognition. Hence, the possibility that Goshen-Gottstein and Moscovitch's new association priming was explicitly contaminated cannot be completely ruled out.

Pecher and Raaijmakers (1999, see also Pecher & Raaijmakers, 2004, for an analogous study using a conceptual animacy decision task) claimed to have found automatic new association priming in lexical decision and perceptual identification tasks. Using an extensive training program similar to the one in Dagenbach et al. (1990), their participants learned both related and unrelated word pairs by performing multiple sessions of paired-associate learning and lexical decision tasks in the study phase. Their participants were then given a lexical decision task, with the context word and target being sequentially presented at 140-ms SOA on each trial, or a perceptual identification task in which the context word and target were rapidly presented and sandwiched by a forward mask and a backward mask. The sequence of events in each perceptual identification trial was forward mask, context word, target, and backward mask. In either task, participants responded only to the target. Pecher and Raaijmakers reported significant new association priming in the lexical decision task but not in the perceptual identification task. (They did not find any old association priming in either task.) In Experiment 2, Pecher and Raaijmakers' participants studied related and unrelated pairs in multiple sessions of a paired-associate learning task and perceptual identification tasks in the study phase. In the test phase, they received either a lexical decision task with forward masked context word and target being sequentially presented with 60-ms SOA on each trial or a perceptual identification task identical to the one used in Experiment 1. After collapsing across the old association priming and new association priming, Pecher and Raaijmakers obtained significant priming in the perceptual identification task, but not in the lexical decision task.[30]

Pecher and Raaijmakers' (1999) short-SOA (140 ms) and masked-prime manipulations made it less likely that their participants might use explicit strategies in the lexical decision and perceptual identification tasks. The new association priming they found should be

---

[30] The Cohen's $ds$ of Pecher and Raaijmakers' (1999) new association priming were large (.71) for their 20 ms effect in Experiment 1's lexical decision task and very small (.14) for their 6% effect in Experiment 2's perceptual identification task. The $t$ of this latter new association priming was computed based on their reported standard errors.

relatively strategy-free, compared with those found in previous studies (e.g., McKoon & Ratcliff, 1979). However, two methodological concerns need to be considered before their new association priming can be regarded as automatic. First, Pecher and Raaijmakers' new association priming in Experiment 1 was overestimated by their use of inappropriate recombined pairs (see also Carroll & Kirsner, 1982; den Heyer, 1986 for a similar problem). To describe that, we use the examples provided in their paper. Suppose that the related to-be-recombined study pair is bread-cow and the unrelated to-be-recombined study pair is milk-harbor. (What the related or unrelated intact pairs are is not relevant here.) At test, the related and unrelated recombined pairs were made up by cross-recombining the previously studied pairs—the related and unrelated recombined test pairs were milk-cow and bread-harbor. In other words, Pecher and Raaijmakers retained the relatedness of intact pairs but switched the relatedness of recombined pairs (a) from "related" at study to "unrelated" at test for assessing the new association priming and (b) from "unrelated" at study to "related" at test for assessing the old association priming (see another example in Table 2 R-i and UR-i pairs). Because Pecher and Raaijmakers' participants extensively studied a small set (64 in total) of related and unrelated pairs in multiple sessions, they might expect to see a related or unrelated target after a specific prime was presented, for example, they might expect to see a related target after seeing bread (since it was paired up with cow before) and an unrelated target after seeing milk (since it was paired up with harbor before). At test, the "relatedness" status of actual targets they saw for related and unrelated recombined pairs, milk-cow and bread-harbor, respectively, were unexpected. Hence, their RTs and accuracy to these recombined pairs might be slowed down in the lexical decision task and lower in the perceptual identification task, respectively, thereby overestimating the new association priming that had presumably been produced by novel associations participants learned in the experiment.[31] One could argue that this expectancy also occurs in a new association priming paradigm involving only unrelated pairs—participants might expect to see REASON-house rather than OBSERVE-house after they studied REASON-house. The latter case, however, actually measures the priming of a new association between reason and house because participants do not have an expectation to the relatedness status of the target. But what Pecher and Raaijmakers measured was the facilitation (i.e., priming) of the new association and the RT/accuracy costs of the expectation violation participants had to the unrelated targets after they saw the context word, which had been paired up with a related target at study. In short, it is unclear whether Pecher and Raaijmakers' small "automatic" new association priming (i.e., 20 ms and 6% in lexical

---

[31] Goshen-Gottstein and Moscovitch (1995a, see also Durgunoglu & Neely, 1987; Neely & Durgunoglu, 1985) resolved the confound between the relatedness statuses at study and at test for recombined pairs and measured new association priming and old association priming by using *UR-a* and *R-a* pairs shown in Table 2. Their unrelated recombined test pairs were formed by unrelated study pairs (study: REASON-house, OBSERVE-wolf; test: OBSERVE-house) and their related recombined test pairs were formed by related study pairs (study: WINDOW-house, DOOR-knob; test: DOOR-house). As claimed by the authors, these recombined pairs for old association priming measure how the study of episodically and semantically related pairs primes the lexical decision performance beyond the effect contributed by its pre-existing association. Unlike other lexical decision studies (e.g., Carroll & Kirsner, 1982; den Heyer, 1986; Pecher & Raaijmakers, 1999), Goshen-Gottstein and Moscovitch did not find significant old association priming in their double-item lexical decision task when the effect was measured by these *R-a* pairs. (Using these pairs, Neely and Durgunoglu even reported numerically, yet statistically non-significant, negative old association priming in a series of experiments using the single-item lexical decision task.) Based on these findings, the presence of old association priming seems to depend on the choice of recombined pairs.

decision and perceptual identification tasks, respectively) would be found had they used the appropriate recombined pairs (see Footnote 28) in their experiments.

In their subsequent study using an animacy decision task (see Table 1), Pecher and Raaijmakers (2004) did partially resolve the problem of recombined pairs in their 1999 paper. They now constructed the unrelated recombined test pairs (umbrella-ship) by recombining two studied unrelated pairs (umbrella-moon and harp-ship). Hence, participants' responses to these unrelated recombined test pairs were unlikely slowed down by the expectation violation they experienced when they expected unrelated targets but received related targets. However, they did not use the same manipulation for their related condition—their related recombined test pairs (nail-hammer) were still formed by two studied unrelated pairs (nail-car and coat-hammer). As participants received both related and unrelated pairs in the animacy decision task, the violation of expectancy (when participants received related recombined pairs) might indirectly influence their responses to the unrelated recombined pairs even though the latter pairs did not violate their expectations. Thus, even though Pecher and Raaijmakers also found small yet significant new association priming in their animacy decision task, it is still unclear whether this effect was actually strategy-free.

To resolve the confound in Pecher and Raaijmakers' (1999, 2004) recombined pairs, researchers should recombine the studied unrelated pairs for the recombined unrelated test pairs and recombine the studied related pairs for the recombined related test pairs. This might equate the participants' expectancy to the relatedness status across intact and recombined test contexts. To directly examine the effect of expectation violation in new association priming, researchers may use the neutral pairs (e.g., XXX-cow) to measure the facilitation for intact pairs and the inhibition for recombined pairs. Pecher and Raaijmakers (1999, Experiment 1, see also Durgunoglu & Neely, 1987; Neely & Durgunoglu, 1985) did use a neutral baseline (BLANK-cow) in their lexical decision task in the study and test phases. Measured against this baseline, the facilitation (neutral minus intact) and inhibition (recombined minus neutral) was 17 ms and -3 ms for new association priming, and 14 ms and 14 ms for old association priming. Although the intact pairs showed a small facilitation, the virtually non-existent (-3 ms) and even reversed (14 ms) inhibition seems to contradict our above analyses.[32] However, because Pecher and Raaijmakers did not include the neutral baseline in their analyses, these facilitation and inhibition effects could not be verified statistically. Also, because their neutral baseline pairs were studied in the study phase and identically represented in the lexical decision task in the test phase, participants might also have developed the associations between BLANK and some targets. It is unclear whether and how this "expectation" might have facilitated, slowed down or had no effect on the participants' responses given that they had also encountered the expectation violation when they responded to the recombined pairs. Finally, using the same word BLANK as a neutral prime might indeed be problematic (see Jonides & Mack, 1984, for discussing the pros and cons of using a neutral baseline). To our knowledge, no study has attempted to tear apart the facilitatory and inhibitory components of new association priming, as has been done in some short-term semantic priming studies (e.g., Neely, 1976, 1977). Future research should use a less problematic neutral baseline (e.g., non-

---

[32] Measured against the neutral primes (XXX-*cow*), Durgunoglu and Neely (1987, see also Neely & Durgunoglu, 1985) found that the facilitation or inhibition of item repetition priming/new association priming depended on some subtle characteristics in their tasks, such as the inclusion of extralist semantic primes or the blocking of short- and long-SOA trials. Hence, more research needs to be done to pinpoint the conditions in which the facilitation and inhibition of new association priming occur.

studied pronounceable non-words) to measure the facilitation and inhibition in new association priming and how they interact with other variables such as proportion of studied test pairs. This line of research could shed light on the automaticity of new association priming—if the activation automatically occurs for new verbal associations, there should not be any inhibitory new association priming according to some spreading activation theories (cf. Neely, 1977; Posner & Snyder, 1975).

One could argue that all of the above criticisms might not be in line with what some theorists postulate concerning how prospective expectancy strategy is operated (cf. Neely, 1977; Neely et al., 1989). According to those theories, participants' expectancy to the target was unlikely operating in Pecher and Raaijmakers (1999, 2004) because the prime-target SOAs (300 ms) they used were too short to allow participants to trigger the expectancy mechanism when they see the prime. However, on the one hand, the assumption of automatic short-term semantic priming might not be applied to new association priming; on the other hand, because Pecher and Raaijmakers' participants extensively learned specific unrelated word pairs before doing the primed lexical decision task, they might expect a specific target after they saw the context word in the lexical decision task. This was not the same as the typical situation in a semantic priming experiment where participants often strategically generate a set of related items when they see the prime. Thus, the prospective "expectancy" mechanism, if any, participants used in the new association priming paradigm might not necessarily be the same as the one used in the short-term semantic priming experiments. Future research should tear apart the prospective expectancy mechanisms that operate in short-term semantic priming and in new association priming.

Finally, even the new association priming in Pecher and Raaijmakers' (1999) masked perceptual identification task might not necessarily be automatic. Masson and Bodner (2003, but see Grossi, 2006) showed that participants' performance on a masked-prime item repetition priming lexical decision task depends on the list context (e.g., the proportion of related prime-target pairs), indicating that participants could develop a retrospective strategy to make their lexical decisions even when they are not aware of the masked prime during the task. When participants identify the target preceded by a masked prime, they could retrospectively recruit the stored memory trace of the masked prime to facilitate their current identification for the target. However, several methodological differences in Masson and Bodner vs. Pecher and Raaijmakers disallow a direct comparison between the two studies. For instance, while Masson and Bodner only forward-masked the prime but not the target and used a lexical decision task, Pecher and Raaijmakers sandwiched both prime and target by forward and backward masks and used a perceptual identification task. Future studies should manipulate the list context (e.g., the proportion of studied test items) to test whether the retrospective memory recruitment mechanism might also operate in the masked new association priming paradigm.

In summary, almost none of the new association priming studies using a speeded implicit memory test has provided convincing evidence for the automaticity of new association priming except perhaps Pecher and Raaijmakers' (1999) masked-prime perceptual identification task. Most of these new association priming studies had limitations in their experimental design (e.g., inappropriate recombined pairs or susceptible to the use of predictive lexicality strategy) or included procedures (e.g., long SOA) that did not satisfy the conditions for establishing that the obtained new association priming was automatic. In short, contrary to what some researchers (e.g., Zeelenberg et al., 2003) have assumed, even speeded implicit memory tests might not necessarily guarantee that the new association priming they yield is automatic and strategy-free.

## DICHOTOMY OF EPISODIC MEMORY VS. SEMANTIC MEMORY

Before concluding the current review, it is important to note that the central claim of this literature review (i.e., the automaticity of new association priming has not been well supported) could shed light on the distinction between episodic and semantic memory, a topic that has been debated (but not yet resolved) in memory research for over 30 years. In this final section, we first define semantic and episodic memory based on Tulving's (1972, 1983) conceptualization. Then we use Carr, Dagenbach, VanWieren et al.'s (1994) criteria to evaluate whether the new association priming reported in previous studies is mediated by episodic or semantic memory. Finally, we discuss three recent new association priming studies (Dagenbach et al., 1990; Pecher & Raaijmakers, 1999, 2004) that are the most relevant to the discussion regarding the episodic-semantic memory distinction.

In his influential chapter in *Organization of Memory,* Tulving (1972, see also Tulving, 1983, *Elements of Episodic Memory*) proposed two different (episodic vs. semantic) memory systems. Semantic memory consists of abstract knowledge such as word meanings and the relations among words, whereas episodic memory consists of memories for personally experienced specific events that are organized according to their temporal (e.g., when did it happen?) and spatial characteristics (e.g., where did it happen?). Because the two systems presumably differ in the organization of their contents, the rules governing information retrieval, and the susceptibility to interference, they have been investigated by different kinds of memory tests. Episodic memory is often assessed by explicit memory tests, where an explicit reference is made to the study episodes. Tulving (1983, 1984) also differentiates semantic associations from episodic associations. Semantic associations are those expressed in a free association task, in which people produce the first word that comes to mind in response to a cue word. These semantic associations exist by virtue of people's knowledge and entail meaningful relations among words. Episodic associations, such as paired-associates acquired within experiments, entail the temporal co-occurrence of two words learned in some study episodes.[33]

---

[33] Tulving (2002) recently defined episodic memory as one of the neuropsychological memory systems (see also Schacter & Tulving, 1994), subserved by a widely distributed network of cortical and subcortical brain regions. He argued that it is the "only memory system that allows people to consciously re-experience past experiences…about happenings in particular places at particular times, or about 'what,' 'where,' and 'when'" (p. 3). The distinction between semantic and episodic memory is that "episodic memory is evolved of semantic memory: Semantic memory appeared long before episodic memory" (p. 6). He questioned whether the memory tasks used in the laboratory are able to test a single memory system, as he mentioned, "In terms of memory systems, all tasks are 'multiply determined'" (p. 6, see also Tulving, 1991). To support the distinction between episodic and semantic memory systems, Tulving cited evidence *only* from neuroimaging studies and from experimental studies using clinical populations in his 2002 review, without even a single reference to any experimental studies using a healthy young population. This is not surprising given his view that traditional laboratory experiments are almost always concerned with "what", rather than "where" and "when", and thus unable to reveal the genuine picture of episodic memory. To our knowledge, no new association priming study has been reported to test this new conceptualization of episodic memory. Hence, we stick to Tulving's 1972 and 1983 definitions in the following discussion.

In contrast to Tulving's (1972, 1983) differentiation between episodic and semantic memories, some researchers argued against the necessity of postulating episodic vs. semantic memory (Anderson & Ross, 1980; N. J. Cohen et al., 1997; Hintzman, 1986; McKoon, Ratcliff, & Dell, 1986; Squire & Zola, 1998). Take Hintzman's MINVERA2 model as an example (see also Hintzman, 1988). Whenever an experience occurs, such as learning a Latin word adamo (to fall in love with someone), a memory trace is stored. If adamo is encountered several times, it is stored on each occurrence together with some contextual information (e.g., where and when adamo was encountered). If memory for adamo is then probed with a cue that includes the context encountered before (e.g., during a date), a specific trace that matches with the context is activated. This specific trace is thus analogous to episodic memory for adamo. However, if the cue includes only adamo that is not with any context previously encountered (e.g., reading a novel in Latin), all traces containing this Latin word may be activated and the resulting context is more abstract (which is an overall average of different previous contexts). Thus, the system computes more or less abstract information according to the cue that is used to access memory. Based on this trace-strength retrieval mechanism, Hintzman posited that there is no need to distinguish episodic and semantic memory systems for explaining the memory performance in the explicit and implicit memory tests (see also Tenpenny, 1995, for a similar view).

Subsequent studies reported evidence supporting (e.g., Roediger, 1984) or questioning (e.g., Anderson & Ross, 1980; McKoon, Ratcliff, & Dell, 1986; Neely & Payne, 1983) the episodic-semantic memory distinction, some of which involved the new association priming paradigm. Rather than exhaustively reviewing these studies, in the following discussions, we focus on three more recent new association priming studies (Dagenbach et al., 1990; Pecher & Raaijmakers, 1999, 2004). For the reviews of those studies prior to 1989, readers are referred to Neely (1989) and Tulving (1983). Neely provided a recipe of experimental controls that should be implemented before a functional dissociation can be used to support or refute the episodic-semantic memory distinction. Carr et al. (1994) also proposed several criteria to assess whether task performance is mediated by episodic or semantic memory. We elaborate Carr et al.'s criteria below and use them to evaluate what new association priming can tell us about the episodic-semantic memory distinction.

a) Because episodic memory is unique to particular episodes of experience and semantic memory can be accessed in different contexts, the novel associations that are formed within experiments should be stored in episodic memory, whereas the old associations (i.e., related pairs) should be stored in semantic memory. Because the new episodic associations being exposed once or twice in previous studies should be unlikely added to semantic memory, the priming for these associations should be mediated by episodic memory. Because the episodic memory trace of study pairs that are presented more frequently in the study phase might be more likely added to semantic memory, assuming that the explicit memory tests measure purely episodic memory, the explicit vs. implicit functional dissociation would be more likely to occur when there is large, rather than small, number of study-pair presentations. To verify this hypothesis in prior studies including both implicit and explicit memory measures (see Table 4 and Functional dissociation section), after eliminating those experiments that violated the retrieval intentionality criterion (cf. Neely, 1989; Schacter et al., 1989), we categorize the remaining experiments, by the number of their study-pair presentations (see the # of P column), into two groups: the study pairs were presented only once (N=45) vs. more than once (N=16). The post-hoc observation contradicts the above prediction: there were more explicit vs. implicit functional dissociations in the studies where the study pairs were presented only once (50%) than more than once (19%). Moreover, all dissociations found in the "more than once" group were from the studies that presented the study pairs only twice (Graf & Schacter, 1989; Marsolek, Schacter, & Nicholas, 1996). Although this pattern might be largely distorted by vastly different manipulations across experiments, the fact that new association priming and explicit memory performance were not always functionally dissociated indicates that they might sometimes be mediated by the same underlying construct—episodic memory.

b)  As per the theory of skill acquisition, the speed in retrieving a memory trace (e.g., a word, an event, or a procedure) is closely related to the number of exposures for that trace (e.g., Logan, 1988, 1990). The more frequently a trace is exposed, the faster it can be retrieved, and in turn, the more likely its retrieval may become automatized. As an episodic memory trace has been encountered only a few times but a semantic memory trace has been encountered so many times, the retrieval of an episodic memory trace should be slower and more effortful than that of a semantic memory trace (see Logan, 1988, for more discussions).[34] Because the automaticity of priming has been regarded as a signature of accessing semantic knowledge (Neely, 1977; Posner & Snyder, 1975), the existence of automatic new association priming could be interpreted as showing that the new episodic associations have been added to semantic memory. However, as reviewed above, automatic new association priming has not been conclusively found in prior new association priming studies. Hence, based on this criterion, new association priming is likely mediated by episodic memory, rather than by semantic memory.

c)  Because episodic, but not semantic, memory is accompanied by information regarding the context whenever it is retrieved, densely amnesic patients should have difficulty forming or retrieving information from episodic memory and yet they might have relatively intact semantic memory (which had been developed prior to the onset of their amnesia). Because episodic associations should be multiply exposed before they are added to semantic memory, densely amnesic patients are typically unable to show any new association priming because they might not even establish the episodic associations at first. Hence, it is not surprising that in previous research, albeit with very few exceptions (e.g., Goshen-Gottstein et al., 2000), amnesic patients with zero explicit memory ability failed to show any new association priming (see Amnesic research section). This once again suggests that new association priming is likely mediated by episodic memory.

d)  While the reinstatement of the original context is critical for the retrieval of episodic memory traces, it is not so for semantic memory because one's knowledge should be equally accessible across a wide range of contexts. If new association priming is mediated by semantic memory, it should be of equal magnitude whether or not the

---

[34] One could argue that depending on the time lag between learning information in an episode and the testing of that information, memory performance might be enhanced in the retrieval of episodic traces due to recency effects. To our knowledge, the potential recency effect in new association priming has not yet been investigated in prior new association priming literature.

study and test contexts are the same. If the prime of an unrelated pair is presented in an implicit memory test, its episodically related target also becomes activated to the same degree, regardless of the context with which that prime has been studied. This is not likely the case because previous studies have shown that new association priming is attenuated when the presentation format of unrelated word pairs was changed from simultaneous at study to sequential at test (e.g., Goshen-Gottstein & Moscovitch, 1995a), when the presentation modality of unrelated word pairs was switched from auditory at study to visual at test (e.g., Schacter & Graf, 1989) and when the task was changed from perceptual identification task at study to lexical decision task at test (e.g., Pecher & Raaijmakers, 1999). Hence, given that semantic memory is context independent, the new association priming reported in these studies was unlikely mediated by semantic memory.

Based on Carr et al.'s (1994) criteria and the findings of new association priming studies, new association priming is more likely mediated by episodic memory than by semantic memory. This claim is counter-intuitive in light of episodic-semantic memory distinction because new association priming occurs in implicit memory tests that participants presumably perform without retrieving information from any specific study episodes (episodic memory). If semantic memory and episodic memory systems are functionally distinct and the information in these two systems can be accessed independently (Tulving, 1983), the reinstatement of episodically associated context words should never influence the performance on a semantic memory test. As a result, the findings of new association priming showed that episodic and semantic information are likely to be stored in the same memory system and therefore, there is no need to posit two different memory systems.

One could argue that the new association priming findings can be accommodated in the distinct episodic and semantic memory systems if one assumes (a) the explicit contamination in implicit (semantic) memory tests or (b) the addition of new episodic associations to semantic memory. First, even though new association priming can be mediated by episodic memory, it may not necessarily be problematic to the episodic-semantic memory distinction because participants might use the explicit-memory retrieval strategy to perform the implicit memory test. The fact that new association priming is mediated by episodic, but not semantic memory could be attributed to participants' treating the semantic (implicit) memory test as an episodic (explicit) memory test and/or using their available episodic information to enhance their task performance (e.g., Durgunoglu & Neely, 1987). Thus, the findings of new association priming do not necessarily provide evidence against the distinction between episodic and semantic memory.

Second, if new association priming were actually mediated by novel associations newly stored in semantic memory, it would not be problematic for the episodic-semantic memory distinction. Dagenbach et al. (1990, see also Sherry & Schacter, 1987) considered that after an episodic association has been extensively studied, it can be added to semantic memory. The new association priming observed under this circumstance might occur automatically and thus be mediated by semantic memory, but not by episodic memory. However, although Dagenbach et al. did show significant yet small new association priming after unrelated study pairs were studied intensively, as we mentioned above, their new association priming might likely be overestimated by their use of inappropriate recombined pairs (see also the Speeded implicit memory tests section). Thus, it is not clear whether their small, apparently automatic, new association priming would be replicated had they used the more appropriate recombined pairs (see Footnote 28 and Table 2).

Similar to Dagenbach et al. (1990), Pecher and Raaijmakers (1999) intensively trained their participants with unrelated word pairs in multiple study-test sessions and found new association priming in the lexical decision or perceptual identification tasks. Given that (a) the multiple exposures of study pairs might make it more likely for their participants to add the new episodic associations to semantic memory and (b) the short SOA (140 ms) and masked-prime (60 ms) manipulations might minimize the participants' explicit-memory retrieval strategy, Pecher and Raaijmakers might have demonstrated automatic new association priming that was mediated by semantic information in a semantic (implicit) memory test, supporting the episodic-semantic memory distinction. However, this conclusion may be undermined by three concerns about their experimental design and findings. The first one, the use of inappropriate recombined pairs as the baseline of new association priming, is discussed in the Speeded implicit memory tests section. The following are the other two concerns that weaken Pecher and Raaijmakers' evidence for the episodic-semantic memory distinction.

If the maximum strength of episodic memory traces of an association is equal for the pre-experimentally related and unrelated pairs and if episodic associations are added to semantic memory, new association priming should be stronger than old association priming because learning effects usually show a negatively accelerated curve (e.g., Newell & Rosenbloom, 1981). Given a fixed amount of learning (e.g., exposure time to the word pairs), the learning effect should be greater for the unrelated word pairs that are freshly built into semantic memory than for the related word pairs that have already had strong associations in memory. However, this Study-Pair Relatedness (related vs. unrelated) × Test Context (intact vs. recombined) interaction was found only in Pecher and Raaijmakers' Experiment 1 (lexical decision task), but not in their Experiment 2 (perceptual identification task). Using a similar multiple study-test procedure, Schrijnemakers and Raaijmakers (1997) observed this interaction in only one of their three experiments that used the lexical decision task. Finally, Pecher and Raaijmakers (2004, Experiment 2) even observed a marginal interaction that was in the opposite direction—old association priming was greater than new association priming. As commented on by Schrijnemakers and Raaijmakers, "…it remains uncertain whether the…priming effect of the new associations was due to a newly formed semantic code or to a weaker episodic code…" (p. 129). Therefore, due to the absence of a Study-Pair Relatedness × Test Context interaction, Raaijmakers and his colleagues' finding seems not to agree with that new associations have been added to semantic memory. (This interaction was actually reported in some new association priming studies, e.g., Durgunoglu & Neely, 1987, Goshen-Gottstein & Moscovitch, 1995a.)

There is another reason that Pecher and Raaijmakers' (1999) new association priming might not necessarily have been mediated by semantic memory. In each training session of their study phase, they sequentially gave their participants three tasks on unrelated word pairs: a paired-associate learning task, a cued-recall task and a lexical decision (or perceptual identification) task. The implicit memory test given at the end of the experiment could be the same as or different from the task their participants did when they learned the study pairs (i.e., lexical decision or perceptual identification task). Pecher and Raaijmakers found significant new association priming only when the study task (lexical decision/ perceptual identification) and test task (lexical decision/perceptual identification) were the same, but not when they were different. By definition, information that is strongly related to a specific context (e.g., type of study task) should not be integrated into semantic memory and the retrieval from semantic memory should be context-independent (Tulving, 1983, 1984). If a new episodic association is added to semantic memory, the priming mediated by this association should be of equal magnitude whether or not the context presented at test are the same as the one presented at study (see Carr et al.'s, 1994, criterion d). Hence, because Pecher and Raaijmakers (see also Pecher & Raaijmakers, 2004; Schrijnemakers & Raaijmakers, 1997) found a study-test task compatibility effect on new association priming (i.e., the effect occurs *only* when the study and test tasks are the same), the effect is unlikely to be mediated solely by semantic memory.

However, Pecher and Raaijmakers (1999, 2004) offered an alternative explanation for the study-test task compatibility effect of their new association priming, based on the assumption that their new association priming did occur automatically. To explain how new associations being accessed automatically in semantic memory could still be context-dependent, they argued that the retrieval from semantic memory, rather than being abstract and static, may interact "dynamically" with the study or test context. The new association priming occurs when a word pair is presented in the same task at study and at test. The more similar the study task and test task, the larger the overlap in the interpretation of the target according to the context word between study and test, and in turn, the greater the new association priming. Vriezen, Moscovitch, and Bellos (1995) also found that the occurrence of item repetition priming was sensitive to the overlap in processing demand between study and test. They failed to find item repetition priming in a classification task when the same item was judged in different semantic domains at study (e.g., size decision) and at test (e.g., animacy decision) but found item repetition priming when the same item was judged in the same semantic domain at study and at test. The reinstatement of identical processing demand (i.e., the same item and the same task to be performed) seems to serve as an a effective retrieval cue for that particular context of prior study episodes, thus producing the strongest item repetition priming, akin to the view of transfer appropriate processing (Roediger et al., 1989). The findings that supported this view have also been reported in other item repetition priming studies (e.g., Hughes & Whittlesea, 2003, but see Vaidya et al., 1997, Experiment 7). Unlike these item repetition priming studies, Pecher and Raaijmakers used different perceptual implicit memory tests (perceptual identification vs. lexical decision in 1999) at study and at test or the presence or absence of animacy decision task at study (in 2004) to examine the context-dependency of new association priming.

Nonetheless, the validity of Pecher and Raaijmakers' (1999, 2004) "context-dependent" semantic memory explanation might hinge on a questionable assumption (i.e., the automaticity of new association priming). Even if the issues associated with this assumption could be clarified, Pecher and Raaijmakers' study-test task compatibility effect might still not be strong evidence for the context-dependency of semantic memory because the effect was actually very small and, strictly speaking, not statistically supported. When their study task was the lexical decision task, their new association priming at test was 20 ms in lexical decision task and 3% in perceptual identification task; when their study task was the perceptual identification task, their new association priming at test was 11 ms in the lexical decision task and 6% in the perceptual identification task. Pecher and Raaijmakers did not verify statistically the 3% vs. 6% (or 20 ms vs. 11 ms) difference, nor did they report the significance of the critical Study Task (perceptual identification vs. lexical decision) × Test Task (perceptual identification vs. lexical decision) × Test Context (intact vs. recombined) interaction,[35] which is essential for showing the study-test task compatibility effect on new association priming. Indeed, even Pecher and Raaijmakers acknowledged, "...because all priming effects in our experiments were rather small, we should not conclude that there is no transfer [of new association priming across a non-identical study and test types] at all." (p. 611). Thus, more evidence, such as including a classification task with different semantic domains at study and at test, should be sought to test the context dependency of semantic memory, an important issue for the episodic-semantic memory distinction.

Even if Pecher and Raaijmakers' (1999) study-test task compatibility effect could be statistically supported, the effect would also be explained by response priming, indicating that the new association priming would likely be mediated by episodic memory. As Spieler and Balota (1996, see also Laver, 2009) pointed out, when a new association priming paradigm involves identical responses in the study task and in the test task (e.g., in a continuous lexical decision task, participants make lexical decision responses to both study and test pairs, see Table 1), the new association priming observed might be partially attributed to the output or motor forms of response priming. The participants could acquire the response association between the word pair and its required response (or between the two individual items within a pair and their required response), in addition to the episodic association between the two items of a pair. Because Pecher and Raaijmakers' (1999, see also animacy decision in Pecher & Raaijmakers, 2004) participants produced identical lexical decision responses or perceptual identification responses to the unrelated word pairs at study and at test and were given extensive training sessions, new associations might be formed between two unrelated words in episodic memory through repeated co-occurrence of the words, as well as in procedural memory through the repeated production of the same response to specific word pairs. Both of these memories could contribute to the observed new association priming. Hence, the study-test task compatibility effect that occurred in the lexical decision and perceptual identification tasks might at least partially reflect the participants' inability to take advantage of the response mapping they acquired in the lexical decision (or perceptual identification) study task to generate responses or to judge the lexicality in the subsequent perceptual identification (or lexical decision) test task. Finally, regarding the episodic-semantic memory distinction, the possibility that new association priming depends on a reinstatement of a specific stimulus-to-response mapping that participants acquired at study could also suggest that the new association priming is mediated by episodic memory, rather than by semantic memory.

In summary, because the automaticity of new association priming has not been generally established and the new association priming itself is likely mediated by episodic memory (e.g., participants could use the episodic and/or response information to facilitate their responses in implicit memory tests), the implications of new association priming for the episodic-semantic memory distinction remain as ambiguous as what they were 20 years ago (See Tulving, 1983; McKoon et al., 1986; Neely, 1989 for reviews).

---

[35] The scaling difference in perceptual identification and lexical decision tasks (measured in proportion with smaller variances vs. in RTs with larger variances) might complicate the pattern of this interaction.

# Conclusion

In this chapter, we evaluated whether or not verbal new association priming *can* occur automatically. Based on the existing verbal new association priming data, the answer is "probably not". Despite using a wide range of experimental techniques to test the automaticity of new association priming (e.g., process dissociation procedure and test awareness), almost none of the prior studies was immune to methodological and/or theoretical limitations. The most plausible demonstration of automatic new association priming was Pecher and Raaijmakers' (1999) masked-prime perceptual identification experiments (with the prime-target SOA as short as 60 ms). Given that the conscious, recollected information may not be available until 500 ms after the onset of the test item, it is difficult to solely attribute the new association priming obtained under this circumstance to the participants' use of an explicit-memory retrieval strategy. As mentioned above, this finding could be explained by Masson and Bodner's (2003) retrospective episodic recruitment account—when participants make a decision to the target preceded by a masked prime, they may retrospectively recruit the stored memory trace of the masked prime to facilitate their current recognition of the target. Regardless of the explanation for Pecher and Raaijmakers' masked new association priming, it is important to note that their effect was very small (less than 10% in a perceptual identification task and 20 ms in a lexical decision task), and hence needs to be replicated before it could be used to support the automaticity of new association priming. As mentioned above, this masked new association priming could be explained by the retrospective memory recruitment account. However, it should be noted that this account itself was quite vague and difficult to test. Apparently, the only way to disconfirm this account is to find a null masked priming effect, which was, in fact, reported at least once in the published masked item repetition priming literature (see Grossi, 2006). Of course, whether or not an account should be rejected based on the null finding is debatable. In short, it seems safe to conclude that the automaticity of new association priming is not fully supported by prior new association priming observed with healthy young adults.

Similarly, almost none of the new association priming studies involving amnesic patients provides clear evidence for the automaticity of new association priming. Fewer than half of them reported significant new association priming as well as an explicit vs. implicit functional dissociation for this clinical population, contradicting most of the previous item repetition priming studies. Moreover, except for very few cases (e.g., Goshen-Gottstein et al., 2000), amnesic patients' intact new association priming might likely be contaminated by their use of an explicit-memory retrieval strategy because in these studies, the presumably "amnesic" patients are often shown to have residual explicit memory (e.g., as indicated by their performance on a standardized memory assessment or an explicit memory test). Hence, future researchers should conduct more research on densely amnesic patients, who have zero explicit memory ability, and/or drug-induced healthy young adults (e.g., Midazolam), who should also be incapable of using any explicit-memory retrieval strategy. The neuroimaging technique (e.g., Badgaiyan et al., 2003) also seems to be promising to verify whether new association priming occurs via a mediation of explicit memory processes. However, at this point, the bulk of the evidence seems not to support the view that new association priming occurs automatically. This stands in contrast to the data showing that item repetition priming does occur automatically (see Roediger & McDermott, 1993, for a review). Hence, more research in this domain should be done to seek out evidence that converges with behavioral findings for or against the automaticity of new association priming.

## ACKNOWLEDGMENT

A substantial portion of this chapter was written in partial fulfillment of the requirements for a Ph.D. degree for the first author at the University at Albany, State University of New York. We thank the chair, Jim Neely, and the other two committee members, Jeanette Altarriba and Tram Neill for their comments. Please address all correspondence to Chi-Shing Tse, Department of Educational Psychology, The Chinese University of Hong Kong, New Territories, Hong Kong, China. E-mail: cstse@cuhk.edu.hk.

## REFERENCES

Aggleton, J. P., & Saunders, R. C. (1997). The relationships between temporal lobe and diencephalic structures implicated in anterograde amnesia. In A. R. Mayes, & J. J. Downes (eds.), *Theories of organic amnesia* (pp. 49-71). UK: Psychology Press.

Allen, S. W., & Jacoby, L. L. (1990). Reinstating study context produces unconscious influences of memory. *Memory & Cognition, 18*, 270-278.

Anderson, J. R., & Ross, B. H. (1980). Evidence against an episodic-semantic distinction. *Journal of Experimental Psychology: Human Learning and Memory, 6*, 441-466.

Badgaiyan, R. D., Schacter, D. L., & Alpert, N. M. (1999). Auditory priming within and across modalities: Evidence from positron emission tomography. *Journal of Cognitive Neuroscience, 11*, 337-348.

Badgaiyan, R. D., Schacter, D. L., & Alpert, N. M. (2003). Priming of new associations: a PET study. *Neuroreport, 14*, 2475-2479.

Barry, E. (2007). Does conceptual implicit memory develop? The role of processing demands. *Journal of Genetic Psychology, 168,* 19-36

Bentin, S., & Moscovitch, M. (1988). The time course of repetition effects for words and unfamiliar faces. *Journal of Experimental Psychology: General, 117,* 148-160.

Bower, G. H. (1996). Reactivating a reactivation theory of implicit memory. *Consciousness and Cognition, 5*, 27-72.

Bowers, J. S., & Schacter, D. L. (1990). Implicit memory and test awareness. *Journal of Experimental Psychology: Learning, Memory and Cognition, 16*, 404-416.

Bowers, J. S., & Schacter, D. L. (1993). Priming of novel information in amnesic patients: Issues and data. In M. E. J. Masson, & P. Graf (eds.), *Implicit memory: New directions in cognition, development, and neuropsychology* (pp. 303-326). NJ: Erlbaum.

Brooks, B. M. (1999). Primacy and recency in primed free association and associative cued recall. *Psychonomic Bulletin & Review, 6*, 479-485.

Brown, J. S., & Carr, T. H. (1993). Limits on perceptual abstraction in reading: Asymmetric transfer between surface forms differing in typicality. *Journal of Experimental Psychology: Learning, Memory and Cognition, 19*, 1277-1296.

Calkins, M. W. (1896). Association: An essay analytic and experimental. *Psychological Monographs, 1,* 1-56.

Carlesimo, G. A., Perri, R., Costa, A., Serra, L., & Caltagirone, C. (2005). Priming for novel between-word associations in patients with organic amnesia. *Journal of the International Neuropsychological Society, 11,* 566-573.

Carr, T. H., Dagenbach, D., VanWieren, D., Carlson-Radvansky, L. A., Alejano, A. R., & Brown, J. S. (1994). Acquiring general knowledge from specific episodes of experience. In M. Moscovitch, & C. Umilta (eds.), *Attention and performance 15: Conscious and non-conscious information processing* (pp. 697-724). MA: MIT Press.

Carroll, M., & Kirsner, K. (1982). Context and repetition effects in lexical decision and recognition memory. *Journal of Verbal Learning and Verbal Behavior, 21,* 55-69.

Cave, C. B., & Squire, L. R. (1992). Intact and long-lasting repetition priming in amnesia. *Journal of Experimental Psychology: Learning, Memory and Cognition, 18,* 509-520.

Cermak, L. S., Bleich, R. P., & Blackford, S. P. (1988a). Deficits in the implicit retention of new associations by alcoholic Korsakoff patients. *Brain and Cognition, 7,* 312-323.

Cermak, L. S., Blackford, S. P., O'Connor, M., & Bleich, R. P. (1988b). The implicit memory ability of a patient with amnesia due to encephalitis. *Brain and Cognition, 7,* 145-156.

Challis, B. H., & Roediger, H. L. (1993). The effect of proportion overlap and repeated testing on primed word fragment completion. *Canadian Journal of Psychology, 47,* 113-123.

Chen, S., & Yang, Z. (1991). Effects of interference upon explicit and implicit memory. *Acta Psychologica Sinica, 4,* 8-14.

Christensen, H., & Birrell, P. (1991). Explicit and implicit memory in dementia and normal aging. *Psychological Research, 53,* 149-161.

Chun, M. M. (2005). Drug-induced amnesia impairs implicit relational memory. *Trends in Cognitive Sciences, 9,* 355-357.

Chun, M. M., & Phelps, E. A. (1999). Memory deficits for implicit contextual information in amnesic subjects with hippocampal damage. *Nature Neuroscience, 2,* 844-847.

Cohen, J. (1988). *Statistical power analysis for the behavioral sciences.* (2nd ed.). NJ: Erlbaum.

Cohen, N. J., & Eichenbaum, H. (1993). *Memory, amnesia, and the hippocampal system.* MA: MIT Press.

Cohen, N. J., Poldrack, R. A., & Eichenbaum, H. (1997). Memory for items and memory for relations in the procedural/declarative memory framework. In A. R. Mayes, & J. J. Downes (eds.), *Theories of organic amnesia (pp.* 131-178). UK: Psychology Press.

Crowder, R. (1976). *Principles of learning and memory.* NJ: Erlbaum.

Curran, T., & Hintzman, D. L. (1995). Violations of the independence assumption in process dissociation. *Journal of Experimental Psychology: Learning, Memory and Cognition, 21,* 531-547.

Curran, T., & Hintzman, D. L. (1997). Consequences and causes of correlations in process dissociation. *Journal of Experimental Psychology: Learning, Memory and Cognition, 23,* 496-504.

Curran, T., & Schacter, D. L. (1997). Implicit memory: What must theories of amnesia explain? In A. R. Mayes, & J. J. Downes (eds.), *Theories of organic amnesia (pp.* 37-47). UK: Psychology Press.

Dagenbach, D., Horst, S., & Carr, T. H. (1990). Adding new information to semantic memory: How much learning is enough to produce automatic priming? *Journal of Experimental Psychology: Learning, Memory and Cognition, 16,* 581-591.

De Houwer, J., Thomas, S., & Baeyens, F. (2001). Association learning of likes and dislikes: A review of 25 years of research on human evaluative conditioning. *Psychological Bulletin*, *127*, 853-869.

Deese, J., (1965). *The structure of associations in language and thought.* Baltimore: John Hopkins Press.

Den Heyer, K. (1986). Manipulating attention-induced priming in a lexical decision task by means of repeated prime-target presentations. *Journal of Memory and Language*, *25*, 19-42.

Dew, I. T. Z, Bayen, U. J., & Giovanello, K. S.(2007). Implicit relational memory in young and older adults. *Journal of Psychology, 215,* 25-34.

Dew, I.T.Z., & Giovanello, K. (2010). Differential age effects for implicit and explicit conceptual associative memory. *Psychology and Aging, 25,* 911-921.

DeSchepper, B., & Treisman, A. (1996). Visual memory for novel shapes: Implicit coding without attention. *Journal of Experimental Psychology: Learning, Memory and Cognition, 22*, 27-47.

Diamond, R. J., & Rozin, P. (1984). Activation of existing memories in anterograde amnesia. *Journal of Abnormal Psychology, 93*, 98-105.

Dorfman, J. (1994). Sublexical components in implicit memory for novel words. *Journal of Experimental Psychology: Learning, Memory and Cognition, 20*, 1108-1125.

Dunn, J. C., & Kirsner, K. (1988). Discovering functionally independent mental processes: The principle of reversed association. *Psychological Review*, *95*, 91-101.

Durgunoglu, A. Y., & Neely, J. H. (1987). On obtaining episodic priming in a lexical decision task following paired-associate learning. *Journal of Experimental Psychology: Learning, Memory and Cognition, 13*, 206-222.

Ellmore, T.M., Stouffer, K., & Nadel, L. (2008). Divergence of explicit and implicit processing speed during associative memory retrieval. *Brain Research, 1229,* 155-166

Eichenbaum, H., & Cohen, N. J. (2001). *From conditioning to conscious recollection: Memory systems of the brain.* NY: Oxford University Press.

Ergis, A. M., Van der Linden, M., & Deweer, B. (1998). Priming for new associations in normal aging and in mild dementia of the Alzheimer type. *Cortex, 34*, 357-373.

Fay, S., Isingrini, M., & Pouthas, V. (2005). Does priming with awareness reflect explicit contamination? An approach with a response-time measure in word-stem completion. *Consciousness and Cognition, 14*, 459-473.

Fleischman, D. A., & Gabrieli, J. D. E. (1998). Repetition priming in normal aging and Alzheimer's disease: A review of findings and theories. *Psychology and Aging, 13*, 88-119.

Fleischman, D.A., Vaidya, C.J., Lange, K. L., & Gabrieli, J. D. E. (1997). A dissociation between perceptual explicit and implicit memory processes. *Brain and Cognition, 35*, 42-57.

Gabrieli, J.D.E., Keane, M.M., Zarella, M.M., & Poldrack, R. A. (1997). Preservation of implicit memory for new associations in global amnesia. *Psychological Science, 8*, 326-329.

Gooding, P. A., Mayes, A. R., & van Eijk, R. (2000). A meta-analysis of indirect memory tests for novel material in organic amnesics. *Neuropsychologia, 38,* 666-676.

Gooding, P. A., Mayes, A. R., van Eijk, R., Meudell, P. R., & MacDonald, F. L. (1999). Do novel associative word-stem completion and cued recall share the same memory retrieval processes? *Memory, 7,* 323-343.

Goshen-Gottstein, Y., & Moscovitch, M. (1995a). Repetition priming for newly formed and pre-existing associations: Perceptual and conceptual influences. *Journal of Experimental Psychology: Learning, Memory and Cognition, 21,* 1229-1248.

Goshen-Gottstein, Y., & Moscovitch, M. (1995b). Repetition priming effects for newly formed associations are perceptually based: Evidence from shallow encoding and format specificity. *Journal of Experimental Psychology: Learning, Memory and Cognition, 21,* 1249-1262.

Goshen-Gottstein, Y., Moscovitch, M., & Melo, B. (2000). Intact implicit memory for newly formed verbal associations in amnesic patients following single study trials. *Neuropsychology, 14,* 570-578.

Graf, P., & Komatsu, S. (1994). Process dissociation procedure: Handle with caution! *European Journal of Cognitive Psychology, 6,* 113-129.

Graf, P., & Schacter, D. L. (1985). Implicit and explicit memory for new associations in normal and amnesic subjects. *Journal of Experimental Psychology: Learning, Memory and Cognition, 11,* 501-518.

Graf, P., & Schacter, D. L. (1987). Selective effects of interference on implicit and explicit memory for new associations. *Journal of Experimental Psychology: Learning, Memory and Cognition, 13,* 45-53.

Graf, P., & Schacter, D. L. (1989). Unitization and grouping mediate dissociations in memory for new associations. *Journal of Experimental Psychology: Learning, Memory and Cognition, 15,* 930-940.

Graf, P., Squire, L. R., & Mandler, G. (1984). The information that amnesic patients do not forget. *Journal of Experimental Psychology: Learning, Memory and Cognition, 10,* 164-178.

Graf, P., Shimamura, A. P., & Squire, L. R. (1985). Priming across modalities and priming across category levels: Extending the domain of preserved function in amnesia. *Journal of Experimental Psychology: Learning, Memory and Cognition, 11,* 386-396.

Gronlund, S. D., & Ratcliff, R. (1989). Time course of item and associative information: Implications for global memory models. *Journal of Experimental Psychology: Learning, Memory and Cognition, 15,* 846-858.

Grossi, G. (2006). Relatedness proportion effects on masked associative priming: An ERP study. *Psychophysiology, 43,* 21-30.

Hayman, C. A., MacDonald, C. A., & Tulving, E. (1993). The role of repetition and associative interference in new semantic learning in amnesia: A case experiment. *Journal of Cognitive Neuroscience, 5,* 375-389.

Henson, R. N. (2003). Neuroimaging studies of priming. *Progress in Neurobiology, 70,* 53-81.

Henson, R. N. (2005). What can functional neuroimaging tell the experimental psychologist? *Quarterly Journal of Experimental Psychology, 58,* 193-233.

Hintzman, D. L. (1986). "Schema abstraction" in a multiple-trace memory model. *Psychological Review, 93,* 411-428.

Hintzman, D. L. (1988). Judgments of frequency and recognition memory in a multiple-trace memory model. *Psychological Review*, *95*, 528-551.

Hintzman, D. L., & Curran, T. (1995). When encoding fails: Instructions, feedback, and registration without learning. *Memory & Cognition*, *23*, 213-226.

Hintzman, D. L., & Curran, T. (1997). Comparing retrieval dynamics in recognition memory and lexical decision. *Journal of Experimental Psychology: General*, *126*, 228-247.

Hirshman, E. (2004). Ordinal process dissociation and the measurement of automatic and controlled processes. *Psychological Review*, *111*, 553-560.

Hirshman, E., Passannante, A., & Arndt, J. (2001). Midazolam amnesia and conceptual processing in implicit memory. *Journal of Experimental Psychology: General*, *130*, 453-465.

Horton, K. D., Wilson, D. E., Vonk, J., Kirby, S. L., & Nielsen, T. (2005). Measuring automatic retrieval: A comparison of implicit memory, process dissociation, and speeded response procedures. *Acta Psychologica*, *119*, 235-263.

Howard, D. V., Fry, A. F., & Brune, C. M. (1991). Aging and memory for new associations: Direct versus indirect measures. *Journal of Experimental Psychology: Learning, Memory and Cognition, 17,* 779-792.

Hughes, A. D., & Whittlesea, B. W. A. (2003). Long-term semantic transfer: An overlapping-operations account. *Memory & Cognition, 31*, 401-411.

Jacoby, L. L. (1983). Perceptual enhancement: Persistent effects of an experience. *Journal of Experimental Psychology: Learning, Memory and Cognition*, *9*, 21-38.

Jacoby, L. L. (1991). A process dissociation framework: Separating automatic from intentional uses of memory. *Journal of Memory and Language*, *30*, 513-541.

Jacoby, L. L. (1998). Invariance in automatic influences of memory: Toward a user's guide for the process-dissociation procedure. *Journal of Experimental Psychology: Learning, Memory and Cognition, 24*, 3-26.

Jacoby, L. L., & Dallas, M. (1981). On the relationship between autobiographical memory and perceptual learning. *Journal of Experimental Psychology: General, 110*, 306-340.

Jacoby, L. L., Toth, J. P., & Yonelinas, A. P. (1993). Separating conscious and unconscious influences of memory: Measuring recollection. *Journal of Experimental Psychology: General, 122*, 139-154.

James, W. (1890/1950). *The principles of psychology*. NY: Dover.

Jenkins, V., Russo, R., & Parkin, A. J. (1998). Levels of processing and single word priming in amnesic and control subjects. *Cortex*, *34*, 577-588.

Jennings, J. M., & Jacoby, L. L. (1993). Automatic versus intentional uses of memory: Aging, attention, and control. *Psychology and Aging*, *8*, 283-293.

Jiang, N., & Forster, K. I. (2001). Cross-language priming asymmetries in lexical decision and episodic recognition. *Journal of Memory and Language*, *44*, 32-51.

Johnson, M. K. (1992). MEM: Mechanisms of recollection. *Journal of Cognitive Neuroscience, 4*, 268-280.

Johnson, M. K., & Chalfonte, B. L. (1994). Binding complex memories: The role of reactivation and the hippocampus. In D.L. Schacter, & E. Tulving (eds.), *Memory systems 1994* (pp. 311-350). MA: MIT Press.

Jonides, J., & Mack, R. (1984). On the cost and benefit of cost and benefit. *Psychological Bulletin*, *96*, 29-44.

Keane, M. M., Gabrieli, J. D. E., Monti, L. A., Fleischman, D. A., Cantor, J. M., & Noland, J. S. (1997). Intact and impaired conceptual memory processes in amnesia. *Neuropsychology, 11*, 59-69.

Kinoshita, S. (1999). Priming for novel associations: Evidence for an attentional component. *Memory, 7*, 385-404.

Kinoshita, S. (2001). The role of involuntary aware memory in the implicit stem and fragment completion tasks: A selective review. *Psychonomic Bulletin & Review, 8*, 58-69.

Laver, G. D. (2009). Adult aging effects on semantic and episodic priming in word recognition. *Psychology and Aging, 24,* 29-39.

Light, L. L., Kennison, R., Prull, M. W., La Voie, D., & Zuelling, A. (1996). One-trial associative priming of non-words in young and older adults. *Psychology and Aging, 11*, 417-430.

Logan, G. D. (1988). Toward an instance theory of automatization. *Psychological Review, 95*, 492-527.

Logan, G. D. (1990). Repetition priming and automaticity: Common underlying mechanisms? *Cognitive Psychology, 22*, 1-35.

Mace, J. H. (2003). Involuntary aware memory enhances priming on a conceptual implicit memory test. *American Journal of Psychology, 116*, 281-290.

Mace, J. H. (2005). Experimentally manipulating the effects of involuntary conscious memory on a priming task. *American Journal of Psychology, 118*, 159-182.

Marsolek, C. J., Schacter, D. L., & Nicholas, C. D. (1996). Form-specific visual priming for new associations in the right cerebral hemisphere. *Memory & Cognition, 24*, 539-556.

Masson, M. E. J., & Bodner, G. E. (2003). A retrospective view of masked priming: Toward a unified account of masked and long-term repetition priming. In S. J. Lupker, & S. Kinoshita (eds.), *Masked priming: The state of the art (pp. 57-94).* NY: Psychology Press.

Mayes, A. R., & Gooding, P. (1989). Enhancement of word completion priming in amnesics by cueing with previously novel associates. *Neuropsychologia, 27*, 1057-1072.

McDermott, K. B., & Roediger, H. L. (1996). Exact and conceptual repetitions dissociate conceptual memory tests: Problems for transfer appropriate processing theory. *Canadian Journal of Experimental Psychology, 50*, 57-71.

McKone, E., & Murphy, B. (2000). Implicit false memory: Effects of modality and multiple study presentations on long-lived semantic priming. *Journal of Memory and Language, 43*, 89-109.

McKone, E., & Slee, J. A. (1997). Explicit contamination in "implicit" memory for new associations. *Memory & Cognition, 25,* 352-366.

McKoon, G., & Ratcliff, R. (1979). Priming in episodic and semantic memory. *Journal of Verbal Learning and Verbal Behavior, 18*, 463-480.

McKoon, G., & Ratcliff, R. (1986). Automatic activation of episodic information in a semantic memory task. *Journal of Experimental Psychology: Learning, Memory and Cognition, 12,* 108-115.

McKoon, G., Ratcliff, R., & Dell, G. S. (1986). A critical evaluation of the episodic-semantic distinction. *Journal of Experimental Psychology: Learning, Memory and Cognition, 12*, 295-306.

Melinger, A., & Dobel, C. (2005). Lexically-driven syntactic priming. *Cognition, 98*, 11-20.

Merikle, P. M., & Reingold, E. M. (1991). Comparing direct (explicit) and indirect (implicit) measures to study unconscious memory. *Journal of Experimental Psychology: Learning, Memory and Cognition, 17*, 224-233.

Meyer, D.E., & Schvaneveldt, R.W. (1971). Facilitation in recognizing pairs of words: Evidence of a dependence between retrieval operations. *Journal of Experimental Psychology, 90*, 227-234.

Micco, A., & Masson, M. E. J. (1991). Implicit memory for new associations: An interactive process approach. *Journal of Experimental Psychology: Learning, Memory and Cognition, 17*, 1105-1123.

Monti, L.A., Gabricli, J.D.E., Wilson, R.S., Beckett, L.A., Grinnell, E., Lange, K.L., & Reminger, S.L. (1997). Sources of priming in text re-reading: Intact implicit memory for new associations in older adults and in patients with Alzheimer's disease. *Psychology and Aging, 12*, 536-547.

Moscovitch, M. (1994). Cognitive resources and dual-task interference effects at retrieval in normal people: The role of the frontal lobes and medial temporal cortex. *Neuropsychology, 8*, 524-534.

Moscovitch, M., Goshen-Gottstein, Y., & Vriezen, E. (1994). Memory without conscious recollection: A tutorial review from a neuropsychological perspective. In C. Umilta, & M. Moscovitch (eds.), *Attention and performance 15: Conscious and non-conscious information processing* (pp. 619-660). MA: MIT Press.

Moscovitch, M., Winocur, G., & McLachlan, D. (1986). Memory as assessed by recognition and reading time in normal and memory impaired people with Alzheimer's disease and other neurological disorders. *Journal of Experimental Psychology: General, 115*, 331-347.

Mulligan, N. W., Guyer, P. S., & Beland, A. (1999). The effects of level-of-processing and organization on conceptual implicit memory in the category exemplar production test. *Memory & Cognition, 27*, 633-647.

Murdock, B. B. (1982). A theory for the storage and retrieval of item and associative information. *Psychological Review, 89*, 609-626.

Musen, G., & Squire, L. R. (1993). Implicit learning of color-word associations using a Stroop paradigm. *Journal of Experimental Psychology: Learning, Memory and Cognition, 19*, 789-798.

Mutter, S.A., Howard, D.V., Howard, J.H., & Wiggs, C.L. (1990). Performance on direct and indirect tests of memory after mild closed head injury. *Cognitive Neuropsychology, 7*, 329-346.

Nairne, J. S. (2005). The functionalist agenda in memory research. In A. F. Healy (ed.), *Experimental cognitive psychology and its applications* (pp. 115-126). Washington DC: American Psychological Association.

Neely, J. H. (1976). Semantic priming and retrieval from lexical memory: Evidence for facilitatory and inhibitory processes. *Memory & Cognition, 4*, 648-654.

Neely, J. H. (1977). Semantic priming and retrieval from lexical memory: Roles of inhibitionless spreading activation and limited-capacity attention. *Journal of Experimental Psychology: General, 106,* 226-254.

Neely, J. H. (1989). Experimental dissociations and the episodic/semantic memory distinction. In H. L. Roediger, & F. I. M. Craik (eds.), *Varieties of memory and consciousness: Essays in honor of Endel Tulving* (pp. 229-270). NJ, Erlbaum.

Neely, J. H., & Durgunoglu, A. Y. (1985). Dissociative episodic and semantic priming effects in episodic recognition and lexical decision tasks. *Journal of Memory and Language, 24*, 466-489.

Neely, J. H., & Kahan, T. A. (2001). Is semantic activation automatic? A critical re-evaluation. In H. L. Roediger, J. S. Nairne, I. Neath, & A. M. Suprenant (eds.), *The nature of remembering: Essays in honor of Robert G. Crowder* (pp. 63-93). Washington DC: American Psychological Association Press.

Neely, J. H., Keefe, D. E., & Ross, K. L. (1989). Semantic priming in the lexical decision task: Roles of prospective prime-generated expectancies and retrospective semantic matching. *Journal of Experimental Psychology: Learning, Memory and Cognition, 15*, 1003-1019.

Neely, J.H., & Payne, D.G. (1983). A direct comparison of recognition failure rates for recallable names in episodic and semantic memory tests. *Memory & Cognition, 11*, 161-171.

Neill, W. T., Beck, J. L., Bottalico, K. S., & Molloy, R. D. (1990). Effects of intentional versus incidental learning on explicit and implicit tests of memory. *Journal of Experimental Psychology: Learning, Memory and Cognition, 16*, 457-463.

Newell, A., & Rosenbloom, P. S. (1981). Mechanisms of skill acquisition and the power law of practice. In J. R. Anderson (ed.), *Cognitive skills and their acquisitions*. NJ: Erlbaum.

Nicolas, S., & Carbonnel, S. (1996). Implicit memory for new associations: The pictorial influence. *Psychological Research, 59*, 145-156.

Nilsson, L. G., Backman, L., & Karlsson, T. (1989). Priming and cued recall in the elderly, alcohol intoxicated and sleep deprived subjects: A case of functionally similar memory deficits. *Psychological Medicine, 19*, 423-433.

Norman, D., & Shallice, T. (1986). Attention to action: Willed and automatic control of behavior. In R. Davidson, G. Schwartz, & D. Shapiro (Eds.), *Consciousness and Self-Regulation: Advances in Research and Theory*. (pp. 1-18). NY: Plenum.

O'Hanlon, L., Wilcox, K. A., & Kemper, S. (2001). Age differences in implicit and explicit associative memory: Exploring elaborative processing effects. *Experimental Aging Research, 27*, 341-359.

Paller, K. A., & Mayes, A. R. (1994). New association priming of word identification in normal and amnesic subjects. *Cortex, 30*, 53-73.

Park, H., Quinlan, J. J., Thornton, E. R., & Reder, L. M. (2004). The effect of midazolam on visual search: Implications for understanding amnesia. *Proceedings of the National Academy of Sciences, 101*, 17879-17883.

Pecher, D., & Raaijmakers, J. G. W. (1999). Automatic priming effects for new associations in lexical decision and perceptual identification. *Quarterly Journal of Experimental Psychology, 52*, 593-614.

Pecher, D., & Raaijmakers, J. G. W. (2004). Priming for new associations in animacy decision: Evidence for context dependency. *Quarterly Journal of Experimental Psychology, 57*, 1211-1231.

Pilotti, M., Bergman, E. T., Gallo, D. A., Sommers, M., & Roediger, H. L. (2000). Direct comparison of auditory implicit memory tests. *Psychonomic Bulletin & Review, 7*, 347-353.

Polster, M. R., McCarthy, R. A., O'Sullivan, G., Gray, P. A., & Park, G. R. (1993). Midazolam-induced amnesia: implications for the implicit/explicit memory distinction. *Brain and Cognition, 22*, 244-265.

Posner, M. I., & Snyder, C. R. (1975). Facilitation and inhibition in the processing of signals. In P. M. Rabbitt, & S. Dornic (eds.), *Attention and performance: Vol. 5* (pp. 669-682). CA: Academic Press.

Rajaram, S., & Coslett, H. B. (2000a). Acquisition and transfer of new verbal information in amnesia: Retrieval and neuroanatomical constraints. *Neuropsychology, 14,* 427-455.

Rajaram, S., & Coslett, H. B. (2000b). New conceptual associative learning in amnesia: A casc study. *Journal of Memory and Language, 43*, 291-315.

Ratcliff, R., Van Zandt, T., & McKoon, G. (1995). Process dissociation, single-process theories, and recognition memory. *Journal of Experimental Psychology: General, 124*, 352-374.

Reingold, E. M. (2003). Interpreting dissociations: The issue of task comparability. *Cortex, 39*, 174-176.

Reingold, E. M., & Goshen-Gottstein, Y. (1996a). Automatic retrieval of new associations under shallow encoding conditions. *Consciousness and Cognition, 5*, 117-130.

Reingold, E. M., & Goshen-Gottstein, Y. (1996b). Separating consciously controlled and automatic influences in memory for new associations. *Journal of Experimental Psychology: Learning, Memory and Cognition, 22,* 397-406.

Reingold, E. M., & Toth, J. P. (1996). Process dissociations versus task dissociations: A controversy in progress. In G. D. M. Underwood (ed.), *Implicit cognition* (pp. 159-202). NY: Oxford University Press.

Richardson-Klavehn, A., Clarke, A. J. B., & Gardiner, J. M. (1999). Conjoint dissociations reveal involuntary "perceptual" priming from generating at study. *Consciousness and Cognition, 8*, 271-284.

Richardson-Klavehn, A., & Gardiner, J. M. (1998). Depth-of-processing effects on priming in stem completion: Tests of the voluntary-contamination, conceptual-processing, and lexical-processing hypotheses. *Journal of Experimental Psychology: Learning, Memory and Cognition, 24*, 593-609.

Richardson-Klavehn, A., Gardiner, J. M., & Java, R. I. (1994). Involuntary conscious memory and the method of opposition. *Memory, 2*, 1-29.

Richardson-Klavehn, A., Gardiner, J. M., & Java, R. I. (1996). Memory: Task dissociations, process dissociations and dissociations of consciousness. In G. D. M. Underwood (ed.), *implicit cognition* (pp. 85-158). NY: Oxford University Press.

Richardson-Klavehn, A., Lee, M. G., Joubran, R., & Bjork, R. A. (1994). Intention and awareness in perceptual identification priming. *Memory & Cognition, 22*, 293-312.

Roediger, H. L. (1984). Does current evidence from dissociation experiments favor the episodic/semantic distinction? *Behavioral and Brain Sciences*, *7*, 252-254.

Roediger, H. L. (1990). Implicit memory: Retention without remembering. *American Psychologist, 45*, 1043-1056.

Roediger, H. L. (2003). Reconsidering implicit memory. In J. S. Bowers, & C. Marsolek (eds.), *Re-thinking implicit memory* (pp. 3-18). UK: Oxford University Press.

Roediger, H. L., Marsh, E. J., & Lee, S. C. (2002). Varieties of memory. In D.L. Medin, & H. Pashler (eds.), *Steven's handbook of experimental psychology volume 2: Memory and cognitive processes.* (3rd ed.) (pp. 1-41). NY: John Wiley & Sons.

Roediger, H.L., & McDermott, K.B. (1993). Implicit memory in normal human subjects. In F. Boller, & J. Grafman (eds.), *Handbook of Neuropsychology; Vol. 8* (pp. 63-131). Amsterdam: Elsevier.

Roediger, H. L., Weldon, M. S., & Challis, B. H. (1989). Explaining dissociations between implicit and explicit measures of retention: A processing account. In H. L. Roediger, & F. I. M. Craik (eds.), *Varieties of memory and consciousness: Essays in honor of Endel Tulving* (pp. 3-39). NJ: Erlbaum.

Rugg, M. D., Fletcher, P. C., Chua, P. M., & Dolan, R. J. (1999). The role of the pre-frontal cortex in recognition memory and memory for source: An fMRI study. *Neuroimage, 10*, 520-529.

Rybash, J. M. (1994). Aging, associative priming, and test awareness. *Aging and Cognition, 1*, 158-173.

Rybash, J. M., Santoro, K. E., & Hoyer, W. J. (1998). Adult age differences in conscious and unconscious influences on memory for novel associations. *Aging, Neuropsychology and Cognition, 5*, 14-26.

Schacter, D. L. (1987). Implicit memory: History and current status. *Journal of Experimental Psychology: Learning, Memory and Cognition, 13*, 501-518.

Schacter, D. L. (1990). Perceptual representation systems and implicit memory: Toward a resolution of the multiple memory systems debate. *Annals of the New York Academy of Sciences, 608,* 543-571.

Schacter, D.L. (1994). Priming and multiple memory systems: Perceptual mechanisms of implicit memory. In D. L. Schacter, & E. Tulving (eds.), *Memory systems 1994* (pp. 233-268). MA: MIT Press.

Schacter, D.L., Alpert, N.M., Savage, C.R., Rauch, S.L., & Albert, M.S. (1996). Conscious recollection and the human hippocampal formation: Evidence from positron emission tomography. *Proceedings of the National Academy of Sciences, 93*, 321-325.

Schacter, D. L., & Badgaiyan, R. D. (2001). Neuroimaging of priming: New perspectives on implicit and explicit memory. *Current Directions in Psychological Science, 10*, 1-4.

Schacter, D. L., Bowers, J. S., & Booker, J. (1989). Intention, awareness, and implicit memory: The retrieval intentionality criterion. In J. C. Dunn, & S. Lewandowsky (eds.), *Implicit memory: Theoretical issues* (pp. 47-65). NJ: Erlbaum.

Schacter, D. L., & Buckner R. L. (1998). Priming and the brain. *Neuron, 20*, 185-195.

Schacter, D. L., & Graf, P. (1986a). Effects of elaborative processing on implicit and explicit memory for new associations. *Journal of Experimental Psychology: Learning, Memory and Cognition, 12*, 432-444.

Schacter, D. L., & Graf, P. (1986b). Preserved learning in amnesic patients: Perspectives from research on direct priming. *Journal of Clinical and Experimental Neuropsychology, 8,* 727-743.

Schacter, D. L., & Graf, P. (1989). Modality specificity of implicit memory for new associations. *Journal of Experimental Psychology: Learning, Memory and Cognition, 15,* 3-12.

Schacter, D. L., & McGlynn, S. M. (1989). Implicit memory: Effects of elaboration depend on unitization. *American Journal of Psychology, 102,* 151-181.

Schacter, D. L., & Tulving, E. (1994). What are the memory systems of 1994? In D. L. Schacter, & E. Tulving (eds.), *Memory systems 1994* (pp. 1-38). MA: MIT Press.

Schrijnemakers, J. M. C., & Raaijmakers, J. G. W. (1997). Adding new word associations to semantic memory: Evidence for two interactive learning components. *Acta Psychologica, 96,* 103-132.

Sherry, D. F., & Schacter, D. L. (1987). The evolution of multiple memory systems. *Psychological Review, 94*, 439-454.

Shimamura, A. P., & Squire, L. R. (1984). Paired-associate learning and priming effects in amnesia: A neuropsychological study. *Journal of Experimental Psychology: General, 113*, 556-570.

Shimamura, A. P., & Squire, L. R. (1989). Impaired priming of new associations in amnesia. *Journal of Experimental Psychology: Learning, Memory and Cognition, 15*, 721-728.

Silberman, Y.., Miikkulainen, R., & Bentin, S. (2005). Associating unseen events: semantically mediated formation of episodic associations. *Psychological Science, 16,* 161-166.

Smith, M. C., MacLeod, C. M., Bain, J. D., & Hoppe, R. B. (1989). Lexical decision as an indirect test of memory: Repetition priming and list-wide priming as a function of type of encoding. *Journal of Experimental Psychology: Learning, Memory and Cognition, 15,* 1109-1118.

Spieler, D. H., & Balota, D. A. (1996). Characteristics of associative learning in younger and older adults: Evidence from an episodic priming paradigm. *Psychology and Aging, 11*, 607-620.

Squire, L. R. (1992). Memory and the hippocampus: A synthesis from findings with rats, monkeys, and humans. *Psychological Review, 99*, 195-231.

Squire, L. R., & Zola, S. M. (1998). Episodic memory, semantic memory, and amnesia. *Hippocampus, 8*, 205-211.

Srinivas, K., Culp, D., & Rajaram, S. (2000). On associations between computers and restaurants: Rapid learning of new associations on a conceptual implicit memory test. *Memory & Cognition, 28*, 900-906.

Stadler, M.A., & Frensch, P.A. (1998). *Handbook of implicit learning.* Thousand Oaks, CA: Sage.

Tenpenny, P. L. (1995). Abstractionist versus episodic theories of repetition priming and word identification. *Psychonomic Bulletin & Review, 2*, 339-363.

Thompson-Schill, S. L., D'Esposito, M., Aguirre, G. K., & Farah, M. J. (1997). Role of left prefrontal cortex in retrieval of semantic knowledge: A re-evaluation. *Proceedings of the National Academy of Science, 94*, 14792-14797.

Toth, J. P., Reingold, E. M., & Jacoby, L. L. (1994). Toward a re-definition of implicit memory: Process dissociations following elaborative processing and self-generation. *Journal of Experimental Psychology: Learning, Memory and Cognition, 20*, 290-303.

Tse, C.-S., & Neely, J. H. (2005). Assessing activation without source monitoring in the DRM paradigm. *Journal of Memory and Language, 53,* 532-550.

Tulving, E. (1972). Episodic and semantic memory. In E. Tulving and W. Donaldson (eds.), *Organization of memory* (pp. 381-403). NY: Academic Press.

Tulving, E. (1983). *Elements of episodic memory.* NY: Oxford University Press.

Tulving, E. (1984). Relations among components and processes of memory. *Behavioral and Brain Sciences, 7*, 257-268.

Tulving, E. (1991). Concepts of human memory. In L. Squire, G. Lynch, N. M. Weinberger, & J. L. McGaugh (eds.), *Memory: Organization and locus of change* (pp. 3-32). NY: Oxford University Press.

Tulving, E. (2002). Episodic memory: From mind to brain. *Annual Review of Psychology, 53,* 1-25.

Tulving, E., Hayman, C. A., & MacDonald, C. A. (1991). Long-lasting perceptual priming and semantic learning in amnesia: A case experiment. *Journal of Experimental Psychology: Learning, Memory and Cognition, 17,* 595-617.

Tulving, E., & Schacter, D.L. (1990). Priming and human memory systems. *Science, 247,* 301-306.

Turriziani, P., Fadda, L., Caltagirone, C., & Carlesimo, G. A. (2004). Recognition memory for single items and for associations in amnesic patients. *Neuropsychologia, 42,* 426-433.

Uttl, B., Graf, P., & Cosentino, S. (2003). Implicit memory for new associations: Types of conceptual representations. In C. J. Marsolek, & J. S. Bowers (eds.), *Re-thinking implicit memory* (pp. 302-323). UK: Oxford University Press.

Vaidya, C. J., Gabrieli, J. D. E., Keane, M. M., & Monti, L. A. (1995). Perceptual and conceptual memory processes in global amnesia. *Neuropsychology, 9,* 580-591.

Vaidya, C.J., Gabrieli, J.D.E., Keane, M. M., Monti, L. A., Gutierrez-Rivas, H., & Zarella, M. M. (1997). Evidence for multiple mechanisms of conceptual priming on implicit memory tests. *Journal of Experimental Psychology: Learning, Memory and Cognition, 23,* 1324-1343.

Vakil, E., & Oded, Y. (2003). Comparison between three memory tests: Cued recall, priming and saving closed-head injured patients and controls. *Journal of Clinical and Experimental Neuropsychology, 25,* 274-282.

Van der Linden, M., Bruyer, R., & Dave, B. (1992). Effect of aging on implicit and explicit memory for new associations. *Current Psychology of Cognition, 12,* 223-237.

Verfaellie, M., Croce, P., & Milberg, W. P. (1995). The role of episodic memory in semantic learning: An examination of vocabulary acquisition in a patient with amnesia due to encephalitis. *Neurocase, 1,* 291-304.

Verfaellie, M., Martin, E., Page, K., Parks, E., & Keane, M. M. (2006). Implicit memory for novel conceptual associations in amnesia. *Cognitive, Affective, & Behavioral Neuroscience, 6,* 91-101.

Vriezen, E.R., Moscovitch, M., & Bellos, S.A. (1995). Priming effects in semantic classification tasks. *Journal of Experimental Psychology: Learning, Memory and Cognition, 21,* 933-946.

Warrington, E. K., & Weiskrantz, L. (1968). A study of learning and retention in amnesic patients. *Neuropsychologia, 6,* 283-291.

Warrington, E. K., & Weiskrantz, L. (1970). Amnesic syndrome: Consolidation or retrieval? *Nature, 228,* 628-630.

Warrington, E. K., & Weiskrantz, L. (1974). The effect of prior learning on subsequent retention in amnesic patients. *Neuropsychologia, 12,* 419-428.

Weldon, M. S., Roediger, H. L., Beital, D. A., & Johnston, T. R. (1995). Perceptual and conceptual processes in implicit and explicit tests with picture fragment and word fragment cues. *Journal of Memory and Language, 34,* 268-285.

White, K. K., Abrams, L., & Byrd, A. L. (2009). Generation, intentionality of processing at encoding and retrieval, and age-related associative deficits. *Memory, 17,* 481-492.

Yang, J., Weng, X., Guan, L., & Kuang P. (1999). Effects of level of processing and word pair types on forming memory for new associations. *Acta Psychologica Sinica, 31*, 257-265.

Yang, J., Weng, X., Guan, L., Kuang P., Zhang, M., Sun, W., & Yu, S. (2002). Frontal lobe participated in priming for new associations: An evidence from patients with frontal lobe lesions. *Acta Psychologica Sinica, 34*, 36-42.

Yang, J., Weng, X., Guan, L., Kuang P., Zhang, M., Sun, W., Yu, S., & Patterson, K. (2003). Involvement of the medial temporal lobe in priming for new associations. *Neuropsychologia, 41*, 818-829.

Yang, J., Meckingler, A., Xu, M., & Zhao, Y. (2008). Decreased parahippocampal activity in associative priming: Evidence from an event-related fMRI study. *Learning & Memory, 18*, 703-710.

Yonelinas, A. P., & Jacoby, L. L. (1994). Dissociations of processes in recognition memory: Effects of interference and of response speed. *Canadian Journal of Experimental Psychology, 48*, 516-534.

Zeelenberg, R., Pecher, D., & Raaijmakers, J. G. W. (2003). Associative repetition priming: A selective review and theoretical implications. In C. J. Marsolek, & J. S. Bowers (eds.), *Re-thinking implicit memory* (pp. 261-283). UK: Oxford University Press.

In: Psychology of Memory
Editors: Dannie M. Hendrix and Orval Holcomb

ISBN: 978-1-61942-633-7
© 2012 Nova Science Publishers, Inc.

*Chapter 2*

# APPLICATIONS OF MEMORY TO THE REAL WORLD: WHAT EMOTIONS AND STRESS HAVE TAUGHT US ABOUT THE NATURE OF MEMORY IN EVERYDAY EXPERIENCES

## *Lening A. Olivera-Figueroa[1,2], Marie France Marin[1,3] and Sonia J. Lupien[1,2]*

[1]Centre for Studies on Human Stress, Fernand Seguin Research Centre,
Louis-H. Lafontaine Hospital, Montréal, Québec, Canada
[2]Department of Psychiatry, Faculty of Medicine,
Université de Montréal, Montréal, Quebec, Canada
[3]Department of Physiology, Faculty of Medicine,
Université de Montréal, Montréal, Quebec, Canada

## ABSTRACT

Throughout the last century, numerous advances have been achieved in the field of memory research that have significantly increased our understanding of the brain structures and mechanisms underlying memory processes. Particularly, over the past few decades a great deal of attention has been devoted to the different ways by which memories can be modulated. For example, emotion is known to be a potent memory modulator, as emotionally arousing experiences have been shown to be better remembered than neutral ones. Moreover, stress and stress hormones have also been shown to modulate memory in complex ways. Given the relevance of emotions and stress in the development and maintenance of certain clinical conditions that involve at their core memory problems, such as post-traumatic stress disorder (PTSD) and depression, there is an impending need to further our current understanding of the roles these two aspects play on the memory problems behind these conditions. As a means to address these scientific inquiries, the present chapter aims to synthesize the current general literature about memory in relation to emotion and stress, in order to provide a perspective on how this body of knowledge could be translated to the clinical treatment for memory-affected conditions. The first section of this book chapter will cover the main memory categories, the stages underlying memory formation, the brain areas involved within each of those processes, as well as the modulating role of emotion on memory. In the second section, the chapter will detail the effects of stress and stress hormones on the modulation of memories. Finally, the last section will address potential new directions that could guide future memory studies, such as accounting for the role of sex differences, as well as through the development of novel, ecologically valid memory paradigms. As such, we suggest that by considering the previously described variables in innovative memory paradigms that closely match reality, future memory research will translate more effectively the knowledge generated through these methods into the development and improvement of therapeutic approaches for memory-related clinical conditions.

## SECTION 1 – MEMORY

### 1.1. Introduction

Decades of research on memory have continuously shown the essential role this cognitive function has on enabling consciousness of the sense of self in living organisms (Tulving, 1987). This bears incredible relevance for humans, as memories of daily experiences is what constitutes the identity of individuals (LeDoux, 2003). For these reasons, the sense of self, the identity and the personality of individuals can be affected by mental illnesses that involve at their core memory problems (Brewin, 2011). Examples of this are the intrusive memories that characterize some symptoms of various psychiatric conditions, such as the persistent re-experiencing of a traumatic event in Post Traumatic Stress Disorder (PTSD), as well as the recurrent thoughts of death observed in ruminating patients who suffer from a Major Depressive Episode (American Psychiatric Association). Thus, there is a need to enhance our understanding of the memory mechanisms underlying these conditions. This would not only increase our comprehension of the memory functions, but could also eventually yield novel ways of preventing and treating the memory problems involved in these clinical conditions. However, it is first essential to understand these processes in healthy individuals. In particular, the first section of this chapter highlights the role of specific brain areas in the processing of memories, the description of the various stages behind memory formation, the main categorizations of human memory as well as the modulatory effects of emotions and different pharmacological or environmental manipulations on memory.

### 1.2. Brain Areas Involved in Memory

Research on the memory systems has revealed the role of certain brain regions, such as the prefrontal cortex, the amygdala and the hippocampus, on processing particular types of information. Of these areas, the prefrontal cortex is known for its contributions for learning, working memory, and retrieval. Furthermore, from a global perspective, the prefrontal cortex has been shown to operate as a gating structure that controls and monitors the processing of information that is represented in other brain areas. In the case of the amygdala, it has been shown to be mostly associated with emotional processing and memory. However, the brain area that has been studied the most in the memory field is the hippocampus (Squire, 1992).

Particularly, it has been shown to play an important role on all stages of memory, namely encoding, consolidation and retrieval (Davis & Gaskell, 2009; Lepage, Habib, & Tulving, 1998; Spaniol et al., 2009; Wais, 2008; Wang & Morris, 2010).

## 1.3. Stages of Memory Formation

In order for a memory to be properly formed, it first needs to undergo encoding. This stage of memory occurs when a mental representation of information is initially processed in the short-term memory (STM) system of an individual (Best, 1968; Schwartz, 1976), which deals with the holding of information for a duration of a few seconds. This newly learned information then undergoes a time-dependent process known as consolidation.

Per se, consolidation consists of the transferring of information from STM to long-term memory (LTM), as a means to stabilize the memory trace and properly store it (Müller & Pilzecker, 1900). Due to the ephemeral nature of this new memory trace (McGaugh, 1972), it remains very unstable and labile at first (Dudai, 1996). However, once the consolidation phase begins to take place, the malleability decreases, leading to a progressive stabilization of the memory trace (Glickman, 1961). Hence, once stored in the LTM system, memories are thought to be relatively stable (McGaugh, 1966, 2000) and available for later access. As such, the use of stored information results in the process of retrieval, where a memory is re-accessed. This can occur through recognition, when a cue serves the role of reminder of a previous memory, or by free recall, where retrieval occurs in the absence of a cue.

## 1.4. Novel Insights into Memory Formation Processes: The Reconsolidation Model

As presented above, psychology has long conceived memory to function in accordance to the phases of encoding, consolidation, and retrieval. However, in the past decades this notion has been extended by the notion of reactivation, where individuals get reminded of past experiences by a cue or stimulus. As such, reactivation reflects yet another daily life phenomenon, since memories are constantly recalled either voluntary or involuntarily by individuals. Examples of this are victims of traumatic experiences who are known to constantly re-experience these events involuntarily, in the form of intrusive thoughts, as well as voluntarily, when telling their accounts of the transpired events to authorities, prosecutors, and therapists. However, one important aspect of memories is the fact that they are not static, but rather malleable. As such, research has found memories to be able to change after their reactivation through a process now known as reconsolidation.

### 1.4.1. Definition and Timing of Memory Reconsolidation

Formally, reconsolidation refers to the update that a memory trace goes through after its reactivation, which results in another round of the consolidation process, now allowing the incorporation of new details to the original memory trace. When this occurs, memories become labile again, as during consolidation, rendering them vulnerable to changes. As such, during this lability period the memory trace can be modified, decreased or increased (Nader,

Schafe, & LeDoux, 2000). Animal research suggests the timing of this window of opportunity for manipulations to emerge around to 3 to 10 minutes after the memory reactivation, lasting for about an hour (Monfils, Cowansage, Klann, & LeDoux, 2009). The reconsolidation update is then thought to be completed 6 hours following the reactivation (Duvarci & Nader, 2004; Nader, Schafe, & Le Doux, 2000). On humans, reconsolidation is thought to possess similar timing characteristics (Schiller & Phelps, 2011).

To date, pharmacological interventions and behavioral interventions present the most implemented methods for manipulating memory reconsolidation (Baratti, Boccia, & Blake, 2009; Diergaarde, Schoffelmeer, & De Vries, 2008). Therefore, as a means to understand the underpinnings of memory reconsolidation, we will now cover the background history of this emerging memory field.

### 1.4.2. Historical Background of the Reconsolidation Model

Altogether, reconsolidation represents a phenomenon that dates back to the sixties, when the reactivation of consolidated memory traces was shown to induce retrograde amnesia through electroconvulsive shock in rats (Misanin, Miller, & Lewis, 1968). This phenomenon remained largely dormant after the publication of the previously referenced study, until the year 1999, when another animal study showed that the beta-blocker propranolol impairs the memory for emotional tasks after a reactivation trial, following consolidation (Przybyslawski, Roullet, & Sara, 1999). A year after this finding, another animal study revealed that infusion of the protein synthesis inhibitor anisomycin was also capable of blocking memory reconsolidation (Nader, Schafe, & Le Doux, 2000). However, due to the toxic properties of this drug on humans, propranolol remained the most promising drug to potentially work on the reconsolidation memory of humans.

Subsequent research throughout the past decades has sought to study whether this phenomenon also occurs in humans. In doing so, a new excitement for this old phenomenon has been ignited through findings that show how certain pharmacological agents as well as some behavioral manipulations, are capable to block memory reconsolidation in humans (Schiller & Phelps, 2011).

## 1.5. Role of Emotions and Arousal on the Formation of Memories

Among various factors that are known to affect the formation of memory, we can highlight preliminary emotion and arousal, due to their impacting role on characterizing memories. Altogether, emotions are defined as changes in mind and body states, triggered by a brain system that responds to the content of an individual's actual or recalled perception (Bechara & Naqvi, 2004). As such, emotions represent the complex physiological and psychological states that indicate an occurrence of value, typically highlighted by arousal (Dolan, 2002). This latter term is defined as a condition of excitement that varies from a low point, such as during sleep states, to a high point, usually characterized by intense, overwhelming excitement (Lupien & Brière, 2000). In some cases, emotion and arousal can lead to secretion of stress hormones, such as glucocorticoids (GCs) and catecholamines. The secretion of these hormones then modulates the strength of the memory trace encoded and consolidated for this experience at the level of the hippocampus (LeDoux, 2002, 2003). This happens due to the high salience of the circumstances eliciting a specific emotion at hand, which prompts cognitive resources to attribute more attention focus during the encoding of an event of emotional nature than for a neutral one. By consequence, these processes facilitate the consolidation of emotionally relevant memories. Altogether, the described processes on how emotional experiences magnify the intensity of memories have been confirmed across numerous studies (McGaugh, 2000; Prado-Alcala & Quirarte, 2007).

## 1.6. Different Memory Categories: Implicit and Explicit Memory

In order to properly categorize memory, a taxonomy has been designed to describe the ramifications of the LTM system's two broad classes: implicit memory (also known as non-declarative memory) and explicit memory (also known as declarative memory) (Squire & Zola, 1996). Prominent models of the memory system have long based the distinction between these two memory categories on whether encoding and retrieval occur in a conscious state, or outside awareness (Squire & Zola, 1996). Implicit memory has been characterized by an unconscious learning and retrieval of material (Schacter, 1987). As such, it contrasts from its counterpart, explicit memory, for which both the learning and the recollection of information occur inside states of conscious awareness (Tulving, 1987). However, the consolidation process remains unconscious in both explicit and implicit memory, since it occurs spontaneously through the passage of time, notably during sleep (Axmacher, Draguhn, Elger, & Fell, 2009).

More precisely, for implicit memory, the information processed stems from unconscious and automatized cognitive skills learning through rules or procedures, sensorimotor learning (procedural memory), associative learning (classical conditioning), and priming. On the other hand, the source for explicit memory tends to come from conscious facts (semantic memory) or experiences (episodic memory). These have led to subcategories within both implicit and explicit memory.

### 1.6.1. Types of Implicit Memory

#### 1.6.1.1. Procedural Memory

Procedural memory is the type of memory that handles the procedures required to perform different actions and skills, such as riding a bicycle, driving a car, and teeth brushing (Squire, 1986). To acquire a particular skill during encoding, the individual first needs to attain a proper cognitive and schematic comprehension of the task that needs to be learned. This is followed by an associative phase, which involves the continuous repetition of the task, in order to properly consolidate it. During this associative phase, the memory system proceeds on discarding ineffective actions in favor of effective ones. Following this, the autonomous phase begins, characterized by a sharper discrimination of stimuli, as well as by a decreased need to involve thought process when retrieving the memory to execute the task. Therefore, the formation of this type of memory is considered complete once the learning of the task becomes engrained and perfected in the individual, rendering its memory retrieval automatic.

### 1.6.1.2. Classical Conditioning

Another type of learning that involves implicit memory is classical conditioning. It consists of the associative learning that gets formed after pairing a neutral conditioned stimulus (CS) with an unconditioned stimulus (US), which by itself is known to naturally elicit specific and unconditioned responses (UR) (Pavlov, 1927). An example of this is fear conditioning, where an aversive stimulus (US), like an electric shock, is paired with a neutral stimulus (CS), such as lights, tones, and/or contexts, yielding fear responses, such as freezing or startle (UR). Because of the association between the US and the CS, the fear response can be elicited by the presentation of the CS alone, which is called a conditioned response (CR) (Hermans, Craske, Mineka, & Lovibond, 2006). In order for a classical conditioning memory to be formed, it requires the pairing of either one very potent CS-US association presentation, or various learning trials.

### 1.6.1.3. Priming

Priming consists of an increase in the sensitivity to recognize stimuli following prior experience with either the same stimuli, or similar ones, that share perceptual, conceptual or semantic resemblances. It occurs unconsciously, through the perceptual identification of stimuli, such as words and objects. For example, one priming task involves the initial presentation of a list of words to participants, followed by the presentation of only a fragment of the words (i.e. "emo" for the word "emotion") (Squire, 1986). In terms of its formation, a single exposure of the stimulus, such as the complete word "emotion", has been shown to be sufficient to prime the memory for this word when presented with a segment of it, in this case with 'emo'. This demonstrates the capacity of priming to be able to be formed at once, on the spot.

### *1.6.2 Types of Explicit Memories*

### 1.6.2.1. Semantic Memory

Of the subcategories of explicit memory, semantic memory involves the recall of concepts and meanings without relevance to personal experiences (Windhorst, 2005). A simple example of this type of memory is the knowledge that cars are a method of transportation and not a type of food, without the necessity to remember a particular personal experience in order to retrieve this knowledge. It is important to keep in mind that this memory type can be modulated by culture, since different ethnic groups tend to have different meanings for circumstances and experiences.

### 1.5.2.2. Episodic Memory

In contrast to semantic memory, episodic memory processes the detailed recall of specific events, circumstances and experiences of an individual (Tulving, 1972). It can be formed from a single experience, without the need for multiple exposures to the same event. Besides this, another relevant characteristic of episodic memory is cognitive complexity, since this type of memory tends to involve conceptual, emotional, temporal and/or sensory elements of information. As such, the combination of all these elements allow these memories to be recalled more vividly (Wheeler, Stuss, & Tulving, 1997). For these reasons, episodic memories tend to include details that remain irrelevant to the main characteristics of the memory, such as remembering that the location of the church where a couple got married was next to a museum. On the matter of retrieval, the associations and elements of this type of memory are stored in a manner allowing these aspects to be retrieved individually (Henke, 2010). For example, one could recall the smell of flowers at a park previously visited, without necessary remembering other memory aspects, such as the nearby locations to the park. Furthermore, it is important to point out that the time construct bears a lot of relevance for episodic memory since they are usually engrained in a manner that follows time sequences in terms of seconds, minutes and hours (Raes, Hermans, Williams, & Eelen, 2007). Importantly, the strength of these memories would tend to decrease through the passage of time unless they become linked to autobiographical knowledge.

### 1.6.2.3. Autobiographical Memory

Autobiographical memories deal with the recollection of experiences relevant to a person's life. It involves elements from episodic memory, such as specificity, cognitive complexity and time, while also incorporating some concepts from semantic memory, like the meanings and concepts attributed to beliefs and attitudes (Conway & Pleydell-Pearce, 2000; Raes, et al., 2007). In contrast to episodic memory, autobiographical memory is composed mainly by the most important details of a personal memory, with unimportant and impersonal details getting gradually forgotten through the passage of time. For example, an accountant can have a general memory of how busy the administrative duties of the first post-university job were during the tax report' season.

### 1.6.2.4. Emotional Memory

Another important characteristic that highly impacts the meaning that an individual attributes to their memories is emotion. As such, the processing of the emotions resulting from an experience leads to the formation of the explicit memory subcategory known as emotional memory. Regarding the methodology usually employed to study emotional memory, researchers generally present emotional words, pictures or movies, as a means to induce this affective state in individuals (Lupien, 2009).

Despite the contributions of these described methods to the emotional memory field, it is important to point out that in real life, the memories for excessively emotional events present a more robust salience for the individuals living them. On the case of extremely arousing, traumatic events, such as the terrorist attacks of September 11th 2001 (9/11) in New York City and the Pentagon, a phenomenon denominated "flashbulb memories" tends to occur (Conway et al., 1994). Across flashbulb memories, relevant details, like the image of the airplanes hitting the twin towers, as well as information not directly related to the traumatic event, such as where the person was when he/she first heard about the event, get imprinted on the individual's memory. For these reasons, despite being categorized as the extreme form of emotional memory, flashbulb memories present elements of both episodic and autobiographical memory. This flashbulb memory involves the vivid nature of episodic memories, as well as the personal relevance of the event, in line with the precepts of autobiographical memory. On this matter, it is important to mention that another aspect that amplifies the relevance of this memory is the central attention devoted by the cognitive and psychological resources towards such an extremely salient event. Altogether, this occurs as an evolutionary mechanism to ensure the survival of an organism when facing an extremely emotional, stressful and/or dangerous situation. For instance, exposure to a violent crime leads witnesses to better recall the weapon (of central relevance during such an arousing event), when compared to other details that at the moment seem peripheral, such as the face of the perpetrator (Brown, 2003).

## 1.7. Objectivity and Veracity of Memories

Based on the reviewed methods, memory tasks involving the recall of personal events that comprise elements from episodic, emotional and/or autobiographical memories have more ecological validity, due to the increased value and importance that they represent for the individuals. However, it is important to acknowledge that there is an important challenge to account for the veracity and objectivity of individuals' self-reported memories from their past.

This difficulty on determining the genuinely and objectivity of a memory can be attributed to the brain left hemisphere's role of "the interpreter", which constructs theories to assimilate perceived information into a comprehensible whole, as a coping mechanism to deal more effectively with similar future events (Gazzaniga, 2000). On the other hand, high accuracy of information is maintained on the right hemisphere of the brain, due to the fact that this hemisphere does not engage with interpretative processes, but rather depends on rationalizations to correlate information from our past with current stimuli (Gazzaniga, 2000). Thus, we can say that the brain possesses a tendency to accommodate our memories to daily life situations by either reinforcing or modifying their recall (Schacter, 2001), in a manner that greatly affects the objectivity of memories.

### 1.7.1. False Memories

To address the issue of the veracity of autobiographical memories, research has been conducted in the past few decades on the phenomenon of false memory. False memory consists of the distorted recollection of events, as well as the recall of events that did not happen (Loftus, 1996; Wade et al., 2007; Zhu et al., 2010). This has been theorized to occur through three different mechanisms. The first is when a memory is attributed to an incorrect source (misattribution), like when an individual remembers an event as having occurred two years ago in his home town, when in fact it really happened five years ago in his parents' city. The second is when a memory for an event that never occurred is suggested or implanted in an individual (suggestibility). For example, this could be the case when an individual falsely believes the idea of him having attended a party after hearing some friends' account of having seen him there. Another example of suggestibility can be observed in crime witnesses, whose recollections of the transpired events are eventually altered by reading different interpretations of the event, as described in newspapers and other media. The third and final false memory mechanism is known as bias (Schacter, 2001). It tends to occur when the present line of thoughts and emotions alters the memory recall of past events. This can be observed in individuals undergoing the break up of a romantic relationship, whose vision of their past relationships tends to become tainted and perceived as completely negative, as a result of their current feelings of sadness. Thus, as described above, the memory capacity is vulnerable to different manipulations.

## 1.8. Memory Modulation

Knowledge of the various mechanisms involved in the different types of memories have led the field to further investigate the factors that can modulate memories. Particularly, memories have been shown to be malleable in a manner that depends on the timing of the intervention. Commonly, these methods involve the introduction of an intervention, either pharmacological or environmental, at a specific time so that a given memory phase (i.e., encoding, consolidation, retrieval) is modulated. To do so, the timing of the intervention needs to take into account the time window of each phase, as well as the pharmacokinetics of the drug in consideration.

### 1.8.1. Modulation of Memory Encoding

To modulate the encoding memory phase, an intervention needs to be implemented either before or during the moment when the individual first attains exposure of the task to be learned. One way to modulate memories at this stage is to administer pharmacological drugs before or during the encoding phase. On this matter we can highlight substances that act on the central noradrenergic system, such as psychostimulant drugs. For instance, administration of the α2-adrenoceptor antagonist yohimbine prior to the encoding of an emotional story has been shown to result in a better memory recall at a drug-free retrieval test when compared to a placebo-treated group (O'Carroll, Drysdale, Cahill, Shajahan, & Ebmeier, 1999). Similarly, the beta-blocker propranolol has been shown to be efficient at modulating emotional memory encoding. In fact, Cahill and colleagues (Cahill, Prins, Weber, & McGaugh, 1994) showed that a dose of 40 mg of propranolol administered before encoding significantly impaired the drug-free memory retrieval memory of an emotionally arousing story compared to a placebo group. Importantly, this finding has been replicated in other studies (Strange & Dolan, 2004; Strange, Hurlemann, & Dolan, 2003).

### 1.8.2. Modulation of Memory Consolidation

In order to specifically modulate the memory consolidation phase, the intervention needs to be provided during the consolidation window of opportunity for memory manipulations. In other words, it needs to be done after encoding but not too late, since this could lead to the memory stabilization before the intervention is made.

Among various behavioral methodologies, the presentation of positive and negative material represents an effective way to modulate the memory consolidation for material unrelated to these emotional presentations. For example, consolidation of a word-list task has been shown to be enhanced when its learning is followed by exposure to positive and negative pictures (Liu, Graham, & Zorawski, 2008; Nielson & Powless, 2007). Similar results have been obtained when positive or negative video clips were presented after learning (Nielson & Powless, 2007; Nielson, Yee, & Erickson, 2005).

With regards to the pharmacological modulation of memory consolidation, the post-learning administration of various substances has been shown to enhance consolidation. Among many, these substances include glucose (Manning, Parsons, & Gold, 1992), nicotine (Colrain, Mangan, Pellett, & Bates, 1992), norepinephrine (Southwick et al., 2002), epinephrine (Cahill & Alkire, 2003), amphetamine (Soetens, Casaer, D'Hooge, & Hueting,

1995; Soetens, D'Hooge, & Hueting, 1993), and D-Cycloserine (DCS), which is a partial agonist of the NMDA receptor (Kalisch et al., 2009).

### 1.8.3. Modulation of Memory Retrieval

In the case of modulating memory retrieval, an intervention would need to be administered after allowing an original memory trace to be completely consolidated. Then, the modulating intervention would be implemented before testing the recall of the memory. An example of an intervention at this memory phase would be the paradigm known as Retrieval-Induced Forgetting (RIF), which states that repeated retrieval of a given item will strengthen the recall for that item, resulting in a decrease in the retrieval access to other associated items (Anderson, Bjork, & Bjork, 1994). As such, this paradigm is based on strength-dependent competition models of interference.

Due to the fact that nicotine has been associated with increased focus and decreased intrusions in healthy individuals, the RIF paradigm has been used to assess the effects of this cholinergic agonist on affecting the efficient inhibition of irrelevant material. Particularly, nicotine has been observed to increase the inhibition of unpracticed, irrelevant exemplars, thereby reducing interference while benefiting the task at hand (Edginton & Rusted, 2003). Furthermore, nicotine has been shown to increase the retrieval-induced forgetting for episodic list learning (Rusted & Alvares, 2008).

Regarding pharmacological modulations of memory retrieval, administration of the beta-blocker propranolol at the retrieval memory phase has been shown to abolish the enhancement of declarative memories for emotional items (Kroes, Strange, & Dolan, 2010).

### 1.8.4. Modulation of Memory Reconsolidation

As mentioned above, recent findings have shown how certain pharmacological and behavioral interventions are capable to block memory reconsolidation in humans (Schiller & Phelps, 2011). Therefore, the following two subsections present some of the most relevant findings on the diverse methods that have thus far been observe to be effective at modulating human memory reconsolidation.

#### 1.8.4.1. Pharmacological Modulations of Memory Reconsolidation

In the case of pharmacological modulations of memory reconsolidation, several drugs have been first tested across learning paradigms on animals. Some of these drugs cannot be directly applied to humans due to various reasons, such as them being toxic, as in the case of anisomycin. For other drugs, such as ondansetron (Davidson et al., 2007), scopolamine (Kelley, Anderson, & Itzhak, 2007; Zhai et al., 2008), ketamine (Zhai, et al., 2008), midazolam (Robinson, Armson, & Franklin, 2011; Robinson & Franklin, 2010), and saralasin (Frenkel, Maldonado, & Delorenzi, 2005; Frenkel, Suarez, Maldonado, & Delorenzi, 2010), continuous animal research is being conducted, as a mean to determine whether or not enough substantial evidence supports translational research to apply them on human populations. As such, research on these drugs' effects on reconsolidation could present potential interesting pathways to eventually extend studies on this memory mechanism to humans.

In addition to the above-described drugs, some have indeed shown enough promise on animal studies to allow translational research to be implemented on humans. Propranolol has thus far been the drug to show the highest potential to serve as an emotional memory reconsolidation blocker. Support for this hypothesis has been observed across healthy individuals (Kindt, Soeter, & Vervliet, 2009; Kroes, et al., 2010; Soeter & Kindt, 2010), as well as on PTSD patients (Brunet et al., 2008; Brunet et al., 2011). However, various articles addressing the efficacy of this drug to block emotional memory reconsolidation have yielded negative findings in healthy populations (de Quervain, Aerni, & Roozendaal, 2007; Schwabe et al., 2009; Tollenaar, Elzinga, Spinhoven, & Everaerd, 2009b, 2009c), as well as in individuals diagnosed with PTSD (Hoge et al., 2011). Therefore, due to this conundrum, the scientific community is still debating on whether the propranolol's effects on reducing the strength of emotional memory could indeed be caused as result of memory reconsolidation blockade, or whether this effect is the result of an interference of the drug on emotional memory retrieval (Schiller & Phelps, 2011).

Besides propranolol, the effectiveness of several other drugs on manipulating reactivated emotional memories has also been tested. Among these, metyrapone has recently been shown to exert a long-lasting reduction of the emotional memory retrieval of a slide show presentation (Marin, Hupbach, Maheu, Nader, & Lupien, 2011). Similarly, systemic administration of the glucocorticoid antagonist mifepristone (RU486) has also been shown to block the reconsolidation of cue-conditioned fear memories in rats (Pitman et al., 2011). Thus, based on the positive findings observed with propranolol, metyrapone, and mifepristone, further research on these drugs will help elucidate whether they could also present the potential to serve as pharmacological adjuncts to treat PTSD. However, an important aspect to consider in future studies assessing the memory effects of each of these drugs on the PTSD condition is their different brain mechanisms. Propranolol is known to target the adrenergic system by acting on the sympathetic adrenomedullary (SAM) axis, whereas metyrapone and mifepristone both act on the GCs system through their action on the hypothalamus-pituitary-adrenal (HPA) axis (although through different pathways). Therefore, more studies are needed to understand the exact mechanism by which stress hormones could be potential targets to block memory reconsolidation of negative memories.

### 1.8.4.2. Behavioral Modulations of Memory Reconsolidation

With regards to behavioral modulations of memory reconsolidation, Monfils and colleagues developed a novel approach which combines principles from reconsolidation blockade with extinction of conditioned fear (Monfils, et al., 2009). Here, extinction refers to the decrement of a fear response that results when the conditioned stimulus (CS) is presented repeatedly in the absence of the unconditioned stimulus (US), leading to a gradual decrease of the conditioned response (Myers & Davis, 2007). On Monfils' paradigm, extinction gets administered during the reconsolidation lability window after a single isolated reactivation trail. Through this method, fear memory responses have been shown to be attenuated permanently in rats, as evidenced by a test conducted on these memories one month later.

A translational research project was then conducted, in an effort to test the application of the principles of this methodology in humans (Schiller et al., 2010). In this study, conditioned fear responses were updated with an extinction procedure after reactivating the fear memory with a single trail. Similarly to the previous animal study, this paradigm yielded a significant reduction in the expression of fear. Furthermore, this effect was shown to be persistent one year later, as well as exclusive to the original fear memory, without affecting other memories. Altogether, these studies present an incredible potential for the treatment of fear-related problems, such as PTSD and phobias (Quirk & Milad, 2010; Quirk et al., 2010). Further human studies implementing this combined extinction/reconsolidation blockade paradigm across PTSD populations will be needed in order to determine whether it can permanently attenuate fear symptoms in PTSD patients by reducing the traumatic memory trace.

## SECTION 2 – STRESS AND MEMORY

### 2.1. Introduction to Stress and Memory

As observed in the previous section, different modulators can impact memory throughout its various phases. Among many modulating factors, stress has been widely studied in relation to its effect on memory (Lupien & Brière, 2000; Schwabe, Joels, Roozendaal, Wolf, & Oitzl, 2011). Therefore, the present section will be devoted to the history behind the stress concept, its definition and characteristics, its relation and differentiation from emotion, as well as the direct effects of stress and stress hormones on the modulation of memories, across all three memory phases.

#### 2.1.1. Stress

Historically, the use of the term "stress" can be traced all the way to the 1930's. During that time, the term was employed within the field of physics to describe the pressure and strain that certain forces can cause on a physical body or an object, which under extreme circumstances could lead to a breaking point. This conception of the term stress then began to be applied to the health and biology field by the endocrinologist Hans Selye, who made a parallel with the medical field. Inspired by this, Dr. Selye theorized in 1936 that stress represented an unspecified syndrome, caused by a dysregulation of an individual's homeostasis, which in turn was due to pressure from a diverse amount of noxious sources (Selye, 1998).

Several researchers disagreed with Selye's idea about stress as an unspecific phenomenon since many circumstances of psychological nature were considered to specifically trigger stress responses (Mason, 1971). To address this conundrum, Dr. John Mason and colleagues conducted experiments addressing how the human stress response system could be altered by psychological stressors, such as bereavement (Hofer, Wolff, Friedman, & Mason, 1972) and parachute jumping. Through these studies, Dr. Mason was able to identify three specific characteristics, that when present in a situation, evoke a physiological stress response in humans. These are novelty (Fishman, Hamburg, Handlon, Mason, & Sachar, 1962), unpredictability, and low sense of control (Mason, 1968a, 1968b). In addition to these characteristics, socially-evaluative circumstances that represent a threat to the ego of an individual, were also recently found to yield a stress response (Dickerson & Kemeny, 2004).

In order to study stress in laboratory conditions, various tasks involving the application of psychological and/or physical stressors have been developed. In human research, the most common psychological stressors are: the Trier Social Stress Test (TSST) (Kirschbaum, Pirke, & Hellhammer, 1993), the Yale Inter-Personal Stressor (YIPS) (Stroud, Tanofsky-Kraff, Wilfley, & Salovey, 2000), the Montreal Imaging Stress Task (MIST) (Dedovic et al., 2005), and the Leiden Public Speaking Task (LPST) (Westenberg et al., 2009). To induce physical stressors, the most applied one is the Cold Pressor Test (CPT) (McRae et al., 2006). As a means to cover both the social and physical spectrums of stress, the Socially Evaluated Cold-Pressor Test (SECPT) has recently been developed (Schwabe, Haddad, & Schachinger, 2008).

### 2.1.2. Stress Hormone Systems: Basal and Reactive

To deal with real-life stressors (physical and/or psychological), organisms have a built in stress system, which is important for many normal and basal bodily functions, as well as for the response to perceived stressful situations. For the normal body functions, a stream of cortisol exists in the blood, called the resting or basal cortisol levels, which follows a circadian rhythm (Liddle, 1966). In humans, this rhythm is characterized by the presence of higher levels of cortisol in the morning and lower levels of cortisol in the afternoon and night (de Weerth, Zijl, & Buitelaar, 2003; Van Cauter & Turek, 1995).

When the brain detects a threat or a stressor, two interrelated systems get activated. One is the sympathetic adrenomedullary (SAM) axis, which initiates the fight-or-flight response through the secretion of the catecholamine hormones (adrenaline and noradrenaline) from the adrenal medulla, as commanded by the hypothalamus' perception of arousal (Poole, Hunt Matheson, & Cox, 2012). The second is the hypothalamic-pituitary-adrenal (HPA) axis, which is also initiated by the hypothalamus. What distinguishes the two processes is that the HPA axis acts through the release of the corticotropin-releasing factor (CRF) by the hypothalamus, which promotes the release of the adrenocorticotropic hormone (ACTH) from the pituitary which in turn stimulates the cortex of the adrenal glands to induce the release of glucocorticoids (GCs), known as cortisol in humans (Lupien, McEwen, Gunnar, & Heim, 2009). The increase in cortisol levels that occurs in response to a stressor is referred to as reactive cortisol levels.

### 2.1.3. Differences between Stress and Emotions

We can note that stress bears striking similarities with emotion, such as coming from an identifiable source, provoking body reactions, increasing arousal, and occurring for a brief period of time that extends its intensity impact in a conscious manner on individuals (Lupien, 2009). However, there are various characteristics that differentiate stress from emotion, as defined in section 1. One of these differences is that although stress evokes emotions on almost all circumstances, an emotion does not necessarily involve stress. For example, information about tragic events on distant countries can yield an emotional reaction in an individual, without inducing a stress response, since the event could bear no relevance to the individual's life in his current environment. In contrast, a stressor of either physical or psychological nature causes both an emotional and stress reaction (Lupien & Brière, 2000).

### 2.1.4. Effects of Stress on Cognition

GCs are liposoluble and have the capacity to cross the blood-brain-barrier and bind to either one of two GCs receptor subtypes, known as the mineralocorticoid (MR; type I) and the glucocorticoid (GR; type II) receptors (Lupien & McEwen, 1997). MR and GR are located throughout various brain areas, including the hippocampus, the prefrontal cortex, and the amygdala (Lupien & McEwen, 1997). Given that these brain regions are well-known for their role in different cognitive functions, such as memory and the regulation of emotions, the impact of stress on these different functions has therefore been widely studied (Lupien &

Brière, 2000). As such, the following section will address the differential effects of stress and stress hormones across the known categories and stages of memories.

## 2.2. Impact of Stress and Stress Hormones on Memory Encoding

Throughout the past two decades, some studies have been conducted to elucidate the influence of stress and stress hormones on the encoding memory phase. These are covered below.

### 2.2.1. Impact of Stress and Stress Hormones on Implicit Memory Encoding

Thus far, only one study has specifically addressed the effects of stress hormones on the encoding phase of an implicit memory subcategory, in this case a procedural memory. In this study, Romer and colleagues compared the effects of 30 mg of cortisol with a placebo when administered one hour before exposure to a 5 choice serial reaction time task (SRTT), involving second-order conditional (SOC) sequences (Romer, Schulz, Richter, Lass-Hennemann, & Schachinger, 2011). After analyzing the reaction time and response accuracy for this task, the administration of cortisol was shown to impair the encoding of implicit sequence learning, when compared to the placebo group.

### 2.2.2. Impact of Stress and Stress Hormones on Explicit Memory Encoding

Regarding the impact of stress on episodic memory encoding, no study has thus far assessed this in a manner independent of emotion. Thus, the following subsection concentrates on the role of stress and stress hormones on emotional memory encoding.

So far, the majority of studies addressing the effects of stress on emotional memory encoding have focused on the impact of stress hormones, like noradrenaline and cortisol, on emotionally relevant material, usually compared to neutral information. As discussed before on section 1, decreasing noradrenaline before the encoding emotional stimuli decreases the memory recall for this material (Chamberlain, Muller, Blackwell, Robbins, & Sahakian, 2006). With regards to the glucocorticoid system, elevated levels of cortisol due to a stressor administered at the time of encoding have been shown to enhance the memory for emotional material (Buchanan & Lovallo, 2001; Kuhlmann & Wolf, 2006; Payne et al., 2007; Putman, Van Honk, Kessels, Mulder, & Koppeschaar, 2004). However, stress induced before the time of encoding has been shown to impair the encoding of neutral memories (Payne, et al., 2007). As such, high levels of both noradrenaline and cortisol promote encoding of emotional memories, whereas increased levels of cortisol impair neutral memories encoding.

## 2.3. Impact of Stress and Stress Hormones on Memory Consolidation

The following sections present the current literature addressing the effects of stress on memory consolidation.

## 2.3.1. Impact of Stress and Stress Hormones on Implicit Memory Consolidation

In an attempt to test the effects of stress on real world situations, Eich and Metcalfe (Eich & Metcalfe, 2009) assessed the stress effects of marathon running on the implicit and explicit memory of runners. For this study, the researchers chose marathon running as the stressor due to its resulting effects of dehydration, immune suppression, and increment in cortisol levels, which has been shown to be up to four times higher than the levels induced by the TSST (Cook, Ng, Read, Harris, & Riad-Fahmy, 1987). To properly address this question, an explicit cued recall task, as well as an implicit word-stem completion task, known to yield priming effects (Graf & Schacter, 1985), were administered to a marathon group (n=141) and a control group (n=120). For the control group, all participants were recruited and tested for the learning and recall of the tasks between 1 to 3 days prior to the marathon. However, for the marathon group, the recruitment and administration of the learning tasks were conducted at the reception area designated for the race. The memory for these tasks was assessed 30 minutes following the completion of the marathon, thereby targeting the early phase of consolidation. Following marathon running, implicit memory was enhanced whereas explicit memory was impaired. Regarding the limitations of this study, we can mention that because delayed memory was not assessed, this study failed to address the long-term effects of its findings, limiting the interpretation to the early phase of consolidation. Thus, future studies could test the retention at least 24hours following the learning and the stress procedures, as a mean to clarify the effects of stress on implicit memory consolidation.

## 2.3.2. Impact of Stress and Stress Hormones on Explicit Memory Consolidation

Regarding the effects of stress on consolidation for episodic memory, Beckner and colleagues conducted a study assessing the impact of stress on verbal memory (Beckner, Tucker, Delville, & Mohr, 2006). There, participants were stressed with a socially evaluated public speaking task immediately following exposure to a film (consolidation group) or before memory retrieval for that film (retrieval group) to then compare them to a group of individuals who were never stressed (control group). The results demonstrated that stress exposure led to an increase in memory consolidation for the neutral verbal material.

To test the effects of a physical stressor on memory consolidation, Andreano and Cahill exposed participants to either the cold-pressor test (CPT) or a control condition immediately following the presentation of a neutral story and then test the memory for this story one week later (Andreano & Cahill, 2006). All participants exposed to the CPT showed an increase in cortisol levels, but only men in that condition showed an enhanced memory for the story. However, the authors mentioned that the menstrual cycles of female participants were not considered and that this could have yielded different results. The impact of sex differences and menstrual cycle phases on the effects of stress on memory will be discussed further in section 3.

Following on the factors that influence the effects of stress on episodic memory consolidation, Joëls and colleagues theorized that stress-induced memory consolidation enhancement occurs only when both the stressor, as well as the memory acquisition phase are contextually related (Joels, Pu, Wiegert, Oitzl, & Krugers, 2006). To test this, Smeets and colleagues presented participants with personality-related words, such as "anxious" and "modest", and memory-related words, like "knowledge" and "intellect". Then, participants were exposed to either one of two modified versions of the TSST: one where the participant had to give a speech on a personality-related theme, and another one where the speech focused on a memory-related theme. In addition to these, a group not exposed to stress served as controls. Through these methods, stress was shown to enhance only the recall of context-congruent personality-related words, when compared to both the memory-stress and control groups (Smeets, Giesbrecht, Jelicic, & Merckelbach, 2007). In doing so, support was found for Joëls's conception of acute stress as a memory consolidation enhancer for material where the stressor matches the to-be-remembered material. However, this effect appeared to be specific for personality words. The authors proposed that the latter finding could be attributed to the personal material being of more relevance for individuals than the memory related words.

Regarding the relevance of stress hormones on the consolidation of emotional memories, several studies have addressed the roles of cortisol and catecholamines. Buchanan and colleagues exposed half of the participants to 20 neutral, 10 unpleasant moderately arousing words, and 10 highly unpleasant arousing words arousal words one hour before stress exposure through a Cold Pressor Test (CPT). Meanwhile, the other half of the study participants were subjected to warm water, in order to serve as controls. Ten minutes after exposure to the stress conditions, a delayed free recall task and a recognition memory test were conducted to assess the early phase of memory consolidation. Across this study, mildly arousing words were shown to be less recalled in individuals exposed to the Cold Pressor Test (CPT) when compared to the warm water control group. Importantly, this effect was only observed in individuals who exhibited an increase in cortisol in response to the CPT (responders).

In order to assess the effects of stress on memory with stimuli of more cognitive complexity, Preuss and Wolf conducted a study where participants were exposed to the TSST or a control condition after presenting all of them with neutral and emotional (positive and negative) pictures, paired with a brief narrative (Preuss & Wolf, 2009). At a delayed free recall test conducted 24 hours later, memory for neutral, but not for positive or negative material, appeared enhanced in the stressed group. This increased memory for neutral stimuli was correlated with increases in cortisol levels induced by the TSST. In doing so, these data demonstrated that stress can enhance weak and/or fragile memories lacking emotional implication, like neutral memories. As such, this study contrasts the data previously found by other laboratories where emotional memory consolidation has been shown to be enhanced by cortisol administration (Buchanan & Lovallo, 2001; Kuhlmann & Wolf, 2006), as well as by post-learning exposure to stress (Abercrombie, Speck, & Monticelli, 2006; Cahill, Gorski, & Le, 2003; Smeets, Otgaar, Candel, & Wolf, 2008). To explain the lack of effects on emotional items, the authors suggested various possibilities. One is that the task used by Preuss and Wolf may not have detected any memory enhancement for emotional stimuli due to a ceiling effect, where the emotional memories were not able to exhibit any further improvement. Another possible explanation comes from the complexity of the task, since it involved the pairing of a narrative to neutral and emotional pictures, whereas in the other studies, pictures were presented without additional information being attached to them. Finally, the authors propose that the findings could also be due to an inverted U-shape relationship between cortisol and arousal, where low and high cortisol levels in the absence of a stressor would increase emotional memory consolidation at optimal arousal levels. Regarding neutral memories, cortisol would then only yield enhancing effects on these memories in the presence of a stressor.

As a mean to address the discrepancy between the aforementioned study and the previously established literature, Yonelinas and colleagues assessed the effects of stress produced by skydiving on the recognition of neutral and negative pictures presented to participants either before they boarded an aeroplane to skydive (stress group), or remained on the ground (control group) (Yonelinas, Parks, Koen, Jorgenson, & Mendoza, 2011). To assess the early phase of memory consolidation, a recognition test for the previously presented stimuli was administered 2-hour following completion of the skydive. The results showed that the stress of jumping from a plane caused an increase in cortisol levels, as well as an enhancement in the recognition memory for neutral pictures, but not for negative pictures, thereby supporting Preuss and Wolf's findings. However, this memory increase was only found in males, suggesting possible sex differences in stress reactivity and/or memory processes. As such, one potential explanation for the lack of effects in women could be that they reacted less to the stressor. To address this issue, the authors proposed the explanation that the skydive may have not been stressful enough to yield a memory enhancement for women. However, due to the lack of scientific evidence to support this statement, a follow-up study is warranted that can objectively address the authors' suggested differential responses between men and women to stress related to skydiving. Nonetheless, the findings from this study highlight the importance of taking into account sex differences on studies conducted on studies assessing the impact of stress on memory.

Inspired by these findings, Lass-Hennemann and colleagues conducted a study on how stress can affect people's memory of strangers' personality traits after a first impression (Lass-Hennemann, Kuehl, Schulz, Oitzl, & Schachinger, 2011). Students were presented with portraits accompanied by a positive or negative behavioral description, before stressing half of them by submerging their hands in ice-cold water. The following day, new portraits, as well as the previous ones, were presented with single-word trait-adjectives. Participants were then asked to write the trait adjective for the portraits presented earlier. This procedure showed that stress-exposed students recalled better the positive personality traits associated with the portraits presented the day before, compared to control students, who recalled better negative traits. Thus, these results indicate that exposure to a physical stressor following an emotional task can affect the consolidation of first impressions in a manner dependent of valence. Moreover, the authors interpreted this finding as an indication that during physically stressful circumstances, people have a predisposition to remember better genuine potential helpers. One interesting way to follow-up on this finding would be to replicate this study's methodology using psychological stressors. Doing so could help increase the psychology field's understanding of the impact stress has on individual's first impressions.

So far, the described studies have not disentangled role of each class of stress hormones, namely cortisol and catecholamines, on memory. Maheu and colleagues investigated the effects of both cortisol and catecholamines on declarative memory using a slide story task containing neutral and emotional information (Maheu, Joober, Beaulieu, & Lupien, 2004). There, the administration of two doses of 750 mg of metyrapone, a cortisol synthesis inhibitor, was found to impair the declarative memory for both emotional and neutral slides when measured one week later, but not five minutes after slide show viewing. Regarding noradrenaline, a memory reduction for the emotional slides was observed both at the short-term and long-term recalls with a dose of 80 mg of propranolol (Maheu, et al., 2004). Importantly, noradrenaline modulation did not impact the neutral memory at either time point. Altogether, these results show the differential roles that both catecholamines and cortisol play in the encoding and consolidation processes of emotional memories, as noradrenaline appears to contribute on the immediate organization of emotional memories, whereas cortisol appear to be responsible for transferring both neutral and emotional information from the short-term to the long-term memory system.

Given the circadian rhythm of cortisol, as well as the fact that a large part of consolidation is thought to occur during sleep (Axmacher, et al., 2009), Wegner and colleagues sought to investigate the role of cortisol on memory consolidation during sleep (Wagner, Degirmenci, Drosopoulos, Perras, & Born, 2005). Using a double-blind randomized controlled trial in healthy men, the authors measured the effects of the cortisol synthesis inhibitor metyrapone on memory for emotional and neutral texts, a task previously shown to elicit sleep-associated consolidation (Wagner, Gais, & Born, 2001). In this experiment, participants first read the texts between 10:30–11:30 PM, and then ingest either 3g of metyrapone or a placebo before going to sleep at midnight. A retrieval test was conducted at 11am the following day. Overall, metyrapone was shown to suppress cortisol during sleep, which resulted in an impairment of neutral memory consolidation, as well as in an enhancement of emotional memory consolidation. As such, the metyrapone-induced memory impairment for the neutral texts stands in agreement with the decreased LTM for neutral slides observed with metyrapone by Maheu and colleagues (Maheu, et al., 2004). In contrast, the metyrapone-enhancement effect for emotional texts opposes the general findings in the literature, since low cortisol has been shown to lower consolidation of emotional memories. The authors of the study suggested this discrepancy to be possibly rooted in the physiologic differences underlying the "offline" states that the human brain goes through during sleep (Stickgold, Hobson, Fosse, & Fosse, 2001).

## 2.4. Impact of Stress and Stress Hormones on Memory Retrieval

After having reviewed the impact of stress and stress hormones on memory encoding and consolidation, we will now cover their impact on retrieval.

### 2.4.1. Impact of Stress and Stress Hormones on Implicit Memory Retrieval

Only one study has addressed the effects of stress hormones (cortisol and noradrenaline) on implicit memory retrieval, in addition to also assessing explicit memory retrieval (Schwabe, et al., 2009). To study implicit memory, the procedural memory task known as the five choice serial reaction time task (SRTT) was implemented. Besides this, explicit emotional memory was assessed through the administration of a list comprised of 24 words, distributed in the following manner: 8 neutral, 8 positive, and 8 negative. Twenty-four hours later after having learned the task, participants were asked to ingest either 40 mg of propranolol or a placebo, followed by exposure to stress through the Socially Evaluated Cold-Pressor Test (SECPT), or a control group, where subjects submerged their hands in warm water. This led to 4 different groups based on their pharmacological interventions and treatment conditions (propranolol/stress; propranolol/control; placebo/stress; and placebo/control). Subjects' retention for the SRTT and words was then tested. Overall, stress exposition, propranolol administration or the combination of these two methods all failed to yield any effects on procedural memory retrieval. As such, this study suggests that implicit memory retrieval does not appear to be affected by either stress hormone (noradrenaline or cortisol). The results from this study on explicit emotional memory will be discussed on the subsections below.

### 2.4.2. Impact of Stress and Stress Hormones on Explicit Memory Retrieval

When considering the relationship of stress and stress hormones with the retrieval of explicit episodic memories, most research has suggested impairing effects of stress on this memory phase. Although in general cortisol appears to facilitate memory consolidation, the opposite appears to be the case with regards to retrieval, since most studies show that elevated levels of cortisol impair the retrieval of episodic memories (de Quervain et al., 2003; de Quervain, Roozendaal, Nitsch, McGaugh, & Hock, 2000; Wolf et al., 2001). Moreover, both very high (Het, Ramlow, & Wolf, 2005) and very low levels of cortisol (Lupien et al., 2002) have been shown to impair the capacity to retrieve already consolidated memory traces, suggesting an inverted-U shape relationship between circulating levels of cortisol and memory retrieval capacities (Lupien & McEwen, 1997).

To address the role of context on the influence of stress on memory retrieval, Schwabe and colleagues recently addressed whether the resemblances of the retrieval context to the learning context can modulate memory performance. More precisely, they sought to test whether the impairing effects of stress on memory retrieval could be cancelled by matching the learning and retrieval contexts (Schwabe & Wolf, 2009). For this study, the design involved either an exposure to the TSST or a control condition, followed by a cued-recall test to assess the memory retrieval of an object location task, presented 24 hours earlier in a vanilla-scented room. Twenty minutes after the stress or control exposure, one group's memory retrieval was assessed in the same room where the learning took place (familiar context), while another group's retrieval was tested in a different room (unfamiliar context). Through this experiment, stress was shown to reduce memory performance in the unfamiliar context, but not in the familiar learning context. Altogether, this study shows that the matching of learning and retrieval contexts abolishes the impairing effects of stress on memory retrieval.

Due to the high valence that physical pain involves, Schwegler and colleagues investigated the effects of cortisol on the recall of previous pain experiences in healthy young men (Schwegler et al., 2010). To address this, male participants were exposed to either pictures only, or pairings of pictures with a heat-pain stimulus, as a mean to create a contextual memory of the picture to the heat-pain. The next day, 20 mg of cortisol or a placebo were administered one hour before presenting all the pictures to the participants. Their task was to identify whether those pictures were paired or not with a pain stimulus the previous day. Through these methods, cortisol, compared to a placebo, was shown to decrease the number of correctly recalled picture-pain associations, thereby reducing the retrieval of explicit contextual pain memory.

To address the roles of both noradrenaline and cortisol on memory retrieval, de Quervain and colleagues (de Quervain, et al., 2007) exposed participants to emotional words. Twenty-four hours later, participants were randomly assigned to one of the four groups: 25 mg of cortisol, 40 mg of propranolol, co-administration of both drugs or placebo. One hour after this, participants were tested for their recall of the emotional words. The results demonstrated an impairing effect of cortisol on the retrieval of highly arousing words. However, the group that received only propranolol did not have any effects on retrieval. Interestingly, concurrent administration of a low dose of 40 mg of propranolol with 25 mg of cortisol an hour before memory recall testing prevented the impairing effect of cortisol to appear. These findings were further addressed by Schwabe and colleagues on the study discussed at the top of this subsection, concerning stress' effects on memory retrieval (Schwabe, et al., 2009). In contrast to the results found by de Quervain and colleagues, retrieval of emotional words was enhanced by endogenous increases in cortisol, induced through the Socially Evaluated Cold Pressor Test (SECPT). However, this effect was blocked by propranolol administration. Importantly, propranolol administration without the presence of stress failed to cause any effects on memory retrieval. Based on the findings from these two studies, the role of noradrenaline on explicit emotional memory retrieval appears to be mediated by the type of activation on the glucocorticoid system. Particularly, cortisol administered exogenously appears to impair memory retrieval processes, whereas induced endogenous cortisol increases promote enhancements of these memories. Nonetheless, both cortisol effects are blocked by propranolol's influence on the noradrenergic system.

A recent study tested the long-term memory retrieval effects of low levels of cortisol for emotional and neutral material (Marin, et al., 2011). In this study, healthy individuals were presented with a slide show task involving neutral and emotional segments. Three days later, participants were randomly assigned to one of the three groups: a single dose of metyrapone (750 mg), two 750 mg doses of metyrapone or placebo. Following the drug administration, memory retrieval was tested. The results demonstrated that the administration of the double dose of metyrapone impaired the emotional memory retrieval, when compared to the placebo and single dose metyrapone groups.

To explore whether stress and stress hormones might also exert effects on personally relevant memories, two studies have addressed the influence of stress and cortisol on autobiographical memories. First, Buss and colleagues (Buss, Wolf, Witt, & Hellhammer, 2004) administered either 10 mg of hydrocortisone (which is a synthetic form of glucocorticoid) or placebo to healthy men students an hour before asking them to take the Autobiographical Memory Test (AMT) (Williams & Broadbent, 1986). There, subjects treated with cortisol were shown to generate fewer neutral autobiographical memories, as compared to the placebo group. To further address this matter, a subsequent study was conducted on the effects of stress induced through the TSST on autobiographical memories in healthy young men (Tollenaar, Elzinga, Spinhoven, & Everaerd, 2009a). The results showed that the stressor failed to yield any effects on the specificity of the subject's autobiographical memory. Altogether, these results suggest that exogenous increases of cortisol, but not endogenous, can decrease the specificity of autobiographical memory retrieval in healthy individuals and this effect seems specific to neutral memories.

## 2.5. Effects of Stress on Memory Reconsolidation

As reported above, stress influences memory processes in different ways. Therefore, the idea of studying the direct effects of stress on reactivated memories also presents a novel approach to understand how this phenomenon could impact previously formed memories. Insofar, few studies have addressed this issue. Moreover, those studies that have indeed been conducted have all focused on explicit memory reconsolidation only. On one hand, stress induced through the SPECT after memory reactivation has been shown to impair the reconsolidation of neutral autobiographical memories (Schwabe & Wolf, 2010). On the other hand, exposure to stress through the TSST after reactivating the memories of a slide story involving neutral and emotional segments have yielded long-lasting memory enhancement only for the emotional memory traces (Marin, Pilgrim, & Lupien, 2010). Because autobiographical and emotional memories are both categorized as explicit memories, these findings suggest differential roles of stress on these explicit memory subcategories. Altogether, stress appears to affect explicit memory reconsolidation in a manner dependent of emotion.

## 2.6. Effects of Stress and Stress Hormones on False Memories

Due to the fact that memories are malleable, false memory research represents another avenue through which the effects of stress on memory can be measured. Thus far, very few studies have sought this question. The first study addressed the impact of stress on participants' ability to accurately recognize words across the Deese Roediger McDermott (DRM) paradigm (Payne, Nadel, Allen, Thomas, & Jacobs, 2002). Participants were assigned either to the TSST (stress group) or to a control condition, to then be presented with semantically related words (like candy, sour, sugar, bitter, chocolate, cake). This was followed with a subsequent memory test, involving previously presented words, non-presented words, unrelated "distractor" words, and semantically related but non-presented "critical lure" words (such as "sweet"). Through these methods, stress was shown to increase the false recognition of semantically related words never presented in the study. Thus, this study suggested that stress could potentiate false memories.

These findings prompted Smeets and colleagues to conduct a follow-up study, where participants were exposed to the Cold Pressor Stressor (CPS) before encoding, during consolidation, before retrieval of emotional and neutral stimuli from the DRM word list paradigm, or served as controls (Smeets, Otgaar, et al., 2008). There, recall for neutral-false words was shown to be higher than for emotional-false words at all memory stages (encoding, consolidation and retrieval), thereby suggesting that neutral memories are more susceptible to false information incorporation. However, both emotional and neutral false recall failed to yielded any significant relationship to cortisol.

Subsequent research on false memory's relationship with stress has found partial support for the described findings on impaired memory retrieval, as false memories retrieval has been shown to be suppressed by cortisol (Diekelmann, Wilhelm, Wagner, & Born, 2011). As such, the authors suggest that the occurrence of false memories could be attributed to a failure in retrieval monitoring, which refers to the capacity to discriminate between a sense of familiarity, caused by external presentations, and an internal generation of associations. Because retrieval monitoring can be enhanced by acute physical stress (Smeets et al., 2008), as well as by psychological stress (Smeets et al., 2006), the authors theorize that cortisol may exert an improvement effect on memory retrieval, which could result in a reduction of false memory production. Therefore, stress would prevent individuals from generating false memories during retrieval.

## 2.7. Summary on the Effects of Stress and Stress Hormones Across the Different Memory Stages

When analyzing the presented literature on stress and stress hormones' effects across all stages of memory formation, various general observations can be made. First, the presence of stress before or during the encoding phase appears to enhance explicit memories, particularly episodic and emotional, while impairing implicit memories. Second, stress increases consolidation for emotional memories. Moreover, for the consolidation of neutral memory, some controversy exists due to discrepant findings in the literature. However, despite this conundrum, recent research suggests that stress can also enhance neutral memory consolidation. Among the mediating factors are the co-existing high levels of noradrenaline and cortisol. Regarding the stress hormones, the proposed idea of catecholamines contributing to the immediate organization of emotional memories, while cortisol transferring short-term memories (STM) into long-term memories (LTM) could be explained by the mechanisms of each of these hormones. Here, the catecholamines' influence on immediate memory organization would be theorized to result as a function of the SAM axis, which is related to rapid action in the wake of a stressor. On the other hand, cortisol's effects on the transition from STM to LTM could be attributed to HPA axis activation, which is characterized by a more delayed mechanism of action. Third, in contrast to encoding and consolidation, stress impairs memory retrieval for episodic and emotional material. However, these stress effects have recently been shown to be abolishable by matching the learning and retrieval contexts, as well as by concomitant administrations of propranolol. With these results in mind, the next section will address the limitations from the stress and memory field, as well as the novel directions through which future research can be guided in these areas.

## SECTION 3 - NEW DIRECTIONS IN STRESS, MEMORY AND EMOTION RESEARCH

### 3.1. Limitations of Current Literature Addressing Stress and Memory

When discussing the reviewed literature on stress and memory, it is important to point out some of the limitations of these studies. Addressing these limitations could shed some light into new directions on which future research could be focused, in order to ensure a proper progression on the elucidation of the effects of stress on memory.

#### 3.1.1. Importance to Address Sex Differences
Because most human studies on stress and memory are based on animal research paradigms, careful consideration needs to be addressed to the limitations of these models. One particular limitation that is worth noting is the tendency of most animal research studies to be exclusively conducted on male species, as a way to avoid the biological irregularities associated with the hormonal system of female organisms. This pattern from the animal research field has also lead the majority of human research to be performed in men, under the assumption that the findings from these studies can be generalized to women. These interpretations can be inaccurate, since many psychopathologies present strong differences

between men and women. Examples of this are findings that show mood and anxiety disorders to be more commonly observed in women (McLean & Anderson, 2009), particularly on unipolar depression (Usall, 2001), as well as on PTSD (Olff, Langeland, Draijer, & Gersons, 2007; Tolin & Foa, 2006). Meanwhile, men suffering from schizophrenia exhibit more risk to complete suicide than women with this condition (Lester). Furthermore, sex differences have also been observed in treatment response to psychiatric conditions, such as depression, where women are more vulnerable to chronic and recurrent episodes (Usall, 2001). Ironically, despite this increased outcome risk, women have been shown to respond better than men to SSRI anti-depressant treatments (Khan, Brodhead, Schwartz, Kolts, & Brown, 2005).

### 3.1.1.1. Sex Differences on Stress Reactivity

Besides the aforementioned sex differences across clinical psychopathologies, men and women have also been observed to differ in terms of stress reactivity and memory capacities. On stress reactivity towards the TSST, men have been shown to exhibit larger increases in adrenocorticotropic hormone (ACTH), which indicates that men react more to this stress task than women in general (Kirschbaum, Kudielka, Gaab, Schommer, & Hellhammer, 1999). On the other hand, women have been shown to exhibit greater negative affect (NA) reactivity than men when exposed to other laboratory stressors, such as viewings of a Holocaust video (Schmaus, Laubmeier, Boquiren, Herzer, & Zakowski, 2008). Similarly, following completion of the TSST, women, compared to men, have also been reported to show more fear, irritability, confusion and decreased happiness (Kelly, Tyrka, Anderson, Price, & Carpenter, 2008). Altogether, these findings indicate that men react more physiologically than women to many stressors, whereas women report a more robust subjective stress response.

### 3.1.1.2. Sex Differences on Memory Capacities

Regarding the processing of memories, numerous differences have been observed on the way women and men process explicit memories. Particularly, across studies on episodic and autobiographical memories, women have exhibited enhanced memory for specific details (Pillemer, Wink, DiDonato, & Sanborn, 2003; Seidlitz & Diener, 1998), more accurate recall (Bloise & Johnson, 2007), as well as faster access to childhood memories (Davis, 1999). These findings suggest a predisposition of women to develop a more enhanced autobiographical memory capacity than men (Andreano & Cahill, 2009). However, due to the numerous complexities that episodic and autobiographical memories entail, other factors should be taken into account when assessing sex differences among these memory capacities, such as the degree of emotion involvement within these memories.

### 3.1.2. Beyond Sex Differences: The Impact of Menstrual Cycle and Oral Contraceptive Use on Memory and Stress

Besides the described sex differences, contrasts in the maturation processing of the reproductive systems of men and women present another relevant aspect that needs to be addressed in studies involving memory and stress. Even though the maturity of the reproductive system begins at puberty for both men and women, in females this developmental stage also represents the beginning of menstruation. This process is composed of various phases, known as the follicular phase, the ovulatory phase, and the luteal phase.

During the luteal menstrual phase, higher concentrations of progesterone than estrogen are present, whereas women undergoing the follicular phase present higher estrogen than progesterone levels. As such, women can hardly be considered as a single group, since the hormonal changes associated with each menstrual cycle phase represent a differential variable among females. Thus, one possible explanation for some lack of effects observed across women in some studies assessing the effects of stress hormones on memory processing could stem from the fact that the menstrual cycle phase was not considered. Given that sexual hormones such as testosterone, estradiol and progesterone could play modulatory roles on the expression and processing of stress, memory and emotions, it is crucial to take variations of these hormones into account (Andreano & Cahill, 2009; Newhouse et al., 2010; van Wingen, Mattern, Verkes, Buitelaar, & Fernandez, 2008; van Wingen et al., 2007). Moreover, the hormonal effects of oral contraceptives (OC) represent another potentially confounding variable when trying to generalize research findings to the overall population.

Few studies have thus far addressed the differential roles of the menstrual cycle and oral contraceptives in stress' effects on memory across all stages. With regards to memory encoding, women using OC have been shown to exhibit decreased memory recognition for emotional and neutral pictures presented after TSST exposure, in comparison to women who do not use OC and men (Cornelisse, van Stegeren, & Joels, 2011).

With regards to memory consolidation under stress, estrogen and progesterone have been shown to play opposite roles. First, when progesterone levels are elevated in the mid-luteal phase, high cortisol levels induced by the cold-pressor stress (CPS) have been positively correlated with memory consolidation for a reading task presented prior stress exposure (Andreano, Arjomandi, & Cahill, 2008). In contrast, the same study showed a trend in the follicular phase, where reactive cortisol levels appear to be lower, which correlated with a lower memory consolidation process.

Moreover, men and those women undergoing their early follicular phase exhibit greater extinction memory compared to women in their late follicular phase (Milad et al., 2006). In the same vein, low estradiol levels in women appear to be related to impairments in consolidation of memory extinction (Milad et al., 2010). Given that a majority of the therapies for people living with post-traumatic stress disorder use extinction principles, these findings underlie the importance of taking into account a women's menstrual cycle phase in order to obtain optimal treatment outcomes.

Finally, when looking at the role of the menstrual cycle phase on the effects of stress on memory retrieval, some contradictory findings have been observed. First, cortisol induces memory impairments for women in the follicular (n=13) and luteal (n=14) menstrual cycle phases, but not in those who use OC (n=20). This suggests a possible decreased sensitivity towards acute cortisol elevations in the later group of women (Kuhlmann & Wolf, 2005). In contrast to the described menstrual cycle findings, Schoofs and Wolf did not observe any impairing effects of stress, presented through the TSST, for the retrieval of positive, negative and neutral nouns in women undergoing the luteal phase, when compared to a control group that was not exposed to stress (Schoofs & Wolf, 2009). The authors suggest that the discrepancy between these two studies with regards to the luteal phase may reflect a reduced sensitivity to the retrieval-memory impairing effects of cortisol, depending on whether it is endogenously or exogenously induced.

## 3.2. Future Directions for Studies Addressing the Effects of Stress on Implicit Memory

As evidenced in Section 2, most research on the effects of stress on memory has thus far been addressed on explicit memory, largely neglecting implicit memory. In doing so, a large gap in the advancement of the memory research field has been left unaddressed, since implicit memory capacity is as essential for human life as explicit memory. Therefore, conducting experiments to test the effects of stress on each subcategory of implicit memory (procedural memory, classical conditioning and priming), across each memory phase (encoding, conditioning and retrieval), present an interesting approach to increase our understanding of memory's mechanisms.

Among ideas for future studies on stress and implicit memories, it would be interesting to study how psychosocial and physical stress could affect the procedural memory capacities of athletes from sports that involve a routine in movements (like gymnastics and artistic skating), as well as from competitive sports, such as boxing, and wrestling. On classical conditioning, human studies could be conducted to assess how stress and stress hormones could modulate learned associations related to appetite, such as the extreme conditioned fear, resistant to extinction, that have been hypothesized to underlie eating disorders, such as anorexia nervosa (Strober, 2004). Doing so could provide insight on the role stress plays on the relationship between conditioning and eating disorders.

## 3.3. Future Directions for Studies Addressing the Effects of Stress on Memory Reconsolidation

Due to the small amount of studies that have thus far addressed the effects of stress on memory reconsolidation, as reported in section 2, additional studies are warranted on this area. Because the only published studies on stress and reconsolidation have only dealt with autobiographical (Schwabe & Wolf, 2010) and emotional memories (Marin, et al., 2010), future studies could also assess the effects of stress on the reactivation of other explicit memories, such as semantic memories. Moreover, exploratory research could also be conducted to test if stress could affect the reconsolidation of implicit memories. These studies could definitely assist the memory research field on achieving a complete comprehension of the effect of stress on the update of memory across all of its known subcategories.

## 3.4. Future Directions for Studies Addressing the Effects of Stress on False Memory Reconsolidation

As evidenced by the findings from false memory research reported in section 2, this field presents another avenue that can help further the knowledge of stress's effects on memory. One way to accomplish this could be to assess the relationship between stress and false memory through methods that bear more striking resemblances to real-life circumstances than the Deese Roediger McDermott (DRM) word list paradigm. To serve such purposes, the misinformation paradigm was developed, as a means to study the misattribution characteristics of false memories (Loftus, Miller, & Burns, 1978). It involves the presentation of an event, followed by the administration of post event information (PEI), to then test the memory for the event. Due to the fact that this task involves the exposure of additional information to previously exposed material, the notion of memory reactivation could also be incorporated to studies of stress's effects on false memory. For instance, if false information were to be given to an individual during a stress period following the reactivation of a real memory, it would be interesting to determine whether the original memory is more likely to be changed than under non-stressful conditions. Some real life example of circumstances where the described scenario could be observed are court meetings and police interviews. Due to the stressful discomfort that these activities represent for crime victims, it is essential to determine whether the memories of these individuals are vulnerable to integrate misinformation during these procedures and the extent to which stress modulates this relationship.

Moreover, during the aftermath of a crime, victims are in a situation in which their memories for the event is constantly updated by exposure to printed, TV-related, online and radio-transmitted news articles on the reported crime. As such, the exposure to diverse perspectives of what transpired can also lead false information to become assembled to the original memory, for example about some features of the perpetrator's face. These projects could help authorities better understand how false information acquired after a crime can lead a victim to wrongly identify an individual as the crime perpetrator.

## 3.5. Future Directions for Studies on Sex Differences: Memory Reconsolidation and False Memories

Based on the reviewed literature within this section, employing the reconsolidation update mechanisms to future studies on memory and stress that account for sex differences represent a promising new avenue for memory research. Among various reasons, the incorporation of the sex variable in reconsolidation paradigms results is important to address because women tend to retrieve more efficiently life events (Andreano & Cahill, 2009), an effect attributed to their capacity to recall significantly more emotional information than men (Davis, 1999). Moreover, through these emotional interactions involving the reactivation of memories, the possibilities become higher in women to incorporate misattributions, false suggestion and biases to their original recollections (Bauste & Ferraro, 2004). Evidence for this increased vulnerability of women to reactivate information comes from statistics on depression, where women have been shown to possess an increased likelihood to ruminate about their problems (Nolen-Hoeksema, 1987; Strauss, Muday, McNall, & Wong, 1997). Thus, in order to properly address this matter, future research on stress and false memory reconsolidation should also account for sex differences. Furthermore, by also addressing the variables of menstrual cycle and gonadal hormones' variations on these proposed studies, our understanding of the differential ways in which stress and emotions influence memory accuracy in men and women could be expanded in a more comprehensive manner.

## 3.6. General Conclusion

This chapter has reviewed the interrelation between the fields of memory, stress and emotion. In doing so, novel approaches for the study of these phenomena have been suggested, as a means to offer researchers and clinicians in these areas an overview regarding the directions towards which the stress and memory field is heading at. Therefore, from the data presented here, it can be concluded that the stress and emotion fields have definitely taught us invaluable lessons with regards to the nature of memory on everyday experiences. As such, future studies should focus more on accounting for the role of sex differences in these phenomena, as well as on developing novel, ecologically valid memory paradigms that closely match reality. Doing so will undoubtedly help on translating more effectively the knowledge generated through these methods into the development and improvement of therapeutic approaches for memory-related clinical conditions.

## REFERENCES

Abercrombie, H. C., Speck, N. S., & Monticelli, R. M. (2006). Endogenous cortisol elevations are related to memory facilitation only in individuals who are emotionally aroused. *Psychoneuroendocrinology, 31*(2), 187-196.

American Psychiatric Association. (2000). *Diagnostic and statistical manual of mental disorders : DSM-IV-TR* (4th ed.). Washington, DC: American Psychiatric Association.

Anderson, M. C., Bjork, R. A., & Bjork, E. L. (1994). Remembering can cause forgetting: retrieval dynamics in long-term memory. *Journal of Experimental Psychology: Learning, Memory, and Cognition, 20*(5), 1063-1087.

Andreano, J. M., Arjomandi, H., & Cahill, L. (2008). Menstrual cycle modulation of the relationship between cortisol and long-term memory. *Psychoneuroendocrinology, 33*(6), 874-882.

Andreano, J. M., & Cahill, L. (2006). Glucocorticoid release and memory consolidation in men and women. *Psychological Science, 17*(6), 466-470.

Andreano, J. M., & Cahill, L. (2009). Sex influences on the neurobiology of learning and memory. *Learning and Memory, 16*(4), 248-266.

Axmacher, N., Draguhn, A., Elger, C. E., & Fell, J. (2009). Memory processes during sleep: beyond the standard consolidation theory. *Cellular and Molecular Life Sciences, 66*(14), 2285-2297.

Baratti, C. M., Boccia, M. M., & Blake, M. G. (2009). Pharmacological effects and behavioral interventions on memory consolidation and reconsolidation. *Brazilian Journal of Medical and Biological Research, 42*(2), 148-154.

Bauste, G., & Ferraro, F. R. (2004). Gender differences in false memory production. *Current Psychology, 23*(3), 238-244.

Bechara, A., & Naqvi, N. (2004). Listening to your heart: interoceptive awareness as a gateway to feeling. *Nature Neuroscience, 7*(2), 102-103.

Beckner, V. E., Tucker, D. M., Delville, Y., & Mohr, D. C. (2006). Stress facilitates consolidation of verbal memory for a film but does not affect retrieval. *Behavioral neuroscience, 120*(3), 518-527.

Best, R. M. (1968). Encoding of memory in the neuron. *Psychological Reports, 22*(1), 107-115.

Bloise, S. M., & Johnson, M. K. (2007). Memory for emotional and neutral information: gender and individual differences in emotional sensitivity. *Memory, 15*(2), 192-204.

Brewin, C. R. (2011). The nature and significance of memory disturbance in posttraumatic stress disorder. *Annual Review of Clinical Psychology, 7*, 203-227.

Brown, J. M. (2003). Eyewitness memory for arousing events: Putting things into context. *Applied Cognitive Psychology, 17*(1), 93-106.

Brunet, A., Orr, S. P., Tremblay, J., Robertson, K., Nader, K., & Pitman, R. K. (2008). Effect of post-retrieval propranolol on psychophysiologic responding during subsequent script-driven traumatic imagery in post-traumatic stress disorder. *Journal of Psychiatric Research, 42*(6), 503-506.

Brunet, A., Poundja, J., Tremblay, J., Bui, E., Thomas, E., Orr, S. P., et al. (2011). Trauma reactivation under the influence of propranolol decreases posttraumatic stress symptoms and disorder: 3 open-label trials. *Journal of Clinical Psychopharmacology, 31*(4), 547-550.

Buchanan, T. W., & Lovallo, W. R. (2001). Enhanced memory for emotional material following stress-level cortisol treatment in humans. *Psychoneuroendocrinology, 26*(3), 307-317.

Buss, C., Wolf, O. T., Witt, J., & Hellhammer, D. H. (2004). Autobiographic memory impairment following acute cortisol administration. *Psychoneuroendocrinology, 29*(8), 1093-1096.

Cahill, L., & Alkire, M. T. (2003). Epinephrine enhancement of human memory consolidation: interaction with arousal at encoding. *Neurobiology of Learning and Memory, 79*(2), 194-198.

Cahill, L., Gorski, L., & Le, K. (2003). Enhanced human memory consolidation with post-learning stress: interaction with the degree of arousal at encoding. *Learning and Memory, 10*(4), 270-274.

Cahill, L., Prins, B., Weber, M., & McGaugh, J. L. (1994). Beta-adrenergic activation and memory for emotional events. *Nature, 371*(6499), 702-704.

Chamberlain, S. R., Muller, U., Blackwell, A. D., Robbins, T. W., & Sahakian, B. J. (2006). Noradrenergic modulation of working memory and emotional memory in humans. *Psychopharmacology (Berl), 188*(4), 397-407.

Colrain, I. M., Mangan, G. L., Pellett, O. L., & Bates, T. C. (1992). Effects of post-learning smoking on memory consolidation. *Psychopharmacology (Berl), 108*(4), 448-451.

Conway, M. A., Anderson, S. J., Larsen, S. F., Donnelly, C. M., McDaniel, M. A., McClelland, A. G., et al. (1994). The formation of flashbulb memories. *Memory & Cognition, 22*(3), 326-343.

Conway, M. A., & Pleydell-Pearce, C. W. (2000). The construction of autobiographical memories in the self-memory system. *Psychological Review, 107*(2), 261-288.

Cook, N. J., Ng, A., Read, G. F., Harris, B., & Riad-Fahmy, D. (1987). Salivary cortisol for monitoring adrenal activity during marathon runs. *Hormone Research, 25*(1), 18-23.

Cornelisse, S., van Stegeren, A. H., & Joels, M. (2011). Implications of psychosocial stress on memory formation in a typical male versus female student sample. *Psychoneuroendocrinology, 36*(4), 569-578.

Davidson, C., Gopalan, R., Ahn, C., Chen, Q., Mannelli, P., Patkar, A. A., et al. (2007). Reduction in methamphetamine induced sensitization and reinstatement after combined pergolide plus ondansetron treatment during withdrawal. *European Journal of Pharmacology, 565*(1-3), 113-118.

Davis, P. J. (1999). Gender differences in autobiographical memory for childhood emotional experiences. *Journal of Personality and Social Psychology, 76*(3), 498-510.

Davis, M. H., & Gaskell, M. G. (2009). A complementary systems account of word learning: neural and behavioural evidence. *Philosophical Transactions of the Royal Society B: Biological Sciences, 364*(1536), 3773-3800.

de Quervain, D. J., Aerni, A., & Roozendaal, B. (2007). Preventive effect of beta-adrenoceptor blockade on glucocorticoid-induced memory retrieval deficits. *The American Journal of Psychiatry, 164*(6), 967-969.

de Quervain, D. J., Henke, K., Aerni, A., Treyer, V., McGaugh, J. L., Berthold, T., et al. (2003). Glucocorticoid-induced impairment of declarative memory retrieval is associated with reduced blood flow in the medial temporal lobe. *European Journal of Neuroscience, 17*(6), 1296-1302.

de Quervain, D. J., Roozendaal, B., Nitsch, R. M., McGaugh, J. L., & Hock, C. (2000). Acute cortisone administration impairs retrieval of long-term declarative memory in humans. *Nature Neuroscience, 3*(4), 313-314.

de Weerth, C., Zijl, R. H., & Buitelaar, J. K. (2003). Development of cortisol circadian rhythm in infancy. *Early Human Development, 73*(1-2), 39-52.

Dedovic, K., Renwick, R., Mahani, N. K., Engert, V., Lupien, S. J., & Pruessner, J. C. (2005). The Montreal Imaging Stress Task: using functional imaging to investigate the effects of perceiving and processing psychosocial stress in the human brain. *Journal of Psychiatry and Neuroscience, 30*(5), 319-325.

Dickerson, S. S., & Kemeny, M. E. (2004). Acute stressors and cortisol responses: a theoretical integration and synthesis of laboratory research. *Psychological Bulletin, 130*(3), 355-391.

Diekelmann, S., Wilhelm, I., Wagner, U., & Born, J. (2011). Elevated cortisol at retrieval suppresses false memories in parallel with correct memories. *Journal of Cognitive Neuroscience, 23*(4), 772-781.

Diergaarde, L., Schoffelmeer, A. N., & De Vries, T. J. (2008). Pharmacological manipulation of memory reconsolidation: towards a novel treatment of pathogenic memories. *European Journal of Pharmacology, 585*(2-3), 453-457.

Dolan, R. J. (2002). Emotion, cognition, and behavior. *Science, 298*(5596), 1191-1194.

Dudai, Y. (1996). Consolidation: fragility on the road to the engram. *Neuron, 17*(3), 367-370.

Duvarci, S., & Nader, K. (2004). Characterization of fear memory reconsolidation. *Journal of Neuroscience, 24*(42), 9269-9275.

Edginton, T., & Rusted, J. M. (2003). Separate and combined effects of scopolamine and nicotine on retrieval-induced forgetting. *Psychopharmacology (Berl), 170*(4), 351-357.

Eich, T. S., & Metcalfe, J. (2009). Effects of the stress of marathon running on implicit and explicit memory. *Psychonomic Bulletin and Review, 16*(3), 475-479.

Fishman, J. R., Hamburg, D. A., Handlon, J. H., Mason, J. W., & Sachar, E. (1962). Emotional and adrenal cortical responses to a new experience. Effect of social environment. *Archives of General Psychiatry, 6*, 271-278.

Frenkel, L., Maldonado, H., & Delorenzi, A. (2005). Memory strengthening by a real-life episode during reconsolidation: an outcome of water deprivation via brain angiotensin II. *European Journal of Neuroscience, 22*(7), 1757-1766.

Frenkel, L., Suarez, L. D., Maldonado, H., & Delorenzi, A. (2010). Angiotensin modulates long-term memory expression but not long-term memory storage in the crab Chasmagnathus. *Neurobiology of Learning and Memory, 94*(4), 509-520.

Gazzaniga, M. S. (2000). Cerebral specialization and interhemispheric communication: does the corpus callosum enable the human condition? *Brain, 123 ( Pt 7)*, 1293-1326.

Glickman, S. E. (1961). Perseverative neural processes and consolidation of the memory trace. *Psychological Bulletin, 58*, 218-233.

Graf, P., & Schacter, D. L. (1985). Implicit and explicit memory for new associations in normal and amnesic subjects. *Journal of Experimental Psychology: Learning, Memory, and Cognition, 11*(3), 501-518.

Henke, K. (2010). A model for memory systems based on processing modes rather than consciousness. *Nature Reviews Neuroscience, 11*(7), 523-532.

Hermans, D., Craske, M. G., Mineka, S., & Lovibond, P. F. (2006). Extinction in human fear conditioning. *Biological Psychiatry, 60*(4), 361-368.

Het, S., Ramlow, G., & Wolf, O. T. (2005). A meta-analytic review of the effects of acute cortisol administration on human memory. *Psychoneuroendocrinology, 30*(8), 771-784.

Hofer, M. A., Wolff, C. T., Friedman, S. B., & Mason, J. W. (1972). A psychoendocrine study of bereavement. II. Observations on the process of mourning in relation to adrenocortical function. *Psychosomatic Medicine, 34*(6), 492-504.

Hoge, E. A., Worthington, J. J., Nagurney, J. T., Chang, Y., Kay, E. B., Feterowski, C. M., et al. (2011). Effect of Acute Posttrauma Propranolol on PTSD Outcome and Physiological Responses During Script-Driven Imagery. *CNS Neuroscience & Therapeutics*, no-no.

Joels, M., Pu, Z., Wiegert, O., Oitzl, M. S., & Krugers, H. J. (2006). Learning under stress: how does it work? *Trends in Cognitive Sciences, 10*(4), 152-158.

Kalisch, R., Holt, B., Petrovic, P., De Martino, B., Kloppel, S., Buchel, C., et al. (2009). The NMDA agonist D-cycloserine facilitates fear memory consolidation in humans. *Cerebral Cortex, 19*(1), 187-196.

Kelley, J. B., Anderson, K. L., & Itzhak, Y. (2007). Long-term memory of cocaine-associated context: disruption and reinstatement. *Neuroreport, 18*(8), 777-780.

Kelly, M. M., Tyrka, A. R., Anderson, G. M., Price, L. H., & Carpenter, L. L. (2008). Sex differences in emotional and physiological responses to the Trier Social Stress Test. *Journal of Behavior Therapy and Experimental Psychiatry, 39*(1), 87-98.

Khan, A., Brodhead, A. E., Schwartz, K. A., Kolts, R. L., & Brown, W. A. (2005). Sex differences in antidepressant response in recent antidepressant clinical trials. *Journal of Clinical Psychopharmacology, 25*(4), 318-324.

Kindt, M., Soeter, M., & Vervliet, B. (2009). Beyond extinction: erasing human fear responses and preventing the return of fear. *Nature Neuroscience, 12*(3), 256-258.

Kirschbaum, C., Kudielka, B. M., Gaab, J., Schommer, N. C., & Hellhammer, D. H. (1999). Impact of gender, menstrual cycle phase, and oral contraceptives on the activity of the hypothalamus-pituitary-adrenal axis. *Psychosomatic Medicine, 61*(2), 154-162.

Kirschbaum, C., Pirke, K. M., & Hellhammer, D. H. (1993). The 'Trier Social Stress Test'--a tool for investigating psychobiological stress responses in a laboratory setting. *Neuropsychobiology, 28*(1-2), 76-81.

Kroes, M. C., Strange, B. A., & Dolan, R. J. (2010). Beta-adrenergic blockade during memory retrieval in humans evokes a sustained reduction of declarative emotional memory enhancement. *Journal of Neuroscience, 30*(11), 3959-3963.

Kuhlmann, S., & Wolf, O. T. (2005). Cortisol and memory retrieval in women: influence of menstrual cycle and oral contraceptives. *Psychopharmacology (Berl), 183*(1), 65-71.

Kuhlmann, S., & Wolf, O. T. (2006). Arousal and cortisol interact in modulating memory consolidation in healthy young men. *Behavioral Neuroscience, 120*(1), 217-223.

Lass-Hennemann, J., Kuehl, L. K., Schulz, A., Oitzl, M. S., & Schachinger, H. (2011). Stress strengthens memory of first impressions of others' positive personality traits. *PLoS One, 6*(1), e16389.

LeDoux, J.E. (2002). *Synaptic Self: How our brains become who we are.* New York: Penguin Books.

LeDoux, J.E. (2003). The self: clues from the brain. *Annals of the New York Academy of Sciences, 1001,* 295-304.

Lepage, M., Habib, R., & Tulving, E. (1998). Hippocampal PET activations of memory encoding and retrieval: the HIPER model. *Hippocampus, 8*(4), 313-322.

Lester, D. (2006). Sex differences in completed suicide by schizophrenic patients: a meta-analysis. *Suicide and Life-Threatening Behavior, 36*(1), 50-56.

Liddle, G. W. (1966). Analysis of circadian rhythms in human adrenocortical secretory activity. *Archives of Internal Medicine, 117*(6), 739-743.

Liu, D. L., Graham, S., & Zorawski, M. (2008). Enhanced selective memory consolidation following post-learning pleasant and aversive arousal. *Neurobiology of Learning and Memory, 89*(1), 36-46.

Loftus, E. F. (1996). Memory distortion and false memory creation. *Bulletin of the American Academy of Psychiatry & the Law, 24*(3), 281-295.

Loftus, E. F., Miller, D. G., & Burns, H. J. (1978). Semantic integration of verbal information into a visual memory. *Journal of Experimental Psychology: Human Learning & Memory, 4*(1), 19-31.

Lupien, S. J. (2009). Brains under stress. *Canadian Journal of Psychiatry, 54*(1), 4-5.

Lupien, S. J., & Brière, S. (2000). Memory and Stress. In F. G. (Ed.), *The encyclopedia of stress.* San Diego: Academic Press.

Lupien, S. J., & McEwen, B. S. (1997). The acute effects of corticosteroids on cognition: integration of animal and human model studies. *Brain Research Reviews, 24*(1), 1-27.

Lupien, S. J., McEwen, B. S., Gunnar, M. R., & Heim, C. (2009). Effects of stress throughout the lifespan on the brain, behaviour and cognition. *Nature Reviews Neuroscience, 10*(6), 434-445.

Lupien, S. J., Wilkinson, C. W., Briere, S., Menard, C., Ng Ying Kin, N. M., & Nair, N. P. (2002). The modulatory effects of corticosteroids on cognition: studies in young human populations. *Psychoneuroendocrinology, 27*(3), 401-416.

Maheu, F. S., Joober, R., Beaulieu, S., & Lupien, S. J. (2004). Differential effects of adrenergic and corticosteroid hormonal systems on human short- and long-term declarative memory for emotionally arousing material. *Behavioral Neuroscience, 118*(2), 420-428.

Manning, C. A., Parsons, M. W., & Gold, P. E. (1992). Anterograde and retrograde enhancement of 24-h memory by glucose in elderly humans. *Behavioral and Neural Biology, 58*(2), 125-130.

Marin, M.F., Hupbach, A., Maheu, F. S., Nader, K., & Lupien, S. J. (2011). Metyrapone administration reduces the strength of an emotional memory trace in a long-lasting manner. *The Journal of Clinical Endocrinology & Metabolism, 96*(8), E1221-1227.

Marin, M.F., Pilgrim, K., & Lupien, S. J. (2010). Modulatory effects of stress on reactivated emotional memories. *Psychoneuroendocrinology, 35*(9), 1388-1396.

Mason, J. W. (1968a). A review of psychoendocrine research on the pituitary-adrenal cortical system. *Psychosomatic Medicine, 30*(5), Suppl:576-607.

Mason, J. W. (1968b). A review of psychoendocrine research on the sympathetic-adrenal medullary system. *Psychosomatic Medicine, 30*(5), Suppl:631-653.

Mason, J. W. (1971). A re-evaluation of the concept of "non-specificity" in stress theory. *Journal of Psychiatric Research, 8*(3), 323-333.

McGaugh, J. L. (1966). Time-dependent processes in memory storage. *Science, 153*(742), 1351-1358.

McGaugh, J. L. (1972). The search for the memory trace. *Annals of the New York Academy of Sciences, 193*, 112-123.

McGaugh, J. L. (2000). Memory--a century of consolidation. *Science, 287*(5451), 248-251.

McLean, C. P., & Anderson, E. R. (2009). Brave men and timid women? A review of the gender differences in fear and anxiety. *Clinical Psychology Review, 29*(6), 496-505.

McRae, A. L., Saladin, M. E., Brady, K. T., Upadhyaya, H., Back, S. E., & Timmerman, M. A. (2006). Stress reactivity: biological and subjective responses to the cold pressor and Trier Social stressors. *Human Psychopharmacology, 21*(6), 377-385.

Milad, M. R., Goldstein, J. M., Orr, S. P., Wedig, M. M., Klibanski, A., Pitman, R. K., et al. (2006). Fear conditioning and extinction: influence of sex and menstrual cycle in healthy humans. *Behavioral Neuroscience, 120*(6), 1196-1203.

Milad, M. R., Zeidan, M. A., Contero, A., Pitman, R. K., Klibanski, A., Rauch, S. L., et al. (2010). The influence of gonadal hormones on conditioned fear extinction in healthy humans. *Neuroscience, 168*(3), 652-658.

Misanin, J. R., Miller, R. R., & Lewis, D. J. (1968). Retrograde amnesia produced by electroconvulsive shock after reactivation of a consolidated memory trace. *Science, 160*(3827), 554-555.

Monfils, M. H., Cowansage, K. K., Klann, E., & LeDoux, J. E. (2009). Extinction-reconsolidation boundaries: key to persistent attenuation of fear memories. *Science, 324*(5929), 951-955.

Müller, G. E., & Pilzecker, A. (1900). Experimentelle Beiträge zur Lehre vom Gedächtnis. *Z. Psychol. Ergänzungsband, 1*, 1-300.

Myers, K. M., & Davis, M. (2007). Mechanisms of fear extinction. *Molecular Psychiatry, 12*(2), 120-150.

Nader, K., Schafe, G. E., & Le Doux, J. E. (2000). Fear memories require protein synthesis in the amygdala for reconsolidation after retrieval. *Nature, 406*(6797), 722-726.

Nader, K., Schafe, G. E., & LeDoux, J. E. (2000). The labile nature of consolidation theory. *Nature Reviews Neuroscience, 1*(3), 216-219.

Newhouse, P. A., Dumas, J., Wilkins, H., Coderre, E., Sites, C. K., Naylor, M., et al. (2010). Estrogen treatment impairs cognitive performance after psychosocial stress and monoamine depletion in postmenopausal women. *Menopause, 17*(4), 860-873.

Nielson, K. A., & Powless, M. (2007). Positive and negative sources of emotional arousal enhance long-term word-list retention when induced as long as 30 min after learning. *Neurobiology of Learning and Memory, 88*(1), 40-47.

Nielson, K. A., Yee, D., & Erickson, K. I. (2005). Memory enhancement by a semantically unrelated emotional arousal source induced after learning. *Neurobiology of Learning and Memory, 84*(1), 49-56.

Nolen-Hoeksema, S. (1987). Sex differences in unipolar depression: evidence and theory. *Psychological Bulletin, 101*(2), 259-282.

O'Carroll, R. E., Drysdale, E., Cahill, L., Shajahan, P., & Ebmeier, K. P. (1999). Stimulation of the noradrenergic system enhances and blockade reduces memory for emotional material in man. *Psychological Medicine, 29*(5), 1083-1088.

Olff, M., Langeland, W., Draijer, N., & Gersons, B. P. (2007). Gender differences in posttraumatic stress disorder. *Psychological Bulletin, 133*(2), 183-204.

Pavlov, I. P. (1927). *Conditioned Reflexes: An Investigation of the Physiological Activity of the Cerebral Cortex.* New York: Oxford University Press.

Payne, J. D., Jackson, E. D., Hoscheidt, S., Ryan, L., Jacobs, W. J., & Nadel, L. (2007). Stress administered prior to encoding impairs neutral but enhances emotional long-term episodic memories. *Learning and Memory, 14*(12), 861-868.

Payne, J. D., Nadel, L., Allen, J. J., Thomas, K. G., & Jacobs, W. J. (2002). The effects of experimentally induced stress on false recognition. *Memory, 10*(1), 1-6.

Pillemer, D. B., Wink, P., DiDonato, T. E., & Sanborn, R. L. (2003). Gender differences in autobiographical memory styles of older adults. *Memory, 11*(6), 525-532.

Pitman, R. K., Milad, M. R., Igoe, S. A., Vangel, M. G., Orr, S. P., Tsareva, A., et al. (2011). Systemic mifepristone blocks reconsolidation of cue-conditioned fear; propranolol prevents this effect. *Behavioral Neuroscience, 125*(4), 632-638.

Poole, G., Hunt Matheson, D., & , & Cox, D. N. (2012). *The psychology of health and health care: A canadian perspective* (4th edition ed.). Toronto: Pearson Prentice Hall.

Prado-Alcala, R. A., & Quirarte, G. L. (2007). [The consolidation of memory, one century on]. *Revista de Neurología, 45*(5), 284-292.

Preuss, D., & Wolf, O. T. (2009). Post-learning psychosocial stress enhances consolidation of neutral stimuli. *Neurobiology of Learning and Memory, 92*(3), 318-326.

Przybyslawski, J., Roullet, P., & Sara, S. J. (1999). Attenuation of emotional and nonemotional memories after their reactivation: role of beta adrenergic receptors. *Journal of Neuroscience, 19*(15), 6623-6628.

Putman, P., Van Honk, J., Kessels, R. P., Mulder, M., & Koppeschaar, H. P. (2004). Salivary cortisol and short and long-term memory for emotional faces in healthy young women. *Psychoneuroendocrinology, 29*(7), 953-960.

Quirk, G. J., & Milad, M. R. (2010). Neuroscience: Editing out fear. *Nature, 463*(7277), 36-37.

Quirk, G. J., Pare, D., Richardson, R., Herry, C., Monfils, M. H., Schiller, D., et al. (2010). Erasing fear memories with extinction training. *Journal of Neuroscience, 30*(45), 14993-14997.

Raes, F., Hermans, D., Williams, J. M., & Eelen, P. (2007). A sentence completion procedure as an alternative to the Autobiographical Memory Test for assessing overgeneral memory in non-clinical populations. *Memory, 15*(5), 495-507.

Robinson, M. J., Armson, M., & Franklin, K. B. (2011). The effect of propranolol and midazolam on the reconsolidation of a morphine place preference in chronically treated rats. *Frontiers in Behavioral Neuroscience, 5*, 42.

Robinson, M. J., & Franklin, K. B. (2010). Reconsolidation of a morphine place preference: impact of the strength and age of memory on disruption by propranolol and midazolam. *Behavioral Brain Research, 213*(2), 201-207.

Romer, S., Schulz, A., Richter, S., Lass-Hennemann, J., & Schachinger, H. (2011). Oral cortisol impairs implicit sequence learning. *Psychopharmacology (Berl), 215*(1), 33-40.

Rusted, J. M., & Alvares, T. (2008). Nicotine effects on retrieval-induced forgetting are not attributable to changes in arousal. *Psychopharmacology (Berl), 196*(1), 83-92.

Schacter, D. (1987). Implicit memory: history and current status. *Journal of Experimental Psychology: Learning, Memory, and Cognition, 13*, 501-518.

Schacter, D. (2001). *The sevens sins of memory: How the mind forgets and remembers.* Houghton Mifflin Company, New York.

Schiller, D., Monfils, M. H., Raio, C. M., Johnson, D. C., Ledoux, J. E., & Phelps, E. A. (2010). Preventing the return of fear in humans using reconsolidation update mechanisms. *Nature, 463*(7277), 49-53.

Schiller, D., & Phelps, E. A. (2011). Does reconsolidation occur in humans? *Frontiers in Behavioral Neuroscience, 5*, 24.

Schmaus, B. J., Laubmeier, K. K., Boquiren, V. M., Herzer, M., & Zakowski, S. G. (2008). Gender and stress: differential psychophysiological reactivity to stress reexposure in the laboratory. *International Journal of Psychophysiology, 69*(2), 101-106.

Schoofs, D., & Wolf, O. T. (2009). Stress and memory retrieval in women: no strong impairing effect during the luteal phase. *Behavioral Neuroscience, 123*(3), 547-554.

Schwabe, L., Haddad, L., & Schachinger, H. (2008). HPA axis activation by a socially evaluated cold-pressor test. *Psychoneuroendocrinology, 33*(6), 890-895.

Schwabe, L., Joels, M., Roozendaal, B., Wolf, O. T., & Oitzl, M. S. (2011). Stress effects on memory: An update and integration. *Neuroscience and Biobehavioral Reviews.*

Schwabe, L., Romer, S., Richter, S., Dockendorf, S., Bilak, B., & Schachinger, H. (2009). Stress effects on declarative memory retrieval are blocked by a beta-adrenoceptor antagonist in humans. *Psychoneuroendocrinology, 34*(3), 446-454.

Schwabe, L., & Wolf, O. T. (2009). The context counts: congruent learning and testing environments prevent memory retrieval impairment following stress. *Cognitive, Affective, & Behavioral Neuroscience, 9*(3), 229-236.

Schwabe, L., & Wolf, O. T. (2010). Stress impairs the reconsolidation of autobiographical memories. *Neurobiology of Learning and Memory, 94*(2), 153-157.

Schwartz, M. (1976). Averaged evoked responses and the encoding of perception. *Psychophysiology, 13*(6), 546-553.

Schwegler, K., Ettlin, D., Buser, I., Klaghofer, R., Goetzmann, L., Buddeberg, C., et al. (2010). Cortisol reduces recall of explicit contextual pain memory in healthy young men. *Psychoneuroendocrinology, 35*(8), 1270-1273.

Seidlitz, L., & Diener, E. (1998). Sex differences in the recall of affective experiences. *Journal of Personality and Social Psychology, 74*(1), 262-271.

Selye, H. (1998). A syndrome produced by diverse nocuous agents. 1936. *Journal of Neuropsychiatry & Clinical Neurosciences, 10*(2), 230-231.

Smeets, T., Giesbrecht, T., Jelicic, M., & Merckelbach, H. (2007). Context-dependent enhancement of declarative memory performance following acute psychosocial stress. *Biological Psychology, 76*(1-2), 116-123.

Smeets, T., Jelicic, M., Merckelbach, H., Peters, M., Fett, A., Taverniers, J., et al. (2006). Enhanced memory performance on an internal-internal source monitoring test following acute psychosocial stress. *Behavioral Neuroscience, 120*(6), 1204-1210.

Smeets, T., Otgaar, H., Candel, I., & Wolf, O. T. (2008). True or false? Memory is differentially affected by stress-induced cortisol elevations and sympathetic activity at consolidation and retrieval. *Psychoneuroendocrinology, 33*(10), 1378-1386.

Smeets, T., Sijstermans, K., Gijsen, C., Peters, M., Jelicic, M., & Merckelbach, H. (2008). Acute consolidation stress enhances reality monitoring in healthy young adults. *Stress, 11*(3), 235-245.

Soetens, E., Casaer, S., D'Hooge, R., & Hueting, J. E. (1995). Effect of amphetamine on long-term retention of verbal material. *Psychopharmacology (Berl), 119*(2), 155-162.

Soetens, E., D'Hooge, R., & Hueting, J. E. (1993). Amphetamine enhances human-memory consolidation. *Neuroscience Letters, 161*(1), 9-12.

Soeter, M., & Kindt, M. (2010). Dissociating response systems: erasing fear from memory. *Neurobiology of Learning and Memory, 94*(1), 30-41.

Southwick, S. M., Davis, M., Horner, B., Cahill, L., Morgan, C. A., 3rd, Gold, P. E., et al. (2002). Relationship of enhanced norepinephrine activity during memory consolidation to enhanced long-term memory in humans. *The American Journal of Psychiatry, 159*(8), 1420-1422.

Spaniol, J., Davidson, P. S., Kim, A. S., Han, H., Moscovitch, M., & Grady, C. L. (2009). Event-related fMRI studies of episodic encoding and retrieval: meta-analyses using activation likelihood estimation. *Neuropsychologia, 47*(8-9), 1765-1779.

Squire, L. R. (1986). Mechanisms of memory. *Science, 232*(4758), 1612-1619.

Squire, L. R. (1992). Memory and the hippocampus: a synthesis from findings with rats, monkeys, and humans. *Psychological Reviews, 99*(2), 195-231.

Squire, L. R., & Zola, S. M. (1996). Structure and function of declarative and nondeclarative memory systems. *Proc Natl Acad Sci U S A, 93*(24), 13515-13522.

Stickgold, R., Hobson, J. A., Fosse, R., & Fosse, M. (2001). Sleep, learning, and dreams: off-line memory reprocessing. *Science, 294*(5544), 1052-1057. doi: 10.1126/science.1063530 294/5544/1052 [pii]

Strange, B. A., & Dolan, R. J. (2004). Beta-adrenergic modulation of emotional memory-evoked human amygdala and hippocampal responses. *Proceedings of the National Academy of Sciences of the United States of America, 101*(31), 11454-11458.

Strange, B. A., Hurlemann, R., & Dolan, R. J. (2003). An emotion-induced retrograde amnesia in humans is amygdala- and beta-adrenergic-dependent. *Proceedings of the National Academy of Sciences of the United States of America, 100*(23), 13626-13631.

Strauss, J., Muday, T., McNall, K., & Wong, M. (1997). Response Style Theory revisited: Gender differences and stereotypes in rumination and distraction. *Sex Roles, 36*(11-12), 771-792.

Strober, M. (2004). Pathologic fear conditioning and anorexia nervosa: on the search for novel paradigms. *International Journal of Eating Disorders, 35*(4), 504-508.

Stroud, L. R., Tanofsky-Kraff, M., Wilfley, D. E., & Salovey, P. (2000). The Yale Interpersonal Stressor (YIPS): affective, physiological, and behavioral responses to a novel interpersonal rejection paradigm. Annals of Behavioral Medicine, *22*(3), 204-213.

Tolin, D. F., & Foa, E. B. (2006). Sex differences in trauma and posttraumatic stress disorder: a quantitative review of 25 years of research. *Psychological Bulletin, 132*(6), 959-992.

Tollenaar, M. S., Elzinga, B. M., Spinhoven, P., & Everaerd, W. (2009a). Autobiographical memory after acute stress in healthy young men. *Memory, 17*(3), 301-310.

Tollenaar, M. S., Elzinga, B. M., Spinhoven, P., & Everaerd, W. (2009b). Immediate and prolonged effects of cortisol, but not propranolol, on memory retrieval in healthy young men. *Neurobiology of Learning and Memory, 91*(1), 23-31.

Tollenaar, M. S., Elzinga, B. M., Spinhoven, P., & Everaerd, W. (2009c). Psychophysiological responding to emotional memories in healthy young men after cortisol and propranolol administration. *Psychopharmacology, 203*(4), 793-803.

Tulving, E. (1972). Episodic and semantic memory. In E. Tulving, Donaldson, W. (Ed.), *Organization of memory*. Oxford, England: Academic Press.

Tulving, E. (1987). Multiple memory systems and consciousness. *Human Neurobiology, 6*(2), 67-80.

Usall, I. R. J. (2001). [Gender differences in mood disorders. A literature review]. *Actas Españolas de Psiquiatría, 29*(4), 269-274.

Van Cauter, & Turek, F. (1995). Endocrine and other biological rhythms. In D. G. LJ (Ed.), *Endocrinology* (pp. 2487– 2548). Philadelphia: Saunders.

van Wingen, G., Mattern, C., Verkes, R. J., Buitelaar, J., & Fernandez, G. (2008). Testosterone biases automatic memory processes in women towards potential mates. *Neuroimage, 43*(1), 114-120.

van Wingen, G., van Broekhoven, F., Verkes, R. J., Petersson, K. M., Backstrom, T., Buitelaar, J., et al. (2007). How progesterone impairs memory for biologically salient stimuli in healthy young women. *Journal of Neuroscience, 27*(42), 11416-11423.

Wade, K. A., Sharman, S. J., Garry, M., Memon, A., Mazzoni, G., Merckelbach, H., et al. (2007). False claims about false memory research. *Consciousness and Cognition, 16*(1), 18-28; discussion 29-30.

Wagner, U., Degirmenci, M., Drosopoulos, S., Perras, B., & Born, J. (2005). Effects of cortisol suppression on sleep-associated consolidation of neutral and emotional memory. *Biological Psychiatry, 58*(11), 885-893.

Wagner, U., Gais, S., & Born, J. (2001). Emotional memory formation is enhanced across sleep intervals with high amounts of rapid eye movement sleep. *Learning and Memory, 8*(2), 112-119.

Wais, P. E. (2008). FMRI signals associated with memory strength in the medial temporal lobes: a meta-analysis. *Neuropsychologia, 46*(14), 3185-3196.

Wang, S. H., & Morris, R. G. (2010). Hippocampal-neocortical interactions in memory formation, consolidation, and reconsolidation. *Annual Review of Psychology, 61*, 49-79, C41-44.

Westenberg, P. M., Bokhorst, C. L., Miers, A. C., Sumter, S. R., Kallen, V. L., van Pelt, J., et al. (2009). A prepared speech in front of a pre-recorded audience: subjective, physiological, and neuroendocrine responses to the Leiden Public Speaking Task. *Biological Psychology, 82*(2), 116-124.

Wheeler, M. A., Stuss, D. T., & Tulving, E. (1997). Toward a theory of episodic memory: the frontal lobes and autonoetic consciousness. *Psychological Bulletin, 121*(3), 331-354.

Williams, J. M., & Broadbent, K. (1986). Autobiographical Memory in Suicide Attempters. *Journal of Abnormal Psychology, 95*(2), 144-149.

Windhorst, C. (2005). The slave model of autobiographical memory. *Cognitive Processing, 6*(4), 253-265.

Wolf, O. T., Convit, A., McHugh, P. F., Kandil, E., Thorn, E. L., De Santi, S., et al. (2001). Cortisol differentially affects memory in young and elderly men. *Behavioral Neuroscience, 115*(5), 1002-1011.

Yonelinas, A. P., Parks, C. M., Koen, J. D., Jorgenson, J., & Mendoza, S. P. (2011). The effects of post-encoding stress on recognition memory: examining the impact of skydiving in young men and women. *Stress, 14*(2), 136-144.

Zhai, H., Wu, P., Chen, S., Li, F., Liu, Y., & Lu, L. (2008). Effects of scopolamine and ketamine on reconsolidation of morphine conditioned place preference in rats. *Behavioral Pharmacology, 19*(3), 211-216.

Zhu, B., Chen, C., Loftus, E. F., Lin, C., He, Q., Li, H., et al. (2010). Individual differences in false memory from misinformation: cognitive factors. *Memory, 18*(5), 543-555.

In: Psychology of Memory                    ISBN: 978-1-61942-633-7
Editors: Dannie M. Hendrix and Orval Holcomb      © 2012 Nova Science Publishers, Inc.

*Chapter 3*

# RECOGNITION MEMORY – DISSOCIATING RECOLLECTION AND FAMILIARITY BY FUNCTIONAL CONNECTIVITY OF NEURAL NETWORKS AND GENETIC VARIANCE

## *Denise Dörfel[*][1] and Anke Karl[2]*

[1]Division of Mind and Brain Research, Department of Psychiatry
and Psychotherapy Charité Universitätsmedizin Berlin, Campus Mitte, Charitéplatz 1,
D-10117, Berlin, Germany
[2]University of Exeter, School of Psychology, Clinical Psychology,
Washington Singer Laboratories, Perry Road, EX4 4QG, UK

## INTRODUCTION

The importance of the medial temporal lobes (MTL) for declarative memory, i.e., the memory for events (episodic memory) and facts (semantic memory) was first highlighted by the case of the famous and well-studied patient H.M. He showed severe deficits in remembering his past and was unable to learn new facts and memorize events, that happened after undergoing brain surgery to remove most parts of his medial temporal lobes (MTL) in 1953. Semantic Facts (semantic memory) and autobiographical events (episodic memory) together comprise the declarative memory (Squire, 2004). Interestingly, his performance in procedural memory (where mainly motor skills are stored, e.g. Squire, 2004) and working memory (a system that maintains and stores information in the short term, e.g. Baddeley, 2003) was not affected; i.e.,. H.M. could learn new motor skills but he could not remember that he had learned them. Decades of research have since revealed a network including the medial temporal lobes, in particular the hippocampus, but also the prefrontal cortex and medial and lateral parietal cortex to be involved in remembering events of one's past; i.e., episodic memory (Aggleton and Brown, 2006; Ally, Simons, McKeever, Peers, and Budson, 2008; Burgess, Maguire, and O'Keefe, 2002; Burgess, Maguire, Spiers, and O'Keefe, 2001;

---
[*] Email: denise.doerfel@charite.de

Eichenbaum, 2000; Maguire, 2001). Previously stored declarative information can be tested using different procedures (Schacter and Tulving, 1994). During *Free Recall* a subject would be asked to study a list of words and then, some time later, to recall as many words that they can remember. Free Recall strongly depends on an intact episodic memory. In *Recognition* tasks subjects are asked to decide whether a given item was previously presented at a list of items (old) or whether it was not presented in the original list (new). Surprisingly, H.M. had comparable recognition rates to healthy controls, when the procedures to assess recognition were adapted to his skills (for instance when he could view pictures longer before the recognition response, Freed and Corkin, 1988; Freed, Corkin, and Cohen, 1987). This raised the question if recognition is not only based on episodic memory, like free recall, but relies on an independent process involving other brain structures besides the MTL. Models of recognition memory that state two independent processes, recollection and familiarity (Yonelinas, 2002), might give an explanation of the findings in H.M.s recognition performance. A person is able to judge whether the recognition of a previously learned item is based on a feeling of familiarity that the item was seen before, or because he or she remembers additional details about the study event, such as when or where it occurred (episodic memory). Recollection sometimes is referred to as contextual memory or relational based recognition, whereas familiarity is called non-contextual memory or item-based recognition (not to be confused with semantic memory). Thus, given this dissociation in recognition memory, patients with severe amnesia, as a result of selective brain damage in the MTL, might still have almost intact recognition memory, maintaining some of their quality of life. Extensive research has studied the nature of recollection and familiarity and revealed anatomical and functional substrates of recognition memory in the brain. This research basically developed two opposing views about the relationship between recollection and familiarity and about the association with hippocampal function (Wixted and Squire, 2010; Yonelinas, Aly, Wang, and Koen, 2010).

In this chapter we will review this debate and we will present evidence, by others and our own research, in favor for the two process assumption.

Before we will introduce the two major opposing recognition memory models, we want to give an overview about different procedures to measure recognition memory, in the next section. This might be helpful in understanding how the models predict the empirical data.

## DIFFERENT PARADIGMS FOR MEASUREMENT OF RECOLLECTION AND FAMILIARITY

The most common procedures that are used to measure recollection and familiarity are the Process-Dissociation Procedure (PDP; Jacoby, 1991), the Remember-Know procedure (R/K; Tulving, 1985) and the Receiver Operating Characteristics (ROC; Yonelinas, 2002).

In the PDP, participants study a list of items in two different contexts, and subsequently have to complete two recognition tests. In the inclusion test, participants are asked to identify an item as old if they previously encountered it, regardless of the context in which it was presented. In the exclusion test, participants are asked to identify an item as old only if it was presented in one of the two study contexts. Thus, only the exclusion test is based on recollective memory. A potential limitation of the PDP is that it uses a rather strict measure of recollection — the ability to determine in which study context the item was presented. However, recollecting some other aspect of the study event (e.g., "I remember coughing as the item was studied") would not be measured as recollection. Another potential problem with the procedure is that it uses different test instructions in the inclusion and exclusion conditions, and this may influence the parameter estimates (Yonelinas, 2002). This procedure will not play a further role in this chapter.

In the ROC procedure participants are required to rate the confidence of their recognition memory responses – hence a varying response criterion in the signal detection process. Then a curve is formed by plotting hits and false alarms against one another as a function of confidence. Limitations of the ROC procedure are that it is dependent on several assumptions and it needs a large number of responses from each subject (Yonelinas, 2002).

In the R/K procedure (Eldridge, Sarfatti, and Knowlton, 2002; Gardiner, Ramponi, and Richardson-Klavehn, 2002; Tulving, 1985), subjects are instructed to indicate when a recognition judgment is based on recollection (R – Remember) and when it is based on familiarity in the absence of recollection (K – Know). This method assumes that remember and know are independent, and thus it is consistent with most dual-process models (Yonelinas, 2002). One advantage of this approach is that it provides a very inclusive measure of recollection in the sense that recollection is not limited to what a subject can recollect on PDP test. However, relying on retrospective and introspective subjective reports may be problematic if subjects have no direct access to the processes that support recognition or if their reports are inaccurate. Studies that compared estimates of recollection and familiarity derived from R/K responses with those from other measures, like PDP or item association tests, though, suggest that the R/K procedure results in comparable measures of recollection and familiarity, (Yonelinas, 2001a, 2001b; Yonelinas, 2002).

## MODELS OF RECOGNITION MEMORY: ONE OR TWO PROCESSES?

### Dual Process Models of Recognition Memory

There are different models that assume recognition memory judgments can be based on two distinct forms of memory (for a review see Yonelinas, 2002; Yonelinas, 2010). These models almost commonly assume that first, recollection and familiarity are independent memory retrieval processes; second, recollection is a threshold retrieval process thought to reflect the retrieval of specific information about a study event; third, familiarity is a signal detection process reflecting a continuous index of memory strength; and fourth, the hippocampus is critical for recollection, but not familiarity.

A prominent model, the dual-process signal-detection (DPSD) model combines all these features (Yonelinas, 2001a). In a recognition task, subjects have to decide, whether items from a list have been previously studied. This list contains targets (items that really were on the previous list) as well as foils (items that weren't on the previous list). In the DPSD model, familiarity is assumed to reflect a signal detection process. When recognition only relies on a familiarity process, the memory strength (or confidence) distribution of targets and foils (new items not on the previously learned list) follows a Gaussian distribution. When the memory strength of a studied item is above an individual response criterion, the item is judged as having been recently studied ('old'). Hence, individuals select the most familiar items as previously studied (see review by Yonelinas et al., 2010). In studies using the Receiver Operating Characteristic (ROC) procedure individuals are additionally required to rate their confidence. It is assumed that, familiarity strength varies across a wider range of confidence, with the more familiar items leading to more confident recognition responses. In an ROC curve (i.e., hit rate mapped against false alarm rate) changes in the response criterion would produce a curved, symmetrical ROC, but only if individuals were exclusively relying on familiarity (Yonelinas and Parks, 2007).

On the other hand, recollection reflects a threshold retrieval process whereby individuals recall detailed qualitative information about studied events (e.g., remembering where or when a person was seen before; Yonelinas, 2002). Recollection does not follow a signal detection process because individuals do not recollect qualitative information about every item that they have studied. Rather, on some items, recollection fails to provide any information that discriminates between old and new items. This process is not supported by signal detection theory. It is assumed that recollection will lead to relatively high confidence responses and an ROC curve would look like a hockey-stick with a major linear component when a recognition process relies exclusively on recollection (see Yonelinas et al., 2010). If recognition uses both familiarity and recollection, an ROC curve would be produced that is u-shaped comparable to a familiarity curve, but rather asymmetrical. Empirical investigations in item recognition ROCs strongly support the predictions of the DPSD model. The ROCs are almost always curved and asymmetrical (for review, see Yonelinas and Parks, 2007). Using the R/K distinction, remember responses can be used as a measure of recollection (R), and know responses can be used as a measure of familiarity in the absence of recollection (Yonelinas and Jacoby, 1995). However, another view states that remember and know do not provide measures of distinct recognition processes, rather they reflect high and low confidence and mainly distinguishes strong memories from weak memories (not recollection from familiarity) (Dunn, 2004; Wixted and Mickes, 2010). Therefore, Yonelinas et al. (2010) advise to be cautious with the R/K procedure because under some conditions individuals make 'remember' responses even when they cannot report any specific details about the study event (eg. Rotello, Macmillan, Reeder, and Wong, 2005; Yonelinas, 2001b). In that instance, the procedure cannot be expected to accurately separate recollection and familiarity and this has likely been responsible for much of the described controversy.

The DPSD model predicts two independent processes, which underlie recognition memory. It therefore provides a framework for the understanding of empirical data in healthy subjects and amnesic patients. Additionally, it might be used to test the neural correlates of recognition memory, as will be described later in this chapter.

## One Process Models of Recognition Memory

Alternative views on the recognition process state that single process theories are more viable than dual process theories of recognition memory. For example, Squire, Wixted, and Clark (2007) argue that the distinction between recollection and familiarity is a distinction between strong and weak memories. They do not assume that only familiarity could be described by a classical signal detection approach but rather that familiarity lies at the lower end of a continuum of confidence ratings, whereas recollection reflects the higher end. However, even in the absence of source information, a strong familiarity signal supports high confidence and accuracy (Wixted, Mickes, and Squire, 2010). To combine the signal detection with a dual process approach (Squire et al., 2007; Wixted, 2007) proposed the Unequal Variance Signal Detection (UVSD) model. The authors assume that the distributions of targets and foils in strong memory conditions (i.e. recollection) show an unequal variance whereas weak memory conditions (i.e. familiarity) show an equal distribution. For example, it has been suggested that because of encoding variability, the old item (target) variance will be greater than the new item (foil) variance. The dual process model also predicts greater old than new item variance, but because they assume that new item responses rely on familiarity, whereas old item responses rely on familiarity and recollection (Yonelinas and Parks, 2007).

As with the DPSD approach, applying the UVSD allows an explanation of the differences in Receiver Operating Characteristic (ROC) curves found in recognition memory. The authors suggest that a symmetrical ROC curve, which typically is plotted using only familiarity responses, reflects weak memory rather than the absence of recollection. Asymmetrical ROCs, which result from the plotting of both recollection and familiarity responses, only implies that the target and foil distributions have unequal variance, which is generally a sign of a strong memory. According to some authors (Squire et al., 2007; Wixted, 2007) those ROCs do not imply that recognition is supported by recollection, as suggested by (Yonelinas, 2002). Newer signal-detection models (e.g. Shimamura and Wickens, 2009; Wixted et al., 2010) state that individual test items can be associated with low, medium, or high degrees of recollection and correspondingly low, medium, or high degrees of confidence and accuracy. From this perspective, recollection does not reflect a threshold (or categorical) process, it is described as a continuous process similar to familiarity, except it involves the retrieval of source information, which familiarity does not. From this perspective, memory strength is determined by hierarchical relational binding of feature units, and the strength of memory is construed as the amount of content retrieved.

In summary, there is scientific evidence for both models and the dispute has not yet been solved (Parks and Yonelinas, 2007; Wixted, 2007; Wixted, 2007; Wixted et al., 2010). Empirical evidence for a dual process dissociation in recognition memory comes from studies that investigated deep vs. shallow encoding, generation vs. reading of a word, divided attention, and benzodiazepine administration at encoding. At the retrieval stage, there is evidence for a much more pronounced dissociation between recollection and familiarity by variables like speed, divided attention, change of the perceptual characteristics of a word between study and test, forgetting rates, manipulations of the processing fluency of test items, and the occurrence of false recognition. Additional variables which affect recollection, but leave familiarity largely unaffected, include normal aging, selective hippocampal damage (see patient H.M.) and to some extend frontal lobe damage (for a summary see Yonelinas, 2002). In contrast, Wixted (2007) provided evidence that the UVSD shows a better fit to several empirical data sets than the DPSD.

An important avenue to investigate the mechanisms involved in recollection and familiarity and to shed light on the debate is the investigation of underlying brain circuitries. In the next section we review the neural correlates of recognition memory and how these findings slightly support dual process models, even though one process models and the unequal variance model might not be rejected by the findings.

## Neural Correlates of Recognition Memory and How Findings Support Dual Process Models

The DPSD model predicts that if familiarity reflects a signal detection process, then patients with severe recollection impairments should produce ROCs that are curved and symmetrical (similar to the ROC curves that would be produced if healthy subjects exclusively rely on familiarity). There is empirical evidence supporting this assumption (for review see Yonelinas et al., 2010). Interestingly, a patient with a lesion that did not impact the hippocampus (as is usually the case in amnesia) but rather affected the surrounding perirhinal cortex (PRc) suffered a selective deficit in familiarity. This offered the opportunity to test the prediction of the DPSD model that an individual who had a selective deficit in familiarity would show asymmetrical and flatter ROC curve than typically observed in item recognition. This patient's item recognition ROCs were indeed found to be flattened, precisely as predicted by the DPSD model (Bowles et al., 2007).

A review of neuroimaging and lesion data by Skinner and Fernandes (2007) concluded that there is strong evidence for recollection related activity in anterior and superior frontal regions. Most of the studies utilized the R/K dissociation and report that remember responses are related to a network of brain regions consisting of left dorsolateral prefrontal cortex, and left middle and superior frontal gyrus, (Eldridge, Engel, Zeineh, Bookheimer, and Knowlton, 2005; Eldridge, Knowlton, Furmanski, Bookheimer, and Engel, 2000; Fenker, Schott, Richardson-Klavehn, Heinze, and Duzel, 2005; Henson, Rugg, Shallice, Josephs, and Dolan, 1999; Wheeler and Buckner, 2004; Woodruff, Johnson, Uncapher, and Rugg, 2005). Activity in the anterior prefrontal cortex has been interpreted to reflect successful retrieval of source information (Dobbins and Wagner, 2005), which supports the assumption that remember reflects a recollection process. Whereas activation in right frontal lobe areas has been related to attentional control processes (Cabeza et al., 2003), which would also be necessary for familiarity responses.

Regarding the activation of brain regions during familiarity, Skinner and Fernandes (2007) reported less concordance across the studies. About one third of the studies reported inferior temporal gyrus/fusiform gyrus, parietooccipital cortex, right superior frontal gyrus and precuneus activation during familiarity. Overlapping activity during both recollection and familiarity responses was shown across most of the studies in the right dorsolateral prefrontal cortex (DLPFC) and left precuneus (BA 7). Right DLPFC involvement in familiarity is interpreted as an additional checking and verification behavior (Henson, Rugg, Shallice, and Dolan, 2000) or as an ongoing exhaustive search for details to accompany the feelings of familiarity with an item (Wheeler and Buckner, 2004). These findings might be interpreted as evidence for processes that contribute to both recollection and familiarity maybe in controlling memory strength which would support one process models.

Several studies found strong activation in the lateral parietal cortex associated with recollection responses (Eldridge et al., 2000; Fenker et al., 2005; Henson et al., 1999; Sharot, Delgado, and Phelps, 2004; Skinner and Fernandes, 2007; Wheeler and Buckner, 2004; Woodruff et al., 2005; Yonelinas, Otten, Shaw, and Rugg, 2005). Additionally, Vilberg and Rugg (2008) strongly support the idea that retrieval-related activity in inferior parietal cortex is not only related to correct recognition, but closely tied to successful recollection. The authors assume that the inferior parietal cortex supports the sustained focusing of attention on the contents of working memory, where recollected information is maintained (Ravizza,

Delgado, Chein, Becker, and Fiez, 2004). Left lateral parietal cortex reflects an old/new effect (Kahn, Davachi, and Wagner, 2004; Konishi, Wheeler, Donaldson, and Buckner, 2000; Rugg and Curran, 2007; Rugg, Otten, and Henson, 2002; Wheeler and Buckner, 2003). Thus, it might be activated by both processes. In line with this, a meta-analysis by Vilberg and Rugg (2008) identified a region concentrated around the intraparietal sulcus, the superior parietal cortex (BA 7/40), related to familiarity judgments, and an area localized in the posterior part of inferior parietal cortex (BA 39) consistently associated with recollection based responses. This points to a dissociation between these two processes in the parietal lobe.

Skinner and Fernandes (2007) report another parietal region, the left precuneus (BA 7), to be active during both recollection and familiarity answers. However, there are conflicting results with respect to precuneus activations in recognition memory. It has been implicated to be a key component of a cortical network subserving episodic retrieval (Burgess et al., 2001; Cavanna and Trimble, 2006). By contrast, Vilberg and Rugg (2008) could not report an association of precuneus activity with recollection based responses, the relatively few precuneus effects in their meta-analysis were rather related to familiarity-driven recognition. Nonetheless, the authors suggest that the region may play some role in recollective processing, although what this role might be is currently ambiguous.

In summary, there is some evidence for different brain regions associated with either recollection or familiarity. However, this might not provide enough validation of dual process models. Most of the studies contrast recollection against familiarity responses. Thus, the results indicate that a certain brain region is more active during recollection than familiarity and this might also be true when recollection would reflect a strong memory strength and familiarity a weak memory strength response. However, a study by Yonelinas et al. (2005) did contrast recollection-familiarity judgments to confidence ratings of the recognized items. Thus, the authors could separate high confidence familiarity responses (in other words a strong memory trace based on familiarity) from recollection responses, which are always supposed to be high confident memories.

They found medial and middle frontal, precentral, cingulate, superior and middle temporal, as well as postcentral activation related to recollection responses and not merely to strong memories, which would support one process models of recognition memory. In line with this, Vilberg and Rugg (2007) could not identify any brain region where recognition memory is only related to memory strength, and Skinner and Fernandes (2007) conclude that brain regions sub-serving recollection are not simply those mediating highly confident memory decisions.

In Figure 1 we have plotted the results of our own automated large-scale database searches on neurosynth.org (Yarkoni, Poldrack, Nichols, Van Essen, and Wager, 2011[1]) with the terms 'recollection' and 'familiarity' onto a template brain and confirm the findings of the neural correlates of recognition memory.

When searching for brain activations related to a given term, NeuroSynth performs a meta-analysis by comparing the coordinates reported for studies with and without the term of interest.

To further review the neural correlates of recognition memory and how they contribute to the dual process view we will next have a closer look on the role of the medial temporal lobes.

---

[1] NeuroSynth is a platform for the automatic synthesis of the results of many different neuroimaging studies.

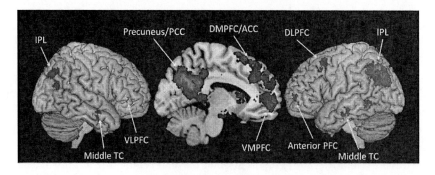

Figure 1. Meta-analytic results of a term based database search (neurosynth.org). Terms: recollection (in red), familiarity (in blue).

## Role of the Medial Temporal Lobe

A core assumption of dual process models of recognition memory is that recollection is dependent on the medial temporal lobes and it is therefore predicted that amnesiacs should exhibit more deficits in recollection than familiarity (Yonelinas, 2002). More precisely, Aggleton and Brown (1999) suggest that relatively selective hippocampal damage disrupts recollection, but not familiarity which instead is dependent on perirhinal cortex. Thus, extensive damage to the temporal lobe can reduce recall (recollection) and recognition (recollection and familiarity) to the same extent (Stark and Squire, 2000), whereas selective hippocampal lesions only reduce recollection (Holdstock et al., 2002). Also, Skinner and Fernandes (2007) concluded that both recollection and familiarity based responses rely on the MTL, although recollection may have a greater reliance on this region than familiarity.

To describe the MTL contribution to recognition memory in more detail, we take a closer look at models by Aggleton and Brown (Aggleton and Brown, 1999; John P. Aggleton and Brown, 2006; Brown and Aggleton, 2001) and Eichenbaum et al. (2007).The authors argue that the hippocampus is responsible for recollection processes, but the perirhinal cortex supports familiarity. Eichenbaum et al. (2007) hypothesize that neocortical input to the perirhinal cortex (PRC) and to the lateral entorhinal area (LEA) comes from association areas that process unimodal sensory information about qualities of objects ("what"). Supporting this assumption, studies that use electrophysiological recordings in monkeys showed that neurons in the anterior parahippocampal region, including the perirhinal cortex, respond strongly to pictures or objects that are new but only weakly when items have been seen previously (for a review see Brown and Aggleton, 2001; Xiang and Brown, 1998). Crucially, fMRI studies assessing non-contextual recognition in humans found decreased activation in the anterior parahippocampal region which contains the perirhinal cortex (e.g. Daselaar, Fleck, and Cabeza, 2006; Fernandez and Tendolkar, 2006; Henson, Cansino, Herron, Robb, and Rugg, 2003). Furthermore, Haskins, Yonelinas, Quamme, and Ranganath (2008) showed, that the perirhinal cortex supports encoding of novel associations in a unitized manner and subsequent associative recognition based on familiarity.

Eichenbaum et al. (2007) further describe that neocortical input to the parahippocampal cortex (PHC) and adjacent medial entorhinal areas (MEA) comes from regions that process polymodal spatial ("where") information. The "what" and "where" signals converge in the hippocampus together with the context in which the items were experienced. Back projections from the hippocampus to the PRC-LEA (the "What" pathway) support recognition judgments of familiarity. Recovery of context and item associations ("what" and "where") are available in the hippocampus and through back projections to the PHC-MEA and constitute the experience of recollection.

Eichenbaum et al. (2007) assume that fMRI activations in the anterior parahippocampal gyrus reflect activations in the perirhinal and lateral entorhinal areas and signal in the posterior parahippocampal region activation of the parahippocampal cortex with or without medial entorhinal area activation. Their review of fMRI results strongly supports the model about the functional organization of the MTL. Studies using ROC and R/K tasks showed that hippocampal and to some extent posterior parahippocampal activation during both encoding and retrieval is consistently higher for recollected than non-recollected items and is generally insensitive to changes in familiarity strength (e.g. Dolcos, LaBar, and Cabeza, 2005; Eldridge et al., 2000; Montaldi, Spencer, Roberts, and Mayes, 2006; Yonelinas et al., 2005). Complementary, anterior parahippocampal activation is generally correlated with familiarity and rarely correlated with item recollection (e.g. Gonsalves, Kahn, Curran, Norman, and Wagner, 2005; Henson et al., 1999). However, the study by Gonsalves et al. (2005) points to a memory strength function in posterior parahippocampal as well as perirhinal cortex. In another meta-analysis, Wais (2008) even concluded that fMRI data alone cannot distinguish between dual process models, which assume that recollection is a threshold process, and signal detection models, which assume that both processes follow a continuous strength signal. This problem still has to be solved.

However, other empirical data further supports the hypothesis of a functional dissociation between recollection and familiarity within the MTL. In a study of healthy aging, Yonelinas et al. (2007) showed that reductions in hippocampal volume were associated with declines in recollection, but not familiarity. Conversely, differences in cortical volume within the entorhinal cortex (EC) were related to familiarity, but not recollection. In line with this, Wolk et al. (2011) reported that recollection was most strongly related to hippocampal volume, whereas familiarity was most directly related to the surrounding entorhinal and perirhinal volume.

In line with this, the same term based meta-analyses that was already described above (neurosynth.org, Yarkoni et al., 2011) revealed that recollection is more associated with hippocampal and posterior parahippocampal whereas familiarity is more related to parahippocampal activation. However, the meta-analysis did not find familiarity activations in anterior parahippocampal regions, hence perirhinal cortex, which is contradictory to Eichenbaum et al.'s model (Figure 2).

In opposition to the dual process theories of recognition memory, Squire et al. (2007) argue that the distinction between recollection and familiarity can be described more effectively by the distinction between strong and weak memories. The authors relate strong memories to hippocampal activity, regardless of whether the item retrieval is accompanied by recollection of context or a feeling of familiarity. Thus, (Squire et al., 2007) summarizes evidence, that selective hippocampal damage impairs recall (which is supposed to specifically reflect recollection) to the same extent than recognition (which comprises familiarity as well as recollection; e.g. Manns, Hopkins, Reed, Kitchener, and Squire, 2003; Rutishauser, Mamelak, and Schuman, 2006). Additionally, a study by Bengner and Malina (2008) found fewer know responses in temporal lobe epilepsy patients with hippocampal sclerosis (HS) as compared with patients without HS. Additionally, there are findings disproving the assumption that in patients with hippocampal damage recollection, measured by associative or source recognition, is impaired while familiarity (single item recognition) is spared (Gold et al., 2006; Stark, Bayley, and Squire, 2002).

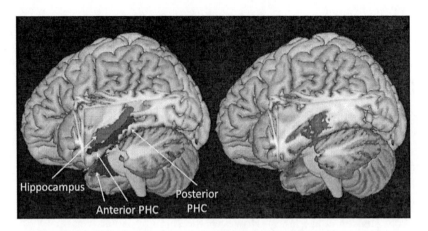

Figure 2. Comparison of the recognition memory model by Eichenbaum et al. (2007) (left, hippocampus in red, parahippocampal cortex in blue) with the results of a term based meta-analysis with the terms recollection (red) and familiarity (blue) (neurosynth.org, (Yarkoni et al., 2011). The cutout of the template brain shows the left MTL.

Other studies, however, show intact recognition memory but affected recall in patients with hippocampal damage (e.g. Holdstock et al., 2002; Mayes, Holdstock, Isaac, Hunkin, and Roberts, 2002; Vargha-Khadem et al., 1997), or severe damage of the connections of hippocampus to diencephalon and other cortical regions (Gilboa et al., 2006). Direct investigations of recollection and familiarity in patients with hippocampal damage revealed pronounced deficits in recollection but not in familiarity (Turriziani, Fadda, Caltagirone, and Carlesimo, 2004; Turriziani, Serra, Fadda, Caltagirone, and Carlesimo, 2008).

Additionally, Skinner and Fernandes (2007) conclude in their review of brain lesion data the estimate of recollection was significantly lower in the MTL compared to non-MTL patient group, though the estimate of familiarity-based responses did not differ across patient groups. Concerning recognition memory in healthy subjects, Shrager, Kirwan, and Squire (2008) found both hippocampus and perirhinal cortex activity during encoding positively correlated to the memory strength of subsequently recognized items as indicated by confidence ratings of the subjects. This is in line with one process models. One limitation of this finding is that the authors only investigated this correlation in the high confidence ratings (4, 5 and 6) but not for the whole memory strength continuum, as would be suggested by signal detection approaches. Additionally, the authors did not collect a recollection vs. familiarity judgment in this study to contrast these two approaches. Another study by Sperling et al. (2003) found that only high confidence recollection in relation to low confidence recollection was associated with anterior hippocampal activity at encoding. However, there was no activation within the hippocampal formation in incorrect, but high confidence memory encoding vs. incorrect but low confidence memory encoding. Therefore, Sperling et al. (2003) suggest that in associative memory formation the anterior hippocampus possibly is binding together items of information rather than creating a feeling of confidence. Other studies (Montaldi et al., 2006; Yonelinas et al., 2005) found that the hippocampus is only activated in recollection compared to high confidence familiarity judgments. Furthermore the hippocampal formation showed no increase in activity with increasing familiarity confidence.

Signal detection (familiarity) and threshold (recollection) assumptions of the dual process model were also tested in a neurocomputational model of the medial temporal lobes (Elfman et al., 2008), the complementary learning systems (CLS) model (Norman and O'Reilly, 2003). The model states that recollection is dependent on the hippocampus, whereas familiarity is subserved by the medial temporal lobe cortex (MTLC), which includes the perirhinal, entorhinal, and parahippocampal cortices. Elfman et al. (2008) found that the hippocampal process produces threshold output functions that lead to U-shaped zROCs (z-transformed ROC-curves) similar to the recollection zROCs (see Yonelinas et al., 2010), whereas the cortical process produces Gaussian signal detection functions and linear zROCs, like familiarity zROCs, which perfectly fits empirical data from source and item recognition studies.

Overall, lesion, fMRI and computational data support functionally distinct processes at the brain systems level underlying recollection and familiarity and are thus in line with the dual-process model (Aggleton and Brown, 1999; Aggleton and Brown, 2006; Aggleton et al., 2005; Brown and Aggleton, 2001; Eichenbaum et al., 2007; Parks and Yonelinas, 2007; Skinner and Fernandes, 2007; Yonelinas et al., 2010).

## *Connectivity of Brain Regions in Recognition Memory*

So far there is support for some brain regions that are exclusively related to recollection and few brain regions that seem to be especially related to familiarity. Additionally, there is growing evidence for overlapping brain regions which are related to both processes. However, a description of how those brain regions are acting in concert to constitute a recollection or a familiarity judgment is still missing.

Functional connectivity of the hippocampus related to recognition memory is described by models of the medial temporal lobes (e.g. Aggleton and Brown, 2006; Eichenbaum et al., 2007). The model by Eichenbaum et al. (see above) suggests that perirhinal cortex receives information from association areas ("what"), whereas the parahippocampal cortex receives input from areas that process polymodal spatial ("where") information. The "what" pathways support judgments of familiarity. The converging of "what" and "when" however, together with the context in which an item was experienced, is supported by the hippocampus and constitutes the experience of recollection. Aggleton and Brown (Aggleton and Brown, 1999; John P. Aggleton and Brown, 2006) established an extended hippocampal system of episodic memory including a medial and a lateral part. The medial part comprises the subiculum, medial mammillary nucleus, anterior medial and anterior ventral thalamic nuclei, and the ventral tegmental nucleus. Via the thalamus it is linked to the prefrontal cortex, including the orbitofrontal, the medial and the dorsolateral part. The lateral part of the extended hippocampal system consists of the presubiculum, postsubiculum, lateral mammillary nucleus, anterior dorsal thalamic nucleus, and the dorsal tegmental nucleus. Both subsystems project over the thalamus to the posterior cingulate/retrosplenial cortex and support episodic memory encoding and retrieval, which is strongly impaired in amnesiacs with lesions comprising at least one of the parts of the system (Aggleton et al., 2000; Dusoir, Kapur, Byrnes, McKinstry, and Hoare, 1990; Harding, Halliday, Caine, and Kril, 2000 ; Spiers, Maguire, and Burgess, 2001; Van der Werf et al., 2003). Further support for the Aggleton and Brown model of episodic memory comes from fMRI studies which consistently report activations in the hippocampus, the dorsolateral and anterior prefrontal cortex, and posterior cingulate/retrosplenial cortex (Fenker et al., 2005; Henson et al., 1999; Jager et al., 2009; Skinner and Fernandes, 2007; Wheeler and Buckner, 2004; Woodruff et al., 2005). But those studies did not investigate the connectivity of those structures. A connectivity study by Habib, McIntosh, Wheeler, and Tulving (2003) investigated the correlations of the hippocampus with other brain regions during encoding of either situationally novel (encountered for the first time at encoding) or situationally familiar (encountered twice before earlier in the experiment) items. The authors showed large-scale neural networks that distinguish between the encoding of situationally novel and situationally familiar items but the same region of the hippocampus participated in these different networks. This would support an overlapping function of the hippocampus in novelty detection as well as context-dependent familiarity during encoding. In an EEG study, Burgess et al. (2002) found that recollection but not familiarity was associated with greater functional connectivity in the gamma frequency range between frontal and parietal sites. An fMRI experiment by Idaka et al. (2006) showed that the inferior frontal gyrus and the intraparietal sulcus were crucial to conscious recollection (deep-encoding of items) whereas activity of the right parietal region was associated to familiarity-based judgment (after shallow encoding of items). Then they conducted structural equation modeling and found that, in the left hemisphere, frontoparietal connectivity was only significant in the deep-encoding condition, which might reflect a stronger connectivity between left frontal and parietal regions during a recollection based process. However, they did not directly contrasted recollection and familiarity on a retrieval level.

The meta-analysis by Skinner and Fernandes (2007) points out the lack of connectivity studies concerning recollection vs. familiarity processes at the stage of memory retrieval. They propose that the connection between frontal, parietal areas and hippocampus may be stronger during recollection than during familiarity responses. They consider it also possible that familiarity is associated with stronger connections between frontal, parietal and perirhinal regions. Further studies have to prove these assumptions.

An interesting study showed that the hippocampal formation is functionally correlated with the inferior parietal lobule, retrosplenial cortex extending into posterior cingulate and precuneus, medial prefrontal cortex, superior frontal cortex, and lateral temporal cortex extending to the temporal pole in a resting state task (Vincent et al., 2006). The authors then reanalyzed the data of two recollection vs. familiarity studies (Shannon and Buckner, 2004; Wheeler and Buckner, 2004). This analysis revealed that the resting state network reported above has strong similarities to the activated recollection areas in the two studies. Thus, one could hypothesize that the brain activations that are related to recollection also work in concert as a recollection-network.

In line with this, the so called Default Mode Network (DMN), a specific network of conjointly fluctuating brain regions in the resting stage, offers the chance to reveal some functional networks involved in recognition memory, because there is striking overlap between the DMN network and commonly recognition related structures (Vincent, Kahn, Snyder, Raichle, and Buckner, 2008; Vincent et al., 2006). Thus, the presence of such a correlation in the DMN (as coherent spontaneous activity between brain regions) would establish a functional relationship which could be available in other functional states, too.

In line with this, Buckner, Andrews-Hanna, and Schacter (2008) have obtained results that suggest that the Precuneus/posterior Cingulate Cortex (pC/PCC), medial PFC and the bilateral intraparietal lobule (IPL), together constitute a "core hub" in the DMN. Additionally, the only interactions between the medial temporal lobes and the rest of the default mode network seem to be between the left MTL and the pC/pCC and the left temporal cortex, respectively (Fransson and Marrelec, 2008; Vincent et al., 2006). Interestingly, a recent fMRI study has demonstrated reduced functional connectivity between the precuneus/PCC and the MTL in patients with amnesic mild cognitive impairment (Sorg et al., 2007; Zhou et al., 2008). The precuneus is a major association area and has wide-spread connections to other cortical and subcortical areas that may subserve a variety of behavioral functions including episodic memory retrieval (for a review see Cavanna and Trimble, 2006).

Overall, functional connectivity of brain regions during recognition memory remains unclear. Particularly, the question whether the different processes of recollection and familiarity can be detected in different, but possibly overlapping, functional brain networks has to be solved.

Therefore, in our own fMRI study (Dörfel, Werner, Schaefer, von Kummer, and Karl, 2009), we aimed to address the issue of functional connectivity of brain regions during recognition memory in humans. In particular, we investigated whether the two different processes of recollection and familiarity are associated with distinct functional brain networks. We will present this study in the next section.

## STUDY: EVIDENCE FOR A DISSOCIATION IN FUNCTIONAL CONNECTIVITY BETWEEN RECOLLECTION AND FAMILIARITY

In our own fMRI study, we hypothesized that only a network supporting recollection involves connectivity of the hippocampus. We also explored the question of whether overlapping areas, i.e. those activated during both recollection and familiarity, show strong functional connectivity to both separate recognition systems.

Thirty right-handed healthy subjects (19 female, mean 23.3 years) participated in this study. The participants had to complete a two-step R/K Procedure (similar to Eldridge et al., 2000). In the study phase, 30 minutes prior to fMRI scanning, subjects had to learn a list of 150 nouns within 7 minutes. Following the procedure in Eldridge et al., the subjects were not explicitly instructed to use any specific strategy. In the recognition phase during fMRI scanning, the subjects were shown 108 old words and 27 new words. In each five-second trial, subjects first saw the word for 3 seconds and within that time period had to decide whether or not they recognized it (first response). Subsequently, for recognized items, they were prompted to decide whether they remembered or knew the item within 2 seconds (second response). This procedure prevents participants from treating R/K judgments as measures of confidence (Hicks and Marsh, 1999) and assures that the Know category is not used for guess responses only (Eldridge et al., 2002).

fMRI analysis revealed different brain areas related to recollection and familiarity, respectively. Recollection based responses activated regions in a left anterior precuneus region and the left angular gyrus which is part of the inferior parietal lobule (IPL). The activated IPL region corresponds to a cluster which is also reported by a meta-analysis of parietal contributions to recollection (Vilberg and Rugg, 2008), and is supposed to reflect something akin to the episodic buffer described by Baddeley (2000), hence maybe a top-down control of working memory content. In contrast, right dorsolateral prefrontal cortex (rDLPFC) was activated only during familiarity based responses. This region is supposed to support familiarity by means of a postretrieval monitoring process or by additional searching for details of the item (Henson et al., 1999; Wheeler and Buckner, 2004).

Previous fMRI studies have demonstrated that precuneus/posterior cingulate areas show greater activity during recollection based judgments (Henson et al., 1999; Wagner, Shannon, Kahn, and Buckner, 2005) or during episodic memory (Burgess et al., 2001). We also found a posterior cingulate/anterior precuneus region activated during recollection based answers. Interestingly, a recent study by Peters et al. (2009) found a very similar active cluster in the left precuneus/posterior cingulate/retrosplenial region during associative as compared to feature-based encoding. Thus, it could be assumed that a defined area in the anterior precuneus plays a role in recollection processes by retrieving spatial or other contextual details (Burgess et al., 2001; Takahashi, Ohki, and Kim, 2008).

In a regions of interest (ROIs) analysis we found activation clusters in the left parahippocampal gyrus and in the bilateral hippocampi only during recollection (see Figure 3). No activation could be found in the perirhinal cortex. Thus, our data also point to the important role of the hippocampal and posterior parahippocampal activations during recollection memory. This is in accordance with models of episodic memory in the MTL (Aggleton and Brown 2006; Eichenbaum, et al. 2007). However, we could not support the hypotheses of perirhinal involvement in familiarity based recognition (Aggleton and Brown 2006).

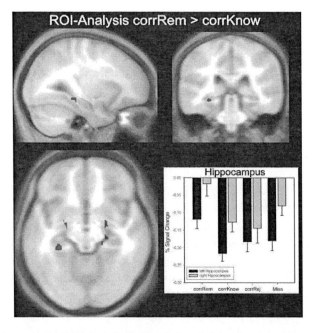

Figure 3. Region of Interest (ROI) analysis including left and right hippocampus and parahippocampal gyrus as well as the perirhinal cortex (BA 35 and 36, borders showed in green lines). BOLD responses in the left posterior parahippocampal gyrus and bilateral hippocampus are higher during corrRem responses compared to corrKnow. Threshold $T_{116} = 2.96$, $p_{corrected} < .05$ (FWE), k = 5. Neither hippocampal nor parahippocampal activation could be found during Knowing. No activation could be found in the perirhinal cortex ($p_{uncorrected} > .001$). (Reprinted from European Journal of Neuroscience, vol. 30, Dörfel et al., 2009, Distinct brain networks in recognition memory share a defined region in the precuneus, p.1952, © 2009 with permission from Wiley Blackwell Publishing Ltd).

Additionally, we found one activation cluster in the medial precuneus (see Figure 4) which was associated with both recollection and familiarity judgments. Although Vilberg and Rugg (2008) related precuneus activations only to familiarity based responses, our findings are in line with findings that link precuneus activation to recollection and episodic memory (Fletcher et al., 1995; Henson et al., 1999; Shallice et al., 1994; Wagner et al., 2005). Tey are also in line with the meta-analysis of Skinner and Fernandes (2007) who found in particular the left precuneus to be associated with both recollection and familiarity. This implies that the precuneus plays an important role in both processes and, on closer inspection, possibly may be divided into different parts maintaining specific functions in recognition memory. For instance, it has been found that the medial part of the bilateral anterior region of the precuneus is more related to episodic memory functions and memory-related imagery activations, whereas the anteromedial part of the precuneus shows a self-reference related function, and the posterior part an Old vs. New memory effect (Cavanna and Trimble, 2006).

In a psychophysiological interaction analysis (PPI) with the overlapping precuneus cluster as a seed region we wanted to gather information about functional connectivity of this region under recollection and familiarity, respectively.

The analysis showed a recollection network including the left middle temporal gyrus and the right superior temporal pole (extending to insula), as well as the left and right hippocampus positively connected with the medial precuneus (see Figure 5).

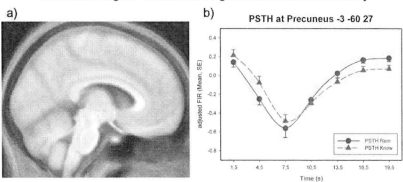

Figure 4. Region of the precuneus that is associated with both Remember (corrRem> Miss) and Know responses (corrKnow> Miss). a) Activation cluster at -3, -60, 27 projected onto a mean image of 56 subjects; $T_{116} = 3.16$, $p_{uncorrected} < .001$. b) Peristimulus time histogram (PSTH) of BOLD signal during corrRem and corrKnow. (Reprinted from European Journal of Neuroscience, vol. 30, Dörfel et al., 2009, Distinct brain networks in recognition memory share a defined region in the precuneus, p.1952, © 2009 with permission from Wiley Blackwell Publishing Ltd)..

This is similar to a study by Takahashi et al. (2008) who found functional connectivity between the medial precuneus and the MTL in a recognition task maybe indicating the retrieval of relational memory. As the lateral temporal gyrus has been implicated in non-relational item-based memory (Konishi, Asari, Jimura, Chikazoe, and Miyashita, 2006), we suggest that at least some recollection trials are accompanied by a fast item-based retrieval process. This familiarity process possibly occurs first and then initiates an additional search for contextual, relational information to come to a correct recognition judgment based on recollection. Interestingly, connectivity studies consider the posterior cingulate/precuneus area as a "core hub" in the so called Default Mode Network (DMN; Buckner et al., 2008;

Fransson and Marrelec, 2008). Vincent et al. (2006) describe the DMN as a network which is strongly related to recollection responses and comprises the hippocampal formation, retrosplenial cortex extending into the posterior cingulate gyrus/precuneus, inferior parietal lobule, medial prefrontal cortex, superior frontal cortex and lateral temporal cortex extending to the temporal pole. Additionally, a DMN study by Fransson and Marrelec (2008) found that the MTL is only connected to the precuneus/posterior cingulate cortex and the left temporal cortex. Additionally, studies of episodic memory (e.g., Burgess et al., 2001; Ranganath, Heller, Cohen, Brozinsky, and Rissman, 2005) have found a network of precuneus, retrosplenial, parahippocampal and hippocampal areas during episodic retrieval as well as encoding.

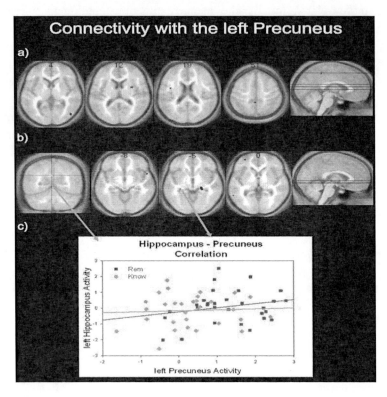

Figure 5. Regions that are functional connected to left Precuneus (b), yellow) during a) Knowing (corrKnow> Miss) and b) Remembering (corrRem> Miss). T > 3.40, $p_{uncorrected}$<.001, extent threshold k = 5. The threshold was lowered to p < .005 in the analysis of negatively connected areas during Remembering. The BOLD time series of these areas are positively (blue) or negatively (red) correlated with the time series of the precuneus during Remember and Know, respectively. c) Region of Interest analysis of the hippocampus: Scatterplots and regression lines of the hippocampus-precuneus correlation in Remembering and Knowing, respectively. (Reprinted from European Journal of Neuroscience, vol. 30, Dörfel et al., 2009, Distinct brain networks in recognition memory share a defined region in the precuneus, p.1953, © 2009 with permission from Wiley Blackwell Publishing Ltd).

Our results do not support a stronger connectivity between perirhinal and parietal regions during familiarity, as suggested by Skinner and Fernandes (2007). Familiarity responses rather were characterized by stronger connectivity of the medial precuneus with the left insula, the right occipital gyrus (BA 18 and 19), and the right middle temporal gyrus. No hippocampal or parahippocampal activity was associated with the precuneus. It is noticeable that we found more areas related to sensory processing, such as BA 18, and insula (for a summary of sensory processing areas see Nieuwenhuys, et al. 2008) in the familiarity network. This is in line with the observation that, compared to recollection, familiarity is more dependent on perceptual processes (Yonelinas and Levy, 2002). Additionally, Montaldi et al. (2006) and Yonelinas et al. (2005) also found that the insula is involved in generating a sense of familiarity.

To sum up, our data and previous findings (for a summary see Cavanna and Trimble, 2006) suggest that the precuneus may be involved in "deciding" whether a recognition response can utilize context information about the item, which would involve hippocampus (recollection), or has to be based on mere perceptual features of the item (familiarity), possibly in cooperation with self-referential and memory-related imagery functions that are also located in the anteromedial precuneus. In line with this, our findings suggest that the anterior medial precuneus area is the region that facilitates the link between episodic memory (hippocampus), nonrelational item-based memory (middle temporal gyrus), the processing of stimuli from the environment coming from primary and secondary sensory areas (somatosensory cortex, insula, BA18) and attention related structures which are associated with retrieval mode (i.e. BA 10, which was negatively correlated to the precuneus in the recollection network). Support for this assumption comes from Naghavi and Nyberg (2005) who showed that BA 7 (including precuneus) is commonly activated across different functions like attention, episodic memory retrieval, working memory and conscious perception. Thus, we revealed new evidence for a dissociation between recollection and familiarity on a brain systems level, but also showed that central brain regions like the precuneus are included in both networks.

We also hypothesized that it is possible to find a dissociation between both recognition processes on a more molecular level. It is suggested, that hippocampal plasticity and long term potentiation (LTP) are the basis of episodic memory (e.g. Neves, Cooke, and Bliss, 2008). Therefore, we assume that recollection, which is hippocampus-dependent, must be more affected by a deficit in hippocampal plasticity. To analyze a factor which directly contributes to LTP and brain plasticity in the hippocampus, we investigated individual differences in Brain Derived Neurotrophic Factor (BDNF) function (as represented by genetic polymorphism) on recognition memory. Before we describe the study in more detail, we want to give a short overview about LTP and the impact of BDNF on LTP.

## LONG TERM POTENTIATION, HIPPOCAMPUS AND MEMORY

One of the basic principles that enable memory formation in the human brain is synaptic Long Term Potentiation (LTP; Bear, Connors, and Paradiso, 2007; Bear and Malenka, 1994; Lynch, 2004).

The early phase of LTP (E-LTP, LTP 1; Blundon and Zakharenko, 2008; Lynch, 2004; Malenka and Bear, 2004; Raymond, 2007) - that lasts approximately 60 minutes – is realized by a NMDA-dependent postsynaptic $Ca2+$ rise and this activates protein kinase C (PKC) and calcium-calmodulin-dependent protein kinase II (CaMKII) (for a detailed description see Lynch, 2004). The activation of the protein kinases lead to a) phosphorylation of the AMPA receptor which results in an enhanced effectiveness of this receptor and/or b) the insertion of entirely new AMPA receptors into the postsynaptic membrane. It remains unclear whether presynaptic changes contribute to E-LTP (Malenka and Bear, 2004; Zakharenko et al., 2003). There is some evidence that the neurotrophin BDNF (Brain Derived Neurotrophic Factor) may contribute to such a process as a retrograde messenger (Poo, 2001) but see (Zakharenko et al., 2003). Additionally, recent data have shown that LTP in the CA-region of the hippocampus consists of the rapidly developing postsynaptic component and a slowly developing presynaptic component (Bayazitov, Richardson, Fricke, and Zakharenko, 2007). Late-phase LTP is believed to mimic the processes involved in memory consolidation. This phase of synaptic strengthening requires protein synthesis (LTP2; Raymond, 2007) and a change in gene transcription (LTP3; Raymond, 2007). The process of gene expression is regulated by transcription factors like cAMP response element binding protein (CREB), which is activated by protein kinase A (PKA), CaMKIV, and mitogen-activated protein kinase (MAPK). Morphological changes that have been reported to accompany late LTP include growth of new dendritic spines, enlargement of preexisting spines and their associated postsynaptic densities (PSDs), which possibly already occurs during E-LTP (Lynch, Rex, and Gall, 2007), and the splitting of single PSDs and spines into two functional synapses (for review see Lynch, 2004; Malenka and Bear, 2004). These changes are supposed to account for the observed long-term strengthening of synapses and therefore may contribute to the consolidation of memories from short-term to long-term memory.

There are multiple modulators on molecular levels that are able to potentiate or impair LTP processes. Among the most prominent factors is the neurotrophin BDNF. The next chapter contains a description of BDNF and its genetic variation followed by an introduction of BDNF as a modulator of LTP.

## The Brain Derived Neurotrophic Factor (BDNF) as Modulator of LTP and Memory Processes

BDNF belongs to the neurotrophin (NT) family.Neurotrophins are signaling molecules that are critical in the development and the function of the vertebrate nervous system by influencing the proliferation, differentiation, plasticity, and survival of neuronal cells (for a summary see (Huang and Reichardt, 2001). BDNF binds to the tropomyosin-related kinase receptor type B (TrkB; for a review see Murer, Yan, and Raisman-Vozari, 2001). When BDNF binds to TrkB, this leads to activation of its catalytic tyrosine kinase domains, which rapidly initiates intracellular signaling cascades which could account for the multiple molecular functions of BDNF including the modulation of LTP (for a review see Bath and Lee, 2006; Murer et al., 2001).

Among the known neurotrophins in humans BDNF is the most highly expressed in the cortex, the limbic structures, the hippocampus, and the cerebellum (Huang and Reichardt, 2001; Murer et al., 2001). BDNF is the only NT that leads to synaptic plasticity (Bath and Lee, 2006). Following this, BDNF should play a major role in hippocampal dependent long-term potentiation underlying episodic memory formation.

To investigate this assumption, several studies used a common single nucleotide polymorphism (SNP) in the BDNF gene, which lies onchromosome 11 (Maisonpierre et al., 1991). This SNP results from a replacement of the base Guanine by Adenine at nucleotide

196 (G196A, dbSNP number rs6265) and producesan amino acid substitution (valine to methionine) at codon 66 in the prodomain of the BDNF protein (val66met; Egan et al., 2003).The sequence variant is located in the 5' pro-BDNF sequence, which encodes the precursor peptide (pro-BDNF) that is proteolytically cleaved to form the mature BDNF protein (Seidah et al., 1996). (Egan et al., 2003) showed that the SNP, though located in the 5' pro-BDNF sequence, and thus unlikely to alter the intrinsic biological activity of the mature protein, affects intracellular processing and secretion of BDNF, leading to impairments in hippocampal function in humans. Dendritic trafficking and synaptic localization are controlled by BDNF's pro-domain, particularly in the region including the Val66Met SNP ('box2/3'), thus having a key role in activity-dependent BDNF secretion (Chen et al., 2005; Egan et al., 2003). Chen et al. (2005) demonstrate that the interaction of BDNF with sortilin, a newly identified neurotrophin receptor, is markedly reduced by the presence of the 66Met allele.

The Met substitution leads to substantial defects in cellular transport (trafficking): (1) decreased variant BDNF distribution into neuronal dendrites, (2) decreased variant BDNF targeting to secretory granules, and (3) subsequent impairment in regulated secretion (Chen et al., 2005; Chen et al., 2004; Egan et al., 2003). Additionally, Met carriers are supposed to exhibit decreased dendritic complexity, fewer neuronal and supporting cells, and increased cell death or decreased neurogenesis during embryological development or over the lifespan (Bath and Lee, 2006). In line with this, studies of brain morphometry repeatedly report smaller hippocampal volumes in Val/Met individuals (Pezawas, et al. 2004; Szeszko, et al. 2005). From this data one could conclude that the BDNF Val66Met polymorphism is able to modulate LTP processes in the hippocampus and other cortical areas and hence may contribute to individual differences in memory performance.

To summarize, BDNF influences the acute synaptic modification, promotes long-term potentiation (LTP) by a presynaptic enhancement of synaptic transmission during high-frequency stimulation (HFS), and participates in the survival and functional differentiation of the neurons and their synapses.

## The BDNF Val66Met Polymorphism and Declarative Memory

There is strong evidence that human carriers of the Met allele show poorer hippocampal-dependent memory performance, because the Met substitution leads to substantial defects in cellular transport of BDNF and this might lead to less efficient LTP in the hippocampus (Bramham and Messaoudi, 2005; Egan et al., 2003). Studies using delayed and immediate recall subtests of the Wechsler Memory Scale (WMS-R) find lower scores in Met/Met carriers compared with homozygote Val/Val subjects (Dempster, et al. 2005; Egan, et al. 2003). Similarly, in recognition memory paradigms BDNF seems to have an effect on performance, such that Val/Val carriers show higher correct identified old words, correct rejections (Hariri et al., 2003), and a higher d' (Goldberg, et al. 2008). However, a study by Hashimoto et al. (2008) could not find an effect on the performance in the recognition of complex scenes. Additionally, recall of words as measured by the California Verbal Learning Test (CVLT), did not show an influence by BDNF polymorphism (Egan, et al. 2003).

At a brain level, the fMRI study by Egan et al. (2003) found an abnormal pattern of hippocampal deactivation during a working memory task in healthy Val/Met individuals. Two similar studies (Hariri et al., 2003; Hashimoto et al., 2008) found Val66Met polymorphism influences mainly on encoding activity in the hippocampal regions than on retrieval activity during a recognition task, such that memory related hippocampal activity was greater in Val/Val carriers. 30% of total variation in recognition memory performance was accounted by BDNF genotype modulation of hippocampal engagement during encoding. But these studies did not differ between recollection and familiarity based recognition. It can be hypothesized, if BDNF Val66Met Genotype modulates the encoding of items through effects on E-LTP in the hippocampus, then recollection answers in a subsequent recognition test must be more influenced by the genotype than familiarity answers. This dissociation possibly can account for the mixed results of BDNF influences on recognition performance found in the literature (Hashimoto et al., 2008). Furthermore, a dissociation between recollection and familiarity by a genetic influence may further support a dual process model of recognition memory. We addressed this question in a genetic imaging study (Dörfel et al., unpublished results) on recollection and familiarity, which will be described in more detail in the next section.

## STUDY: BDNF VAL66MET IS RELATED TO INDIVIDUAL VARIATIONS IN RECOGNTITION MEMORY BASED ON RECOLLECTION

Twenty-six participants (18 females, mean 25.8 years) participated in this study. According to genotypes, these subjects were categorized into two groups: the Val/Val-BDNF group (15 subjects, 11 females) and the Val/Met-BDNF group (11 subjects, 7 females). There were no subjects in the homozygous Met/Met group, due to the infrequent occurrence of this genotype in Caucasians. Subjects had to complete the R/K procedure (Eldridge et al., 2000) during fMRI scanning as already described above.

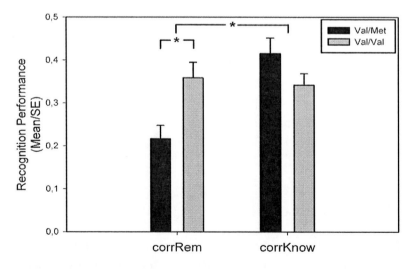

Figure 6. Recognition Memory Performance (hits) in an R/K Task in carriers of the BDNF Val/Met genotype compared to carriers of the BDNF Val/Val genotype. corrRem = Recollection based recognition, corrKnow = Familiarity based Recognition.

Results showed that the performance in recollection based recognition was significantly decreased in BDNF Val/Met carriers as compared to Val/Val carriers, while the performance of familiarity based retrieval and the correct rejection of new items did not vary according to BDNF genotype (see Figure 6). This finding confirms our hypothesis that only recollection-based retrieval should be related to BDNF genotype because BDNF is known to be involved in the LTP in the hippocampus (Lu, Christian, and Lu, 2008; Poo, 2001). Additionally, these results are in line with previous research on recognition memory (Hariri et al., 2003) and add additional information about a specific role of the BDNF gene in recollection based recognition. Furthermore, the specific effect of the BDNF genotype only on recollection supports Dual Process Models of recognition memory (Eichenbaum et al., 2007; Yonelinas, 2002), which state that recollection and familiarity are functionally independent.

## CONCLUSION

The first aim of this chapter was to review the debate about the relationship between recollection and familiarity, two processes of recognition memory.

We presented this debate by describing the most prominent recognition memory models: the dual process signal detection model DPSD (Yonelinas, 2002) and the unequal variance signal detection model UVSD (Wixted, 2007). The second aim of this chapter was to present evidence, by others and our own research, in favor for the DPSD.

This model, and all other dual process models, almost commonly assume that first, recollection and familiarity are independent memory retrieval processes; second, recollection is a threshold retrieval process thought to reflect the retrieval of specific information about a study event; third, familiarity is a signal detection process reflecting a continuous index of memory strength; and fourth, the hippocampus is critical for recollection, but not familiarity.

Results on variables that influence recollection and not familiarity such as different testing circumstances (for a review see Yonelians, 2002),confirm the first assumption.

Additionally, our own preliminary finding that variations in BDNF genotype are associated to recollection performance and not to familiarity performance further supports the argument of different retrieval processes. Also the findings of fMRI studies, which almost exclusively report different neural correlates for recollection and familiarity, respectively (see review by Skinner and Fernandes, 2007), are more in line with the assumption of different retrieval systems than with one, confidence-dependent system. However, more studies have to be conducted that directly compare recollection vs. familiarity based responses (e.g. in an R/K Task) with confidence ratings. Also, there is a lack of connectivity studies, which would prove the assumption of different, dissociable retrieval systems on a neuronal level underling the two processes. Our own study (Dörfel et al., 2009) points in this direction, but still has to be replicated.

The second and third assumptions are supported by findings of different ROC curves in familiarity as compared to familiarity together with recollection-based recognition, but also the USVD approach can explain these different ROC curves (the same is true for z-transformed ROC curves). However, a computational approach showed that the hippocampal process, which is supposed to underlie recollection, produces U-shaped zROCs similar to the recollection zROCs (see Yonelinas et al., 2010), whereas the cortical process produces

Gaussian signal detection functions and linear zROCs, like familiarity zROCs (Elfman et al., 2008). These findings are also in line with the last assumption of the hippocampus being critical for recollection, but not familiarity.

Additionally, this assumption found support by many lesion studies, fMRI studies, including our own (Dörfel et al. 2009) and a review by Skinner and Fernandes (2007). Furthermore, we showed that variations in BDNF function, a neurotrophin which is critical for synaptic plasticity in the hippocampus, only effects recollection performance, not familiarity.

Overall, we consider the dissociation between recollection and familiarity important, because it offers the opportunity to investigate episodic memory and/or hippocampal function with a comparatively simple, standardized procedure, e.g. the R/K task.

In summary, we conclude that dual process models of recognition memory are widely supported by the current data. Future research should replicate the results on brain connectivity during recognition memory as well as on the dissociation by BDNF genotype.

# REFERENCES

Aggleton, J. P., and Brown, M. W. (1999). Episodic memory, amnesia, and the hippocampal-anterior thalamic axis. *Behav. Brain Sci., 22*(3), 425-444.

Aggleton, J. P., McMackin, D., Carpenter, K., Hornak, J., Kapur, N., Halpin, S., . . . Gaffan, D. (2000). Differential cognitive effects of colloid cysts in the third ventricle that spare or compromise the fornix. *Brain*, 123 ( Pt 4), 800-815.

Aggleton, J. P., and Brown, M. W. (2006). Interleaving brain systems for episodic and recognition memory. *Trends in Cognitive Sciences, 10*(10), 455-463.

Aggleton, J. P., Vann, S. D., Denby, C., Dix, S., Mayes, A. R., Roberts, N., and Yonelinas, A. P. (2005). Sparing of the familiarity component of recognition memory in a patient with hippocampal pathology. *Neuropsychologia, 43*(12), 1810-1823.

Ally, B. A., Simons, J. S., McKeever, J. D., Peers, P. V., and Budson, A. E. (2008). Parietal contributions to recollection: Electrophysiological evidence from aging and patients with parietal lesions. *Neuropsychologia. Part Special Issue: What is the Parietal Lobe Contribution to Human Memory?, 46*(7), 1800-1812.

Baddeley, A. (2003). Working memory: looking back and looking forward. [Review]. *Nat. Rev. Neurosci., 4*(10), 829-839.

Bath, K. G., and Lee, F. S. (2006). Variant BDNF (Val66Met) impact on brain structure and function. *Cognitive, Affective, and Behavioral Neuroscience, 6*(1), 79-85.

Bayazitov, I. T., Richardson, R. J., Fricke, R. G., and Zakharenko, S. S. (2007). Slow presynaptic and fast postsynaptic components of compound long-term potentiation. *J. Neurosci., 27*(43), 11510-11521.

Bear, M. F., Connors, B. W., and Paradiso, M. A. (2007). *Neuroscience. Exploring the Brain.* (3. ed.). Philadelphia: Lippincott Williams and Wilkins.

Bear, M. F., and Malenka, R. C. (1994). Synaptic plasticity: LTP and LTD. *Curr. Opin. Neurobiol., 4*(3), 389-399.

Bengner, T., and Malina, T. (2008). Remembering versus knowing during face recognition in unilateral temporal lobe epilepsy patients with or without hippocampal sclerosis. *Brain Cogn.*

Blundon, J. A., and Zakharenko, S. S. (2008). Dissecting the components of long-term potentiation. *Neuroscientist, 14*(6), 598-608.

Bowles, B., Crupi, C., Mirsattari, S. M., Pigott, S. E., Parrent, A. G., Pruessner, J. C., . . . Kohler, S. (2007). Impaired familiarity with preserved recollection after anterior temporal-lobe resection that spares the hippocampus. *Proc. Natl. Acad. Sci. USA, 104*(41), 16382-16387.

Bramham, C. R., and Messaoudi, E. (2005). BDNF function in adult synaptic plasticity: the synaptic consolidation hypothesis. *Progress in Neurobiology, 76*(2), 99-125.

Brown, M. W., and Aggleton, J. P. (2001). Recognition memory: what are the roles of the perirhinal cortex and hippocampus? *Nat. Rev. Neurosci., 2*(1), 51-61.

Buckner, R. L., Andrews-Hanna, J. R., and Schacter, D. L. (2008). The brain's default network: anatomy, function, and relevance to disease. *Ann. NY Acad. Sci., 1124*, 1-38.

Burgess, A. P., and Ali, L. (2002). Functional connectivity of gamma EEG activity is modulated at low frequency during conscious recollection. *Int. J. Psychophysiol., 46*(2), 91-100.

Burgess, N., Maguire, E. A., and O'Keefe, J. (2002). The human hippocampus and spatial and episodic memory. *Neuron, 35*(4), 625-641.

Burgess, N., Maguire, E. A., Spiers, H. J., and O'Keefe, J. (2001). A temporoparietal and prefrontal network for retrieving the spatial context of lifelike events. *Neuroimage, 14*(2), 439-453.

Cabeza, R., Dolcos, F., Prince, S. E., Rice, H. J., Weissman, D. H., and Nyberg, L. (2003). Attention-related activity during episodic memory retrieval: a cross-function fMRI study. *Neuropsychologia, 41*(3), 390-399.

Cavanna, A. E., and Trimble, M. R. (2006). The precuneus: a review of its functional anatomy and behavioural correlates. *Brain, 129*(Pt 3), 564-583.

Chen, Z. Y., Ieraci, A., Teng, H., Dall, H., Meng, C. X., Herrera, D. G., . . . Lee, F. S. (2005). Sortilin controls intracellular sorting of brain-derived neurotrophic factor to the regulated secretory pathway. *J. Neurosci., 25*(26), 6156-6166.

Daselaar, S. M., Fleck, M. S., and Cabeza, R. (2006). Triple Dissociation in the Medial Temporal Lobes: Recollection, Familiarity, and Novelty. *J. Neurophysiol., 96*(4), 1902-1911.

Dobbins, I. G., and Wagner, A. D. (2005). Domain-general and domain-sensitive prefrontal mechanisms for recollecting events and detecting novelty. *Cereb. Cortex, 15*(11), 1768-1778.

Dolcos, F., LaBar, K. S., and Cabeza, R. (2005). Remembering one year later: role of the amygdala and the medial temporal lobe memory system in retrieving emotional memories. *Proc. Natl. Acad. Sci. USA, 102*(7), 2626-2631.

Dörfel, D., Werner, A., Moser, D., Schaefer, M., Von Kummer, R., and Karl, A. (unpublished results). BDNF Val66Met is related to individual Contextual Memory variations – possible implications for increased PTSD risk after trauma?

Dorfel, D., Werner, A., Schaefer, M., von Kummer, R., and Karl, A. (2009). Distinct brain networks in recognition memory share a defined region in the precuneus. *Eur. J. Neurosci., 30*(10), 1947-1959.

Dunn, J. C. (2004). Remember-know: a matter of confidence. *Psychol. Rev., 111*(2), 524-542.

Dusoir, H., Kapur, N., Byrnes, D. P., McKinstry, S., and Hoare, R. D. (1990). The role of diencephalic pathology in human memory disorder. Evidence from a penetrating paranasal brain injury. *Brain*, 113 ( Pt 6), 1695-1706.

Egan, M. F., Kojima, M., Callicott, J. H., Goldberg, T. E., Kolachana, B. S., Bertolino, A., . . . Weinberger, D. R. (2003). The BDNF val66met polymorphism affects activity-dependent secretion of BDNF and human memory and hippocampal function. *Cell, 112*(2), 257-269.

Eichenbaum, H. (2000). A cortical-hippocampal system for declarative memory. *Nat. Rev. Neurosci., 1*(1), 41-50.

Eichenbaum, H., Yonelinas, A. P., and Ranganath, C. (2007). The medial temporal lobe and recognition memory. *Annu. Rev. Neurosci., 30*, 123-152.

Eldridge, L. L., Engel, S. A., Zeineh, M. M., Bookheimer, S. Y., and Knowlton, B. J. (2005). A dissociation of encoding and retrieval processes in the human hippocampus. *J. Neurosci., 25*(13), 3280-3286.

Eldridge, L. L., Knowlton, B. J., Furmanski, C. S., Bookheimer, S. Y., and Engel, S. A. (2000). Remembering episodes: a selective role for the hippocampus during retrieval. *Nat. Neurosci., 3*(11), 1149-1152.

Eldridge, L. L., Sarfatti, S., and Knowlton, B. J. (2002). The effect of testing procedure on remember-know judgments. *Psychon Bull Rev., 9*(1), 139-145.

Elfman, K. W., Parks, C. M., and Yonelinas, A. P. (2008). Testing a neurocomputational model of recollection, familiarity, and source recognition. *J. Exp. Psychol. Learn Mem. Cogn., 34*(4), 752-768.

Fenker, D. B., Schott, B. H., Richardson-Klavehn, A., Heinze, H. J., and Duzel, E. (2005). Recapitulating emotional context: activity of amygdala, hippocampus and fusiform cortex during recollection and familiarity. *Eur. J. Neurosci., 21*(7), 1993-1999.

Fernandez, G., and Tendolkar, I. (2006). The rhinal cortex: 'gatekeeper' of the declarative memory system. *Trends Cogn. Sci., 10*(8), 358-362.

Fletcher, P. C., Frith, C. D., Baker, S. C., Shallice, T., Frackowiak, R. S., and Dolan, R. J. (1995). The mind's eye--precuneus activation in memory-related imagery. *Neuroimage, 2*(3), 195-200.

Fransson, P., and Marrelec, G. (2008). The precuneus/posterior cingulate cortex plays a pivotal role in the default mode network: Evidence from a partial correlation network analysis. *NeuroImage, 42*(3), 1178-1184.

Freed, D. M., and Corkin, S. (1988). Rate of forgetting in H.M.: 6-month recognition. *Behav. Neurosci., 102*(6), 823-827.

Freed, D. M., Corkin, S., and Cohen, N. J. (1987). Forgetting in H.M.: a second look. *Neuropsychologia, 25*(3), 461-471.

Gardiner, J. M., Ramponi, C., and Richardson-Klavehn, A. (2002). Recognition memory and decision processes: a meta-analysis of remember, know, and guess responses. *Memory, 10*(2), 83-98.

Gilboa, A., Winocur, G., Rosenbaum, R. S., Poreh, A., Gao, F., Black, S. E., . . . Moscovitch, M. (2006). Hippocampal contributions to recollection in retrograde and anterograde amnesia. *Hippocampus, 16*(11), 966-980.

Gold, J. J., Smith, C. N., Bayley, P. J., Shrager, Y., Brewer, J. B., Stark, C. E., . . . Squire, L. R. (2006). Item memory, source memory, and the medial temporal lobe: concordant findings from fMRI and memory-impaired patients. *Proc. Natl. Acad. Sci. USA, 103*(24), 9351-9356.

Gonsalves, B. D., Kahn, I., Curran, T., Norman, K. A., and Wagner, A. D. (2005). Memory strength and repetition suppression: multimodal imaging of medial temporal cortical contributions to recognition. *Neuron, 47*(5), 751-761.

Habib, R., McIntosh, A. R., Wheeler, M. A., and Tulving, E. (2003). Memory encoding and hippocampally-based novelty/familiarity discrimination networks. *Neuropsychologia, 41*(3), 271-279.

Harding, A., Halliday, G., Caine, D., and Kril, J. (2000). Degeneration of anterior thalamic nuclei differentiates alcoholics with amnesia. *Brain,* 123 ( Pt 1), 141-154.

Hariri, A. R., Goldberg, T. E., Mattay, V. S., Kolachana, B. S., Callicott, J. H., Egan, M. F., and Weinberger, D. R. (2003). Brain-derived neurotrophic factor val66met polymorphism affects human memory-related hippocampal activity and predicts memory performance. *J. Neurosci., 23*(17), 6690-6694.

Hashimoto, R., Moriguchi, Y., Yamashita, F., Mori, T., Nemoto, K., Okada, T., . . . Ohnishi, T. (2008). Dose-dependent effect of the Val66Met polymorphism of the brain-derived neurotrophic factor gene on memory-related hippocampal activity. *Neurosci. Res., 61*(4), 360-367.

Haskins, A. L., Yonelinas, A. P., Quamme, J. R., and Ranganath, C. (2008). Perirhinal Cortex Supports Encoding and Familiarity-Based Recognition of Novel Associations. *Neuron, 59*(4), 554-560.

Henson, R. N., Cansino, S., Herron, J. E., Robb, W. G., and Rugg, M. D. (2003). A familiarity signal in human anterior medial temporal cortex? *Hippocampus, 13*(2), 301-304.

Henson, R. N. A., Rugg, M. D., Shallice, T., and Dolan, R. J. (2000). Confidence in Recognition Memory for Words: Dissociating Right Prefrontal Roles in Episodic Retrieval. *J. Cogn. Neurosci., 12*(6), 913-923.

Henson, R. N. A., Rugg, M. D., Shallice, T., Josephs, O., and Dolan, R. J. (1999). Recollection and Familiarity in Recognition Memory: An Event-Related Functional Magnetic Resonance Imaging Study. *J. Neurosci., 19*(10), 3962-3972.

Hicks, J. L., and Marsh, R. L. (1999). Remember-know judgments can depend on how memory is tested. *Psychon Bull Rev., 6*(1), 117-122.

Holdstock, J. S., Mayes, A. R., Roberts, N., Cezayirli, E., Isaac, C. L., O'Reilly, R. C., and Norman, K. A. (2002). Under what conditions is recognition spared relative to recall after selective hippocampal damage in humans? *Hippocampus, 12*(3), 341-351.

Hritcu, L., Clicinschi, M., and Nabeshima, T. (2007). Brain serotonin depletion impairs short-term memory, but not long-term memory in rats. *Physiol. Behav., 91*(5), 652-657.

Huang, E. J., and Reichardt, L. F. (2001). Neurotrophins: roles in neuronal development and function. *Annual Review of Neuroscience, 24,* 677-736.

Iidaka, T., Matsumoto, A., Nogawa, J., Yamamoto, Y., and Sadato, N. (2006). Frontoparietal Network Involved in Successful Retrieval from Episodic Memory. Spatial and Temporal Analyses Using fMRI and ERP. *Cereb. Cortex, 16*(9), 1349-1360.

Jacoby, L. L. (1991). A process dissociation framework: Separating automatic from intentional uses of memory. *Journal of Memory and Language, 30*(5), 513-541.

Jager, T., Szabo, K., Griebe, M., Bazner, H., Moller, J., and Hennerici, M. G. (2009). Selective disruption of hippocampus-mediated recognition memory processes after episodes of transient global amnesia. *Neuropsychologia, 47*(1), 70-76.

Kahn, I., Davachi, L., and Wagner, A. D. (2004). Functional-neuroanatomic correlates of recollection: implications for models of recognition memory. *J. Neurosci., 24*(17), 4172-4180.

Konishi, S., Asari, T., Jimura, K., Chikazoe, J., and Miyashita, Y. (2006). Activation shift from medial to lateral temporal cortex associated with recency judgements following impoverished encoding. *Cereb. Cortex, 16*(4), 469-474.

Konishi, S., Wheeler, M. E., Donaldson, D. I., and Buckner, R. L. (2000). Neural correlates of episodic retrieval success. *Neuroimage, 12*(3), 276-286.

Lu, Y., Christian, K., and Lu, B. (2008). BDNF: a key regulator for protein synthesis-dependent LTP and long-term memory? *Neurobiol. Learn Mem., 89*(3), 312-323.

Lynch, G., Rex, C. S., and Gall, C. M. (2007). LTP consolidation: substrates, explanatory power, and functional significance. *Neuropharmacology, 52*(1), 12-23.

Lynch, M. A. (2004). Long-term potentiation and memory. *Physiol. Rev., 84*(1), 87-136.

Maguire, E. A. (2001). Neuroimaging studies of autobiographical event memory. *Philos Trans. R Soc. Lond B Biol. Sci., 356*(1413), 1441-1451.

Maisonpierre, P. C., Le Beau, M. M., Espinosa, R., 3rd, Ip, N. Y., Belluscio, L., de la Monte, S. M., . . . Yancopoulos, G. D. (1991). Human and rat brain-derived neurotrophic factor and neurotrophin-3: gene structures, distributions, and chromosomal localizations. *Genomics, 10*(3), 558-568.

Malenka, R. C., and Bear, M. F. (2004). LTP and LTD: an embarrassment of riches. *Neuron, 44*(1), 5-21.

Manns, J. R., Hopkins, R. O., Reed, J. M., Kitchener, E. G., and Squire, L. R. (2003). Recognition memory and the human hippocampus. *Neuron, 37*(1), 171-180.

Mayes, A. R., Holdstock, J. S., Isaac, C. L., Hunkin, N. M., and Roberts, N. (2002). Relative sparing of item recognition memory in a patient with adult-onset damage limited to the hippocampus. *Hippocampus, 12*(3), 325-340.

Montaldi, D., Spencer, T. J., Roberts, N., and Mayes, A. R. (2006). The neural system that mediates familiarity memory. *Hippocampus, 16*(5), 504-520.

Murer, M. G., Yan, Q., and Raisman-Vozari, R. (2001). Brain-derived neurotrophic factor in the control human brain, and in Alzheimer's disease and Parkinson's disease. *Prog. Neurobiol., 63*(1), 71-124.

Naghavi, H. R., and Nyberg, L. (2005). Common fronto-parietal activity in attention, memory, and consciousness: Shared demands on integration? *Conscious Cogn, 14*(2), 390-425.

Neves, G., Cooke, S. F., and Bliss, T. V. (2008). Synaptic plasticity, memory and the hippocampus: a neural network approach to causality. [Review]. *Nat. Rev. Neurosci., 9*(1), 65-75.

Norman, K. A., and O'Reilly, R. C. (2003). Modeling hippocampal and neocortical contributions to recognition memory: a complementary-learning-systems approach. *Psychol. Rev., 110*(4), 611-646.

Parks, C. M., and Yonelinas, A. P. (2007). Moving beyond pure signal-detection models: comment on Wixted (2007). *Psychol. Rev., 114*(1), 188-202.

Peters, J., Thoma, P., Koch, B., Schwarz, M., and Daum, I. (2009). Impairment of verbal recollection following ischemic damage to the right anterior hippocampus. *Cortex, 45*(5), 592-601.

Poo, M. M. (2001). Neurotrophins as synaptic modulators. *Nature Reviews Neuroscience, 2*, 24-32.

Ranganath, C., Heller, A., Cohen, M. X., Brozinsky, C. J., and Rissman, J. (2005). Functional connectivity with the hippocampus during successful memory formation. *Hippocampus, 15*(8), 997-1005.

Ravizza, S. M., Delgado, M. R., Chein, J. M., Becker, J. T., and Fiez, J. A. (2004). Functional dissociations within the inferior parietal cortex in verbal working memory. *Neuroimage, 22*(2), 562-573.

Raymond, C. R. (2007). LTP forms 1, 2 and 3: different mechanisms for the "long" in long-term potentiation. *Trends Neurosci., 30*(4), 167-175.

Rotello, C. M., Macmillan, N. A., Reeder, J. A., and Wong, M. (2005). The remember response: subject to bias, graded, and not a process-pure indicator of recollection. *Psychon Bull Rev., 12*(5), 865-873.

Rugg, M. D., and Curran, T. (2007). Event-related potentials and recognition memory. *Trends Cogn Sci, 11*(6), 251-257.

Rugg, M. D., Otten, L. J., and Henson, R. N. A. (2002). The neural basis of episodic memory: evidence from functional neuroimaging. *Phil. Trans. R. Soc. Lond. B, 357*(1424), 1097-1110.

Rutishauser, U., Mamelak, A. N., and Schuman, E. M. (2006). Single-trial learning of novel stimuli by individual neurons of the human hippocampus-amygdala complex. *Neuron, 49*(6), 805-813.

Schacter, D. L., and Tulving, E. (1994). *Memory systems of 1994?* Cambridge, MA: MIT Press.

Shallice, T., Fletcher, P., Frith, C. D., Grasby, P., Frackowiak, R. S., and Dolan, R. J. (1994). Brain regions associated with acquisition and retrieval of verbal episodic memory. *Nature, 368*(6472), 633-635.

Shannon, B. J., and Buckner, R. L. (2004). Functional-anatomic correlates of memory retrieval that suggest nontraditional processing roles for multiple distinct regions within posterior parietal cortex. *J. Neurosci., 24*(45), 10084-10092.

Sharot, T., Delgado, M. R., and Phelps, E. A. (2004). How emotion enhances the feeling of remembering. *Nat. Neurosci., 7*(12), 1376-1380.

Shimamura, A. P., and Wickens, T. D. (2009). Superadditive memory strength for item and source recognition: the role of hierarchical relational binding in the medial temporal lobe. *Psychol Rev, 116*(1), 1-19.

Shrager, Y., Kirwan, C. B., and Squire, L. R. (2008). Activity in Both Hippocampus and Perirhinal Cortex Predicts the Memory Strength of Subsequently Remembered Information. *Neuron, 59*(4), 547-553.

Skinner, E. I., and Fernandes, M. A. (2007). Neural correlates of recollection and familiarity: a review of neuroimaging and patient data. *Neuropsychologia, 45*(10), 2163-2179.

Sorg, C., Riedl, V., Muhlau, M., Calhoun, V. D., Eichele, T., Laer, L., . . . Wohlschlager, A. M. (2007). Selective changes of resting-state networks in individuals at risk for Alzheimer's disease. *Proc. Natl. Acad. Sci. USA, 104*(47), 18760-18765.

Sperling, R., Chua, E., Cocchiarella, A., Rand-Giovannetti, E., Poldrack, R., Schacter, D. L., and Albert, M. (2003). Putting names to faces: successful encoding of associative memories activates the anterior hippocampal formation. *Neuroimage, 20*(2), 1400-1410.

Spiers, H. J., Maguire, E. A., and Burgess, N. (2001). Hippocampal amnesia. Neurocase, 7(5), 357-382.

Squire, L. R. (2004). Memory systems of the brain: a brief history and current perspective. *Neurobiol. Learn Mem., 82*(3), 171-177.

Squire, L. R., Wixted, J. T., and Clark, R. E. (2007). Recognition memory and the medial temporal lobe: a new perspective. *Nat. Rev. Neurosci., 8*(11), 872-883.

Stark, C. E., Bayley, P. J., and Squire, L. R. (2002). Recognition memory for single items and for associations is similarly impaired following damage to the hippocampal region. *Learn Mem., 9*(5), 238-242.

Stark, C. E., and Squire, L. R. (2000). Recognition memory and familiarity judgments in severe amnesia: no evidence for a contribution of repetition priming. *Behav. Neurosci., 114*(3), 459-467.

Takahashi, E., Ohki, K., and Kim, D. S. (2008). Dissociated Pathways for Successful Memory Retrieval from the Human Parietal Cortex: Anatomical and Functional Connectivity Analyses. *Cereb. Cortex, 18*(8), 1771-1778.

Tulving, E. (1985). How many memory systems are there? *American Psychologist, 40*(4), 385-398.

Tulving, E. (1985). Memory and consciousness. *Canadian Psychology Psychologie Canadienne, 26*(1), 1-12.

Turriziani, P., Fadda, L., Caltagirone, C., and Carlesimo, G. A. (2004). Recognition memory for single items and for associations in amnesic patients. *Neuropsychologia, 42*(4), 426-433.

Turriziani, P., Serra, L., Fadda, L., Caltagirone, C., and Carlesimo, G. A. (2008). Recollection and familiarity in hippocampal amnesia. *Hippocampus, 18*(5), 469-480.

Van der Werf, Y. D., Scheltens, P., Lindeboom, J., Witter, M. P., Uylings, H. B., and Jolles, J. (2003). Deficits of memory, executive functioning and attention following infarction in the thalamus; a study of 22 cases with localised lesions. *Neuropsychologia*, 41(10), 1330-1344.

Vargha-Khadem, F., Gadian, D. G., Watkins, K. E., Connelly, A., Van Paesschen, W., and Mishkin, M. (1997). Differential effects of early hippocampal pathology on episodic and semantic memory. *Science, 277*(5324), 376-380.

Vilberg, K. L., and Rugg, M. D. (2007). Dissociation of the neural correlates of recognition memory according to familiarity, recollection, and amount of recollected information. *Neuropsychologia, 45*(10), 2216-2225.

Vilberg, K. L., and Rugg, M. D. (2008). Memory retrieval and the parietal cortex: a review of evidence from a dual-process perspective. *Neuropsychologia, 46*(7), 1787-1799.

Vincent, J. L., Kahn, I., Snyder, A. Z., Raichle, M. E., and Buckner, R. L. (2008). Evidence for a Frontoparietal Control System Revealed by Intrinsic Functional Connectivity. *J. Neurophysiol.*, 90355.

Vincent, J. L., Snyder, A. Z., Fox, M. D., Shannon, B. J., Andrews, J. R., Raichle, M. E., and Buckner, R. L. (2006). Coherent spontaneous activity identifies a hippocampal-parietal memory network. *J. Neurophysiol., 96*(6), 3517-3531.

Wagner, A. D., Shannon, B. J., Kahn, I., and Buckner, R. L. (2005). Parietal lobe contributions to episodic memory retrieval. *Trends Cogn. Sci., 9*(9), 445-453.

Wais, P. E. (2008). FMRI signals associated with memory strength in the medial temporal lobes: a meta-analysis. *Neuropsychologia, 46*(14), 3185-3196.

Wheeler, M. E., and Buckner, R. L. (2003). Functional dissociation among components of remembering: control, perceived oldness, and content. *J. Neurosci., 23*(9), 3869-3880.

Wheeler, M. E., and Buckner, R. L. (2004). Functional-anatomic correlates of remembering and knowing. *Neuroimage, 21*(4), 1337-1349.

Wixted, J. T. (2007). Dual-process theory and signal-detection theory of recognition memory. *Psychol. Rev., 114*(1), 152-176.

Wixted, J. T. (2007). Spotlighting the probative findings: Reply to Parks and Yonelinas (2007). *Psychological Review, 114*(1), 203-209.

Wixted, J. T., and Mickes, L. (2010). A continuous dual-process model of remember/know judgments. *Psychol. Rev., 117*(4), 1025-1054.

Wixted, J. T., Mickes, L., and Squire, L. R. (2010). Measuring recollection and familiarity in the medial temporal lobe. *Hippocampus, 20*(11), 1195-1205.

Wixted, J. T., and Squire, L. R. (2010). The role of the human hippocampus in familiarity-based and recollection-based recognition memory. *Behav. Brain Res., 215*(2), 197-208.

Wolk, D. A., Dunfee, K. L., Dickerson, B. C., Aizenstein, H. J., and DeKosky, S. T. (2011). A medial temporal lobe division of labor: insights from memory in aging and early Alzheimer disease. *Hippocampus, 21*(5), 461-466.

Woodruff, C. C., Johnson, J. D., Uncapher, M. R., and Rugg, M. D. (2005). Content-specificity of the neural correlates of recollection. *Neuropsychologia, 43*(7), 1022-1032.

Xiang, J. Z., and Brown, M. W. (1998). Differential neuronal encoding of novelty, familiarity and recency in regions of the anterior temporal lobe. *Neuropharmacology, 37*(4-5), 657-676.

Yarkoni, T., Poldrack, R. A., Nichols, T. E., Van Essen, D. C., and Wager, T. D. (2011). Large-scale automated synthesis of human functional neuroimaging data. [Research Support, N.I.H., Extramural]. *Nat. Methods, 8*(8), 665-670.

Yonelinas, A. P. (2001a). Components of episodic memory: the contribution of recollection and familiarity. *Philos. Trans. R. Soc. Lond B Biol. Sci., 356*(1413), 1363-1374.

Yonelinas, A. P. (2001b). Consciousness, control, and confidence: the 3 Cs of recognition memory. *J. Exp. Psychol. Gen., 130*(3), 361-379.

Yonelinas, A. P. (2002). The Nature of Recollection and Familiarity: A Review of 30 Years of Research. *Journal of Memory and Language, 46*(3), 441-517.

Yonelinas, A. P., Aly, M., Wang, W. C., and Koen, J. D. (2010). Recollection and familiarity: examining controversial assumptions and new directions. *Hippocampus, 20*(11), 1178-1194.

Yonelinas, A. P., and Jacoby, L. L. (1995). Dissociating automatic and controlled processes in a memory-search task: beyond implicit memory. *Psychol. Res., 57*(3-4), 156-165.

Yonelinas, A. P., and Levy, B. J. (2002). Dissociating familiarity from recollection in human recognition memory: different rates of forgetting over short retention intervals. *Psychon Bull Rev., 9*(3), 575-582.

Yonelinas, A. P., Otten, L. J., Shaw, K. N., and Rugg, M. D. (2005). Separating the brain regions involved in recollection and familiarity in recognition memory. *J. Neurosci., 25*(11), 3002-3008.

Yonelinas, A. P., and Parks, C. M. (2007). Receiver operating characteristics (ROCs) in recognition memory: a review. *Psychol. Bull, 133*(5), 800-832.

Yonelinas, A. P., Widaman, K., Mungas, D., Reed, B., Weiner, M. W., and Chui, H. C. (2007). Memory in the aging brain: doubly dissociating the contribution of the hippocampus and entorhinal cortex. *Hippocampus, 17*(11), 1134-1140.

Zakharenko, S. S., Patterson, S. L., Dragatsis, I., Zeitlin, S. O., Siegelbaum, S. A., Kandel, E. R., and Morozov, A. (2003). Presynaptic BDNF required for a presynaptic but not postsynaptic component of LTP at hippocampal CA1-CA3 synapses. *Neuron, 39*(6), 975-990.

Zhou, Y., Dougherty, J. H., Jr., Hubner, K. F., Bai, B., Cannon, R. L., and Hutson, R. K. (2008). Abnormal connectivity in the posterior cingulate and hippocampus in early Alzheimer's disease and mild cognitive impairment. *Alzheimers Dement, 4*(4), 265-270.

In: Psychology of Memory
Editors: Dannie M. Hendrix and Orval Holcomb

ISBN: 978-1-61942-633-7
© 2012 Nova Science Publishers, Inc.

*Chapter 4*

# NEURAL SUBSTRATES OF RECOLLECTION AND FAMILIARITY: FURTHER BRIDGING HUMAN AND ANIMAL RECOGNITION MEMORY USING TRANSLATIONAL PARADIGMS

## *Magdalena M. Sauvage*[*]

Mercator Research Group1, Medicine faculty,
RUB, Universitätsstraße 150, 44 801 Bochum, Germany
Center for Memory and Brain, Boston University,
2 Cummington St, Boston 02215, MA, US

## ABSTRACT

The medial temporal lobe (MTL) of the brain is crucial for recognition memory, as shown by the severe memory deficits found in aging, and in patients with amnesia who have damage to this brain region. Recognition memory is thought to rely on two retrieval processes: the familiarity and the recollection processes, that are differentially affected in aging or following MTL damage (recollection is impaired while familiarity is relatively spared), and the characteristics of these processes have been discussed since the time of Aristotle. Familiarity is defined as a vague feeling of 'déjà-vu', for example when one recognizes a person but cannot identify this person by name. In contrast, recollection requires the integration of several features belonging to the event to be recognized, for example the identity of the person taking part to this event, and the spatial or temporal contexts of the event. Two major controversies currently fuel the debates in human recognition memory: 1) whether the familiarity and the recollection processes are truly qualitatively distinct processes, or whether they reflect different memory strengths of the same process; and 2) whether both processes share the same neural substrate: the hippocampus (HIP), or whether the HIP supports recollection only, and the cortex surrounding the HIP, the parahippocampal region (ParaHIP), supports familiarity. These conflicting findings are mainly based on the interpretation of Receiver Operating

[*] Correspondence should be addressed to Magdalena Sauvage, Mercator Research Group1 (fam), Medicine faculty, RUB, Universitätsstraße 150, 44 801 Bochum, email: magdalena.sauvage@rub.de; Tel: +49(0)234 32-26739, Fax: +49(0)23432-14504.

Characteristic (ROC) functions by the two leading models of recognition memory used to analyze memory performance in humans. Indeed, those models report either a selective recollection deficit following hippocampal damage (the dual process model), or an impairment of both the recollection and the familiarity processes (the one process model). This discrepancy is suggested to stem, at least in part, from the limited spatial resolution of standard human imaging techniques, which does not allow for a precise identification of the extent of the MTL damage in amnesic patients, and prevents a clear assessment of whether the damage is truly restricted to the HIP, or whether it also extends to the adjacent ParaHIP, which could in turn explain the additional familiarity deficits reported in some studies. In this chapter, after introducing those two main models of recognition memory, I will first report how we developed new translational paradigms (human standard recognition memory tasks adapted to rats) using rats to investigate whether the HIP supports only recollection, or both processes. Second, I will report how we addressed the first controversy in this field: whether familiarity and recollection are distinct processes, by evaluating memory performance of control rats with those new translational paradigms. Then, I will show how we tackled the second major controversy in human recognition memory: whether the HIP supports selectively the recollection process, or both processes, by studying memory performance of rats with hippocampal damage with our new animal ROC paradigms across memory demands. Finally, I will present recent data that extend beyond those controversies, and aim at elucidating whether the ParaHIP is functionally segregated in terms of its involvement in the familiarity and the recollection processes. In summary, studies mentioned in this chapter provide compelling evidence that the recollection and the familiarity processes are qualitatively distinct processes, that the HIP supports recollection (and not familiarity), and that the ParaHIP is functionally segregated in terms of familiarity and recollection.

**Keywords:** ROC, recollection, familiarity, episodic recognition memory, hippocampus, MEC, PRc

# INTRODUCTION

The characteristics of the familiarity and the recollection processes have been discussed since the time of Aristotle, and the evaluation of the contribution of familiarity and recollection to recognition memory performance has also drawn much attention since the 70's. Familiarity is generally described as a vague feeling of déjà–vu, for example when one meets a person, but cannot identify this person by name or by any other information related to a previous encounter. Familiarity is commonly thought as a continuous index of memory strength, and a fast and automatic process (Yonelinas and Jacoby, 1994, 1996; see for reviews Mandler, 1980; 2008). In contrast, the recollection process involves the retrieval and the integration of different qualitative features of the event to be remembered, such as the temporal and spatial contexts of this event, and is thought be a controlled and effortful threshold search process (see for a review Yonelinas 2002). The recollection and the familiarity processes are believed to be initiated in parallel, but familiarity judgements were found to fade faster than the recollection ones (Hockley, 1991, 1992; Yonelinas and Levy, 2002). Moreover, familiarity-based responses were shown to exhibit different spatial and temporal distributions than those based on recollection in event related potentials studies, suggesting that familiarity and recollection have distinct kinetics, hence could be distinct processes, and could have different neural substrates (Curran 2000, Duezel et al, 1997; Smith

1993; Kilmesh et al 2001). However, studies on amnesic patients with damage to the MTL focusing on the investigation of the specific neural substrates of familiarity or recollection did not report a very consistent picture, which led to major controversies in human recognition memory. Thus, part of the studies focusing on patients with damage circumscribed to the HIP report selective recollection deficits and spared familiarity, suggesting that the HIP selectively supports recollection (Aggleton and Shawn, 1996; Vargha-khaden et al, 1997; Yonelinas et al 1998; Holdstock et al, 2000; Mayes et al, 2001; Duezel et al, 2001; Yonelinas et al 2002; Quamme et al, 2004; Aggleton et al 2005; Barbeau et al, 2005; Brandt et al, 2008; Turriziani et al, 2008; Vann et al, 2009; Bowles et al, 2010; Martin et al 2011; see for reviews Montaldi and Mayes, 2010; Yonelinas et al, 2010). In contrast, other studies report deficits in both recollection and familiarity following damage to the HIP, suggesting that the HIP supports both the familiarity and the recollection processes (Reed and Squire, 1997; Manns and Squire 1999; Stark et al 2000; Manns et al 2003; Wais et al, 2006; Kirwan et al, 2009; Smith et al, 2011, Song et al, 2011, see for a review Wixted and Squire 2010). This discrepancy has been suggested to stem, at least in part, from an inaccurate estimation of the MTL damage in patients, and the familiarity deficits to possibly be caused by damage extending to the ParaHIP instead of being restricted to the HIP. Indeed, due to the limited spatial resolution of the standard human imaging techniques, it is very challenging to define with precision the outer edges of a brain lesion, such that it is extremely difficult to define in patients with MTL damage, whether the damage is circumscribed to the HIP, or whether it also extends to the ParaHIP which is directly adjacent (Figure 1). A similar limitation is observed in functional magnetic resonance imaging (fMRI) studies, which does not allow for a precise assessment of the source of task-induced brain activity when regions are adjacent. Thus, because of those technical limitations, no consensus had emerged from the literature regarding the identity of the neural substrates of familiarity and recollection, and the question of 1) whether recollection and familiarity are distinct processes, and 2) whether they have a common neural substrate, has thus been fuelling the debates in humans and animal recognition memory for the past decades.

Fortunately, the MTL is exceptionally conserved across species (Figure 1; Manns and Eichenbaum, 2006), and one way to address these controversies was to study 1) whether memory performance could rely on either process without significant contribution of the other process, and 2) to perform lesions restricted to the HIP in animals, and to assess whether recollection only, or recollection and familiarity would be affected by this lesion. The only caveat, at the time, was that no animal behavioral tasks allowed for the quantitative evaluation of the contribution of recollection or familiarity to recognition memory performance. Hence, to address this issue, we adapted standard human recognition memory tasks allowing for such a distinction to rats, which allow for data to be analyzed and collected in the exact same manner than it is done in humans. Generating those behavioral tasks and validating them as proper translational paradigms enabled us to investigate whether recollection and familiarity were distinct processes. Subsequently, we investigated the specific contribution of the HIP to recollection and familiarity by combining those translational paradigms with lesions restricted to the HIP. Finally, we adopted a similar lesion approach to study the role of the ParaHIP in recollection and familiarity.

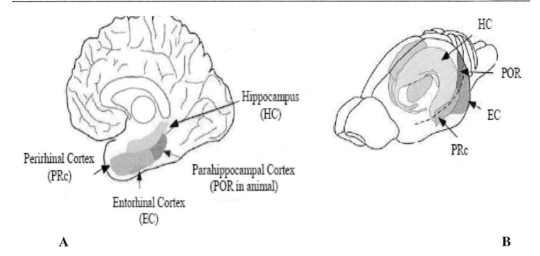

A                                                                                                    B

Figure 1. *Medial temporal brain areas*: A. in humans (Burwell and Furtak, 2008); B in rats (Furtak et al, 2007).

# I. NEW TRANSLATIONAL BEHAVIORAL TASKS TO STUDY RECOLLECTION AND FAMILIARITY

## I.1. Recollection and Familiarity in Humans: Receiver Operating Characteristics (ROC) Functions

In humans, one of the standard methods to analyze recognition memory is to plot receiver operating characteristic (ROC) functions based on the performance of subjects (see for reviews: Yonelinas and Parks, 2007; Wixted et al 2007). Thus, episodic recognition memory in humans is usually assessed by presenting a study list of items to a subject (for example: a list of words appearing on a screen, one word at a time) and, after a delay, by testing the memory for those words by presenting a longer list of items that includes the same items intermixed with an equal number of new items, again one at a time. During this recognition phase, the subject is asked whether the item presented was part of the study list ('old' item), or whether it was not ('new' item). Based on the responses collected, the probability of correct recognition of a study list item (p'hit') is plotted as a function of the probability of incorrect recognition of a new item (p'false alarm') across confidence levels, that vary from 'very' to 'less' sure that an item at test belonged to the study list or from 'very' to 'less' sure that the item did <u>not</u> belong to the study list. Subsequently, the best fitting curve is defined to generate a ROC function based on the model of recognition memory chosen for the analysis of the data. Quite a few of those models exist, and among them, two models are used in routine to study episodic recognition memory in humans: the dual-process model and the one-process model (see for reviews: Yonelinas, 2002; Yonelinas and Parks, 2007; Wixted et al, 2007, respectively).

## I.2. Interpretation of the ROC Functions within the Frame of the Dual-and the One-process Models of Recognition Memory

### I.2.1. The Dual-process Model

The dual-process model suggests that recollection and familiarity are qualitatively distinct processes that contribute to recognition memory. Familiarity reflects the 'quantitative' memory strength of the target to remember (hence familiarity is considered as a continuous process), while recollection would reflect a search process focused on the retrieval of 'qualitative' information related to the remembered event. Within the frame of this model, recollection and familiarity cooperate under certain conditions, as it is the case for the recognition of single items, but can also lead to successful recognition memory performance independently of each other. For example: recognition memory performance relies primarily on the familiarity process in aging, while performance is principally supported by recollection for associative recognition memory (Howard et al, 2006; Peters and Daum 2008; Yonelinas, 1997; Arndt and Reder, 2001; Slotnick et al, 2000; Rotello et al, 2000; Kelley and Wixted, 2001). Moreover, studies using the dual-process model to analyze recognition memory performance report that familiarity and recollection have distinct neural substrates: the HIP for recollection and the surrounding temporal cortex, the ParaHIP, for familiarity (Yonelinas et al, 2002; Aggleton et al, 2005; Bowles et al, 2007; Yonelinas et al, 2007; Wolk et al, 2011; see for reviews Eichenbaum et al, 2007; Diana et al, 2007; Montaldi and Mayes 2010). Using this model, two distinct indices can be generated from the analysis of ROC functions: one recollection index (R) and one familiarity index (F) (see Yonelinas, 1994 and Yonelinas and Parks, 2007 for details on the calculation of the indices). Within the frame of this model, the y-intercept of the ROC (R) reflects an estimate of the contribution of the recollection process to recognition memory performance. The familiarity index (F), which is calculated as the distance between the peaks of the normal distribution of the familiarity for 'old' or 'new' items, is indirectly reflected by the degree of curvilinearity of the ROC function (Figure 2A) and reveals the contribution of familiarity to recognition memory performance. In other words, within the frame of the dual-process model, when ROC functions are linear and have a y-intercept different from zero (e.g. asymmetric when compared to the main diagonal that represents chance level), the recollection process contributes primarily to recognition memory performance (Figure 2B). In contrast, when ROC functions are curvilinear and their y-intercept does not differ from zero (eg, the function is fully curvilinear and symmetric compared to the main diagonal), memory performance is essentially based on familiarity (Figure 2C). Finally, curvilinear and asymmetric ROC functions reflect the contribution of both familiarity and recollection to the performance, respectively (Figure 2A). Based on this interpretation of the ROC functions, studies using the dual-process model of recognition memory to analyze performance of amnesic patients with damage to the hippocampus have reported selective deficits in recollection, while familiarity was relatively spared, suggesting that the hippocampus supports recollection but not familiarity (Yonelinas et al 1998; Yonelinas et al 2002; Aggleton et al, 2005; Vann et al, 2009; Bowles et al, 2010; Martin et al 2011; see for a review Yonelinas et al, 2010).

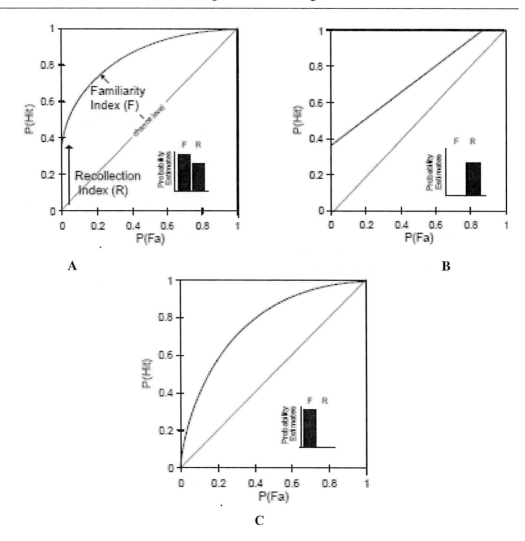

Figure 2. *Idealized human ROC functions for recognition memory*. Recollection (R) and familiarity (F) indices are shown as bar diagrams (see Yonelinas and Parks, 2007 for detailed calculations) A. ROC curve for single item recognition memory: the function is asymmetrical and curvilinear, reflecting the contribution of recollection and familiarity to recognition memory. B. ROC curve for associative recognition memory (memory for pairs): the function is asymmetrical and linear, suggesting that recognition memory performance is primarily based on recollection. C. ROC curve for single item recognition memory when a response deadline is applied: the function is symmetric and curvilinear reflecting a performance principally based on familiarity.

### *I.2.2. The One-process Model*

A second model that is also used in the human literature to study recognition memory is the 'one-process' model, which in contrast to the dual-process model, suggests that familiarity and recollection are one and the same qualitative process that differ in the memory strength that they reflect. This model posits that the familiarity process reflects a weaker memory strength than recollection, and grows into recollection as memory strength increases. Within the frame of this model, the degree of curvilinearity of the ROC function reflects the sum of the strengths of memory components, and its asymmetry reflects a greater variability in strength for the 'old' than for 'new' items (see for a review Wixted et al, 2007). A consequence of the assumption that familiarity and recollection are one and the same process is that recognition memory performance cannot rely on recollection without a contribution of the familiarity process. Hence, in light of this model, ROC functions are always curvilinear (e.g. never linear, if recognition memory is successful) and vary only in how distant the curve lies from the main diagonal: the further away from the diagonal, the stronger the memory strength (Wais et al, 2006). Another consequence of the same assumption is that, familiarity and recollection should have the same neural substrate: the HIP, as reported by other studies focusing on patients with amnesia with damage thought to be restricted to the MTL (Reed and Squirc, 1997; Manns and Squire 1999; Manns et al 2003; Kirwan et al, 2009; Smith et al, 2011, Song et al, 2011, see for a review Wixted and Squire 2010).

## I.3. Animal ROC Paradigms

In an attempt to shed some light on two major controversies in human recognition memory: 1) whether the recollection and the familiarity processes are distinct (or one and the same process), and 2) whether the hippocampus supports both recollection and familiarity (or only the recollection process), we adapted human ROC paradigms to rats with the aim of collecting and analyzing data using the same methodological tools used in humans, to bridge further human and animal recognition memory. Thus, Eichenbaum and colleagues (Boston University, USA) developed in 2004 the first ROC paradigm for animals using rats' innate ability to discriminate odors and to forage (Fortin et al, 2004). As previously mentioned, humans ROC paradigms consist in three experimental phases: a 'study', a 'delay' and a 'recognition' phase. During the study phase, target stimuli are presented to the subject, one at a time. After the delay, the memory for the target stimuli is tested by presenting once again the target stimuli ('old' stimuli) intermixed with an equal number of stimuli that have not been experienced during the 'study' phase ('new' stimuli), and subjects are asked which stimuli are 'new' or 'old' and how confident they are about their responses. Subsequently, the probability of a hit (correct recognition of the study phase targets) is plotted as a function of the probability of a false alarm (incorrect recognition the new stimuli) across confidence levels to obtain a ROC function. Since vision is the primary sense for humans, but not of rodents, Fortin and colleagues used odors (simple household spices such as coriander, cumin etc…) mixed in sand contained in cups as target stimuli to take advantage of the innate ability of rats to discriminate between odors. Every day a unique list of 10 odors (chosen out of a pool of 40 odors) was presented during the 'study phase' one at a time, and after a delay, the same odors ('old' odors) were presented again during the recognition phase, this time intermixed with 10 odors that had not been presented during the study phase ('new' odors; Figure 3A). Sampling of each odor during the study phase was ensured by placing a small piece of cereal in each cup. To indicate whether the odors were 'new' or 'old', rats were trained on a delayed-non-matching to sample rule before collecting data for the ROC function. When the odor was 'old', rats were trained to go toward the stimulus cup, refrain digging and go to the back of the cage to receive a reward, if the response was correct (see figure 3B). When the odor was 'new', animals were trained to dig in the stimulus cup where they would find a piece of reward, if they were correct. To avoid for behavioural responses to be guided by the detection of rewards in the stimulus cups, all cups contained a piece of reward. In the cup containing a 'new' odor, rats could retrieve the reward by digging, while they could not in cups containing 'old' odors since the reward was trapped under a wire mesh. To evaluate the level of confidence of the rats for each response and plot the corresponding ROC function, Fortin and colleagues developed a very elegant system based on varying the amount of effort that rats had to put to retrieve the reward by varying the size of the stimulus cups, and the amount of reward placed in the cup, or at the back of the cage (figure 3C). In brief, rats confident about their responses would typically put quite some efforts to retrieve the reward even if it meant digging into a very deep cup. In contrast, if they were not confident, they would typically choose to adopt the behavioural responses (dig or repress digging) that could yield the largest reward. Based on this principle, five combinations of size of cups and reward yielding an increasing number of false alarm were defined (bias level 5 to 1). Each bias level was used once a week in a pseudo-random manner (one bias per session, 20 trials per session), and the number of hit and fa collected. Once performance on a given bias was stable (within 0.2 p(hit) or p(fa) of each other), four to five sessions per bias were averaged, ROC functions were plotted, and ROC indices were generated using the exact same analytical methods than in humans (see Yonelinas, 1994; Yonelinas and Parks, 2007 for details).

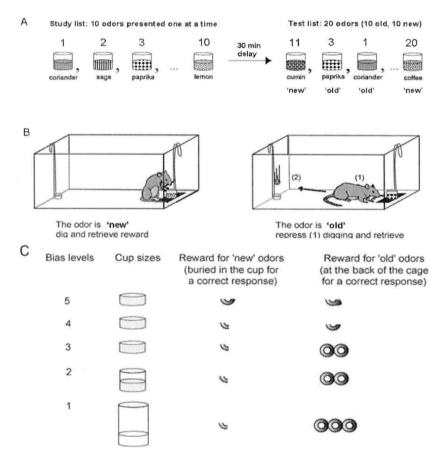

Figure 3. *Example of ROC paradigm in rats*. A. Sequence of odor presentations on the sample and test phases (Fortin et al, 2004). B. Non-matching-to-sample rule (Sauvage et al, 2010b). C. Bias levels obtained by varying cup heights and payoff ratios of cereal rewards (Sauvage et, 2008).

In summary, a typical ROC session in animals or in humans would consist in presenting a study list of stimuli one at a time (odors for animals, visual stimuli for humans) and, after a delay, memory for those stimuli was tested by presenting the same stimuli ('old') intermixed with 'new' stimuli. The number of correct recognition of an 'old' stimulus (hit) and the number of incorrect recognition of a 'new' stimulus (false alarm) across bias levels was collected, ROC functions plotted on the basis of the p(hit) and p(fa), the best fitting curve defined and the quantitative indices of recollection and familiarity generated to reflect the extent of the contribution of familiarity and recollection to recognition memory performance. Once the animal behavioural paradigms were designed, we investigated whether those latter tasks were proper translational paradigms by studying whether ROC functions in animals were varying to a similar extent than human ROC functions when subjected to the same manipulations. This series of experiments also allowed us to establish whether recollection and familiarity were distinct processes, or whether they reflected different strengths of the same process.

## II. ARE ANIMAL ROC PARADIGMS TRULY TRANSLATIONAL? ARE FAMILIARITY AND RECOLLECTION QUALITATIVELY DISTINCT PROCESSES?

The first requirement for animal ROC paradigms to be proper translational tools is to ensure that the contribution of familiarity and recollection to recognition memory performance in rats are comparable to those of humans across memory demands. To address this issue, we studied animal ROC functions of rats performing on a single item recognition memory paradigm as well as on tasks that would favor the contribution of either the recollection process or the familiarity process (associative recognition memory task for recollection; single item recognition memory task with deadline for familiarity). In addition, revealing that recognition memory performance could rely on either process, independently of the other, would also constitute evidence that those processes are distinct.

### II.1. Familiarity and Recollection in Item Recognition Memory

The first step of the validation of animal ROC paradigms as translational tasks was taken by Fortin and colleagues in 2004 who studied ROC functions for the memory of single items in rats. In this study, the authors first analyzed the function in a model-independent manner, as performed in the subsequent studies, by comparing the polynomial and linear regressions to assess whether the ROC function was linear or curvilinear, and by calculating the slope of the z-transformed ROC function to test for asymmetry. The authors reported that rat ROC functions for the memory of single items were curvilinear and asymmetrical (Figure 4A). These results were further confirmed by analysing the data with the dual-process model of recognition memory to evaluate the contribution of familiarity and recollection to item recognition memory. Indeed, the y-intercept (R) and the familiarity index (F) were found to be different from zero, revealing a significant contribution of recollection and familiarity, through the asymmetry and the curvilinearity of the ROC function, respectively. In light of the data obtained in humans for single item recognition, this result suggested that both the recollection and the familiarity processes contribute to recognition memory in animals and humans (compare Figure 2A and 4A; Yonelinas, 1994; Fortin et al, 2004; see for reviews Eichenbaum et al, 2009; Sauvage, 2010), revealing that the animal ROC paradigm was an appropriate translational tool to study single item recognition memory. Moreover, those data revealed that the recollection and the familiarity processes cooperated to achieve successful single item recognition memory performance. To further study whether animal ROC functions would be similar to that of humans under further memory demands, and investigate whether recollection and familiarity could also vary independently under specific conditions, we generated ROC functions in rats under conditions that would favour the contribution of familiarity or favour the contribution of recollection. We first studied recognition memory performance of single items under speeded conditions, which is reported to favour the use of familiarity over that of recollection, by introducing a response deadline in the original ROC paradigm for single item recognition memory. We subsequently generated ROC functions based on the performance of rats on an associative recognition memory task, known to rely primarily on recollection.

## II.2. Item Recognition Memory under Speeded Conditions Relies on Familiarity, and not Recollection

The familiarity process is described as a rapid and automatic process, while recollection is thought to be slower and conceptually driven (see for reviews Yonelinas, 2002; Mandler, 1980; 2008). Thus, results from studies using technical approaches, such as process dissociation procedures, response deadlines, evoked response potentials and electroencephalograms converged into revealing that familiarity–based judgments are completed faster than recollection-based judgments (Smith, 1993; Yonelinas and Jacoby, 1994, Hintzman and Curran, 1994; 1998; Duzel et al, 1997; Mc Elree, et al, 1999; Curran, 2004; Woodruff et al, 2006). To investigate whether familiarity alone could support successful recognition memory, we tested the memory of rats for single odors as described in Fortin et al, 2004, but this time we applied a response deadline by limiting the time available for the animals to complete a trial. This manipulation aimed at allowing for familiarity-based judgements to be completed, but not recollection-based judgements. To assess the effect of applying such a deadline, we first evaluated the memory performance of animals without deadline, and plotted the corresponding ROC function. As expected, the no-deadline condition yielded a typical single item recognition memory ROC function: curvilinear and asymmetrical, reflecting the contribution of familiarity and recollection to recognition memory performance, respectively (similar to Figure 4A). This first step also enabled us to measure the average response duration for each animal at each of the 5 bias levels, and to tailor the response deadlines to each animal. Subsequently, memory performance was assessed in the same animal, but this time a deadline was applied by giving to the animal half the time they originally took to respond. As a consequence of this deadline, the ROC function remained curvilinear, but, from asymmetrical became symmetrical (y-intercept not different from 0), reflecting a selective decrease of the contribution of recollection to recognition memory performance, while that of familiarity was spared (Figure 4B; Sauvage et al, 2010a). These results revealed that recognition memory performance under speeded conditions relies essentially on the familiarity process, while the contribution of recollection to this performance was negligible. These findings were also recently confirmed by a human ROC study that aimed at further bridging human and animal recognition memory by performing the same task than that performed in the latter study and generating ROC functions, but this time in humans (Koen et al, 2011). In summary, our data suggest that recognition memory performance could be supported by the familiarity process without a significant contribution of the recollection process, and that ROC functions mirror functions obtained in humans under speeded conditions. To complete the validation of the task as a translational paradigm, and to further investigate whether recollection and familiarity would behave as distinct processses under other conditions, we investigated the shape of ROC functions for associative recognition memory, which has been suggested to principally rely on the recollection process in humans.

## II.3. Recollection Contributes to Associative Recognition Memory, not Familiarity

Asymmetrical and linear ROC functions, reflecting a strong contribution of the recollection process and a lack of contribution of the familiarity process to recognition performance have been reported in a number of independent studies (Yonelinas, 1997; Arndt and Reder, 2001; Slotnick et al, 2000; Rotello et al, 2000; even by the most fervent partisan of the one-process model: Kelley and Wixted, 2001). However, because linear ROCs have been rarely reported in studies using the one-process model, the finding of linear ROCs remained long controversial. To test whether associative recognition memory relied solely on the recollection process, we developed a new associative ROC paradigm involving the recognition of odors paired with media (Sauvage et al, 2008). The principle of this task is that rats can separately attend to odors and media as distinct dimensions when presented at once as an odor-medium pair (Birrell et al, 2000). To test associative recognition memory performance, we adapted the ROC protocol described in the previous section by presenting odor-medium pairs instead of simple odours. Odors were still simple household spices (cumin, thyme etc...), but this time, were mixed with different media (sand, cotton balls...); one odor with one medium per stimulus cup, generating a pool of 110 pairs to choose from. In brief, to assess associative recognition memory performance, rats were presented with a study list of 10 odor-medium pairs (for example: thyme mixed with sand, and cumin mixed with beads), one at a time. After a delay, the memory for those pairs was tested using a delayed-non-matching to sample rule by presenting the same ten pairs intermixed with ten pairs that had not been presented during the study phase ('new' rearranged pairs composed of the same media and odors than those presented during the study phase, but not the same pairings; for example thyme mixed with beads). Using this paradigm, we collected p(hit) and p(fa) for each bias level and, using the standard analysis methods for ROC functions in animals, we were able to show that the rat ROC function for associative recognition memory was linear and asymmetrical, reflecting a strong contribution of recollection and a negligible contribution of familiarity to memory performance (Figure 4C; Sham). In summary, our results support previous findings in humans reporting that recollection primarily supports associative recognition memory, without requiring a significant contribution of familiarity to memory performance. These results gave further support to the 'dual-process' theory, which suggests that recollection and familiarity are qualitatively distinct processes that can cooperate under certain conditions, but can also support successful recognition memory performance based solely on one or the other process. In contrast, those results do not support the one-process model view, which predicts that memory performance cannot be supported by the recollection process without the contribution of familiarity. In reaction to these findings, partisans of the one-process model argued that the linearity of the ROC function for associative recognition memory could be due to the use of differential reward payoffs to manipulate the decision criteria of the animals (bias levels) rather than from a selective use of recollection (Wixted and Squire, 2008; see Eichenbaum et al, 2008 for comments). However, a simple visual inspection of the rat ROC function for single odor recognition memory shows that it is possible to obtain a curvilinear ROC function with the exact same differential reward payoffs but different memory demands (compare Figure 4A, B and C), suggesting that the shape of ROC functions is tied to memory demands and not related to the use of differential payoff rewards. More precisely, Wixted and Squire speculated that the use of differential reward payoffs could lead to a 'differential outcomes effect' (DOE), and explain the linearity of the ROC function with no ties to a specific recollection deficit. A differential outcomes effect is observed when animals learn faster (as measured by an increase in performance accuracy), after hundreds of repetitions, stimulus-response reward combinations that yield a larger reward than those which yield a smaller one. For example: animals would learn faster to push a lever when a green light is on if they receive a large reward, than when they would learn to respond to a red light if the reward is smaller. The main reason why this interpretation is erroneous is that our results lead to a pattern opposite to that predicted if a DOE would be at stake. Indeed, in our experiment: accuracy is the highest when there is no difference between the reward obtained for the 'new' or 'old' stimuli (bias 5; 1/2 froot loop in both cases) and is the lowest for Bias 1, which yields the largest difference between rewards for the 'new' stimulus and the 'old' stimuli (¼ compared to 3 froot loops). Hence, a careful reading of the DOE literature makes it obvious that the differential outcomes effect is not at work in our study, and that the linearity of the rat ROC function for associative recognition memory is tied to memory demands, and not to the use of differential payoff rewards (Eichenbaum et al, 2008). In conclusion, we have reported in this study that the ROC function for associative recognition in rats is linear, demonstrating that recollection can support recognition memory performance without significant contribution of the familiarity process, which suggests that familiarity and recollection are distinct processes. Moreover, we could show that the animal ROC function for associative recognition memory is similar to that of humans validating further the animal ROC paradigms as proper translational tasks.

In conclusion, in the second part of this chapter, we have gathered evidence from rats with 'healthy' hippocampus that familiarity and recollection could support recognition memory independently of each other, supporting the claim that familiarity and recollection are qualitatively distinct processes, and that their respective contribution depends on the memory demands of the task. Moreover, we validated the animal ROC paradigms as appropriate translational paradigms by demonstrating that animal ROC functions vary to the same extent than human ROC functions do when subjected to similar manipulations. In the third part of the chapter, we will focus on shedding some light on a second important controversy fuelling the field of human recognition memory which is whether the hippocampus supports recollection only, or whether it supports both recollection and familiarity. Indeed, the neural substrates for recollection and familiarity remain controversial in humans principally because of the difficulty of precisely defining the extent of the brain damage in patients with amnesia, and because of the impossibility of identifying precisely the source of memory-induced activity in brain areas that are adjacent. To address this issue, we combined behavioural animal ROC paradigms to lesions circumscribed to the hippocampus, and evaluated the effect of those lesions on the contribution of familiarity and recollection to single item- and associative recognition memory. Furthermore, we studied memory performance of old rats, as a physiological model of hippocampal dysfunction.

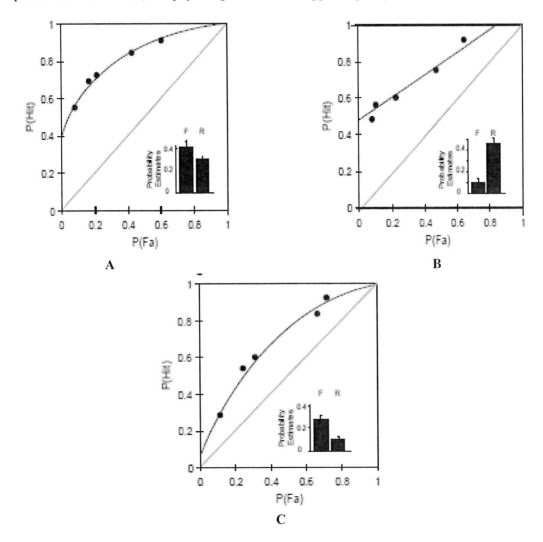

Figure 4. *Animal ROC paradigms are translational, and recollection and familiarity are distinct processes.* Recollection (R) and familiarity (F) indices are shown as bar diagrams. Rat ROC functions are comparable to human ones' under the same memory demands, suggesting rat ROC tasks are proper translational paradigms. A. ROC function for single item recognition memory (Fortin et al, 2004); B. ROC function for single item recognition memory with a response deadline (Sauvage et al, 2010a); C: ROC function for associative recognition memory (Sauvage et al, 2008). Recognition memory performance could rely on familiarity or recollection, independently of each other, suggesting that the familiarity and the recollection processes are distinct.

# III. Does the HIP Support Both Familiarity and Recollection, or only Recollection?

Studies in animals that did not use ROC functions have suggested for the HIP a predominant role in recollection, while the ParaHIP would play a critical role in familiarity in recognition memory (Eichenbaum et al, 1994; Aggleton and Brown, 1999; Brown and Aggleton, 2001; see for a review Eichenbaum et al, 2007). In addition, evidence from human studies using ROC paradigms and focusing on the ParaHIP are rather consensual, and support the claim that, at least part of the ParaHIP (the perirhinal cortex: PRc, and the entorhinal cortex: EC) plays a preponderant role in familiarity (Bowles et al, 2007; Yonelinas et al, 2007; Haskins et al, 2008; Ford et al, 2010; see for reviews Diana et al, 2007; 2009; Yonelinas et al, 2010). In contrast, results emerging from studies focusing on the contribution of the HIP to familiarity and recollection are rather conflicting. Indeed, as mentioned in the introduction, some human fMRI and behavioral studies report selective recollection deficits in amnesic patients with damage restricted to the hippocampus, as reflected by a y-intercept of the ROC function significantly reduced in amnesic patients, while the curvilinearity of the function is spared (see for reviews Eichenbaum et al, 2007; Montaldi and Mayes 2010; Yonelinas et al, 2010). In contrast, others studies report familiarity and recollection deficits in the same type of patients, as reflected by an alteration of both the asymmetry and the curvilinearity of ROC functions (see for reviews Wixted and Squire 2004; 2010). Moreover, studies from the latter laboratory have suggested that activity in the HIP and the PRc was correlated to the memory strength of remembered items rather than tied to the specific contribution of those brain areas to the recollection or the familiarity processes (Shrager et al, 2008; see for a review Squire et al, 2007). A possible explanation for the discrepancy between those results is that damage to the brain in the latter studies was not restricted to the HIP, but also extended to the cortex adjacent to the HIP: the ParaHIP. To test whether damage truly restricted to the HIP would lead to selective recollection deficits, or impair both familiarity and recollection, we combined our animal ROC paradigms with stereotactic lesions unequivocally restricted to the HIP (as it is possible to control for with histological stainings in animals), and studied the performance of HIP lesioned-rats on tasks with different memory demands (single item- or associative recognition memory). In addition, I also report results from an aging study on single item recognition memory used as a model of physiological hippocampal dysfunction.

## III.1. Hippocampal Lesion Impairs Recollection, but not Familiarity in Item Recognition Memory

Fortin and colleagues had the first shot at investigating the effect of a selective hippocampal lesion on familiarity and recollection, and reported a significant drop of the y-intercept of the ROC function while its curvilinearity remained unaffected, consistent with a selective deficit in recollection and a performance principally relying on the familiarity process (Figure 5A, Hippocampus). This finding was the first evidence that damage unequivocally restricted to the HIP selectively impaired recollection without affecting familiarity, suggesting that the HIP supports recollection, but not familiarity. Overall memory performance in the HIP-lesioned group was slightly, but significantly lower when compared to controls'. Hence it was argued by the partisan of the one-process model, that hippocampal lesions could have affected overall memory strength rather than the recollection process per-se. Fortin and colleagues tested this hypothesis by lowering the overall memory performance of control rats by increasing the delay from 30 to 75 min between the study phase and the recognition phase of the memory task in a subsequent experiment, and by evaluating the effect of this manipulation on the contribution of recollection and familiarity to recognition memory. Against the predictions of the one-process model, decreasing memory strength affected selectively the familiarity process, but not the recollection process (Figure 5B). Indeed, the ROC function for single item recognition memory of controls, which was originally asymmetrical and curvilinear with a standard delay of 30 min (Figure 5A: Sham), became linear and asymmetrical when the delay between study phase and recognition phase was increased to 75 min (Figure 5B), reflecting a drop in familiarity, and not recollection. This latter result clearly contrasted with the effect obtained following the HIP lesion, which led to a curvilinear and symmetrical ROC reflecting a significant decrease in recollection (Figure 5A, Hippocampus). This manipulation clearly showed that reducing overall memory strength did not affect recollection, but significantly affected the familiarity process, and therefore could not account for the recollection deficit observed following hippocampal damage in this experiment.

In conclusion, this first study showed clearly that the hippocampus supports recollection in animals, which is in line with findings in the human literature within the frame of both the one-model- and the dual-process models. In addition, the findings that familiarity was not affected by hippocampal damage (eg HIP does not support familiarity) was in agreement with part of the human literature. Next, to test whether the contribution of the HIP to recollection or familiarity was depending on the type of insults inflicted to the HIP, Eichenbaum and colleagues investigated whether these results would further hold in the physiological model of hippocampal dysfunction that is aging.

## III.2. Hippocampal Dysfunction in Aging also Impairs Recollection, and not Familiarity

Reduced hippocampal function in aging was found in humans and animals, and was paralleled by selective recollection deficits, and relatively spared familiarity in humans (Rosenzweig and Barnes, 2003; Wilson et al., 2006; Daselaar et al, 2006; Duarte et al, 2006; Howard et al, 2006; Prull et al, 2006; Duverne et al, 2007; Peters and Daum, 2008). To test whether physiological dysfunction of the HIP would have the same effect than hippocampal lesion on recollection and familiarity in rats, Eichenbaum and colleagues compared the memory performance for single odors of old (22-24 months old) memory-impaired rats with the performance of old rats without memory impairments, and control rats (young rats). Since old rats tend to overall participate less to tasks than controls, independently of whether they are memory-impaired or not, the ROC paradigm for single item recognition memory was slightly modified to bring them to a similar level of participation than the controls. In brief, only one size of target cup was used, reward ratio and reward type were slightly altered, and the delay between study and recognition phases was reduced to 15 min (Robitsek et al, 2008). Those changes did not affect the performance of controls, which yielded a typical ROC function for single item recognition memory (asymmetrical and curvilinear), reflecting the contribution of recollection and familiarity to recognition memory, respectively. In addition, old 'memory-unimpaired' rats displayed a similar ROC function than controls'. In striking contrast, the ROC function of memory-impaired rats was symmetrical and curvilinear, revealing a selective loss of recollection and a performance relying principally on the familiarity process (Figure 5C). These results mirrored those obtained following lesions of the HIP on the same single odor recognition memory task, and confirmed that the HIP supports recollection, and not familiarity independently of the type of insults inflicted to the HIP (physiological or lesion). In addition, to study whether the contribution of the HIP to recollection and familiarity depend on memory demands or could be generalized to other types of memory, we studied next the effect of hippocampal damage on memory performance in an associative recognition memory task.

## III.3. Lesion of the Hippocampus Impairs Recollection, but Increases the Contribution of Familiarity in Associative Recognition Memory

Previous human studies have shown that patients with amnesia, who perform poorly on associative recognition memory tasks with pairs of unrelated stimuli, could perform significantly better when tested with compound words; words that are based on the combination of two other words that can be encoded either as a pair of unrelated words, or unitized as a single word (for example: fireman, motherboard, etc…; Giovanello et al, 2003; 2006). Indeed, in the latter case amnesic patients can rely on the familiarity process, spared in those patients, to remember such pairs of words as opposed to primarily relying on recollection as it is the case for healthy subjects with intact HIP (Quamme et al, 2007; Yonelinas et al, 1997). To further study the contribution of the HIP to familiarity and recollection in associative recognition memory, we investigated the recognition memory performance for pairs in rats with and without hippocampal lesion using the associative ROC paradigm described in Sauvage et al, 2008. Briefly, rats were presented with a study list of ten odors paired with media, and recognition memory performance was subsequently assessed by presenting the same pairs intermixed with rearranged odor-medium pairs. As described in the first part of this chapter, the sham-operated animals displayed a standard ROC function for associative recognition memory, reflecting the contribution of recollection with a negligible contribution of familiarity to memory performance (eg. the ROC function was asymmetrical and linear, respectively; Figure 5D, Sham). At difference, the ROC function for hippocampal-lesioned rats suggested that performance was principally relying on the familiarity process, while the recollection process was significantly altered by hippocampal lesion (the ROC function curvilinear and almost symmetrical, respectively: Figure 5D; Hippocampus). Even more interesting, further statistical analysis of the recollection and familiarity indices revealed that hippocampal lesion significantly decreased the contribution of the recollection process to memory performance, but significantly increased that of familiarity (Sauvage et al, 2008). Thus, these findings confirm the results of human studies reporting that the HIP supports recollection. More importantly, this study brought the first clear evidence, in the human and animal literature, that the HIP is unlikely to be the neural substrate of familiarity, given that the contribution of the familiarity process to recognition memory increases significantly following hippocampal damage. In line with another assumption of the one-process model, partisans of this theory suggested an alternative interpretation of those data. Assuming that the recollection process was a more 'demanding' process (a term that remains to be clarified) than the familiarity process, and that the lesion of the HIP were not total, it was suggested that hippocampal lesion could reduce significantly the contribution of the recollection process to recognition memory, but that enough resources would still be available to complete the 'less demanding' familiarity judgments. Technical and theoretical considerations render this hypothesis rather unlikely. Indeed, the lesions of the HIP involved numerous small lesions (twenty-four total; twelve per hemisphere), that were performed stereotactically (e.g. spread along the rostro-caudal, dorso-ventral and medio-lateral axis in a regular manner) leaving even the remaining hippocampal 'bits' definitively disconnected and unlikely to be functional. Moreover, if in line with the one-process model theory, the HIP was truly supporting both the recollection and the familiarity process, and the less 'demanding' process (familiarity) were to be selectively spared by HIP lesion, one would expect familiarity-based judgements to be spared, but a significant increase of the contribution of familiarity to recognition memory as observed in the present experiment would still remain to be explained. Finally, a global 'memory strength' effect cannot account for the latter findings because overall recognition memory performance did not significantly differ between the Hippocampus group and the Sham rats in this experiment. Taken together, those results suggested that hippocampal-lesioned rats recognize the pairs presented during the study phase to a similar level than controls, only, they used a familiarity-based strategy by unitizing both stimulus elements of the pair into a single one (for example 'cumin-scented sand' instead of cumin and sand) instead of recollection–based judgements as it is the case for controls. Such a strategy has been reported in hippocampal-lesioned rats in previous studies (Eichenbaum et 1994), and in patients with amnesia tested for the recognition memory of compounds words (Giovanello et al, 2006; Quamme et al 2007). In conclusion, this study brought the first clear evidence that the HIP does not support familiarity, given that the contribution of familiarity to recognition memory increases following hippocampal lesion. Moreover, these findings suggest that the role of the HIP in recollection can be generalized to other memory demands than single item recognition memory, as it is the case in humans. These results, together with the fact that familiarity and recollection were found to vary in an opposite manner under the same manipulations, brought further support to the claim that familiarity and recollection are qualitatively distinct processes.

In summary, in the third part of this chapter, we have brought evidence based, this time, on hippocampal damage that the HIP supports recollection and not familiarity, as shown by a significant reduction of the contribution of recollection to memory performance following hippocampal damage in single item and associative recognition memory. We also reported that the contribution of familiarity to memory performance was either: not affected by hippocampal damage, or was even significantly increased, suggesting that the HIP is not the neural substrate of the familiarity process. Finally, we reported the first compelling evidence that familiarity and recollection are distinct processes, since they can vary in an opposite manner under a given manipulation. Of note, it is important to underline that results from animal ROC studies are not the product of model-dependent analysis, since data are systematically analyzed first with model-independent parameters (linear and polynomial regressions) to evaluate the shape of the ROC functions, and only then, ROC indices for recollection and familiarity are generated using the dual-process model (Fortin et al, 2004; Robitsek et al, 2008; Sauvage et al, 2008, 2010a, 2010c for details and Sauvage, 2010b for a

172                              Magdalena M. Sauvage

review). Moreover, each data set was concurrently analyzed with the single-process model which confirmed the dual-process findings by revealing that hippocampal dysfunction selectively eliminates one parameter of the ROC function, specifically the inequality of variances between 'old' and 'new' items. By contrast, no changes were observed in the second one-process model parameter of the ROC function, d', that reflects the difference in memory strength between 'old' and 'new' items. In summary, analysis with the one-process model confirmed that hippocampal dysfunction selectively eliminates one parameter supporting the identification of old items, which is comparable to altering the recollection process in the dual-process theory, and left intact another parameter comparable to familiarity. In the final part of this chapter, I report further studies that go beyond the role of the HIP in recollection and familiarity, and focus on identifying the contribution of the ParaHIP to recollection and familiarity.

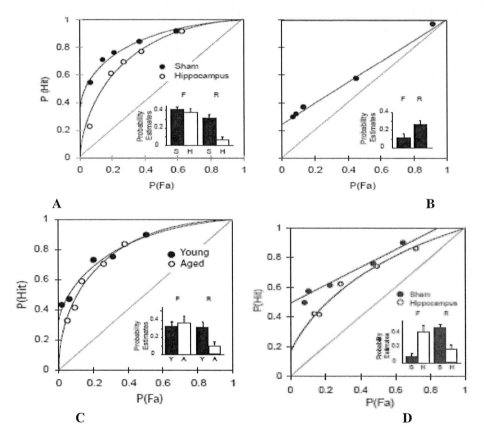

Figure 5. The hippocampus supports recollection and not familiarity, independently of the memory demands and independently of the type of insults (Sauvage et al, 2010b). Hippocampal damage eliminates recollection-based performance while sparing the familiarity process in a single item recognition memory in young (A) and aged (C) rats, as reflected by a drop of the y-intercept of the function (Fortin et al, 2004; Robitsek et al, 2008). The same damage impairs recollection, but significantly increases familiarity in associative recognition memory, as reflected by an additional increase in the curvilinearity of the ROC function (D) (Sauvage et al, 2008). In contrast to lesioning the hippocampus, reducing memory strength by extending the delay between the study and the recognition phases for control rats (Sham) led to a selective reduction of the contribution of familiarity to recognition memory performance, suggesting that reduced memory strength cannot account for the recollection deficit observed following hippocampal lesion (B).

# IV. Is the Parahippocampal Region Functionally Segregated in Terms of Familiarity and Recollection in Recognition Memory?

Recent human and animal studies have suggested that specific areas of the parahippocampal region, could contribute to different aspects of memory function (see for reviews Eichenbaum et al, 2007; Lipton et Eichenbaum, 2008; Diana et al, 2007; 2009). Familiarity of individual items are suggested to be principally processed by the perirhinal cortex (PRc) and the lateral entorhinal cortex (LEC), while the postrhinal cortex (POR; parahippocampal cortex in humans) and the medial entorhinal cortex (MEC) would preferentially process the spatial and temporal context in which items have been experienced, hence supporting rather recollection. Subsequently, both the item and contextual information would be combined within the HIP. However, no direct evidence of this functional segregation can be found in the human literature given the difficulty of teasing apart the precise location of memory-related brain activity within the adjacent areas of the MTL in humans, and the rarity of the cases showing restricted lesions to one or the other areas of the parahippocampal region. Hence, to tackle this issue we applied our standard approach by combining stereotactic lesions with animal behavioural ROC paradigms, and focused on investigating the contribution of the different areas of the parahippocampal region to recollection and familiarity in recognition memory starting with a brain area that could provide to the HIP information required for recollection-based judgements:the MEC, and pursuing by focusing on the PRc to investigate the neural substrate of familiarity.

## IV.1. The MEC Is Selectively Involved in Recollection, but not Familiarity in Item Recognition Memory

Most of the recent studies on the MEC emphasize its role in spatial navigation and path integration due to the recent discovery of the grid cells in the caudal MEC, which are suggested to code for space in a metric manner (Fyhn et al, 2004; Hafting et al 2005, see for reviews Mc Naughton et al, 2006; Moser and Moser, 2008). The MEC is one of the major inputs of the HIP and receives major and direct projections from the PHc (see for a review Van Strien et al, 2009). Human fMRI studies have reported a strong involvement of the PHc and the HIP in the recollection of single item and associations (Eldridge et al, 2000; Cansino et al, 2002; Yonelinas et al, 2005; Woodruff et al, 2005; Aminoff et al 2008; Suchan et al, 2008). In contrast, the contribution of the MEC to recollection has been principally extrapolated from its anatomical projections with the PHc and the HIP. Hence, direct evidence of a critical and/or selective contribution of the MEC to the recollection process in recognition memory was missing. To test whether the MEC contributes selectively to recollection, we performed restricted lesions of the MEC and investigated the effect of these lesions on recollection and familiarity using our standard ROC paradigm for item recognition memory (Sauvage et al, 2010c). In contrast to the sham-lesioned rats, that displayed a typical curvilinear and asymmetrical ROC function reflecting the contribution of both processes to memory performance (Figure 6A: Sham), the ROC function of MEC-lesioned rats remained curvilinear, but became symmetrical (y-intercept not different from 0; Figure 6A: MEC). This suggested a selective reduction of the contribution of recollection to memory performance and spared familiarity, as observed previously in rats with hippocampal dysfunction (Figure 5A, MEC). These findings demonstrated a selective role of the MEC in recollection, and not familiarity. Moreover, since MEC damage in our study impaired performance on a non-spatial (odor) recognition memory task, these findings also suggested a broader role of the MEC in recognition memory than a dedicated role in spatial memory. These findings are supported by recent electrophysiological studies reporting that MEC cells of rats performing on a left/right working memory alternation task signal which of the two episodes is ongoing, hence MEC activity seems not to only reflect the spatial context of events experienced, but also their temporal context (Lipton et al., 2007; Lipton and Eichenbaum, 2008). Our findings brought direct evidence that the MEC process information necessary for recollection and suggest that the MEC could constitute one of the sources of information necessary for the HIP to complete recollective-based judgements. To test further the hypothesis of a functional segregation of the parahippocampal region in recollection and familiarity, Eichenbaum and colleagues investigated next the contribution of the PRc to recollection and familiarity in single item recognition memory.

## IV.2. The PRc Process Familiarity, and not Recollection

Numerous human and animal studies point towards a critical and selective role of the PRc in familiarity in recognition memory. Thus, fMRI studies in humans have reported a high correlation between PRc activity and the use of familiarity-based judgements in tasks taxing for recognition memory (Davachi et al., 2003; Henson et al., 2003; Ranganath et al., 2003; Montaldi et al., 2006; Suchan et al, 2008; Haskins et al, 2008; Ford et al, 2010). Moreover, ablation of the PRc in a patient who suffered from an intractable case of epilepsy led to selective familiarity deficits, while the contribution of recollection to recognition memory remained intact (Bowles et al, 2007). Furthermore, previous animal studies have suggested that the PRc could preferentially process information required to achieve behavioral responses based on familiarity (Eichenbaum et al, 1994, Aggleton and Brown, 1999; Brown and Aggleton 2001). To confirm that the PRc played a critical role in familiarity and to investigate whether the parahippocampal region was functionally segregated in terms of its contribution to recollection and familiarity in recognition memory, Eichenbaum and colleagues decided to adopt a standard ROC approach. However, because the PRc is directly located above the LEC on the dorso-ventral axis (see Figure 1), a lesion approach was unlikely to lead to a specific lesion of the PRc, but rather to a lesion of the PRc–LEC (by diffusion of the medium used to induce lesions) and thereby prevent the assessment of the specific contribution of the PRc to familiarity and recollection. Hence, the authors decided on an alternative strategy and targeted a brain area that provides major excitatory inputs to the PRc (the amygdala), but does not belong to the MTL. Depriving the PRc from amygdala inputs leads to PRc dysfunction, and the effect of this dysfunction was assessed using the standard ROC paradigm for single item recognition. The ROC function for amygdala-lesioned animals for single item recognition memory was found to remain asymmetrical, but instead of being curvilinear as observed in controls, the ROC function of lesioned rats became linear, suggesting a selective reduction of the contribution of familiarity to memory performance while that of recollection was not significantly altered (Figure 6B: Sham versus

Amygdala; Farovik et al, 2011). These data provided compelling evidence that the PRc subserves familiarity rather than recollection, and gave further support to the hypothesis of a functional segregation of the parahippocampal region into a 'familiarity' stream of information processing that would include the PRc, and a 'recollection' steam of information processing that would comprise the MEC.

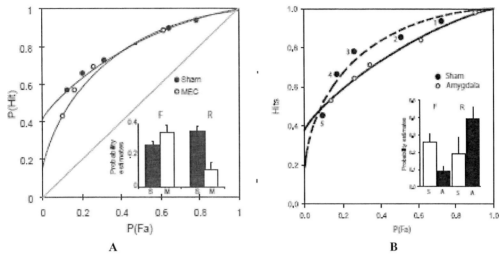

Figure 6. *The parahippocampal region is functionally segregated in terms of recollection and familiarity.* A. A significant and specific reduction of the y-intercept of the ROC function following MEC damage reveals that the MEC plays a critical role in recollection (Sauvage et al, 2010c). B. Prc dysfunction following amygdala lesion led to a selective alteration of the curvilinearity of the ROC function, suggesting a determinant role of the PRc in familiarity (Farovik et al, 2011).

## CONCLUSION

Developing new translational ROC paradigms enabled us to contribute to solve two major controversies that fuelled human recognition memory for the past two decades, principally because of technical limitations. Thus, using animal ROC paradigms, we were able to accumulate clear evidence that the familiarity and the recollection processes are qualitatively distinct processes. Indeed, we showed that recognition memory performance could rely on either the familiarity process or the recollection process, independently of each other, in experiments with intact and hippocampal-damaged rats. Moreover, we reported that recollection and familiarity could even vary in an opposite manner under specific conditions, which goes against the one-process theory that familiarity and recollection reflect the same process, and differ only in memory strength. In addition, we clearly demonstrated that the HIP supports the recollection process, and not the familiarity process since hippocampal dysfunction impairs recollection while sparing familiarity in single item recognition memory, and even significantly increases the contribution of familiarity to the recognition memory for pairs of items (associative recognition memory). These translational paradigms also enabled us to further dissect the pathways involved in the processing of information that are necessary to complete familiarity- and recollection-based judgments by revealing that the parahippocampal region is functionally segregated into two distinct streams of information processing: onethat includes the PRc, and supports preferentially familiarity-type information, and a second that principally supports processes recollective-type information and includes the MEC. The profound translational character of the animal ROC paradigms has been clearly demonstrated while adopting an 'animal to human' approach by numerous studies confirming that animal ROC functions vary in a similar manner than humans' under the same memory demands. In addition, as a counterpart to this approach, recent human studies have built upon results originally described in animal ROC paradigms to study human recognition memory performance, and thus, strengthened the bridge between human and animal recognition memory that constitutes ROC paradigms (Koen et al, 2011). Given the success of this approach, in terms of translational research and the many questions that remain to be elucidated in the domain of memory function, we are confident that the use of the animal ROC paradigms combined with more standard approaches and new technologies, will contribute to significant progress in the characterization of the neural substrates of familiarity and recollection in recognition memory.

## ACKNOWLEDGMENTS

These experiments were funded by the grants MH71702, MH51520, MH52090 and AG09973, and the Mercator Stiftung.

## REFERENCES

Aggleton JP, Brown MW. (1999) Episodic memory, amnesia, and the hippocampal-anterior thalamic axis. *Behav Brain Sci.*22(3):425-44; discussion 444-89.

Aggleton, J.P., Vann, S.D., Denby, C., Dix, S., Mayes, A.R., Roberts, N., Yonelinas, A.P.(2005). Sparing of the familiarity component of recognition memory in a patient with hippocampal pathology. *Neuropsychologia.*43(12):1810-23.

Aminoff, E., Gronau, N., Bar, M. (2007) The parahippocampal cortex mediates spatial and nonspatial associations. *Cereb Cortex.* 17(7):1493-503.

Arndt, J., & Reder, L.M. (2002). Word frequency and receiver-operating characteristic curves in recognition memory: Evidence for a dual-process interpretation. *Journal of Experimental Psychology: Learning, Memory, and Cognition.* 28(5):830-42.

Atkinson, R.C., Juola, J.F. (1973). Factors influencing speed and accuracy of word recognition, In S.Kornblum (Ed.), *Attention and performance* (Vol.4,pp.583-612) new york: Academic Press.

Atkinson, R.C., Juola, J.F. (1974). Search and decision processes in recognition memory. In D.H. krantz, R.C. Atkinson.RD. Luce (Eds.).*Contemporary developments in mathematical psychology* (pp.243-293). San Francisco: W.H. Freeman.

Bar, M., Aminoff, E., Schacter, D.L. (2008) Scenes unseen: the parahippocampal cortex intrinsically subserves contextual associations, not scenes or places per se. *J Neurosci.* 20; 28 (34): 8539-44.

Barbeau, E.J., Felician, O., Joubert, S., Sontheimer, A., Ceccaldi, M., Poncet, M. (2005) Preserved visual recognition memory in an amnesic patient with hippocampal lesions. *Hippocampus*. 15(5):587-96.

Birrell, J.M. & Brown, V.J. (2000). Medial frontal cortex mediates perceptual attentional set shifting in the rat. *J. Neurosci*. 20, 4320–4324.

Bowles, B., Crupi, C., Mirsattari, S.M., Pigott, S.E., Parrent, A.G., Pruessner, J.C., Yonelinas, A.P., Köhler, S. (2007). Impaired familiarity with preserved recollection after anterior temporal-lobe resection that spares the hippocampus. *Proc Natl Acad Sci USA*. 9;104(41):16382-7.

Bowles B, Crupi C, Pigott S, Parrent A, Wiebe S, Janzen L, Köhler S. (2010) Double dissociation of selective recollection and familiarity impairments following two different surgical treatments for temporal-lobe epilepsy. *Neuropsychologia*. 48(9):2640-7.

Brandt, K.R., Gardiner, J.M., Vargha-Khadem, F., Baddeley, A.D., Mishkin, M. (2008) Impairment of recollection but not familiarity in a case of developmental amnesia. *Neurocase*.15(1):60-5.

Brown, M. W. & Aggleton, J. P. (2001) Recognition memory: what are the roles of the perirhinal cortex and hippocampus? *Nature Rev. Neurosci*. 2, 51–61.

Burwell RD, Furtak SC. (2008).Recognition memory: can you teach an old dogma new tricks? *Neuron*. 28;59(4):523-5.

Craik, F.I., & Byrd, M. (1982). Aging and cognitive deficits: the role of attentional resources. In: *Aging and cognitive processes* (Craik FI, Trehub S, eds), pp51–110.

Curran, T. (2004). Effects of attention and confidence on the hypothesized ERP correlates of recollection and familiarity. *Neuropsychologia* 42:1088–106.

Daselaar, S.M., Fleck, M.S., Dobbins, I.G., Madden, D.J., Cabeza, R. (2006). Effects of healthy aging on hippocampal and rhinal memory functions: an event related fMRI study. *Cereb Cortex* 16:1771–1782.

Diana, R.A., Yonelinas, A.P., Ranganath, C. (2007). Imaging recollection and familiarity in the medial temporal lobe: a three-component model. *Trends Cogn Sci*. 11(9):379-86.

Diana, R.A., Yonelinas, A.P., Ranganath, C. (2009). Medial Temporal Lobe Activity during Source Retrieval Reflects Information Type, not Memory Strength. *J Cogn Neurosci. online*.

Duarte, A,, Ranganath, C., Trujillo, C., Knight, R.T. (2006). Intact recollection memory in high performing older adults: ERP and behavioral evidence. *J. Cogn. Neurosci*. 18(1):33–47.

Duverne, S., Habibi, A., Rugg, M.D. (2008). Regional specificity of age effects on the neural correlates of episodic retrieval. *Neurobiol Aging*. 29(12):1902-16.

Duzel, E.,Yonelinas, A.P., Mangun, G.R., Heinzem, H.J., Tulving, E. (1997). Event-related brain potential correlates of two states of conscious awareness in memory. *Proc. Natl. Acad. Sci. USA*. 94(11):5973–78.

Düzel, E., Vargha-Khadem, F., Heinze, H.J., Mishkin, M. (2001) Brain activity evidence for recognition without recollection after early hippocampal damage. *Proc Natl Acad Sci U S A*. 98(14):8101-6.

Eichenbaum, H. (1994) *in Memory Systems* (eds. Schacter, D.L., Tulving, E.) 147–202 Q5 (MIT Press, Cambridge, Massachusetts).

Eichenbaum, H., Otto, T. & Cohen, N. J. (1994). Two functional components of the hippocampal memory system. *Behav. Brain Sci*. 17, 449–472, 472–518.

Eichenbaum, H., Yonelinas, A.R. & Ranganath, C. (2007). The medial temporal lobe and recognition memory.*Annu. Rev. Neurosci.* 30, 123–152.

Eichenbaum, H., Sauvage, M., Fortin, N., and Yonelinas, A.P. (2008) "ROCs in Rats? Response to Wixted and Squire". *Learning and Memory.* 26;15(9):691-3.

Eichenbaum H, Fortin N, Sauvage M, Robitsek RJ, Farovik A.(2010) An animal model of amnesia that uses Receiver Operating Characteristics (ROC) analysis to distinguish recollection from familiarity deficits in recognition memory. *Neuropsychologia.* 48(8):2281- 9.

Farovik A, Place R.J, Miller D.R., Eichenbaum H. (2011). Amygdala lesions selectively impair familiarity in recognition memory. *Nat Neurosci.* 14(11):1416-7.

Ford JH, Verfaellie M, Giovanello KS. (2010) Neural correlates of familiarity-based associative retrieval. *Neuropsychologia.* 48(10):3019-25.

Fortin, N.J., Wright, S.P., Eichenbaum, H. (2004). Recollection-like memory retrieval in rats is dependent on the hippocampus. *Nature.* 9;431(7005):188-91.

Furtak SC, Wei SM, Agster KL, Burwell RD. (2007) Functional neuroanatomy of the parahippocampal region in the rat: the perirhinal and postrhinal cortices.*Hippocampus.* 17(9):709-22.

Fyhn, M., Molden, S., Witter, M.P., Moser, E.I., Moser, M.B. (2004). Spatial representation in the entorhinal cortex. *Science.* 27, 305 (5688), 1258-64.

Giovanello KS, Verfaellie M, Keane MM. (2003) Disproportionate deficit in associative recognition relative to item recognition in global amnesia. *Cogn Affect Behav Neurosci.* 3(3):186-94.

Giovanello, K.S., Keane, M.M., Verfaellie, M.(2006). The contribution of familiarity to associative memory in amnesia. *Neuropsychologia.* 44(10):1859-65.

Hafting, T., Fyhn, M., Molden, S., Moser, M.B., Moser, E.I. (2005). Microstructure of a spatial map in the entorhinal cortex. *Nature.* 436(7052):801-6.

Haskins, A.L., Yonelinas, A.P., Quamme, J.R., Ranganath, C. (2008). Perirhinal cortex supports encoding and familiarity-based recognition of novel associations.*Neuron.* 28;59(4):554-60.

Hockley, W. E. (1991). Recognition memory for item and associative information: A comparison of forgetting rates. In E. William, E. Hockley, & E. S. Lewandowsky (Eds.), *Relating theory and data: Essays on human memory in honor of Bennet B. Murdock* (pp. 227–248).

Hockley, W. E. (1992). Item versus associative information: Further comparisons of forgetting rates. *Journal of Experimental Psychology: Learning, Memory, and Cognition,*18(6), 1321–1330.

Hintzman, D.L., Curran, T. (1994). Retrieval dynamics of recognition and frequency judgments:evidence for separate processes of familiarity and recall. *J. Mem. Lang.* 331:1–18.

Hintzman, D.L., Caulton, D.A., Levitin, D.J. (1998). Retrieval dynamics in recognition and list discrimination: further evidence of separate processes of familiarity and recall. *Mem Cognit.* 26(3):449-62.

Holdstock, J. S., Mayes, A. R., Cezayirli, E., Isaac, C. L.,Aggleton, J. P., & Roberts, N. (2000). A comparison of egocentric and allocentric spatial memory in a patient with selective hippocampal damage. *Neuropsychologia*, 38(4), 410–425.

Howard, M.W., Bessette-Symons, B., Zhang, Y., Hoyer, W.J. (2006). Aging selectively impairs recollection in recognition memory for pictures: evidence from modelling and receiver operating characteristic curves. *Psychol Aging.* 21:96–106.

Kelley, R., Wixted, J.T.(2001) On the nature of associative information in recognition memory. *J Exp Psychol Learn Mem Cogn.* 27(3):701-22.

Kirwan CB, Wixted JT, Squire LR. (2010) A demonstration that the hippocampus supports both recollection and familiarity. *Proc Natl Acad Sci U S A.* 107(1):344-8.

Knowlton, B.J., Squire, L.R.(1995) Remembering and knowing: two different expressions of declarative memory. *J Exp Psychol Learn Mem Cogn.* 21(3):699-710.

Koen, J.D., Yonelinas, A.P. (2011) From humans to rats and back again: bridging the divide between human and animal studies of recognition memory with receiver operating characteristics.Learn Mem. 18(8):519-22.

Lipton, P.A., Eichenbaum, H. (2008) Complementary roles of hippocampus and medial entorhinal cortex in episodic memory. *Neural Plast.* 2008: 258467.

Mandler, G. (1980). Recognizing: The judgment of previous occurrence. *Psychological Review, 87,* 252–271.

Mandler, G. (2008) Familiarity breeds attempts: A critical review of dual process theories of recognition. *Perspectives in Psychological Science,* 3(5), 392-401.

Manns JR, Squire LR. (1999) Impaired recognition memory on the Doors and People Test after damage limited to the hippocampal region. *Hippocampus.* 9(5):495-9.

Manns, J. R., Hopkins, R.O., Reed, J.M., Kitchener, E. G. & Squire, L. R. (2003). Recognition memory and the human hippocampus. *Neuron.* 37, 171–180.

Manns, J.R., Eichenbaum, H. (2006) Evolution of Declarative Memory. *Hippocampus* 16:795–808.

Martin CB, Bowles B, Mirsattari SM, Köhler S. (2011) Selective familiarity deficits after left anterior temporal-lobe removal with hippocampal sparing are material specific.*Neuropsychologia.* 49(7):1870-8.

Mayes, A. R., Isaac, C. L., Holdstock, J. S., Hunkin, N. M.,Montaldi, D., Downes, J. J., MacDonald, C., Cezayirli, E., & Roberts, J. N. (2001). Memory for single items, word pairs, and temporal order of different kinds in a patient with selective hippocampal lesions. *Cognitive Neuropsychology,* 18(2), 97–123.

McNaughton, B.L., Battaglia, F.P., Jensen, O., Moser, E.I., Moser, M.B. (2006). Path integration and the neural basis of the 'cognitive map'. Nat Rev Neurosci. 7 (8), 663-78.

McElree, B., Dolan, P.O., Jacoby, L.L. (1999). Isolating the contributions of familiarity and source information to item recognition: a time course analysis. *J. Exp. Psychol. Learn Mem. Cogn.*253:563–82.

Montaldi, D., Spencer, T.J., Roberts, N., Mayes, A.R. (2006) The neural system that mediates familiarity memory. *Hippocampus.*16(5):504-20.

Montaldi D, Mayes AR. (2010) The role of recollection and familiarity in the functional differentiation of the medial temporal lobes.*Hippocampus.* 20(11):1291-314.

Moser, E.I., Moser, M.B. (2008). A metric for space. Hippocampus. *18*(12), 1142-56.

Peters J, Daum I. (2008) Differential effects of normal aging on recollection of concrete and abstract words. *Neuropsychology.* 22(2):255-61.

Prull, M.W., Dawes, L.L., Martin, A.M. 3rd., Rosenberg, H.F., Light, L.L. (2006). Recollection and familiarity in recognition memory: adult age differences and *Psychology: Human Learning and Memory.* 28(6),1499–1517.

Quamme, J. R., Yonelinas, A. P., Widaman, K. F., Kroll, N. E. A., &Sauve, M. J. (2004). Recall and recognition in mild hypoxia: Using covariance structural modelling to test competing theories of explicit memory. *Neuropsychologia. 42*, 672–691.

Quamme, J.R., Yonelinas, A.P., Norman, K.A.(2007). Effect of unitization on associative recognition in amnesia. *Hippocampus.* 17(3):192-200.

Reed, J. M., & Squire, L. R. (1997). Impaired recognition memory in patients with lesions limited to the hippocampal formation. *BehavioralNeuroscience, 111*, 667–675.

Robitsek, R.J., Fortin, N.J., Koh, M.T., Gallagher, M., Eichenbaum, H. (2008). Cognitive aging: a common decline of episodic recollection and spatial memory in rats. *J Neurosci.* 28(36):8945-54.

Rosenzweig, E.S., Barnes, C.A. (2003). Impact of aging on hippocampal function: plasticity, network dynamics, and cognition. *Prog Neurobiol.*69:143–179.

Rotello, C. M., Macmillan, N. A., & Van Tassel, G. (2000).Recall-to-reject in recognition: Evidence from ROC curves. *Journal of Memory and Language*, 43(1),67–88.

Sauvage, M., Fortin N.J., Owens, C.B., Yonelinas, A.P., Eichenbaum, H. (2008). Recognition memory opposite effects of hippocampal damage on recollection and familiarity. *Nat. Neurosc.* 11(1):16-8.

Sauvage, M., Beer, Z., Eichenbaum, H. (2010a) Recognition memory: adding a response deadline eliminates recollection but spares familiarity". *Learn Mem.* 13;17(2):104-8.

Sauvage MM. (2010b). ROC in animals: uncovering the neural substrates of recollection and familiarity in episodic recognition memory. *Conscious Cogn.* 19(3):816-28.

Sauvage, M., Beer, Z., Ho, L., Eichenbaum, H. (2010c) The Medial Entorhinal Cortex: a selective role in recollection-based memory, J Neurosci. 2010 Nov 17;30(46):15695-9.

Schacter, D.L., Verfaellie, M., Anes, M.D. (1997) Illusory memories in amnesic patients: conceptual and perceptual false recognition. *Neuropsychology.* 11(3):331-42.

Shrager, Y., Kirwan, C.B., Squire, L.R. (2008). Activity in both hippocampus and perirhinal cortex predicts the memory strength of subsequently remembered information. *Neuron.* 28; 59(4):547-53.

Slotnick, S. D., Klein, S. A., Dodson, C. S., & Shimamura, P. (2000). An analysis of signal detection and threshold models of source memory. *Journal of Experimental Psychology: Human Learning and Memory.* 28(6),1499–1517.

Smith, M.E. (1993). Neurophysiological manifestations of recollective experience during recognition memory judgments. *J. Cog. Neurosci.* 5(1):1–13.

Smith CN, Wixted JT, Squire LR.(2011) The hippocampus supports both recollection and familiarity when memories are strong. *J Neurosci.* 31(44):15693-702.

Song Z, Wixted JT, Hopkins RO, Squire LR. (2011) Impaired capacity for familiarity after hippocampal damage. Proc Natl Acad Sci U S A. 108(23):9655-60.

Squire, L.R., Stark, C.E.L. & Clark, R.E. (2004). The medial temporal lobe. *Annu. Rev. Neurosci. Review.* 27, 279–306.

Squire, L.R., Wixted, J.T., Clark, R.E.(2007). Recognition memory and the medial temporal lobe: a new perspective. *Nat Rev Neurosci.* 8(11):872-83.

Suchan, B., Gayk, A.E., Schmid, G., Köster, O., Daum, I. (2008) Hippocampal involvement in recollection but not familiarity across time: a prospective study. *Hippocampus.* 18(1):92-8.

Stark, C. E. & Squire, L. R. (2000).Functional magnetic resonance imaging (fMRI) activity in the hippocampal region during recognition memory. *J. Neurosci.* 20, 7776–7781.

Turriziani, P., Fadda, L., Caltragirone, C., & Carlesimo, G. A. (2004). Recognition memory for single items and for associations in amnesic patients. *Neuropsychologia*, *42*, 426–433.

Turriziani, P., Serra, L., Fadda, L., Caltagirone, C., Carlesimo, G.A. (2008) Recollection and familiarity in hippocampal amnesia. *Hippocampus*. 18(5):469-80.

Vann, S.D., Tsivilis, D., Denby, C.E., Quamme, J.R., Yonelinas, A.P., Aggleton, J.P., Montaldi, D., Mayes, A.R. (2009) Impaired recollection but spared familiarity in patients with extended hippocampal system damage revealed by 3 convergent methods. *Proc Natl Acad Sci U S A*. 106(13):5442-7.

Van Strien, N.M., Cappaert, N.L., Witter, M.P. (2009). The anatomy of memory: an interactive overview of the parahippocampal-hippocampal network. *Nat Rev Neurosci*. 10(4):272-82. Review.

Vargha-Khadem, F., Gadian, D.G., Watkins, K.E., et al.(1997). Differential effects of early hippocampal pathology on episodic and semantic memory. *Science*, 277(5324), 376–380.

Wais, P.E., Wixted, J.T., Hopkins, R.O., Squire, L.R. (2006) The hippocampus supports both the recollection and the familiarity components of recognition memory. *Neuron*. 2;49(3):459-66.

Wilson, I.A., Gallagher, M., Eichenbaum, H., Tanila, H. (2006). Neurocognitive aging: prior memories hinder new hippocampal encoding. *Trends Neurosci*. 29:662– 670.

Wixted, J.T., Squire, L.R. (2004) Recall and recognition are equally impaired in patients with selective hippocampal damage. *Cogn Affect Behav Neurosci*. 4(1):58-66. Review.

Wixted, J.T. (2007). Dual-process theory and signal-detection theory of recognition memory.*Psychol Rev*.114(1):152-76.

Wixted, J.T., Squire, L.R. (2008) Constructing receiver operating characteristics (ROCs) with experimental animals: cautionary notes. *Learn Mem*. 26;15(9):687-90.

Wixted JT, Squire LR. (2010) The role of the human hippocampus in familiarity-based and recollection-based recognition memory. *Behav Brain Res*. 215(2):197-208.

Wolk DA, Dunfee KL, Dickerson BC, Aizenstein HJ, DeKosky ST. (2011). A medial temporal lobe division of labor: insights from memory in aging and early Alzheimer disease. *Hippocampus*. 21(5):461-6.

Woodruff CC, Johnson JD, Uncapher MR, Rugg MD. (2005). Content-specificity of the neural correlates of recollection. *Neuropsychologia* 43:1022–32.

Woodruff, C.C., Hayama, H.R., Rugg, M.D. (2006). Electrophysiological dissociation of the neural correlates of recollection and familiarity. *Brain Res*. 1100(1):125–35.

Yonelinas, A.P. (1994). Receiver-operating characteristics in recognition memory: evidence for a dual-process model. *J. Exp. Psychol. Learn Mem. Cogn*. 20(6):1341–54.

Yonelinas, A.P., Jacoby, L.L.(1994). Dissociations of processes in recognition memory: effects of interference and of response speed. *Can J Exp Psychol*. 48(4):516-35.

Yonelinas, A.P.(1997) Recognition memory ROCs for item and associative information: the contribution of recollection and familiarity. *Mem Cognit*.25 (6):747-63.

Yonelinas, A.P., Kroll, N.E., Dobbins, I., Lazzara, M., Knight, R.T. (1998). Recollection and familiarity deficits in amnesia: convergence of remember-know, process dissociation, and receiver operating characteristic data. *Neuropsychology*. 12, 323-339.

Yonelinas, A.P. (1999). The contribution of recollection and familiarity to recognition and source memory judgments: a formal dual-process model and an analysis of receiver operating characteristics. *J. Exp. Psychol. Learn Mem. Cogn*. 25:1415–34.

Yonelinas, A.P. (2002). The nature of recollection and familiarity: a review of 30 years of research. *J. Mem. Lang.* 46:441–517.

Yonelinas, A.P., Kroll NE, Quamme, J.R., Lazzara, M.M., Sauvé, M.J., Widaman, K.F., Knight, R.T. (2002). Effects of extensive temporal lobe damage or mild hypoxia on recollection and familiarity. *Nature Neurosci.* 5, 1236–1241.

Yonelinas, A.P., Parks, C.M. (2007). Receiver operating characteristics (ROCs) in recognition memory: a review. *Psychol Bull.*133 (5):800-32.

Yonelinas, A.P., Widaman, K., Mungas, D., Reed, B., Weiner, M.W., Chui, H.C. (2007). Memory in the aging brain: doubly dissociating the contribution of the hippocampus and entorhinal cortex. *Hippocampus.*17(11):1134-40.

Yonelinas AP, Aly M, Wang WC, Koen JD. (2010) Recollection and familiarity: examining controversial assumptions and new directions. *Hippocampus.* 20(11):1178-94.

In: Psychology of Memory  
Editors: Dannie M. Hendrix and Orval Holcomb

ISBN: 978-1-61942-633-7  
© 2012 Nova Science Publishers, Inc.

*Chapter 5*

# WORKING MEMORY SPAN TASKS: THE EFFECTS OF TASK STRUCTURE AND ADMINISTRATION AND SCORING PROCEDURES

### *Helen St. Clair-Thompson*
University of Hull, UK

## ABSTRACT

Measures of working memory, requiring both the processing and storage of information, are widely used across a number of domains of psychology. This is in part because working memory scores serve as useful predictors of cognitive skills such as comprehension, problem solving and intelligence. However, there are no standard administration and scoring procedures for working memory tasks. For example, some researchers administer set sizes in ascending order, whilst others prefer a randomized order. Some investigators assign scores of the total number of stimuli in perfectly recalled trials, whilst others calculate the proportion of stimuli recalled correctly throughout the entire task. The current chapter begins with a brief overview of working memory span tasks, and then reviews a number of variations in task structure, administration and scoring procedures. The focus is on the effects of these variations on working memory scores and the predictive ability of working memory tasks. The practical implications of the findings are described, for instance working memory tasks are more predictive of higher order cognition if set sizes are presented in a randomized order and if proportion scoring is used. The findings are then discussed in relation to current theoretical accounts of working memory. It is suggested that the effects of many of the variations in administration and scoring reflect the degree which scores capture variance from active control or executive-attentional resources. More generally, it is suggested that researchers need to consider administration and scoring methods when employing working memory span tasks.

# INTRODUCTION

Working memory is a cognitive system responsible for both the processing and storage of information during cognitive tasks (e.g. Baddeley, 1986), that underpins our capacity for complex thought (Baddeley, 2007). Over recent decades working memory has become a widely useful, scientifically productive construct. It plays an important role in contemporary global models of cognition (e.g. Anderson & Lebiere, 1998; Cowan, 1995; see also Conway, Kane, Bunting, & Hambrick et al., 2005). It serves as a useful predictor of a wide range of cognitive abilities, such as mathematics, comprehension, and problem solving (e.g. DeStefano & LeFevre, 2004; Engle, 2002; Seigneuric, Ehrlich, Oakhill, & Yuill, 2000). It also accounts for a significant portion of variance in general intelligence (e.g. Conway, Kane & Engle, 2003; Engle, Tuholski, Laughlin, & Conway, 1999; Kane & Engle, 2002; Kyllonen, 1996). Measures of working memory are therefore widely used across a number of domains of psychology (Conway et al., 2005; Friedman & Miyake, 2005; Miyake, 2001).

There are several theoretical models of working memory which differ in their views of the nature, structure, and function of the memory system (e.g. for a review see Conway, Jarrold, Kane, & Towse, 2007; Miyake & Shah, 1999). According to one of the most popular models (Baddeley, 2000; Baddeley & Hitch, 1974) working memory consists of four components. There are two domain specific short-term memory systems; the phonological loop that is responsible for the maintenance of auditory information, and the visuo-spatial sketchpad that is specialised for dealing with visual and spatial information. These are governed by a central executive system, often likened to a mechanism of attentional control (e.g. Engle & Kane, 2004; Engle, Kane, & Tuholski, 1999; Kane, Conway, Hambrick, & Engle, 2007, Kane & Engle, 2000; Kane, Hambrick, & Conway, 2005). Baddeley (2000) added the fourth component, the episodic buffer. This is responsible for integrating information from the subsystems of working memory and long term memory.

Another theoretical approach defines working memory as the ability to control attention to maintain information in the face of distraction (e.g. Engle & Kane, 2004; Kane, Bleckley, Conway, & Engle, 2001; Oberauer & Kliegel, 2001). Specifically, this approach proposes a limited attentional resource which is partially drawn away from the primary task by irrelevant information. This includes stimuli which require a response but also information that attracts attention involuntarily (see also Oberauer, Lange, & Engle, 2004). A detailed description of each approach to working memory is outside of the scope of this review, but models of working memory will be referred to throughout the chapter in relation to research using working memory tasks.

Irrespective of the theoretical approach to working memory, working memory can be assessed using a range of measures (e.g. for a review see Oberauer, 2005), but the most commonly used are working memory span tasks which require both the processing and storage of information. For example, in reading span (Daneman & Carpenter, 1980) participants read aloud a series of sentences, and then attempt to recall the final word of each sentence in sequence. In counting span (Case, Kurland, & Goldberg, 1982) participants count the number of items in a series of arrays and then recall the successive tallies of each array. In operation span participants carry out arithmetic operations whilst maintaining words (e.g. Turner & Engle, 1989).

These working memory span tasks have been shown to be both reliable and valid measures of working memory capacity. When tasks are used with adults estimates of internal consistency, including split-half correlations and Cronbach's alpha, typically range from .70 to .90 (e.g. Conway et al., 2005; Engle, Tuholski, et al., 1999; Miyake, Friedman, Retiinger, Shah, & Hegarty, 2001; Oberauer, SuB, Schulze, Wilhelm, & Witmann, 2000). Test-retest correlations commonly range from .70 to .80 (e.g. Friedman & Miyake, 2004; Klein & Fiss, 1999). Reliability estimates are also reasonable when working memory span measures are used with children (e.g. Hitch, Towse, & Hutton, 2001; Pickering & Gathercole, 2001). The validity of the tasks is evidenced in the significant correlations between working memory span scores and performance on a wide range of other cognitive skills during both childhood and adulthood (e.g. see Alloway, Gathercole, Kirkwood, & Elliot, 2009; Conway et al., 2005).

Despite their popularity in research and assessment no standard administration and scoring methods exist for working memory tasks (see also, Conway et al., 2005; Friedman & Miayke, 2005). However, recent research has suggested that variations in administration and scoring procedures can influence participant's scores on working memory tasks. For example, participants gain higher scores if tasks are participant- paced (e.g. McCabe, 2010; St Clair-Thompson, 2007b), if items to be recalled belong to a different stimulus category than material that was processed (e.g. Conlin, Gathercole, & Adams, 2005a), and if scoring methods give some credit for trials which were not perfectly recalled (Friedman & Miyake, 2005; St Clair-Thompson & Sykes, 2010). Perhaps more importantly, these manipulations also affect the predictive ability of working memory tasks (e.g. McCabe, 2010; St Clair-Thompson, 2007b; St Clair-Thompson & Sykes, 2010; Unsworth & Engle, 2007). There is therefore a need for a review of how and why administration and scoring methods can influence working memory scores and their predictive ability.

The chapter will begin with an overview of working memory span tasks. Variations in task structure, administration and scoring methods will then be described, with a focus on the effects of these variations on working memory scores and their predictive ability. The findings of the studies described are then discussed in relation to current theoretical accounts of working memory.

## OVERVIEW OF WORKING MEMORY SPAN TASKS

Working memory span tasks were designed from the perspective of Baddeley and Hitch's (1974) model of working memory, which defined working memory as a system that could store information in the service of ongoing mental activity. Working memory tasks were therefore created to assess both the processing and storage of information. They interleave the presentation of to-be-remembered stimuli with the presentation of a secondary processing task such as reading or comprehending sentences. The tasks can therefore be distinguished from short-term memory tasks involving the immediate recall of information with no supplementary processing.

The first working memory span task to be developed was the reading span task (Daneman & Carpenter, 1980), in which participants are required to read aloud a series of sentences whilst remembering the last word of each. After each series of sentences participants are required to recall the words in the same order as they were presented. In the original version of the task there were 15 trials, 3 each of 2, 3, 4, 5, and 6 sentences. The trials were presented in ascending order until a participant failed to successfully recall the words in all three trials at a set size. At this point testing was terminated, and a participant was awarded a score of the level at which they correctly recalled the words on 2 out of 3 trials.

Since the development of the reading span task, a wide range of other working memory span measures have been used, with a variety of processing and storage requirements. These involve, for example, judging the veracity of a series of sentences and then recalling the final word of each sentence (Daneman & Carpenter, 1980), making odd-even judgements about digits whilst remembering words (e.g. Conlin, Gathercole, & Adams, 2005b), identifying an odd-one-out shape and remembering spatial locations (e.g. Jarvis & Gathercole, 2003), or carrying out mental rotation whilst remembering locations (e.g. Shah & Miyake, 1996). It is, however, important to note that working memory span tasks predict performance on measures of other cognitive skills irrespective of their processing requirements (e.g. Bayliss, Jarrold, Gunn, & Baddeley, 2003; Conway et al., 2005; Engle, Tuholski, et al., 1999). A number of theoretical approaches consider the executive-attentional component of working memory to be a domain-general resource, with working memory span tasks tapping domain- specific storage, but domain-general processing resources (e.g. Engle, Tuholski et al., 1999; Duff & Logie, 2001). Studies have also revealed that working memory span measures from different processing domains load onto the same factor during factor analysis (e.g. Alloway, Gathercole, & Pickering, 2006).

There are several views of how participants go about completing working memory tasks. Early accounts proposed limited cognitive resources which could be shared between simultaneous processing and storage (e.g. Daneman & Carpenter, 1980; Case et al., 1982). According to this view, more efficient and faster processing leads to additional resources being available to support storage. However, subsequent accounts have challenged resource-sharing theories. Towse and Hitch (1995) manipulated a counting span task in terms of both processing duration and processing difficulty. Children achieved lower scores when the processing was more difficult, but this effect disappeared when controlling for the duration of processing (see also Barouillet & Camos, 2001; Ransdell & Hecht, 2003). These results suggested that processing time was more important than processing difficulty. This lead to a task-switching hypothesis (e.g. Hitch et al.2001; Towse, Hitch, & Hutton, 1998; 2000; 2002). According to this hypothesis participants complete working memory span tasks in a sequential rather than a simultaneous fashion. For example, in the counting span task (Case et al., 1982) they count an array, commit the total to memory, and then count the next array. Thus as soon as a participant is involved in processing there is a time related decay of memory items. This view is consistent with multiple-component models of working memory (e.g. Baddeley, 2000).

Another account of working memory span task performance is the time-based resource-sharing model (e.g. Barrouillet, Bernardin & Camos, 2004; Barrouillet, Gavens, & Vergauwe et al., 2009; Barrouillet, Portrat & Camos, 2011). This model proposes that performance on working memory measures is determined by cognitive cost. Both processing and storage are considered to require attention, with a rapid and frequent switching between the two during working memory task performance. The cognitive cost of a task is a function of the time for which processing captures attention, preventing the refreshing of memory traces. Cognitive cost can therefore be manipulated by increasing the complexity of processing operations, reducing the time available for the refreshing of memory traces, or increasing the number of memory retrievals that a processing task involves. In contrast to the resource-switching approach (e.g. Towse et al., 1998; 2000), which assumes that there is no attempt to maintain memory items during processing, the time-based resource-sharing view assumes that participants switch their attention from processing to storage during processing intervals (for attempts to compare and integrate resource-sharing and time dependent approaches see Barouillet et al., 2004; Jarrold & Bayliss, 2007; Towse, Hitch, & Horton, 2007).

A detailed description of the evidence relating to each account of working memory task performance is outside of the scope of this chapter. However, the theories will be returned to in the chapter in order to assist with the interpretation of the findings of studies into the administration and scoring of working memory measures. We will now move on to these variations in methods, their effects on working memory scores and their predictive ability. Many of the studies described are concerned with the correlations between scores on working memory tasks and other cognitive skills. There is relatively little research examining the effects of task structure, administration and scoring procedures within other research designs, such as those which involve discriminating between groups. Each of the variations in methods is discussed one at a time, although many are interconnected. There is no attempt to weigh the costs and benefits of each in order to decide on one single method, because often the preferred method will depend upon a researcher's particular theory or aims. Rather, the variations are summarised and then discussed in relation to current theories of working memory.

## THE EFFECTS OF TASK STRUCTURE

### Cognitive Load

One important variation in task structure that can influence working memory scores is the cognitive cost of a working memory task (Barrouillet et al. 2004; Barrouillet et al., 2011). For example, Barrouillet et al. (2004) held processing durations constant, and compared performance on working memory tasks with different processing operations. The items to be recalled were the same in each case. More demanding processing operations (e.g. arithmetic) resulted in lower working memory scores than less demanding processing operations (e.g. reading digits). They further demonstrated that working memory span scores were reduced by increasing the number of processing operations to be completed within a given time. Similar results have emerged from reducing the time period allowed for a given number of processing operations (Lepine, Barouillet, & Camos, 2005). Consistent with the time-based resource-sharing theory (e.g. Barrouillet et al. 2004; Barrouillet et al., 2011), these findings suggest that it is important for researchers administering working memory tasks to consider the number and difficulty of the processing operations involved, and also the time allowed to complete these operations within working memory tasks.

Further support for this suggestion has come from research using the counting span task (Case et al., 1982). If counting is made more difficult, requiring a conjunction search rather than a feature search (e.g. Duncan, 1987; Treisman, 1991; Treisman & Gelade, 1980; Treisman & Sato, 1990), or requiring participants to count using an unfamiliar sequence

(Case et al., 1982), then participants achieve lower working memory scores (St Clair-Thompson, 2007a). It has further been suggested that in participants of a high ability counting at an unspecified rate may be an automatic process and thus may not demand executive-attentional resources (e.g. Barrouillet & Camos, 2001; Towse & Hitch, 1997; St Clair-Thompson, 2007a). In such situations counting span may be equated with measures of short-term memory, which require the immediate recall of information with no supplementary processing. If, however, more demanding processing is used then scores are indicative of executive-attentional involvement (St Clair-Thompson, 2007a).

Manipulations to cognitive load also affect the relationships between working memory and cognitive skills. Lepine et al. (2005) revealed that allowing less time for processing operations increased the ability of working memory tasks to predict children's literacy, mathematics, and global scholastic attainment scores. Similarly, St Clair- Thompson (2007a) demonstrated that the more demanding the processing operations in the counting span task, the closer its relationship with reading comprehension and arithmetic. Findings therefore suggest that to be a good measure of working memory a task must be designed to have an adequate cognitive load. Furthermore, if the purpose of using working memory tasks is to predict cognitive skills then this purpose would appear to be better served if measures with a high cognitive cost are used.

## Stimulus Similarity

Although all working memory span tasks involve both processing and storage there are variations in the degree of similarity between what is processed and what is recalled. In some tasks the storage items and processing task are from the same domain, for example reading sentences and recalling words (e.g. Pickering & Gathercole, 2001). However, in others the processing and storage items are from different domains, such as carrying out arithmetic operations and recalling words (e.g. see Unsworth, Heitz, Schrock, & Engle, 2005). Evidence indicates that a high degree of relatedness between material to be processed and stored results in lower working memory scores (e.g. Bayliss et al., 2003; Conlin et al., 2005a; Duff & Logie, 2001). For example, Conlin et al. (2005a) combined sentence span and operation span with remembering either words or digits. The items to be remembered were not a direct product of the processing operations in either case. Memory spans were significantly greater when the items to be recalled belonged to a different stimulus category from the material which was processed (but see Oberauer et al.,2004, for contrasting findings). Stimulus similarity may not, however, influence the predictive ability of working memory tasks. Bunting (2006) compared performance on operation span tasks requiring participants to remember either digits or words. Stimulus similarity did not influence the correlation between operation span and intelligence. However, further research is needed to explore the effect of stimulus similarity on working memory- performance relationships within other domains.

There are a number of possible reasons for the effect of stimulus-similarity. Duff and Logie (2001) argued that differences arose because distinctiveness of processing and storage stimuli allows them to be handled more readily by separate subsystems of working memory, such as the central executive and phonological loop of the multiple- component model of working memory (Baddeley, 2000; Baddeley & Hitch, 1974). However, an alternative account is that stimulus similarity results in interference (e.g. Saito & Miyake, 2004). When processing and storage domains are similar, the representations generated by processing and maintenance overlap. This causes interference and thus poorer recall (see also May, Hasher, & Kane, 1999). This is consistent with suggestions that working memory span tasks assess the ability to handle proactive interference, which builds up across trials (e.g. Bowles & Salthouse, 2003; Bunting, 2006; Conway & Engle, 1994; May et al., 1999). To achieve high scores on working memory tasks individuals must be successful at managing the memory component of the task so as to recall only the items from the current trial and not any previous trials. This should be easy on the first few trials, as few other sets have been remembered and recalled. However, on later trials this will be increasingly difficult as many more items have been presented. This will also become increasingly difficult if there is an overlap between processing and maintenance (e.g. May et al., 1999).

It is, however, important to note that in each of these studies examining stimulus similarity the items to be recalled were not a direct product of the processing task. In many working memory tasks the memory items are generated from the processing activity (e.g. Case et al., 1982; Daneman & Carpenter, 1980). Relationships between processing and storage in working memory span tasks are therefore not always competitive. Depending on the structure of a working memory task there may in fact be a cooperative relationship (see Towse, Hitch, Horton & Harvey, 2010). Towse, Cowan, Hitch, and Horton (2008) compared two versions of a reading span task. In one version the to-be-remembered items were sentence words, and thus were integrated with the processing task. In the other version the to-be-remembered items were words that were independent of the sentences to be processed. Participants achieved higher scores for the integrated condition, and also took longer interword pauses during output (see also Towse et al., 2010). This supported the suggestion that when the opportunity exists, memory for processing operations can be used to reconstruct memory for target items. It is not yet known whether this can also influence the predictive ability of working memory tasks.

To summarise, at the moment there appears to be no consensus about how tasks should be structured regarding the similarity between processing and storage stimuli. Researchers should be aware that increased similarity may place further demands upon the ability to overcome proactive interference. However, semantic similarity may allow opportunities for participants to reconstruct their memory for target items. More research is needed to examine this issue.

## Ascending versus Randomised Format

Traditionally the trials in working memory span tasks are presented so that the number of items to remember increases over successive trials (e.g. Daneman & Carpenter, 1980). However, some researchers prefer to administer the trials in random order (e.g. Unsworth et al., 2005). Studies indicate that the order of presentation can influence working memory scores. For example, Lustig, May, and Hasher (2001) compared performance on tasks in which set sizes were presented in ascending order with those in which they were presented in descending order, with the longest lists being presented first. Participants achieved higher scores in the descending tasks. This was attributed to the descending structure reducing proactive interference (see also May et al., 1999). In an ascending format the largest set sizes are presented last, and are therefore the most influenced by proactive influence (e.g. Keppel

& Underwood, 1962; Wickens, 1970). They are also the most important in determining working memory scores (e.g. Lustig et al., 2001). However, in a descending format fewer sets have previously been remembered and recalled before participants encounter these longest lists. Thus, they are less influenced by proactive interference.

It is, however, important to note that the participants in this study were old adults, and proactive interference is known to differentially lower the performance of old adults compared to young adults (Blalock & McCabe, 2011; Rowe, Hasher, & Turcotte, 2008). Rowe et al. (2008) administered a visuo-spatial working memory task in both ascending and descending formats to both young and old adults. Older adults gained higher scores in descending tasks, consistent with the idea that using a descending structure reduced proactive interference. However, for young adults the opposite pattern was found, with higher scores on ascending tasks. Rowe et al. attributed these findings to the effects of practice, suggesting that for older adults the influence of proactive interference outweighed the effects of practice due to age related declines in inhibitory control, whereas in young adults the influence of practice outweighed the influence of proactive interference (see also Blalock & McCabe, 2011).

Tasks in which set sizes are presented in descending order, however, are not commonly used. The more commonly used methods involve presenting list lengths in an ascending (e.g. Case et al., 1982), or a randomized order (e.g. Unsworth et al., 2005). St Clair-Thompson (in press) found that participants achieved marginally higher scores on randomized tasks than on ascending tasks, this difference being significant for counting recall but not for reading recall. This marginal difference between scores on ascending and randomized tasks could be expected, given that the using randomized rather than descending lists (e.g. Lustig et al., 2001; Rowe et al., 2008) is not such a powerful manipulation of proactive interference. Alternatively, the marginal difference may have resulted from the effects of practice operating in addition to proactive interference (see also Blalock & McCabe, 2011).

The presentation format of working memory span tasks can also influence predictive ability. Lustig et al. (2001) revealed that using a descending rather than ascending order of presentation altered the relationship between working memory scores and prose recall. This is a commonly used measure of language comprehension that can typically be predicted by working memory (e.g. see Daneman & Merikle, 1996). Specifically, when tasks were presented in descending order the correlation between working memory and prose recall was no longer significant (see also Bunting, 2006; May et al., 1999). St Clair-Thompson (in press) further revealed that ascending and randomized tasks differed dramatically in terms of their predictive ability. Only scores on the randomized tasks were significantly related to intelligence.

The reduction in predictive ability of tasks in a descending format can be explained by proactive interference (e.g. Bunting, 2006; Lustig et al., 2001). However, in St Clair-Thompson (in press) the tasks assumed to involve less proactive interference (randomized tasks) were more closely related with general intelligence. One explanation for this finding is that tasks presented in ascending format are more amenable to strategy use. This may be particularly relevant as the working memory tasks used in this study were participant- paced. Although instructed to complete the processing activities (counting or completing the sentences) as quickly as possible, there was no time limit within which participants had to provide their answer. Previous studies have suggested that such participant-paced tasks can allow participants to take additional time to employ memory strategies (e.g. Friedman & Miyake, 2004; St Clair-Thompson, 2007a). This issue will be returned to later. Another possible explanation is that differences between ascending and randomized tasks arise due to participants not being aware of how many stimuli have to be recalled on each trial in randomized tasks. In contrast, in ascending (or descending) tasks participants are aware of the number of items that have to be recalled, or can accurately judge this based on memory of the previous trials. In randomized tasks, maintaining the number of items to be remembered in addition to the stimuli themselves may result in an increased cognitive demand (e.g. Barrouillet et al., 2004), or greater demands on executive-attentional resources (St Clair-Thompson, 2007b). As discussed earlier working memory tasks that are more cognitively demanding are better predictors of cognitive skills (e.g. Lepine et al., 2005; St Clair-Thompson, 2007b). It is, however, worthy of note that the increased employment of memory strategies in ascending tasks, or an increased cognitive demand in randomized tasks, would be expected to lead to higher working memory scores in ascending tasks (e.g. St Clair-Thompson, 2007a; 2007b). This is not the pattern of findings that was observed in the study.

One final explanation of differences between ascending and randomized tasks is also based on participants being aware of how many stimuli are to be recalled on ascending but not randomized tasks. This is that ascending tasks may be more influenced by practice. When the number of to-be-remembered stimuli is known performance may become more automated. Previous research has shown that such practice can reduce the relationship between working memory and general intelligence (Blalock & McCabe, 2011). Further research is needed to explore this possibility, along with other explanations of the cognitive underpinnings of the improved predictive ability of randomized tasks.

It is also worthy of note that there may be practical differences between ascending, descending, and randomized tasks. For example, using an ascending task format allows for testing to be discontinued when a participant fails to correctly recall the to-be-remembered items in all trials at a list length (e.g. Daneman & Carpenter, 1980). This reduces the overall time of task administration, which may be of benefit to both researchers and participants. Descending and randomized tasks do not allow for discontinuation.

Researchers and practitioners employing working memory span tasks therefore need to consider the format of these tasks. A descending task structure has only been used in order to examine the cognitive resources underlying working memory task performance. However, many tasks are available in ascending or randomized formats. These may differ in terms of the involvement of proactive interference (e.g. Lustig et al., 2001), executive- attentional resources, or practice (see also St Clair-Thompson, in press). More research is needed to examine differences between ascending and randomized tasks. Meanwhile, it is suggested that researchers be aware that their choice of task format may influence working memory scores and predictive ability.

## Spoken versus Silent Processing

Another variation in task structure concerns how participants complete the processing activity within working memory tasks. Beaman (2004) compared two versions of an operation span task, in which participants had to solve a series of mathematical problems whilst retaining words for later recall. In one version of the task participants were asked to read the mathematical problems aloud and in the other they read them silently. Participants achieved higher scores when reading them silently. Beaman proposed two possible explanations of this finding. The first was that articulating the operations created an irrelevant auditory-feedback loop that had to be successfully ignored in order to recall the words. The second possibility was that the act of articulating the material was disruptive due to the attentional demands of setting up and running an appropriate articulatory motor program (see also Melser & Klauer, 1999). This may be synonymous with the idea that it resulted in an increased cognitive load or greater demands upon executive-attentional resources (e.g. Barrouillet et al., 2004; St Clair-Thompson, 2007b).

No other studies, however, have directly compared read aloud and read silent versions of working memory span tasks. Further research is also needed to examine whether this variation in administration method influences the relationship between working memory and higher order cognitive skills. It is also worthy of note that there are practical advantages of read silently methods. For example, they can allow for group testing without participants disrupting each other, which is not possible using read aloud versions.

## ISSUES OF ADMINISTRATION

### Experimenter versus Participant Paced Processing

The main variation that has occurred in the administration of working memory span tasks concerns the way in which the timing of the presentation of stimuli is controlled. Tasks are traditionally administered individually, with participants responding to each processing task and encoding the to-be-remembered item, and the experimenter then revealing the next stimulus. However, in some cases the amount of time available for processing is controlled by a computer (e.g. Lepine et al., 2005; Oberauer et al., 2000). In this method the experimenter determines the time allowed for each processing task, and this remains the same for each participant. Alternatively, some researchers have used a method of pacing which involves asking participants to complete practice trials consisting of only processing operations. The average time taken for processing then determines the time allowed during the experimental trials (e.g. Unsworth et al., 2005). Each of these three methods can be contrasted with a self-paced method, in which participants are in complete control of the advancement of the task (e.g. Friedman & Miyake, 2004; Waters & Caplan, 1996). In such cases participants can choose to take additional time to complete the task (e.g. McCabe, 2010; St Clair-Thompson, 2007b).

The administration method used can influence performance on working memory measures. Studies have shown that participant-paced tasks result in higher scores than experimenter-paced tasks (e.g. Friedman & Miyake, 2004; McCabe, 2010; St Clair-Thompson, 2007b) or computer-paced tasks (e.g. Lepine et al., 2005). The differences do not arise due to reliability of the measures. It has therefore been suggested that they result from additional time being taken to employ memory strategies (e.g. Friedman & Miyake, 2004; St Clair-Thompson, 2007b), or from the reduced cognitive load that results from not imposing time constraints (Lepine et al., 2005). The administration method can also influence the predictive ability of working memory tasks. Experimenter- paced tasks and computer-paced tasks show stronger correlations with criterion measures than participant-paced tasks (e.g. Friedman & Miyake, 2004; McCabe, 2010; St Clair-Thompson, 2007b). This indicates that individual differences in strategy use add noise to the correlations of working memory tasks with other cognitive skills (e.g. Engle & Kane, 2004; Turley- Ames & Whitfield, 2003). These findings are also consistent with suggestions from the time-based resource-sharing approach to working memory (e.g. Barrouillet et al., 2004) that reducing the time allowed to complete processing operations can increase the cognitive cost of a task, and therefore improve its predictive ability (see also Lepine et al., 2005; St Clair-Thompson, 2007a).

These findings have important implications, suggesting that researchers should use experimenter-paced or computer-paced tasks. In addition to improving predictive ability there are also other advantages to using computer-paced measures. Computer paced tasks require little experimenter input, and therefore allow for group testing. Recent research has established the reliability and validity of working memory span tasks in such situations (e.g. De Neys, d'Ydealle, Schaeken, & Vos, 2002; Unsworth et al., 2005). Automated versions of working memory span tasks also score themselves, again reducing experimenter time (e.g. Unsworth et al., 2005), and they may allow researchers to conduct web-based research.

## Recall versus Recognition

Many working memory tasks require participants to remember a series of stimuli and recall them in the same order as they were presented (e.g. Daneman & Carpenter, 1980; Pickering & Gathercole, 2001). However, some researchers use a method of recognition rather than recall, requiring participants to choose the to-be-remembered items from a list of given options (e.g. Alptekin & Ercetin, 2009; Unsworth et al., 2005). In this case the number of distracter items can be set by the researcher, with some using as few as two distracters per correct word (e.g. Alptekin & Ercetin, 2009; Chun & Payne, 2004) and others preferring a set of 12 response options per trial (e.g. Unworth et al., 2005). Evidence suggests that recall and recognition tasks can result in different levels of performance. Alptekin and Ercetin (2009) found that participants performed better when given a working memory task involving recognition than a task requiring recall, with less variability also being observed for the recognition measure. Scores on the recall and recognition tasks also differed in terms of their ability to predict reading comprehension, with scores on the working memory task involving recall being better predictors. Alptekin and Ercetin interpreted these results as reflecting a qualitative difference between recall and recognition. Specifically, they described recognition as being driven by two separate mechanisms (see also Unsworth & Engle, 2007). One is a fairly automatic process of familiarity and the other is a controlled process aimed at recovering the target items. Working memory is involved in searching for target items but it is not involved in the former process of familiarity. They further suggested that recall may be more cognitively demanding than recognition, in that item retrieval is based on the ability to retrieve relevant information from a large set of possible items, whereas recognition involves a limited search set.

There is of course much variability in terms of the number of response options that can be provided in recognition tasks. There has been no research examining the differences between recognition tasks with many response options (e.g. Unsworth et al., 2005) and traditional recall tasks. In some cases using a recognition task may not allow for a reduced search set. For example, in counting span (Case et al., 1982) the items to be recalled are usually single digits between 0 and 9. A recognition test could therefore use the same response options.

Further research is therefore needed to explore differences between working memory tasks involving recall and recognition. Meanwhile it is suggested that researchers ensure the cognitive demand of working memory tasks is sufficient by either using recall, or providing a large set of distracter items on each trial.

## ISSUES OF SCORING

### Taking into Account the Processing

Working memory span tasks are dual task measures. Thus, there are at least two sources of data, one from processing and one from storage. However, the common method of scoring working memory tasks does not consider processing performance. This is because processing accuracy is typically close to ceiling, with task instructions emphasising accuracy on the processing task (see also Conway et al., 2005; St Clair-Thompson, 2007b). In addition, performance on the processing component of working memory span tasks is usually positively correlated to performance on the storage component, with participants who are good at maintaining information also performing well on the processing tasks (e.g. Kane, Hambrick & Tuholski et al., 2004; Waters & Caplan, 1996). Although processing does not contribute to a participants score it is, however, important for researchers to monitor processing accuracy to ensure that participants are not attending only to storage at the expense of processing. Therefore, some researchers have proposed that participant's scores should only be used in analysis if processing accuracy is in excess of 85 percent (e.g. Bunting, 2006; Unsworth & Engle, 2006).

Although it seems unnecessary to include accuracy on the processing component in working memory scores it may, however, be worthwhile considering reaction times for the processing operations. Some studies have revealed only a minor association between recall accuracy and reaction time on the processing component of working memory tasks (e.g. Unsworth et al., 2005). Furthermore, reaction times predict unique variance in higher order cognition over and above working memory span scores. For example, Waters and Caplan (1996) found that the addition of processing times to reading span scores increased the correlation between reading span and comprehension. Similarly, Bayliss et al. (2003) demonstrated that processing times were a significant predictor of reading and mathematics in children when statistically controlling for storage capacity. Hitch et al.(2001) also revealed that speeds of processing and memory spans predicted both shared and unique variance in word reading and number skills. Thus, if the goal of a study is to predict as much variance as possible in cognitive skills, including reaction time measures boosts the predictive ability of working memory tasks (e.g. Cowan, Towse, Hamilton, & Saults et al., 2003).

In addition to reaction time, measures of the chronometry of recall may improve the predictive ability of working memory tasks. Cowan et al. (2003) examined overall response durations as well as both interword pauses and preparatory intervals during working memory task recall. Interword pauses refer to silent gaps between the articulation of each item to be recalled, and are thought to reflect search through memory for identification of the next items to be recalled. Preparatory intervals refer to gaps before recall commences, and are thought to involve processes relating to partial rehearsal, response planning and sequence preparation (see also Towse, Cowan, Horton & Whytock, 2008). Cowan et al. found that response durations were significantly correlated with recall ability, and that recall processes were linked to wider achievement domains. Towse et al. (2008) further revealed that recall timing variables partially mediate the relationship between working memory and scholastic attainment, but also predict independent variance in attainment. More research is needed to examine relationships between recall timing and measures of cognitive skills.

## Absolute versus Proportion Correct Scoring

A number of scoring methods can be used for working memory span tasks. Some researchers assign a span score, of the highest level at which a participant successfully recalls the stimuli in the majority of trials (e.g. Daneman & Carpenter, 1980). In this case the task begins with the presentation of one or two items to remember, and the set size is increased over successive trials until the participant's performance falls below a threshold. Once the threshold is reached, testing is discontinued. The maximum number of items correctly recalled before this point (in the majority of trials at that list length) is the span score. A similar method involves counting the total number of stimuli in perfectly recalled trials (e.g. Engle et al., 1999; McNamara & Scott, 2001). Such methods are often referred to as absolute scoring methods (e.g. Unsworth & Engle, 2007).

Another method of scoring involves assigning a score of the proportion of stimuli recalled correctly throughout the task (e.g. Friedman & Miyake, 2000; Kane et al., 2004; Turner & Engle, 1989). In this case experimenters administer all the trials within a task, rather than discontinuing testing. Each element of each trial then contributes to a participant's score. For example, if a participant recalls 3 out of 5 items on a trial they score .60 for that trial. The proportions for all the trials are then averaged, producing a score with a maximum of 1.00. This is often referred to as proportion correct scoring (e.g. Unsworth & Engle, 2007). In some versions of proportion correct scoring higher weights are also assigned to items with a higher memory load. However, researchers have suggested no benefit to this method when compared to that described above (see Conway et al., 2005).

Scores obtained using different methods are typically highly correlated (e.g. Friedman & Miyake, 2005; Klein & Fiss, 1999; Turner & Engle, 1989; Waters & Caplan, 1996). However, some scoring methods demonstrate better psychometric properties (see also, Conway et al., 2005; Friedman & Miyake, 2005). For example, span scores can take only one of a few values, usually between 2 and 6. This greatly limits the sensitivity of the measure (e.g. Oberauer & Suß, 2000). Some scoring methods also result in higher correlations with criterion measures (e.g. Friedman & Miyake, 2005; St Clair-Thompson & Sykes, 2010; Unsworth & Engle, 2007). Friedman and Miyake (2005) compared absolute and proportion correct scoring methods for the reading span task. The proportion correct scores were more closely correlated with Verbal SAT scores than the absolute scores. This difference was not due to reliability, as internal consistency and test- retest reliability were similar for the two methods (see also Unsworth & Engle, 2007). Similar findings were revealed by St Clair-Thompson and Sykes (2010) using working memory tasks with children. Proportion correct scores were a better predictor of scholastic attainment than absolute scores for a range of short-term and working memory measures.

There are several possible explanations for the difference between absolute and proportion correct scoring. Friedman and Miyake suggested that the differences arose because proportion correct scoring may be more sensitive to subtle individual differences. However, Unsworth and Engle (2007) suggested that the scoring methods differ in terms of the cognitive resources they assess. They proposed that working memory comprises of an active maintenance or short-term memory component (primary memory) and controlled search and retrieval processes (secondary memory). Items are thought to be initially maintained in primary memory but then displaced to secondary memory by other incoming items or distracting information. According to this view proportion correct scoring contains more information from long lists, on which participants correctly recalled some but not all items, and thus captures more variance from secondary memory. This view may be synonymous with the idea that proportion correct scoring captures additional variance from executive-attentional resources (e.g. St Clair-Thompson & Sykes, 2010).

A final possibility for the differences between scoring methods is that proportion correct scoring captures additional variance from the ability to handle proactive interference. As noted earlier working memory tasks may assess the ability to handle proactive interference, which builds up across trials (e.g. Bunting, 2006; Lustig et al., 2001; May et al., 1999). As the standard administration of working memory tasks involves presenting the largest set sizes last, these may be the most heavily influenced by proactive interference (e.g. Keppel & Underwood, 1962; Wickens, 1970). As proportion correct scoring methods capture additional variance from long lists it is therefore reasonable to suggest that they may capture more variance from the ability to manage proactive interference. To date there has been no research examining these possible underpinnings of differences between the scoring methods.

In addition to the theoretical implications there are practical implications of research into scoring methods. If the purpose of using working memory tasks is to predict cognitive skills, then researchers should use proportion correct scoring methods. It is, however, worthy of note that this requires the administration of all trials within a task and does not allow for discontinuation.

## SUMMARY OF THE EFFECTS OF TASK STRUCTURE, ADMINISTRATION AND SCORING METHODS

The research reviewed in this chapter has demonstrated that the structure, administration and scoring methods used for working memory tasks have an important impact upon working memory scores and their predictive ability. Table 1 provides a summary of each of the issues that has been addressed. The list of issues is, however, by no means exhaustive. There are several other variations in administration which may impact upon working memory scores and their predictive ability. These include, for example, whether it is necessary to interleave processing between each memory item, or whether similar findings emerge from other tasks (e.g. Schmiedek, Hildebrandt, Lovden, & Wilhelm et al., 2009), and whether it is necessary for participants to engage in serial recall rather than free recall (e.g. see Alptekin & Ercetin, 2009).

**Table 1. A summary of the effects of task structure, administration and scoring methods**

| Variation | Effect on working memory scores | Effect on predictive ability | Relevant references |
|---|---|---|---|
| Cognitive load (manipulating the difficulty or the number of processing operations, or the time allowed for processing) | Increasing cognitive load reduces working memory scores | Increasing cognitive load increases predictive ability | Barrouillet et al. (2004) Lepine et al. (2005) St Clair-Thompson (2007a) |
| Stimulus similarity (when memory items are not generated by the processing task) | Increasing stimulus similarity results in lower working memory scores | Stimulus similarity may have no effect upon predictive ability* | Bayliss et al. (2003) Conlin et al. (2005a) Duff & Logie (2001) Oberauer et al. (2004) |
| Ascending versus randomized lists | Randomized lists lead to marginally higher scores than ascending lists* | Randomized tasks are better predictors of cognitive skills* | St Clair-Thompson (in press) |
| Spoken versus silent processing | Silent processing results in higher scores than spoken processing* | The effects on predictive ability are currently unknown* | Beaman (2004) |
| Experimenter versus participant-paced processing | Participant-paced tasks result in higher scores than experimenter-paced or computer-paced tasks | Experimenter-paced or computer- paced tasks are more predictive of higher order cognition | Friedman & Miyake (2004) Lepine et al. (2005) McCabe (2010) St Clair-Thompson (2007b) |
| Recall versus recognition | Participants achieve higher scores on recognition tasks than recall tasks* | Tasks requiring recall are better predictors of cognitive skills than those requiring recognition* | Alptekin & Ercetin (2009) |
| Including reaction time measures | N/A | Including reaction time measures improves the predictive ability of working memory tasks | Bayliss et al. (2003) Cowan et al. (2003) Waters & Caplan (1996) |
| Absolute versus proportion correct scoring methods | N/A | Proportion correct scores are better predictors of cognitive skills than absolute scores | Friedman & Miyake (2005) St Clair-Thompson & Sykes (2010) Unsworth & Engle (2010) |

*These are issues about which there is relatively little research so the conclusions are somewhat tentative.

Whilst describing the variations in task structure, administration and scoring methods in the current chapter, an attempt has been made to describe the cognitive underpinnings of differences between these methods. It appears that even small manipulations in task structure, administration or scoring can have an important influence upon participant's scores and their predictive ability. This is at least in part because working memory span tasks are complex in their nature. They were designed to assess the ability to process and store information (e.g. Daneman & Carpenter, 1980), but performance is also influenced by domain specific skills such as chunking and rehearsal (e.g. Conway et al., 2005), speed of processing (e.g. Towse et al., 1995), and the ability to resist interference (e.g. Oberauer & Kliegel, 2001). The effects of variations in administration and scoring may therefore arise because the variations alter the extent to which scores capture variance from each of these skills that working memory measures assess. For example, one common theme that has emerged throughout the chapter is that variations in administration and scoring can influence the extent to which working memory scores capture variance from executive-attentional resources (see also St Clair-Thompson, 2007a; St Clair- Thompson & Sykes, 2010). This may be synonymous with the idea of increasing cognitive load (e.g. Barouillet et al., 2004). Alternatively, rather than influencing executive-attentional demands *per se*, variations in administration and scoring may influence the requirement of participants to resist proactive interference (see also Lustig et al., 2001; May et al., 1999). These findings are consistent with suggestions that the predictive power of working memory measures results from a fundamental capacity required by complex activities such as a capability for controlling attention (e.g. Conway & Engle, 1996; Engle et al., 1999) or for coordinating multiple-system functioning (Baddeley, 1990).

## INTERPRETATION WITHIN CURRENT THEORETICAL FRAMEWORKS OF WORKING MEMORY

The research reviewed in this chapter suggests that working memory should be viewed as a flexible system, with the extent to which a task measures executive-attentional resources being determined, in part, by administration and scoring procedures. There are a number of theoretical accounts of working memory which can explain the current results. The results are not inconsistent with the multiple-component model of working memory (Baddeley, 2000; Baddeley & Hitch, 1974) or the controlled attentional view (e.g. Engle & Kane, 2004; Kane et al., 2001) described earlier. However, particularly worthy of note at this stage are two further approaches; the dual-component framework of Unsworth and Engle (2006; 2007) and the continuity approach of Cornoldi and Vechhi (2000).

As mentioned earlier in the chapter Unsworth and Engle (2006; 2007) proposed that working memory comprises of an active maintenance or short-term memory component (primary memory) and controlled search and retrieval processes (secondary memory). During working memory tasks items are thought to be initially maintained in primary memory but then displaced to secondary memory by other incoming items or distracting information, including processing activities. Unsworth and Engle used this theoretical account to explain differences between scoring procedures for working memory tasks. Specifically, they suggested that proportion correct scores, compared to absolute scores, contain more information from long lists, and thus capture more variance from secondary memory. This approach could also be used to account for variations in administration methods. For example, it would seem reasonable to assume that increasing the number of processing activities within a given time limit (e.g. Barouillet et al., 2004) or increasing the complexity of processing activities (e.g. St Clair-Thompson, 2007a), would increase the displacement of items from primary memory, drawing further upon secondary memory. Similarly, an increase in similarity between items to be processed and items to be recalled (e.g. Bayliss et al., 2003), or using ascending rather than descending task formats (e.g. Lustig et al., 2001), would result in greater distraction, and thus greater involvement of secondary memory resources.

In an alternative account, Cornoldi and Vecchi (2000; see also Cornoldi & Vecchi, 2003) developed a model of working memory characterized by two dimensions based on continuum relations. One dimension (the horizontal continuum) relates to the type of material to be processed and recalled, for example verbal, visual, or spatial information. The second dimension (the vertical continuum) relates to the degree of active processing that is required. The model assumes a conical structure, such that greater distances between modalities are postulated in passive processes than in active processes requiring elaboration and integration of information. This model is similar to the controlled attention perspective proposed by Engle and colleagues (e.g. Engle & Kane, 2004; Engle et al., 1999). However, active control is associated to, rather than identified with attention, and control varies along a continuum maintaining modality-specific features (for a comparison of these approaches see Cornoldi & Vecchi, 2003). In terms of accounting for variations in administration and scoring procedures, in this model each working memory task involves a different degree of central and peripheral structures. Therefore, manipulations such as increasing the number or complexity of processing activities (e.g. Barrouillet et al., 2004; St Clair-Thompson, 2007a), or increasing stimulus similarity (e.g. Conlin et al., 2005), would shift a task up the vertical continuum, reflecting a greater involvement of active control.

Cornoldi and Vecchi (2003) provided a comparison of their model with other theoretical accounts. They acknowledged that within the multiple-component model of working memory (e.g. Baddeley, 2000; Baddeley & Hitch, 1974) their vertical continuum could be represented by the degree of coordination between the central executive and domain-specific storage components of working memory. However, they proposed that a continuum is more flexible and allows the identification of a different amount of central control in each task. The research reviewed in this chapter, concerned with task structure, administration and scoring procedures for working memory tasks, suggests that this is an important feature of this model. The findings suggest that a suitable framework of the working memory system must be able to account for how experimental manipulations, including increasing cognitive load (e.g. Barrouillet et al., 2004; Lepine et al., 2005), altering stimulus similarity (e.g. Bunting, 2006), or employing different scoring procedures (e.g. St Clair-Thompson & Sykes, 2010), can lead a task to place increased demands upon executive-attentional resources or active control.

## CONCLUSION

Working memory span tasks, involving both processing and storage, are amongst the most commonly used measures in psychology (see also Conway et al., 2005; Friedman & Miyake, 2005). However, researchers and practitioners continue to use a range of working memory tasks, with different processing and storage requirements, and varying administration and scoring procedures. The current review has outlined a number of variations in task structure, administration and scoring that influence both working memory scores and their predictive ability. The practical implications of the findings are clear. If the aim of research or assessment is to predict higher-order cognition, attainment or intelligence, then there are benefits to using tasks which are cognitively demanding (e.g. Lepine et al., 2005), with list lengths in randomized order (e.g. St Clair-Thompson,in press), tasks which minimise strategy use (e.g. McCabe, 2010), are scored using proportion correct methods (e.g. Friedman & Miyake, 2005), and include indicators of reaction time (e.g. Cowan et al., 2003). Whether these benefits extend to other research designs, for example those in which it is necessary to identify discrete groups such as those of high versus low working memory capacity, remains to be seen. The theoretical implications of the findings, however, are less clear. It is suggested that a number of the variations in administration and scoring alter the demands placed upon executive-attentional resources or active control (see also Barrouillet et al., 2004; St Clair-Thompson, 2007a; St Clair-Thompson & Sykes, 2010). These findings are consistent with a number of theoretical accounts of working memory, but the differing interpretations highlight the need for a better understanding of the cognitive resources underlying working memory task performance.

The research discussed in this chapter also suggests that that the development of standard administration and scoring methods for working memory tasks would be worthwhile. It is possible that differences in administration and scoring procedures may account for contrasting findings in the working memory literature. Unsworth and Engle (2007) suggested that differences between absolute and proportion correct scoring methods for working memory tasks could explain discrepancies regarding impairments of short-term and working memory in patients with schizophrenia or with frontal lobe lesions. Other variations in administration and scoring could possibly explain further discrepancies. Researchers who find such discrepancies should take a task-analysis approach and fully examine the tasks used in relevant studies. There may well be differences in administration and scoring methods. It is also important to note though that researchers may find diverse patterns of findings in different participants groups. For example, there is evidence for qualitative differences in performance on some working memory tasks between children and adults (e.g. St Clair-Thompson, 2010). There may also be differences if comparing typically developing samples to those with neurodevelopmental disorders or neuropsychological impairments. The issues raised in this chapter are therefore important in both cognitive research and research which uses working memory tasks for assessment purposes.

The suggestion that perhaps researchers should develop standard administration and scoring methods for working memory tasks is of course not appropriate across all domains of psychology. Implementing various manipulations in administration and scoring provides important evidence for the cognitive processes underlying performance on working memory tasks, and their relationship with complex cognition. Different administration and scoring methods will continue to be used for this purpose for many years to come. However, there are many studies in psychology in which working memory measures are used with no consideration of administration or scoring methods. It is therefore suggested that researchers need to consider their methods when employing working memory tasks, and when interpreting the relationships between working memory scores and higher-order cognition.

## REFERENCES

Alloway, T.P., Gathercole, S.E., Kirkwood, H.J., & Elliott, J. (2009). The Working memory rating scale: A classroom-based behavioural assessment of working memory. *Learning and Individual Differences, 19*, 242-245.

Alloway, T.P., Gathercole, S.E., & Pickering, S.J. (2006). Verbal and visuo-spatial short-term and working memory in children: Are they separable? *Child Development, 77*, 1698-1716.

Alptekin, C., & Ercetin, G. (2009). Assessing the relationship of working memory to L2 reading: Does the nature of comprehension process and treading span task make a difference? *System, 37,* 627- 639.

Anderson, J. R. & Lebiere, C. (1998). *The atomic components of thought.* Mahwah, NJ: Erlbaum.

Baddeley, A.D. (1986). *Working Memory.* Oxford: Oxford University Press.

Baddeley, A.D. (1990). *Human memory: Theory and practice.* Hillsdale, NJ: Erlbaum.

Baddeley, A.D. (2000). The episodic buffer: a new component of working memory? *Trends in Cognitive Sciences, 11(4),* 417- 423.

Baddeley, A.D. (2007). *Working memory, thought and action.* Oxford: Oxford University Press.

Baddeley, A.D., & Hitch, G. (1974). Working Memory. In Bower, G.H. (Ed.), *The Psychology of Learning and Motivation.* New York: Academic Press.

Barrouillet, P., Bernardin, S., & Camos, V. (2004). Time constraints and resource sharing in adults' working memory spans. *Journal of Experimental Psychology General, 133,* 83-100.

Barrouillet, P., & Camos, V. (2001). Developmental increase in working memory span: Resource sharing or temporal decay? *Journal of Memory and Language, 45,* 1-20.

Barrouillet, P., Gaven's, N., Vergauwe, E., Gaillard, V., & Camos, V. (2009). Working memory span development: A time-based resource sharing model account. *Developmental Psychology, 45, 477- 490.*

Barrouillet, P., Portrat, S., & Camos, V. (2011). On the law relating processing to storage in working memory. Psychological Review, 118, 175- 192.

Bayliss, D.M., Jarrold, C., Gunn, D.M., & Baddeley, A.D. (2003). The complexities of complex span: Explaining individual differences in working memory in children and adults. *Journal of Experimental Psychology General. 132,* 71- 92.

Beaman, C.P. (2004). The irrelevant sound phenomenon revisited: What role for working memory capacity? *Journal of Experimental Psychology: Learning, Memory and Cognition, 30,* 1106-1118.

Blalock, L.D., & McCabe, D.P. (2011). Proactive interference and practice effects in visuospatial memory span task performance. *Memory, 19,* 83-91.

Bowles, R.P., & Salthouse, T.A. (2003). Assessing the age-related effects of proactive interference on working memory tasks using the Rasch model. *Psychology and Aging, 18,* 608-615.

Bunting, M. (2006). Proactive interference and item similarity in working memory. *Journal of Experimental Psychology, Learning, Memory, and Cognition, 12,* 183-196.

Case, R., Kurland, D.M., & Goldberg, J. (1982). Operational efficiency and the growth of short- term memory span. *Journal of Experimental Child Psychology, 33,* 386- 404.

Chun, D.C., & Payne, J.S. (2004). What makes students click: working memory and look-up behaviour. System, 32, 481-504.

Conlin, J.A., Gathercole, S.E., & Adams, J.W. (2005a). Stimulus similarity decrements in children's working memory span. The Quarterly Journal of Experimental Psychology, 58, 1434- 1446.

Conlin, J.A., Gathercole, S.E., & Adams, J.W. (2005b). Children's working memory: investigating performance limitations in complex span tasks. *Journal of Experimental Child Psychology,* 90, 303-17.

Conway, A.R.A., & Engle, R.W. (1994). Working memory and retrieval: A resource dependent inhibition model. Journal of Experimental Psychology General, 123, 354- 373.

Conway, A.R.A., & Engle, R.W. (1996). Individual differences in working memory capacity. More evidence for a general capacity theory. *Memory, 4*, 577-590.

Conway, A.R.A., Kane, M.J., Bunting, M.F., Hambrick, D.Z., Wilhelm, O., & Engle, R.W. (2005). Working memory span tasks: A methodological review and user's guide. *Psychonomic Bulletin and Review, 12*, 769-786.

Conway, A. R. A., Kane, M. J., & Engle, R. W. (2003). Working memory capacity and its relation to general intelligence. *Trends in Cognitive Science, 7*, 547-552.

Conway, A.R.A., Jarrold, C., Kane, M.J., & Towse, J.N. (2007). *Variation in working memory*. NY: Oxford University Press.

Cornoldi, C., & Vecchi, T. (2000). Mental imagery in blind people: The role of passive and active visuo-spatial processes. In M. Heller (Ed.). *Touch, representation, and blindness* (pp 143-181). Oxford: Oxford University Press.

Cornoldi, C., & Vecchi, T. (2003). *Visuo-spatial working memory and individual differences.* Hove, UK: Psychology Press.

Cowan, N. (1995). Attention and memory: An integrated framework. Oxford, England: Oxford University Press.

Cowan, N., Towse, J.N., Hamilton, Z., Saults, J.S., Elliott, E.M., Lacey, J.F., Moreno, M.V., & Hitch, G.J. (2003). Children's working memory processes: A response- timing analysis. Journal of Experimental Psychology General, 132, 113-132.

Daneman, M., & Carpenter, P.A. (1980). Individual differences in working memory and reading. *Journal of Verbal learning and Verbal Behaviour, 19*, 450- 466.

Daneman, M., & Merikle, P.M. (1996). Working memory and language comprehension: a meta-analysis. *Psychonomic Bulletin and Review, 3*, 422-433.

De Neys, W., d'Ydealle, G., Schaeken, W., & Vos, G. (2002). A Dutch, computerised, and group administrable adaptation of the operation span test. *Psychologica Belgica, 42*, 177-190.

DeStefano, D., & LeFevre, J. (2004). The role of working memory in mental arithmetic. *European Journal of Cognitive Psychology, 16*, 353- 386.

Duff, S.C., & Logie, R.H. (2001). Processing and storage in working memory span. *The Quarterly Journal of Experimental Psychology, 54*, 31-48.

Duncan, J. (1987). Attention and Reading: Wholes and parts in shape recognition- A tutorial review. In M. Coltheart (Ed). *Attention and Performance X11: The psychology of reading* (pp 39- 62). Hillsdale NJ: Lawrence Erlbaum.

Engle, R.W. (2002). Working memory capacity as executive attention. *Current Directions in Psychological Science, 11,* 19-23.

Engle, R.W., & Kane, M.J. (2004). Executive attention, working memory capacity, and a two-factor theory of cognitive control. In B. Ross (Ed), *The psychology of learning and motivation* (Vol. 44, pp. 145-199). New York: Elsevier.

Engle, R.W., Kane, M.J., & Tuholski, S.W. (1999). Individual differences in working memory capacity and what they tell us about controlled attention, general fluid intelligence and functions of the prefrontal cortex. In Miyake, A., & Shah, P. (Eds). *Models of working memory: Mechanisms of active maintenance and executive control (*pp. 102-134). London: Cambridge Press.

Engle, R.W., Tuholski, S.W., Laughlin, J.E., & Conway, A.R.A. (1999). Working memory, short- term memory, and general fluid intelligence: A latent variable approach. *Journal of Experimental Psychology General,* 128, 309- 331.

Friedman, N.P., & **Miyake, A.** (2000). Differential roles for spatial and verbal working memory in the comprehension of spatial descriptions. *Journal of Experimental Psychology: General, 129,* , 61–83.

Friedman, N.P., & Miyake, A. (2004). The reading span test and its predictive power for reading comprehension. *Journal of Memory and Language, 31,* 136- 158.

Friedman, N.P., & Miyake, A. (2005). Comparison of four scoring methods for the reading span test. *Behavior Research Methods, Instruments and Computers, 37,* 581-590.

Hitch, G.J., Towse, J.N., & Hutton, U. (2001). What limits children's working memory span: Theoretical accounts and applications for scholastic development. *Journal of Experimental Psychology General, 130,* 184- 198.

Jarrold, C., & Bayliss, D. (2007). Variation in working memory due to typical and atypical development. In A.R.A. Conway, C. Jarrold, M. Kane, & J.N. Towse (Eds.). *Variation in working memory* (pp 134-161). New York: Oxford University Press.

Jarvis, H.L., & Gathercole, S.E. (2003). Verbal and nonverbal working memory and achievements on national curriculum tests at 11 and 14 years of age. *Educational and Child Psychology, 20,* 123- 140.

Kane, M.J., Bleckley, K.M., Conway, A.R.A., & Engle, R.W. (2001). A controlled- attention view of working memory capacity. *Journal of Experimental Psychology: General, 130*, 169-183.

Kane, M.J., Conway, A.R.A., Hambrick, D.Z., & Engle, R.W. (2007). Variation in working memory capacity as variation in executive attention and control. In A.R.A. Conway, C. Jarrold, M.J. Kane, A. Miyake, & J.N. Towse (Eds.). *Variation in working memory* (pp. 21-48). NY: Oxford University Press.

Kane, M.J., & Engle, R.W. (2000). Working memory capacity, proactive interference and divided attention: Limits on long-term retrieval. *Journal of Experimental Psychology, Learning, Memory, and Cognition, 26*, 333-358.

Kane, M.J., & Engle, R.W. (2002). The role of prefrontal cortex in working memory capacity, executive attention, and general fluid intelligence: An individual differences perspective. *Psychonomic Bulletin and Review, 9*, 637- 671.

Kane, M. J., Hambrick, D. Z., & Conway, A. R. A. (2005). Working memory capacity and fluid intelligence are strongly related constructs: Comment on Ackerman, Beier, and Boyle (2004). *Psychological Bulletin, 131,* 66-71.

Kane, M.J., Hambrick, D.Z., Tuholski, S.W., Wilhelm, O., Payne, T.W., & Engle, R.W. (2004). The generality of working memory capacity: A latent variable approach to verbal and visuo-spatial memory span and reasoning. *Journal of Experimental Psychology General, 133,* 189- 217.

Keppel, G., & Underwood, B.J. (1962). Proactive interference in short-term retention of single items. Journal of Verbal Learning and Verbal Behavior, 1, 153-161.

Klein, K., & Fiss, W.H. (1999). The reliability and stability of the Turner and Engle working memory task. *Behavior Research Methods, Instruments, and* Computers, 31, 429- 432.

Kyllonen, P. C. (1996). Is working memory capacity Spearman's g? In I. Dennis & P. Tapsfield (Eds.), *Human abilities: Their nature and measurement* (pp. 49-75). Mahwah, NJ: Erlbaum.

Lepine, R., Barrouillet, P., & Camos, V. (2005). What makes working memory spans so predictive of higher level cognition? *Psychonomic Bulletin and Review, 12,* 165- 170.

Lustig, C., May, C.P., & Hasher, L. (2001). Working memory span and the role of proactive interference. *Journal of Experimental Psychology: General, 130,* 199-207.

May, C.P., Hasher, L., & Kane, M.J. (1999). The role of interference in memory span. *Memory and Cognition, 27,* 759- 767.

McCabe, D.P. (2010). The influence of complex working memory span task administration methods on prediction of higher level cognition and metacognitive control of response times. *Memory and Cognition, 38,* 868- 882.

McNamara, D.S., & Scott, J.L. (2001). Working memory capacity and strategy use. *Memory and Cognition, 29, 10-17.*

Melser, T., & Klauer, K.C. (1999). Working memory and changing-state hypothesis. *Journal of Experimental Psychology: Learning, Memory and Cognition, 25,* 1272-1299.

Miyake, A. (2001). Individual differences in working memory: Introduction to the special issue. *Journal of Experimental Psychology: General*, 130, 163- 168.

Miyake, A., Friedman, N.P., Rettinger, D.A., Shah, P., & Hegarty, M. (2001). How are visuospatial working memory, executive functioning, and spatial abilities related? A latent variable analysis. *Journal of Experimental Psychology: General, 130,* 621–640.

Miyake, A., & Shah, P. (1999). *Models of working memory: Mechanisms of active maintenance and executive control.* New York: Cambridge University Press.

Oberauer, K. (2005). The measurement of working memory capacity. In O. Wilhelm & R.W. Engle (Eds), *Handbook of understanding and measuring intelligence* (pp.393-408). Thousand Oaks: Sage.

Oberauer, K., & Kliegl, R. (2001). Beyond resources: Formal models of complexity effects and age differences in working memory. *European Journal of Cognitive Psychology, 13,* 187-215.Oberauer, K., Lange, E., & Engle, R.W. (2004). Working memory capacity and resistance to interference. *Journal of Memory and Language, 51,* 80-96.

Oberauer, K., & SuB, H.M. (2000). Working memory and interference. A comment on Jenkins, Myerson, Hale and Fry (1999). *Psychonomic Bulletin and Review, 7,* 727- 733.

Oberauer, K., SuB, H.M., Schulze, R., Wilhelm, O., & Wittmann, W. W. (2000). Working memory capacity- facets of a cognitive ability construct. *Personality and Individual Differences, 29,* 1017-1045.

Pickering, S., & Gathercole, S. (2001). Working Memory Test Battery for Children (WMTB-C). London: The Psychological Corporation.

Ransdell, S. and Hecht, S. A. (2003). Time and resource limits on working memory: Cross-age consistency in counting span performance. *Journal of Experimental Child Psychology,* 86, 303-313.

Rowe, G., Hasher, L., & Turcotte, J. (2008). Age differences in visuospatial working memory. *Psychology and Aging, 23,* 79-84.

Saito, S., & Miyake, A. (2004). On the nature of forgetting and the processing-storage relationship in reading span performance. Journal of Memory and Language, 50, 425-443.

Schmiedek, F., Hildebrandt, A., Lovden, M., Wilhelm, O., & Lindenberger, U. (2009). Complex span versus updating tasks of working memory: The gap is not that deep. *Journal of Experimental Psychology: Learning, Memory and Cognition, 35,* 1089-1096.

Seigneuric, A., Ehrlich, M.F., Oakhill, J.V., & Yuill, N.M. (2000). Working memory resources and children's reading comprehension. *Reading and Writing, 13,* 81- 103.

Shah, P., & Miyake, A. (1996). The Separability of Working Memory Resources for Spatial Thinking and Language Processing: An Individual Differences Approach. *Journal of Experimental Psychology General, 125,* 4- 27.

St Clair-Thompson, H.L. (2007a). The effects of cognitive demand upon relationships between working memory and cognitive skills. *Quarterly Journal of Experimental Psychology A, 60,* 1378- 1388.

St Clair-Thompson, H.L. (2007b). The influence of strategies upon relationships between working memory and cognitive skills. *Memory, 15,* 353- 365.

St Clair-Thompson, H.L. (2010). Backwards digit recall: A measure of short-term memory or working memory? *European Journal of Cognitive Psychology, 22,* 286-297.

St Clair-Thompson, H.L. (in press). Ascending versus randomized list lengths in working memory tasks. *Journal of Cognitive Psychology.*

St Clair-Thompson, H.L., & Sykes, S. (2010). Scoring methods and the predictive ability of working memory tasks. *Behavior Research Methods, 42, 969-975.*

Towse, J.N., Cowan, N., Hitch, G.J., & Horton, N. (2008). The recall of information from working memory: insights from behavioural and chronometric perspectives. *Experimental Psychology, 55,* 371-383.

Towse, J.N., Cowan, N., Horton, N., & Whytock, S. (2008). Task experience and children's working memory performance: A perspective from recall timing. *Developmental Psychology, 44,* 695-706.

Towse, J.N., & Hitch, G.J. (1995). Is there a relationship between task demand and storage space in tests of working memory capacity? *The Quarterly Journal of Experimental Psychology, 48A,* 108-124.

Towse, J.N., & Hitch, G.J. (1997). Integrating information in object counting: A role for a central coordination process? *Cognitive Development, 12,* 393- 422.

Towse, J.N., Hitch, G.J., & Horton, N. (2007). Working memory as the interface between processing and retention: A developmental perspective. *Advnaces in Child Development and Behavior, 35,* 219- 251.

Towse, J.N., Hitch, G.J., Horton, N., & Harvey, K. (2010). Synergies between processing and memory in children's reading span. *Developmental Science, 13,* 779- 789.

Towse, J.N., Hitch. G.J., & Hutton, U. (1998). A re-evaluation of working memory capacity in children. *Journal oF Memory and language, 39,* 195- 217.

Towse, J.N., Hitch. G.J., & Hutton, U. (2000). On the interpretation of working memory span in adults. *Memory and Cognition, 28,* 341-348.

Towse, J.N., Hitch. G.J., & Hutton, U. (2002). On the nature of the relationship between processing activity and item retention in children. *Journal of Experimental Child Psychology, 82,* 156- 184.

Treisman, A.M. (1991). Search, similarity, and integration of features between and within dimensions. *Journal of Experimental Psychology, Human Perception and Performance, 12,* 652- 676.

Treisman, A.M., & Gelade, G. (1980). A feature- integration theory of attention. *Cognitive Psychology, 12,* 97- 136.

Treisman, A.M., & Sato, S. (1990). Conjunction search revisited. *Journal of Experimental Psychology: Human Perception and Performance, 16,* 459- 478.

Turley- Ames, K.J., & Whitfield, M.M. (2003). Strategy training and working memory task performance. *Journal of Memory and Language, 49,* 446- 468.

Turner, M.L., & Engle, R.W. (1989). Is working memory capacity task dependent? *Journal of Memory and Language, 28,* 127- 154.

Unsworth, N., & Engle, R.W. (2006). Simple and complex memory span and their relation to fluid abilities: Evidence from list-length effects. *Journal of Memory and Language, 54,* 68-80.

Unsworth, N., & Engle, R.W. (2007). On the division of short-term and working memory: An examination of simple and complex span and their relation to higher order abilities. *Psychological Bulletin, 133,* 1038- 1066.

Unsworth, N., Heitz, R.P., Schrock, J.C., & Engle, R.W. (2005). An automated version of the operation span task. *Behavior Research Methods, 37,* 498-505.

Waters, G.S., & Caplan, D. (1996). The measurement of verbal working memory capacity and its relation to reading comprehension. *Quarterly Journal of Experimental Psychology, 49,* 51-79.

Wickens, D.D. (1970). Encoding categories of words: An empirical approach to meaning. *Psychological Review, 77,* 1-15.

In: Psychology of Memory
Editors: Dannie M. Hendrix and Orval Holcomb

ISBN: 978-1-61942-633-7
© 2012 Nova Science Publishers, Inc.

*Chapter 6*

# CAPACITY LIMITS IN VISUAL SHORT-TERM MEMORY

## *Jean-Francois Delvenne*
Institute of Psychological Sciences, University of Leeds, UK

## ABSTRACT

Visual short-term memory (VSTM) is the system that temporarily holds relevant visual information that is useful for a particular ongoing cognitive task. Most studies on VSTM have particularly focused on its storage capacity. Even though they have not yet resolved the fundamental question of why there is a capacity limit in the first place, those studies have converged to the conclusion that VSTM is extremely limited in capacity, holding only about three to four objects simultaneously. In this chapter, I will review the different techniques that have been used to reveal the capacity limits in VSTM as well as the different factors that have been shown to influence this capacity. This review will consider both behavioural and neuroimaging work.

## 1. INTRODUCTION

Imagine Bob, a healthy young man, watching a movie scene in which an actor is sitting in a car next to his new date. The actor is dressed with a jeans and a red check shirt. The camera then moves to a close-up of the actor's face, full of admiration for his new guest, and finally comes back to the initial shot. His shirt is now a blue check shirt. Bob would notice this evident and unforgivable editing error if he can spot the mismatch between this new information and the old one that must be retrieved from memory since not visible anymore. In other words, Bob needs to have a cognitive system that allows him to encode and store visual information and to make use of it when that information is no longer in view. This system is called *visual short-term memory* (VSTM) (or *visual working memory*).

The very existence of a short-term memory dedicated to the maintenance of recently perceived visual information has only been established at the end of the 60's and in the early 70's. Before that, studies about the storage of visual information were conducted within the context of iconic memory, a very short-lived memory (i.e., less than half a second) and regarded as the persistence of the initial perceptual image (Neisser, 1967; Sperling, 1960). For the visual information to be maintained for longer time than half a second, researchers then thought that the information had to be verbally recoded (Sperling, 1963; 1967). This idea can probably be accredited to the experimental paradigms adopted during that period, which particularly encouraged verbal coding of visual information. For example, in the colour memory study of Brener (1940), coloured slides were serially presented to participants, who then had to verbally report the colour names in the order they were shown. The results revealed that about seven colours could be accurately reported, which coincides, rather predictably given the nature of the recall procedure, to the prototypical verbal memory span of seven items (Miller, 1956). Even in the famous study of Sperling (1960), in which participants were instructed to report all the stimuli that were briefly presented, verbal short-term memory could have play a major role. Not only by the nature of the stimuli that were used (i.e., letters and digits) but also by the task itself that entailed to write down the characters that were reported, requiring therefore a translation of the visually presented information into a verbal code.

The works of Posner in the 60's and Phillips in the 70's have been extremely influential for the acknowledgement of a specific system than can store the visual aspect of information, and that for longer time than the simple persistence of the sensory experience. For instance, Posner and colleagues (Posner & Keele, 1967; Posner, Boies, Eichelman, & Taylor, 1969) conducted a simple letter matching task in which two letters were sequentially presented to participants. The letters were displayed in either upper (e.g., "A") or lower case (e.g., "a"). The task was to decide whether the two letters were the same or different, irrespective of the physical presentation. The results revealed faster response times when the letters had the same appearance as compared to when they visually differed. Those findings suggest, perhaps indirectly, that the visual representation of a stimulus can be stored in memory, and therefore that a VSTM system exists.

A more direct demonstration of the existence of a post-iconic visual memory was provided by Phillips (1974) using a procedure that, for the first time, assessed VSTM performance without being contaminated by verbal short-term memory. Phillips used the change detection paradigm in which two arrays of complex visual stimuli (i.e., partially-filled grids of dots), which were completely unfamiliar and pretty hard to verbally encode, were successively presented to participants and separated by a brief retention interval. The two grids of dots were either similar or different by having one cell more or less filled. The task was to detect a change between the two grids. Various retention interval durations and different levels of complexity, defined by the number of cells, were used. The results revealed that at short retention intervals (<250 ms), change detection performance was high and unaffected by the complexity of the grids. However, at longer intervals, performance declined as a function of the number of cells in the arrays. Those findings clearly demonstrate the distinction between a high-capacity, but short-lived, iconic memory representation and a limited-capacity, but longer-lasting, VSTM representation.

What characterises VSTM the most is probably its extremely limited capacity of storage. As we will see throughout this chapter, research has consistently shown that only a few pieces of information can be simultaneously held in VSTM. This high limitation is commonly exemplified in the literature by the phenomenon known as 'change blindness'. Change blindness refers to the remarkable failure of individuals to notice significant changes in visual scenes when these changes occur across brief perceptual interruptions such as blank intervals, blinks, eye movements, etc. (see the review by Simons & Rensink, 2005). For example, in an experiment conducted in natural, real-world social situation, Simons and Levin (1998) observed that 50% of people in the test did not notice that the man in front of them has turned into a different person after a very brief visual interruption. In view of this, researchers would not be surprised if Bob, our romantic movie fan from the example given at the start of this chapter, actually fails to detect the colour change of the actor's shirt[1]. To detect a change, the initial information has to be first encoded and maintained in memory, and then retrieved to enable the comparison process with the new input. Change blindness can be explained by a breakdown of any of those memory stages (i.e., encoding, storage, retrieval) but basically suggests that our VSTM is quite poor at representing properly a large amount of visual information.

In this chapter, I will first review the different methods and procedures that have been employed to measure the storage capacity of VSTM (section 2). Then, I will provide a synthesis of the different factors that have been found to modulate this capacity (section 3).

# 2. MEASURING THE CAPACITY OF VISUAL SHORT-TERM MEMORY

## 2.1. Behavioural Measures

The capacity of VSTM refers to the maximum of visual items that can be held, and is usually estimated by the number of items that can be correctly recognised or recalled after their presentation (Logie, 1995). Most studies on VSTM capacity have indeed used either a recognition paradigm or report procedure. To some extent, these two methods are similar as they both involve the presentation of a sample array, which consists of one or more visual items that must be remembered, followed by a short retention interval, and finally by a memory test. In addition, in both paradigms, memory performance declines as the number of items in the sample array (i.e., the set size) increases.

In the recognition paradigm, the memory test involves a comparison between a second array (i.e., test array) that follows the retention interval, and the initial sample array. The task typically requires a simple same/different judgement. The test array may consist of either a single-probe or a whole-display. In a single-probe test, only one item is presented at test and the task is to decide whether that particular item comes from the sample array. In a whole-display test (also known as the change detection paradigm – Phillips, 1974), all the items presented within the sample array are shown again at test, except that on some trials one of those items is different. The task requires detecting that change. The observer's ability to match the information between the two sequentially presented arrays, or to detect a mismatch, accounts for his memory capacity. In other words, the assumption behind the failure to

---

[1] Movie editing mistakes are far from being a rarity. For example, according to MovieMistakes.com, 394 editing errors have been found in the movie "Apocalypse Now" (i.e., one error every 25 seconds!), 298 errors in "Harry Potter and the Prisoner of Azkaban", 271 errors in "Star Wars", etc. What is even more extraordinary is the fact that very few viewers, even the most devoted fans, have ever detected a single one of those mistakes.

recognise a previously presented object, or to detect a change, is that the object was not properly encoded, stored, or retrieved from memory.

Although Phillips (1974) was the first to use the recognition paradigm to assess VSTM performance, it cannot be assured that Phillips' results actually provide a pure estimate of VSTM capacity of storage. In Phillips' study, grids of dots were used as stimuli and the simultaneous presentation of the dots may have led participants to encode a configuration of the dots as a gestalt figure rather than a set of distinctive items (e.g., two dots form a line, three dots form a line or a triangle, etc.). As the whole configuration (i.e., the gestalt figure) made by the dots often changes with the addition or removal of one dot, the task could have been based purely on configuration change detection. Importantly, recent research has shown that the encoding of a configuration, as well as the detection of a configuration change, do not necessarily require encoding and maintaining each item individually (Delvenne, Braithwaite, Riddoch, & Humphreys, 2002; Delvenne & Bruyer, 2006; Jiang, Olson & Chun, 2000).

The first convincing and systematic measure of VSTM capacity in a recognition paradigm was provided by Luck and Vogel (1997) (see also Vogel, Woodman, & Luck, 2001, for a full report). Rather than using indistinct items (like the dots in Phillips' study), Luck and Vogel (1997) used simple distinct features, such as different colours and orientated lines (Figure 1). While participants in Phillips's study could have relied on the dots configuration to make their change detection judgments, those from Luck and Vogel's study undeniably had to discriminate between the items and to memorise each of them independently. The authors observed that change detection performance remained almost flawless when there were 4 or less items in the sample array, but declined dramatically and rather consistently with larger numbers of items. This abrupt decrease in memory performance when more than four items are presented led the authors to suggest that the capacity of VSTM is about 3-4 items. The recognition paradigm, as a tool for measuring VSTM capacity, has since been used in many studies (e.g., Alvarez & Cavanagh, 2004; Awh, Barton, & Vogel, 2007; Delvenne & Bruyer, 2004, 2006; Delvenne, Cleeremans, & Laloyaux, 2010; Jiang et al., 2000; Wheeler & Treisman, 2002; Xu, 2002a, amongst many others). Those studies, among which some have used quantitative estimates of capacity using the Pashler/Cowan K equation (Cowan, 2001; Pashler, 1988), have all reached the same conclusion, namely that VSTM is severely limited in storage capacity.

Although the recognition paradigm is a simple procedure that can be used to test the ability to remember an item with sufficient fidelity to discriminate it from a different object, it provides little information about how well the item is remembered. In order to provide a continuous measure of the fidelity of the memory representations, a second class of VSTM studies has recently emerged in which a report procedure is used (Bays, Wu, & Husain, 2011; Umemoto, Drew, Ester, & Awh, 2010; Wilken & Ma, 2004; Zhang & Luck, 2008). For example, Wilken and Ma (2004) have developed a paradigm in which participants were briefly presented with a number of coloured items and then, after a short retention interval, were cued to report the exact colour of one of the items by adjusting a continuous colour wheel (Figure 2). The authors found that the precision of reports declined systematically as the number of items increased, suggesting that as more items are held in memory, the precision of the stored information decreases. Using the same procedure, Zhang and Luck (2008) found that although the rate of random guessing was low from 1 to 3 items, the amount of detail maintained about the items decreased, suggesting that VSTM holds 1 item with greater fidelity than 3 items.

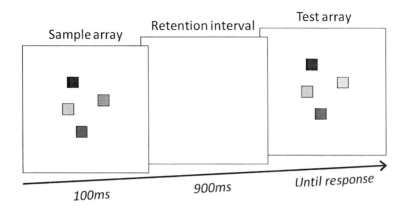

Figure 1. Example of a colour change detection task. The task is to decide whether the colours in the test array are the same as, or different from those in the sample array. Different grey levels represent different colours.

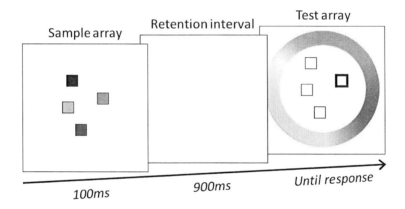

Figure 2. Example of a trial in a report procedure. The task is to retrieve the colour of the cued item and to indicate it on the colour wheel. Different grey levels represent different colours.

## 2.2. Neural Measures

In recent years, Event Related Potentials (ERPs), which measure the electrophysiological activity in the brain, and Functional Magnetic Resonance Imaging (fMRI), which measures the change in blood flow that accompanies neural activity in the brain, have both contributed substantially to our understanding of brain organisation, including VSTM capacity. Contrary to the behavioural memory tasks in which the response is used to make assumptions about what is stored, these techniques can be used to track the on-line maintenance of information dynamically. One conclusion from recent ERPs (Vogel & Machizawa, 2004) and fMRI (Todd & Marois, 2004, 2005; Xu & Chun, 2006) studies is that the capacity limit of VSTM storage is localised to the occipital and posterior parietal cortex, even though VSTM is mediated by a large distributed network of brain regions (e.g., Cohen, Perlstein, Braver, Nystrom, Noll, Jonides, & Smith, 1997; Courtney, Ungerleider, Keil, & Haxby, 1997; Desimone, 1996;

Fuster & Jervey, 1982; Miller, Erickson, & Desimone, 1996; Pessoa, Gutierrez, Bandettini, & Ungerleider, 2002).

ERPs studies used the Contralateral Control Method (Gratton, 1998), which is based on the fact that the visual system is primarily contralaterally organised. For example, Vogel and Machizawa (2004) presented participants with a bilateral display of equal amount of coloured objects in each hemifield. Participants were asked to fix centrally and to remember the items from a single hemifield for one second (Figure 3A). A large, sustained negative deflection, starting approximately 250-300 ms following the onset of the memory array and lasting during the entire retention period, was observed at posterior electrode sites that were contralateral to the attended hemifield. Importantly, the amplitude of this *contralateral delay activity* (CDA) (or *sustained posterior contralateral negativity* - SPCN) was found to be modulated by the number of memory items. Specifically, CDA amplitude was the smallest when there was only one item in the memory array and increased as the number of items increased, reaching an asymptote limit at each individual's behaviourally measured capacity, typically at around 3-4 items (Figure 3B). These findings have since been replicated numerous times rather consistently (e.g., Anderson, Vogel, & Awh, 2011; Delvenne, Kaddour, & Castronovo, 2011; Gao, Xu, Chen, Yin, Shen, & Shui, 2011; Eimer & Kiss, 2009; Ikkai, McCollough, & Vogel, 2010; McCollough, Machizawa, & Vogel, 2007; see the review by Perez & Vogel, *in press*). The strong correlation between the amplitude of CDA and the number of objects held in memory suggests that this component is a good electrophysiological marker of VSTM capacity.

Neuroimaging studies using fMRI have also contributed to the study of VSTM capacity by revealing the involvement of specific brain regions, which are also sensitive to the number of items held in memory. In particular, reminiscent of CDA amplitude, the activity in the intraparietal sulcus (IPS) has been found to be strongly modulated by the number of objects that are held in memory and to also reach an asymptotic limit at around 4 items (Todd & Marois, 2004; 2005; Xu & Chun, 2006). Furthermore, distinct cortical regions, including regions within the IPS, have been found to reflect distinct aspects of VSTM capacity (Xu, 2007, 2009; Xu & Chun, 2006, 2007). Whereas the activity in the inferior IPS has been found to be modulated by the number of locations occupied by the objects in the memory array, those in the superior IPS and the lateral occipital complex (LOC) are sensitive to the complexity of the objects. Note that the functional similarities between the IPS and the CDA, as well as the dorsal, posterior scalp topography of the CDA, strongly suggest that the IPS may be the major source of this wave. Furthermore, the dissociation between the two IPS regions could possibly resolve the current disagreement over whether CDA is primarily sensitive to the number of remembered objects or to the information load (Gao et al., 2011; Gao, Li, Liang, Chen, Yin, & Shen, 2009; Ikkai et al., 2010; Wang, Most, & Hoffman, 2009; Woodman & Vogel, 2008). Since such a large and sustained ERP component is likely to be generated by several coordinated sources of which both IPS regions may play a central role, it is plausible that the CDA amplitude is sensitive to both the number and the complexity of the objects held in memory. This remains an open question and further ERPs studies are needed to identify the temporal dynamics and the interactions between these two aspects of VSTM storage.

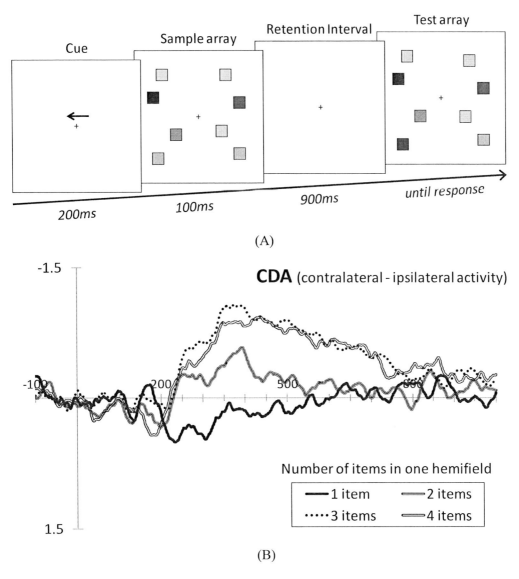

Figure 3. (A) Example of a trial used in ERPs studies. The different grey levels represent different colours. The task is to memorise the colours in the cued hemifield (indicated by the arrow). (B) CDAs (ipsilateral activity subtracted from contralateral activity) at posterior electrode sites for arrays of one, two, three, and four items per hemifield. (Adapted from Delvenne et al., 2011b.).

It is clear that the last 15 years of research into VSTM has come to a consensus according to which VSTM is extremely limited in storage capacity. The limited resources available to maintain visual information in short-term memory is shared between the representations of the items. As I will discuss this in the next section, it appears that both the number and resolution of representations are limited in VSTM (Wilken & Ma, 2004; Alvarez & Cavanagh, 2004; Awh et al., 2007; Scolari, Vogel, & Awh, 2008; Zhang & Luck, 2008) and correspond to separate dimensions of memory ability (Awh et al., 2007; Xu & Chun, 2006).

# 3. FACTORS INFLUENCING THE CAPACITY OF VISUAL SHORT-TERM MEMORY

## 3.1. Verbal Recoding

Intuitively, we may assume that more visual objects can be retained in VSTM if those objects can be named and rehearsed phonologically. However, conflicting evidence exists as to whether the verbal recoding of visual information affects the number of items that can be held in VSTM at all. On the one hand, several studies have shown an increase in VSTM capacity when verbal memory is available to help with retention (Paivio, 1990; Postle, D'Esposito & Corkin, 2005; Silverberg & Buchanan, 2005). On the other hand, other studies have found that VSTM performance is unaffected by the occurrence of a concurrent task that occupies verbal memory (Phillips & Christie, 1977; Pashler, 1988; Vogel et al., 2001; Morey & Cowan, 2004; 2005; Eng, Chen & Jiang, 2005), suggesting that the prevention of verbal encoding does not reduce VSTM capacity. This recurrent failure to find a benefit of verbal recoding of information on VSTM capacity may be attributed either to the similarity between the capacity of verbal and visual short-term memory (Cowan, 2001), and/or to the cost that would be required by such an additional cognitive process of translating a visual object into a verbal code. Nevertheless, because of the current uncertainty of the role of verbal memory in VSTM capacity, the recommendation would be to use procedures that simply prevent verbal recoding of the to-be-remembered visual items. The three most common procedures that have been used in the literature to minimize the role of verbal memory are (1) the use of a brief presentation of the memory items, which would reduce the ability to verbally encode the stimuli (Frick, 1988), (2) the use of meaningless and unfamiliar objects, that are difficult to be named, such as irregular shapes, textures, etc. (e.g., Cermack, 1971; Delvenne & Bruyer, 2004), and (3) the use of a concurrent verbal task (e.g., Delvenne & Bruyer, 2004; Delvenne et al., 2010; Vogel et al., 2001; Wheeler & Treisman, 2002; Xu & Nakayama, 2007).

## 3.2. Individual Differences

While the storage capacity of VSTM in healthy adults might averaged around 3-4 items (Cowan, 2001; Luck & Vogel, 1997), there exist considerable differences across individuals, ranging from 1.5 items to about 5 items (Vogel & Machizawa, 2004; Vogel et al., 2001). It has been recently suggested that individual differences in VSTM capacity might reflect their ability to exclude irrelevant information from entering VSTM (Jost, Bryck, Vogel, & Mayr, 2011; Lee, Cowan, Vogel, Rolan, Valle-Inclan et al., 2010; McNab & Klingberg, 2008; Vogel, McCollough & Machizawa, 2005). For instance, using the Contralateral Control Method (Gratton, 1998), Vogel and colleagues (2005) recorded the electrophysiological activity in participants while they performed a change detection task in which two or four oriented bars were displayed in the cued hemifield. In some trials, all the items were red (i.e., two- and four-targets conditions) whereas in other trials two were red and two were blue (i.e., distracters-present condition). The task was to remember only the red items. Participants were split into two groups based on their K scores (Cowan, 2001; Pashler, 1988): a high and a low capacity group. In high capacity individuals, the CDA amplitude was significantly smaller in the distracters-present condition than in the four-targets condition, but was equivalent to that observed in the two-targets condition, indicating that these individuals were efficient at filtering out the distracters and at preventing them from consuming memory capacity. By contrast, the CDA amplitude in low capacity individuals was larger in the distracters-present condition than that in the two-targets condition, but did not differ from that in the four-targets condition, indicating a high level of inefficiently from these individuals at excluding irrelevant information from entering memory. Furthermore, using the fMRI, McNab and Klingberg (2008) found that the activity in the prefrontal cortex and basal ganglia was a reliable predictor of (1) the extent to which irrelevant information is excluded from being stored in memory, and (2) individual differences in memory capacity. Moreover, the deficit for low-capacity individuals in filtering out irrelevant information appears to be restricted to spatial-based filtering mechanisms and reflects a difficulty in disengaging attention from the location of the distracters (Jost et al., 2011; Fukuda & Vogel, 2009, 2011). When irrelevant items share the same spatial location as relevant items, no differences between low- and high-capacity individuals in the ability to prevent distracters from entering VSTM is observed, suggesting a distinction between the mechanism for the feature-based filtering and that for spatial-based filtering (Zhou, Yin, Chen, Ding, Gao, & Shen, 2011). Specifically, Zhou and colleagues (2011) found that once relevant information enters VTSM, irrelevant high-discriminable information that shares its spatial location is also transferred into VSTM, regardless of VSTM capacity. As we will see in Section 3.5., one possible explanation for the absence of a deficit in feature-based filtering in low-capacity individuals may be that once features share the same spatial location, they are automatically bound into an integrated representation at no cost.

## 3.3. Age

Research in developmental studies has found that the capacity of VSTM increases throughout childhood. For example, it has been shown that infants of a few hours old have a capacity of only one object (Slater, Earle, Morison, & Rose, 1985; Slater & Morison, 1991). While it is acknowledged that the ability to remember one visually presented object is present very early in development, the age at which VSTM maturity is attained is a matter of debate. Some authors have suggested VSTM capacity increases during the first year of life to the adult levels of approximately 4 objects (Rose, Feldman, & Jankowski, 2001; Ross-Sheehy, Oakes, & Luck, 2003). Others have proposed that children might wait until the age of about 5 before they can double in size their capacity of one object (Cowan, Elliott, Saults, Morey, Mattox, et al., 2005; Riggs, McTaggart, Simpson, & Freeman, 2006) and that the full VSTM maturity is only reached at 10-11 years of age (Cowan et al., 2005; Logie & Pearson, 1997; Riggs et al., 2006; Wilson, Scott, & Power, 1987). The distinction between object individuation and identification (Xu, 2007, 2009; Xu & Chun, 2006, 2007, 2009) may provide a possible framework to explain those conflicting findings. Research has shown that whereas infants of 10 months old are able to keep track of more than one object when presented simultaneously at different locations, they can only infer the presence of one object when the objects are presented sequentially at the same location (Xu & Carey, 1996). This suggests that inferring the number of objects present depends greatly on whether the objects occupy distinct spatial locations. Infants may therefore use spatial information to individuate multiple objects very early in development (by using the output from the inferior IPS, responsible for object individuation), but may only process more than one object in more details (object identification) later. Therefore, it is possible that a capacity of 3-4 objects can be found in children at the end of their first year if the task does not entail processing the objects in much detail. Clearly further research is needed to examine this assumption. Note that at the other extreme of the age range, VSTM capacity declines in elderly people (e.g., Hartley, Little, Speer, & Jonides, 2011; Jost et al., 2010). While lifespan changes in VSTM capacity are well documented, the underlying neuronal and functional mechanisms still need to be understood.

## 3.4. The Nature of the Memory Representations

The capacity of VSTM has been shown to be influenced by the nature of the memory representations. For example, VSTM capacity is larger when the to-be-remembered visual items belong to distinct dimensions, such as colour, shape, orientation, texture, etc., as compared to when they all belong to the same single dimension (e.g., colour) (Delvenne & Bruyer, 2004; Wheeler & Treisman, 2002). For instance, using the change detection paradigm (Phillips, 1974), we found that remembering two shapes and two textures (thus four features in total) was easier than remembering four shapes or four textures, suggesting that items from the same dimension compete for capacity, whereas items from different dimensions may be maintained in independent memory stores (Delvenne & Bruyer, 2004). The existence of distinct memory stores for each specific dimension is supported by recent neuroimaging studies that suggest that the neural mechanisms that encode the sensory information are the same as those that store it (Awh & Jonides, 2001; Chelazzi, Miller, Duncan, & Desimone, 1993; Harrison & Tong, 2009; Miller, Erickson, & Desimone, 1996; Postle, 2006; Serences, Ester, Vogel, & Awh, 2009; Supèr, Spekreijse, & Lamme, 2001). For example, Serences and colleagues (2009) used the fMRI and found specific patterns of sustained neural activities for each remembered dimension (i.e., the colour or orientation of a foveally presented grating) in primary visual cortex (V1) during VSTM maintenance. Those patterns were similar to those observed during the encoding of the same stimuli.

In addition, other recent studies have suggested that the complexity of the objects may also influence the number of objects that can be held in memory. VSTM capacity has been shown to decrease as object complexity increases (Alvarez & Cavanagh, 2004; Awh et al., 2007; Eng et al., 2005; Luria & Vogel, 2011; Scolari et al., 2008; Xu & Chun, 2006). For instance, Alvarez and Cavanagh (2004) observed that the capacity of VSTM was approximately four objects when the stimuli were simple coloured squares, but it was reduced to only two objects when the stimuli were random polygons. At the neural level, object complexity may be represented in the superior IPS and the LOC. Xu and Chun (2006) found that the activity in those areas increased with both the number and the complexity of objects held in memory. However, while this activity reached an asymptotic limit at approximately four objects when simple objects were used (i.e., solid shapes), it did not increase above two objects when complex objects were used (i.e., various shaped holes) (see also Song & Jiang, 2006).

The emotionality of the objects has also been suggested to affect VSTM capacity. For example, recent studies have found that VSTM capacity was enhanced for emotional faces, such as angry (and sometimes happy) faces, as compared to neutral faces (Jackson, Wolf, Johnston, Raymond, & Linden, 2008; Jackson, Wu, Linden, and Raymond, 2009; Langeslag, Morgan, Jackson, Linden, & Van Strien, 2009). The perceptual and cognitive mechanisms underlying the VSTM advantage for a particular emotional object are currently unknown. In the case of an angry face, its perception may represent a potential threat situation. Thus, the aptitude to effectively encode and hold in memory the face of an angry individual has perhaps developed particularly well in order to deal effectively with such a potential menace.

## 3.5. The Perceptual Organisation of Visual Information

One of the factors that probably influence the most VSTM capacity is the perceptual organisation of visual information in the visual field. In particular, the integration of several to-be-remembered visual features into a single object can considerably increase the number of features that can be held simultaneously in memory. For example, a shape and a colour will be better remembered if they belong to the same object (i.e., a coloured shape) than if they form two distinct entities. The first compelling demonstration of the effect of feature integration on VSTM capacity was provided by Luck and Vogel (1997). In their landmark study, Luck and Vogel demonstrated that individuals were able to store up to four colours or orientations at a time, but when the colours and orientations were conjoined to form four coloured orientations, they were able to retain all eight features (see Figure 4). The authors replicated these findings with objects containing each four features (colour, size, orientation, and the presence or absence of a gap in the centre of the object). They found that all features (i.e., 16 features) from four objects can be remembered as accurately as four features distributed across four objects. This clearly shows that the integration of features into objects increases substantially the number of features that can be stored in VSTM. Although Luck and Vogel (1997)'s study provides evidence that in some cases VSTM capacity may be defined by the number of integrated objects, studies on object complexity have shown that the formation and encoding of a complex object requires more resources than a simple object and that VSTM capacity decreases as function of object complexity (Alvarez & Cavanagh, 2004; Awh et al., 2007; Eng et al., 2005; Luria & Vogel, 2011; Scolari et al., 2008; Xu & Chun, 2006). This suggests that VSTM capacity may not be only determined by the number of objects, but also by the information load.

The effect of perceptual integration on VSTM capacity greatly depends on the nature and spatial arrangement of features within objects. Features can be bound together in VSTM and stored just as well as a single feature, provided that the features belong to different dimensions (i.e., colour, shape, orientation, etc.). When the features are from the same dimension, the integration of those features into a smaller number of objects has no effect on VSTM capacity (Delvenne & Bruyer, 2004; Olson & Jiang, 2002; Wheeler & Treisman, 2002; Xu, 2002a). For example, four unicoloured objects are stored in memory just as well as two bicoloured objects, suggesting that features from the same dimension compete for memory capacity. In addition, in the real world, most visual objects are composed of multiple parts, each with its own features. For example, a car consists of a combination of different parts (i.e., doors, wheels, windows, etc.), which have each their own shape, size, colour, etc. Studies have shown that memory improves when the features are integrated into the same part of an object, thus sharing the same spatial location, compared to different parts of an object

(Delvenne & Bruyer, 2004; Xu, 2002b). For example, if a shape feature appears on one part of an object and a texture feature on another part of the object, then individuals perform worse when required to remember those features than when the shape and the orientation feature appear on the same part of an object (Delvenne & Bruyer, 2004).

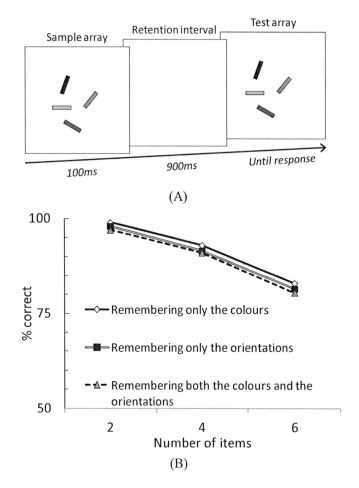

(A)

(B)

Figure 4. (A) Example of a trial adapted from Luck and Vogel (1997). The different grey levels represent different colours. The task is to memorise the colours, the orientations, or both. (B) Results adapted from Luck and Vogel (1997) and showing similar memory performance across the three conditions.

Most of the time in the real world, we are confronted to multiple objects that appear at distinct spatial locations within our visual field. The spatial configuration of a visual display, defined by the spatial relationships between objects, seems to be automatically encoded in VSTM, even prior to the objects themselves (Chun & Jiang, 1998; Jiang et al., 2000). For example, performance at a colour change detection task is reduced if the spatial configuration changes between the memory and test array (Jiang et al., 2000), indicating that an object from a multiple objects display is not independently stored in memory but rather in relation to the others. Moreover, the spatial configuration of a visual scene is not only encoded in VSTM, but it may even help retaining the objects themselves. Memory capacity for objects is reduced if the formation of a spatial configuration is either prevented or useless for detecting a change between a memory and test array (Delvenne et al., 2002; Delvenne & Bruyer, 2006).

## 3.6. Perceptual Expertise

Developmental and aging studies have indicated that once VSTM capacity reaches its maturity in childhood (at about 3-4 items), it remains stable all through adulthood and declines at the end of life. This indirectly suggests that VSTM capacity may be rather inflexible and that the adult human brain does not exhibit plasticity for capacity. However, recent work suggests that extensive experiences with a specific object category can result in superior object identification performance and increase VSTM capacity (see Curby & Gauthier, 2010). For example, VSTM capacity for faces, stimuli for which we are expert, is larger than that for other complex non-face objects, such as clocks and cars (Curby & Gauthier, 2007). Moreover, more upright faces can be remembered than inverted faces (Curby & Gauthier, 2007; Scolari et al., 2008) and more famous faces can be stored in memory than unfamiliar faces provided that the faces are presented upright, that is to say in an orientation that is familiar to us (Jackson & Raymond, 2008). The effect of perceptual expertise on VSTM capacity does not appear to be tied to the face category. Car experts, but not car novices, also demonstrate a VTSM advantage for upright, but not inverted, cars similar to that for faces (Curby, Glazek, & Gauthier, 2009). Importantly, VSTM capacity for upright cars appears to be correlated with each individual's degree of car expertise. The underlying mechanisms responsible for the advantage of perceptual expertise for VSTM capacity remains to be understood. However, one plausible explanation may be that extensive experiences with a particular object category reduce the perceived complexity of the objects, perhaps by a more holistic encoding process that facilitates the integration of features within objects of expertise (Curby & Gauthier, 2010). To further examine the role of perceptual expertise in reducing the perceived perceptual complexity of the objects, it would be interesting in future studies to examine the correspondence between the level of expertise for a particular object category and the neural activity in the superior IPS and LOC, namely the areas that have been shown to be sensitive to the complexity of objects in VSTM (Xu & Chun, 2006).

## 3.7. The Spatial Distribution across the Left and Right Hemifields

Recent data have suggested that the capacity of VSTM can benefit from the division of visual inputs across the two hemifields. For example, using a change detection task, I found that the spatial locations of items were better remembered when the items were split between the left and right side of fixation than when they were all presented within the same single hemifield (Delvenne, 2005). This bilateral benefit in visual information processing is known as the *Bilateral Field Advantage* (BFA) and refers to the fact that visual tasks are processed more accurately and/or more quickly when the visual information is distributed across the vertical meridian than when it is displayed in one hemifield only. Over the last 40 years, studies have revealed this phenomenon in a number of distinctive visual tasks, such as target identification tasks (Awh & Pashler, 2000; Chakravarthi & Cavanagh, 2006; Dimond &

Beaumont, 1971; Scalf, Banich, Kramer, Narechania, & Simon, 2007), target detection tasks (Alvarez & Cavanagh, 2006; Castiello & Umilta, 1992; Reardon, Kelly, & Matthews, 2009), visual enumeration tasks (Delvenne, Castronovo, Demeyere, & Humphreys, 2011), multiple object tracking tasks (Alvarez & Cavanagh, 2005), and matching tasks (Dimond and Beaumont, 1972; Banich & Belger, 1990; Belger & Banich, 1992, 1998; Berger, 1988; Brown, Jeeves, Dietrich, & Burnison, 1999; Collin, McMullen, & Seguin, 2009; Compton, 2002; Davis & Schmit, 1971; Koivisto, 2000; Kraft, Muller, Hagendorf, Schira, Dick, Fendrich, & Brandt, 2005; Kraft, Pape, Hagendorf, Schmidt, Naito, & Brandt, 2007; Liederman, Merola, & Martinez, 1985; Ludwig, Jeeves, Norman, & DeWitt, 1993; Muller, Malinowski, Gruber, & Hillyard, 2003; Norman, Jeeves, Milne, & Ludwig, 1992; Reuter-Lorenz, Stanczak, & Miller, 1999; Sereno & Kosslyn, 1991; Weissman & Banich, 2000; Weissman, Banich, & Puente, 2000; Zhang & Feng, 1999).

If a BFA is observed in visual processing, it is plausible to suggest that a BFA may also be seen in memory, especially considering the close relationship between perception and memory. For instance, it has been shown that the brain regions that are activated during sensory information encoding are also recruited during the maintenance of the information in VSTM (Awh & Jonides, 2001; Chelazzi et al., 1993; Harrison & Tong, 2009; Postle, 2006; Miller et al., 1996; Serences et al., 2009; Supèr et al., 2001). However, although a BFA in visual processing has been rather consistently found, research in VSTM has shown that the occurrence of this effect in memory seems to depend greatly on the nature of the visual information and the task. Specifically, a BFA has been observed in VSTM when the task is dominated by spatial processing, such as remembering multiple spatial locations (Delvenne, 2005) or spatial orientations (Umemoto et al., 2010), detecting the location of a change in a change detection task in which a change appears in all trials (Buschman, Siegel, Roy, & Miller, 2011), and attending to two locations within memory representations (Delvenne & Holt, in press). By contrast, when spatial processing is minimized in the task, the distribution of visual inputs across the two hemifields does not increase VSTM capacity. In particular, no BFA has been found in VSTM when the task entails detecting a non-spatial attribute (i.e., colour) change between two successive displays (Delvenne, 2005; Delvenne et al., 2011b; Mance, Becker, & Liu, 2011; Umemoto et al., 2011; Xu & Nakayama, 2007) or when the task involves reporting letters (Duncan et al, 1999). Clearly, further research is needed to fully understand the BFA in VSTM, to determine its source, and to identify the perceptual and cognitive factors that affect its occurrence.

## CONCLUSION

The last 15 years has seen surge in both cognitive neuroscience and behavioural research on VSTM. Much of this research has been devoted to characterize its capacity limit and to understand the factors that modulate it. At present, there is general agreement that VSTM is extremely limited in the number of items it can store. Although the limitation is estimated to be around 3-4 items, research has also shown that the capacity is affected by a number of factors, which certainly complicates any attempt to provide a pure estimate of VSTM capacity. Specifically, putting on one side the effects of distraction, fatigue, or other external factors that could affect the general performance on a memory task, the number of visual items that you can hold in memory depends on your age, your previous experience with the items, the nature and complexity of the items and how they are perceptually organised within your visual field.

The fact that VSTM capacity is not fixed but can be modulated by different factors strongly suggests that VSTM is limited by some resources that are flexibly allocated. Research on object complexity, in particular, has provided clear evidence that VSTM capacity decreases as function of object complexity (Alvarez & Cavanagh, 2004; Awh et al., 2007; Eng et al., 2005; Luria & Vogel, 2011; Scolari et al., 2008; Xu & Chun, 2006), indicating that the more each item requires resources, the less items can be processed and held in memory simultaneously. How exactly those limited resources are allocated, however, is a question that remains yet to be resolved. Currently, two contrasting views have been proposed. For some researchers, resource allocation is discrete and quantised into 'slots' (Luck & Vogel, 1997; Zhang & Luck, 2008). According to this view, increasing the complexity of the objects may reduce the number of objects (or 'slots') that can be held in memory, but not the resolution of the remembered items. This slot model is an all-or-nothing model, where items are either stored in memory with high-resolution or not retained at all. For other researchers, resource allocation is continuous and divided among the items, with the resolution of the stored items reduced as their number increases (Alvarez & Cavanagh, 2004; Bays & Husain, 2008; Huang, 2010; Wilken & Ma, 2004). Rather than being an all-or-nothing model, this resource model proposes that items can be stored in VSTM with a low resolution.

The recent neural object-file theory, proposed by Xu and Chun (2006, 2007, 2009), could potentially reconcile those two views, as it suggests that VSTM is limited by both a fix number of slots and the complexity of the representations. Specifically, this theory proposes that the inferior IPS selects a fix number of approximately four items via their spatial locations (object individuation) and that the superior IPS and the LOC process a subset of those items in more detail (object identification). If the items are simple and/or do not require much resources, then the capacity of VSTM will be limited by the object individuation stage. By contrast, if the items are complex and/or do require much resources, then only a subset of the selected items will be processed by the object identification stage and VSTM capacity will be reduced accordingly. Thus, the number and resolution of items held in VSTM may represent two distinct attributes of the VSTM representations and they may both define its limitation. Note that given that each hemifield may have some degree of resources independence in visual processing (Alvarez & Cavanagh, 2005; Delvenne, 2005; Buschman et al., 2011), it would be exciting in future studies to examine the correspondence between such hemifield independence and the dichotomy between number and resolution. One possibility, although rather speculative at this stage, has been nicely formulated by Buschman and colleagues (2011): "the two hemifields act like discrete resources, whereas within a hemifield neural information is divided among objects in a graded fashion" (p3).

# REFERENCES

Alvarez, G. A., & Cavanagh, P. (2004). The capacity of visual short-term memory is set both by visual information load and by number of objects. *Psychological Science, 15*, 106–111.

Alvarez, G. A., & Cavanagh, P. (2005). Independent resources for attentional tracking in the left and right visual hemifield. *Psychological Science, 16*, 637–643.

Alvarez, G. A., & Cavanagh, P. (2006). Hemifield independence is a signature of location-based attentional filtering. *Journal of Vision, 6(6)*, 943a.

Anderson, D. E., Vogel, E. K., & Awh, E. (2011). Precision in visual working memory reaches a plateau when individual item-limits are exceeded. *Journal of Neuroscience, 31*(3), 1128-1138.

Awh, E., Barton, B., & Vogel, E. K. (2007). Visual working memory represents a fixed number of items, regardless of complexity. *Psychological Science, 18(7)*, 622-628.

Awh, E., & Jonides, J. (2001). Overlapping mechanisms of attention and working memory. *Trends in Cognitive Sciences, 5(3)*, 119-126.

Awh, E., & Pashler, H. (2000). Evidence for split attentional foci. *Journal of Experimental Psychology: Human Perception and Performance, 26*, 834–846.

Banich, M. T., & Belger, A. (1990). Interhemispheric interaction: How do the hemispheres divide and conquer a task? *Cortex, 26*, 77-94.

Bays, P. M., & Husain, M. (2008). Dynamic shifts of limited working memory resources in human vision. Science, *321*, 851-854.

Bays, P. M., Wu, E. Y., & Husain, M. (2011). Storage and binding of object features in visual working memory. *Neuropsychologia, 49*, 1622-1631.

Belger, A., & Banich, M. T. (1992). Interhemispheric interactions affected by computational complexity. *Neuropsychologia, 30*, 923-929.

Belger, A., & Banich, M. T. (1998). Costs and benefits of integrating information between the hemispheres: a computational perspective. *Neuropsychology, 12,* 380-398.

Berger, J. M. (1988). Interhemispheric cooperation and activation in integration of verbal information. *Behavioural Brain Research, 29*, 193-200.

Brener, R. (1940). An experimental investigation of memory span. *Journal of Experimental Psychology, 26*, 467-482.

Brown, W. S., Jeeves, M. A., Dietrich, R., & Burnison, D. S. (1999). Bilateral field advantage and evoked potential interhemispheric transmission in commissurotomy and callosal agenesis. *Neuropsychologia, 37*, 1154-1180.

Buschman,T. J., Siegel, M., Roy, J. E., & Miller, E. K. (2011) Neural substrates of cognitive capacity limitations. *Proceedings of the National Academy of Sciences, 108*(27), 11252-5.

Cermak, G. W. (1971). Short-term recognition memory for complex free-form figures. *Psychonomic Science, 25*(4), 209–211.

Castiello, U., & Umilta, C. (1992). Splitting focal attention. Journal of Experimental Psychology: Human Perception and Performance, 18(3), 837–848.

Chakravarthi, R., & Cavanagh, P. (2009). Bilateral field advantage in visual crowding. *Vision Research, 49*, 1638-1646.

Chelazzi, L., Miller, E. K., Duncan, J., & Desimone, R. (1993). A neural basis for visual search in inferior temporal (IT) cortex. *Nature, 363*, 345-347.

Chun, M. M., & Jiang, Y. (1998). Contextual cueing: Implicit learning and memory of visual context guides spatial attention. *Cognitive Psychology, 36*, 28-71.

Cohen, J. D., Perlstein, W. M., Braver, T. S., Nystrom, L. E., Noll, D. C., Jonides, J., & Smith, E. E. (1997). Temporal dynamics of brain activation during a working memory task. *Nature*, 386, 604-607.

Collin, C. A., McMullen, P. A., & Seguin, J.-A. (2009). A significant bilateral field advantage for shapes defined by static and motion cues. *Perception, 38*, 1132-1143.

Compton, R. J. (2002). Inter-hemispheric interaction facilitates face processing. *Neuropsychologia, 40*, 2409–2419.

Courtney, S. M., Ungerleider, L. G., Keil, K., & Haxby, J. V. (1997). Transient and sustained activity in a distributed neural system for human working memory. *Nature, 386*, 608-611.

Cowan, N. (2001). The magical number 4 in short-term memory: A reconsideration of mental storage capacity. *Behavioral and Brain Sciences, 24*, 87-114.

Cowan, N., Elliott, E. M., Saults, J. S., Morey, C. C., Mattox, S., et al. (2005). On the capacity of attention: Its estimation and its role in working memory and cognitive aptitudes. *Cognitive Psychology, 51*, 42–100.

Curby, K. M., & Gauthier, I. (2007). A visual short-term memory advantage for faces. *Psychonomic Bulletin and Review, 14(*4), 620-628.

Curby, K. M., & Gauthier, I. (2010). To the Trained Eye: Perceptual Expertise Alters Visual Processing. *Topics in Cognitive Science, 2*, 189–201.

Curby, K. M., Glazek, K., & Gauthier, I. (2009). A visual short-term memory advanatge for objects of expertise. *Journal of Experimental Psychology: Human Perception & Performance, 35*(1), 94–107.

Davis, R., & Schmit, V. (1971). Timing the transfer of information between the hemispheres in man. *Acta Psychologica, 36*, 335-346.

Delvenne, J.-F. (2005). The capacity of visual short-term memory within and between hemifields. *Cognition, 96*, B79–B88.

Delvenne, J.-F., Braithwaite, J. J., Riddoch, M. J., & Humphreys, G. W. (2002). Capacity limits in Visual Short-Term Memory for local orientations. *Current Psychology of Cognition, 21*(6), 681-690.

Delvenne, J.-F., & Bruyer, R. (2004). Does visual short-term memory store bound features? *Visual Cognition, 11*(1), 1-27.

Delvenne, J.-F., & Bruyer, R. (2006). A configural effect in visual short-term memory for features from different parts of an object. *The Quarterly Journal of Experimental Psychology, 59*(9), 1567-1580.

Delvenne, J.-F., Castronovo, J., Demeyere, N., & Humphreys, G. W. (2011a). Bilateral field advantage in visual enumeration. *PLoS ONE 6(3)*: e17743.

Delvenne, J.-F., Cleeremans, A., & Laloyaux, C. (2010). Feature bindings are maintained in visual short-term memory without sustained focused attention. *Experimental Psychology, 57(2)*, 108-116.

Delvenne, J.-F. & Holt, J. L. (*in press*). Splitting attention across the two visual fields in visual short-term memory. *Cognition.* doi:10.1016/j.cognition.2011.10.015

Delvenne, J.-F., Kaddour, L., & Castronovo, J. (2011b). An electrophysiological measure of visual short-term memory capacity within and across hemispheres. *Psychophysiology, 48*, 333-336.

Desimone, R. (1996). Neural mechanisms for human visual memory and their role in attention. *Proceedings of the National Academy of Sciences, USA, 93*, 13494–13499.

Dimond, S. J., & Beaumont, J. G. (1971). Use of two cerebral hemispheres to increase brain capacity. *Nature, 232*, 270-271.

Dimond, S. J., & Beaumont, J. G. (1972). Processing in perceptual integration between and within the cerebral hemispheres. *British Journal of Psychology, 63(4)*, 509-517.

Eimer, M., & Kiss, M. (2010). An electrophysiological measure of access to representations in visual working memory. *Psychophysiology, 47*, 197-200.

Eng, H. Y., Chen, D., & Jiang, Y. (2005). Visual working memory for simple and complex visual stimuli. *Psychonomic Bulletin & Review, 12*, 1127-1133.

Frick, R. W. (1988). Issues of representation and limited capacity in the visuospatial sketchpad. *British Journal of Psychology, 79*, 289-309.

Fukuda, K., & Vogel, E. K. (2009). Human variation in overriding attentional capture. *Journal of Neuroscience, 29*(27), 8726-8733.

Fukuda, K., & Vogel, E. K. (2011). Individual differences in recovery time from attentional capture. *Psychological Science, 22*(3), 361 –368.

Fuster, J. M., & Jervey, J. P. (1982). Neuronal firing in the inferotemporal cortex of the monkey in a visual memory task. *Journal of Neuroscience, 2*, 361-375.

Gao, Z., Li, J., Liang, J., Chen, H., Yin, J., & Shen, M. (2009). Storing fine detailed information in visual working memory—Evidence from event-related potentials. *Journal of Vision, 9*(7), 17, 1-12.

Gao, Z., Xu, X., Chen, Z., Yin, J., Shen, M., & Shui, R. (2011). Contralateral delay activity tracks object identity information in visual short term memory. *Brain Research, 1406*, 30-42.

Gratton, G. (1998). The contralateral organization of visual memory: A theoretical concept and a research tool. *Psychophysiology, 35*, 638-647.

Hartley, A. A., Little, D. M., Speer, N. K., & Jonides, J. (2011). Input, retention, and output factors affecting adult age differences in visuospatial short-term memory. *The journals of gerontology Series B Psychological sciences and social sciences, 6*(4), 435-443.

Harrison, S. A., & Tong, F. (2009). Decoding reveals the contents of visual working memory in early visual areas. *Nature, 458*, 632–635.

Huang, L. (2010). Visual working memory is better characterized as a distributed resource rather than discrete slots. *Journal of Vision, 10*(14):8, 1–8, http://www.journalofvision.org/content/10/14/8, doi:10.1167/10.14.8.

Ikkai, A., McCollough, A. W., & Vogel, E. K. (2010). Contralateral delay activity provides a neural measure of the number of representations in visual working memory. *Journal of Neurophysiology, 103*, 1963-1968.

Jackson, M. C., & Raymond, J. E. (2008). Familiarity enhances visual working memory for faces. *Journal of Experimental Psychology: Human Perception & Performance, 34*(3), 556-568.

Jackson, M. C., Wolf, C., Johnston, S., Raymond, J. E., & Linden, D. E. J. (2008). Neural Correlates of Enhanced Visual Short-Term Memory for Angry Faces: An fMRI Study. *PLoS ONE, 3*(10): e3536. doi:10.1371/journal.pone.0003536.

Jackson, M. C., Wu, C.-Y., Linden, D. E. J., & Raymond, J. E. (2009). Enhanced visual short-term memory for angry faces. *Journal of Experimental Psychology: Human Perception & Performance, 35*(2), 363-374.

Jiang, Y., Olson, I. R., & Chun, M. M. (2000). Organization of visual short-term memory. *Journal of Experimental Psychology: Learning, Memory, & Cognition, 26*, 683-702.

Jost, K., Bryck, R. L, Vogel, E. K., Mayr, U. (2011). Are old adults just like low working memory young adults? Filtering efficiency and age differences in visual working memory. *Cerebral Cortex, 21*, 1147– 1154.

Koivisto, M. (2000). Interhemispheric interaction in semantic categorization of pictures. *Cognitive Brain Research, 9*, 45-51.

Kraft, A., Muller, N. G., Hagendorf, H., Schira, M. M., Dick, S., Fendrich, R. M., & Brandt, S. A. (2005). Interactions between task difficulty and hemispheric distribution of attended locations: Implications for the splitting attention debate. *Cognitive Brain Research, 24(1)*, 19–32.

Kraft, A., Pape, N., Hagendorf, H., Schmidt, S., Naito, A., & Brandt, S. A. (2007). What determines sustained visual attention? The impact of distracter positions, task difficulty and visual fields compared. *Brain Research, 1133(1)*, 123–135.

Langeslag, S. J. E., Morgan, H. M., Jackson, M. C., Linden, D. E. J., & van Strien, J. W. (2009). Electrophysiological correlates of improved working memory for emotional faces. *Neuropsychologia, 47*(3), 887-896.

Lee, E. Y., Cowan, N., Vogel, E. K., Rolan, T., Valle-Inclan, F., et al. (2010). Visual working memory deficits in patients with Parkinson's disease are due to both reduced storage capacity and impaired ability to filter out irrelevant information. *Brain, 133*, 2677–2689.

Liederman, J., Merola, J., & Martinez, S. (1985). Interhemispheric Collaboration in Response to Simultaneous Bilateral Input. *Neuropsychologia, 23*, 673-683.

Logie, R. H. (1995). *Visuo-spatial working memory*. East Sussex, UK: Lawrence Erlbaum Associates.

Logie, R. H., & Pearson, D. G. (1997). The inner eye and the inner scribe of visuo-spatial working memory: Evidence from developmental fractionation. *European Journal of Cognitive Psychology, 9*(3), 241-257.

Luck, S. J., & Vogel, E. K. (1997). The capacity of visual working memory for features and conjunctions. *Nature, 390*, 279–281.

Ludwig, T. E., Jeeves, M. A., Norman, W. D., & DeWitt, R. (1993). The bilateral field advantage on a letter-matching task. *Cortex, 29*, 691-713

Luria, T., & Vogel, E. K. (2011). Shape-color and color-color conjunction stimuli are represented as bound objects in visual working memory. *Neuropsychologia, 49*, 1632–1639.

Mance, I., Becker, M. W., & Liu, T (2011, May 30). Parallel consolidation of simple features into visual short-term memory. *Journal of Experimental Psychology: Human Perception & Performance*. Advance online publication. doi: 10.1037/a0023925.

McCollough, A. W., Machizawa, M. G., & Vogel, E. K. (2007). Electrophysiological measures of maintaining representations in visual working memory. *Cortex, 43*(1), 77-94

McNab, F., & Klingberg, T. (2008). Prefrontal cortex and basal ganglia control access to working memory. *Nature Neuroscience, 11*(1), 103-107.

Miller, G. (1956). The magical number seven, plus or minus two: Some limits on our capacity for processing information. *Psychological Review, 63*, 81-97.

Miller, E. K, Erickson, C. A, & Desimone, R. (1996). Neural mechanisms of visual working memory in prefrontal cortex of the macaque. *Journal of Neuroscience, 16*, 5154 –5167.

Morey, C. C., & Cowan, N. (2004). When do visual and verbal memories conflict: Evidence of cross domain limits in working memory. *Psychonomic Bulletin & Review, 11*, 296-301.

Morey, C. C., & Cowan, N. (2005). When do visual and verbal memories conflict? The importance of working-memory load and retrieval. *Journal of Experimental Psychology: Learning, Memory, and Cognition, 31*, 703-713.

Muller, M. M., Malinowski, P., Gruber, T., & Hillyard, S. A. (2003). Sustained division of the attentional spotlight. *Nature, 424*, 309–312.

Neisser, U. (1967.) *Cognitive psychology*. New York: Appleton-Century-Crofts.

Norman, W. D., Jeeves, M. A., Milne, A., & Ludwig, T. E. (1992). Hemispheric interactions: The bilateral advantage and task difficulty. *Cortex , 28 ,* 623-642.

Olson, I. R., & Jiang, Y. (2002). Is visual short-term memory object based? Rejection of the "strong-object" hypothesis. *Perception&Psychophysics, 64*, 1055–1067.

Pashler, H. (1988). Familiarity and visual change detection. *Perception & Psychophysics, 44*, 369-378.

Phillips, W. A. (1974). On the distinction between sensory storage and short-term visual memory. *Perception & Psychophysics, 16*, 283-290.

Phillips, W. A., & Christie, D. F. M. (1977). Interference with visualization. *Quarterly Journal of Experimental Psychology, 29*, 637-650.

Paivio, A. (1990). *Mental representations: A dual coding approach*. New York: Oxford University Press.

Pashler, H. (1988). Familiarity and visual change detection. *Perception & Psychophysics, 44*, 369-378.

Pessoa, L., Gutierrez, E., Bandettini, P. B., & Ungerleider, L. G. (2002). Neural correlates of visual working memory: fMRI amplitude predicts task performance. *Neuron, 35*, 975-987.

Perez,V. B., & Vogel,E. K. (in press). What ERPs can tell us about Visual Working Memory. In S. J. Luck, & E. Kappenman Eds. Oxford *Handbook of Event-related Potential Components*.

Phillips, W. A. (1974). On the distinction between sensory storage and short-term visual memory. *Perception & Psychophysics, 16*, 283-290.

Posner, M. I., Boies, S. J., Eichelman, W. H., & Taylor, R. L. (1969). Retention of visual and name codes of single letters. *Journal of Experimental Psychology, 79*, 1-16.

Posner, M. I., & Keele, S. W. (1967). Decay of visual information from a single letter. *Science, 158*, 137-139.

Postle, B. R. (2006). Working memory as an emergent property of the mind and brain. *Neuroscience, 139*, 23-38.

Postle, B. R., D'Esposito, M., & Corkin, S. (2005). Effects of verbal and nonverbal interference on spatial and object visual working memory. *Memory & Cognition, 33*, 203-212.

Reardon, K. M., Kelly, J. G., & Matthews, N. (2009). Bilateral Attentional Advantage on Elementary Visual Tasks. *Vision Research, 49(7)*, 692-702.

Reuter-Lorenz, P. A., Stanczak, L., & Miller, A. (1999). Neural recruitment and cognitive aging: Two hemispheres are better than one especially as you age. *Psychological Science, 10*, 494-500.

Riggs, K. J, McTaggart, J., Simpson, A., & Freeman, R. P. J. (2006). The development of visual working memory in 5 to 11 year olds. *Journal of Experimental Child Psychology, 95*, 18-26.

Rose, S. A., Feldman, J. F., & Jankowski, J. J. (2001). Visual short-term memory in the first year of life: Capacity and recency effects. *Developmental Psychology, 37*, 539–549.

Ross-Sheehy, S., Oakes, L. M., & Luck, S. J. (2003). The development of visual short-term memory capacity in infants. *Child Development, 74*, 1807–1822.

Scalf, P., Banich, M. T., Kramer, A. F., Narechania, K., & Simon, C. D. (2007). Double take: Parallel processing by the cerebral hemispheres reduces the attentional blink. *Journal of Experimental Psychology: Human Perception and Performance, 33*, 298–329.

Scolari, M., Vogel, E. K., & Awh, E. (2008). Perceptual expertise enhances the resolution but not the number of representations in working memory. *Psychonomic Bulletin & Review, 15*(1), 215-222.

Serences, J., Ester, E., Vogel, E. K., & Awh, E. (2009). Stimulus-specific delay activity in human primary visual cortex. *Psychological Science, 20(2)*, 207-214.

Sereno, A. B., & Kosslyn, S. M. (1991). Discrimination within and between hemifields: A new constraint on theories of attention. *Neuropsychologia, 29*, 659-675.

Silverberg, N., & Buchanan, L. (2005). Verbal mediation and memory for novel figural designs: A dual interference study. *Brain and Cognition, 57*, 198-209.

Simons, D. J., & Levin, D. T. (1998). Failure to detect changes to people in a real-world interaction. *Psychonomic Bulletin and Review, 5*(4), 644–649.

Simons, D. J., & Rensink, R. A. (2005). Change blindness: Past, present, and future. *Trends in Cognitive Sciences, 9*, 16–20.

Slater, A., Earle, D. C., Morison, V., & Rose, D. (1985). Pattern preferences at birth and their interaction with habituation-induced novelty preferences. *Journal of Experimental Child Psychology, 39*, 37–54.

Slater, A., & Morison, V. (1991). Visual attention and memory at birth. In Weiss M. J. S. & Zelazo, P. R. (eds.), Newborn attention: Biological constraints and the influence of experience. Norwood, NJ: Ablex.

Song J.-H., & Jiang Y. (2006). Visual working memory for simple and complex features: An fMRI study. *NeuroImage, 30*(3), 963-72.

Sperling, G. (1960). The information available in brief visual presentations. *Psychological Monographs: General & Applied, 74*, 1-29.

Sperling, G. (1963). A model for visual memory tasks. *Human Factors, 5*, 19-31.

Sperling, G. (1967). Successive approximations to a model for short-term memory. *Acta Psychologica, 27*, 285-292.

Supèr, H., Spekreijse, H., & Lamme, V. A. F. (2001). A neural correlate of working memory in the monkey primary visual cortex. *Science, 293*, 120 –124.

Todd, J. J., & Marois, R. (2004). Capacity limit of visual short-term memory in human posterior parietal cortex. *Nature, 428*, 751-754.

Todd, J. J., & Marois, R. (2005). Posterior parietal cortex activity predicts individual differences in visual short-term memory capacity. *Cognitive, Affective, and Behavioral Neuroscience, 5*(2), 144-155.

Umemoto, A., Drew, T., Ester, E. F., & Awh, E. (2010). A Bilateral Advantage for Storage in Visual Working Memory. *Cognition, 117*, 69-79.

Vogel, E. K., & Machizawa, M. G. (2004). Neural activity predicts individual differences in visual working memory capacity. *Nature, 428*, 748-751.

Vogel, E. K., McCollough, A. W., & Machizawa, M. G. (2005). Neural measures reveal individual differences in controlling access to working memory. *Nature, 438*, 500–503.

Vogel, E. K., Woodman, G. F., & Luck, S. J. (2001). Storage of features, conjunctions, and objects in visual working memory. *Journal of Experimental Psychology: Human Perception and Performance, 27*, 92-114.

Wang, L., Most, S. B., & Hoffman, J. E. (2009). Contralateral delay activity is sensitive to the spatial distribution of items in working memory: an ERP study. Paper Presented at the *Vision Sciences Society, 9th Annual Meeting*, Naples, Florida.

Weissman, D. H., & Banich, M. T. (2000). Cooperation between the cerebral hemispheres underlies the performance of complex but not simple tasks. *Neuropsychology, 14,* 41-59.

Weissman, D. H., Banich, M. T., & Puente, E. I. (2000). An unbalanced distribution of inputs across the hemispheres facilitates interhemispheric interaction. *Journal of International Neuropsychological Society, 6(3),* 313-321.

Wheeler, M. E., & Treisman, A. M. (2002). Binding in short-term visual memory. *Journal of Experimental Psychology: General, 131*, 48-64.

Wilken, P., & Ma, W. J. (2004). A detection theory account of change detection. *Journal of Vision, 4*(12), 11, 1120–1135.

Wilson, J. T. L., Scott, J. H., & Power, K. G. (1987). Developmental differences in the span of visual memory for pattern. *British Journal of Developmental Psychology, 5*, 249–255.

Woodman, G. F., & Vogel, E. K. (2008). Selective storage and maintenance of an object's features in visual working memory. *Psychonomic Bulletin & Review, 15*(1), 223-229.

Xu, F., & Carey, S. (1996). Infants' metaphysics: the case of numerical identity. *Cognitive Psychology, 30*, 111-153.

Xu, Y. (2002a). Limitations in object-based feature encoding in visual short-term memory. *Journal of Experimental Psychology: Human Perception and Performance, 28*, 458-468.

Xu, Y. (2002b). Integrating color and shape in visual short-term memory for objects with parts. *Perception & Psychophysics, 64*, 1260–1280.

Xu, Y. (2007). The role of the superior intra-parietal sulcus in supporting visual short-term memory for multifeature objects. *Journal of Neuroscience, 27*, 11676-11686.

Xu, Y. (2009). Distinctive neural mechanisms supporting visual object individuation and identification. *Journal of Cognitive Neuroscience, 21*, 511-519.

Xu, Y., & Chun, M. M. (2006). Dissociable neural mechanism supporting visual short-term memory for objects. *Nature, 440*, 91–95.

Xu, Y., & Chun, M. M. (2007). Visual grouping in human parietal cortex. *Proceedings of the National Academy of Sciences, USA, 104*, 18766-18771.

Xu, Y., & Chun, M. M. (2009). Selecting and perceiving multiple visual objects. *Trends in Cognitive Sciences, 13*, 167-174.

Xu, Y., & Nakayama, K. (2007). Visual short-term memory benefit for objects on different 3D surfaces. *Journal of Experimental Psychology: General, 136*, 653-662.

Zhang, W., & Feng, L. (1999). Interhemispheric interaction affected by identification of Chinese characters. *Brain and Cognition, 39,* 93–99.

Zhang, W., & Luck, S. J. (2008). Discrete fixed-resolution representations in visual working memory. *Nature, 452*, 233–235.

Zhou, J., Yin, J., Chen, T., Ding, X., Gao, Z., & Shen, M. (2011). Visual Working Memory Capacity Does Not Modulate the Feature-Based Information Filtering in Visual Working Memory. *PLoS ONE 6*(9), e23873. doi:10.1371/journal.pone.0023873.

In: Psychology of Memory
Editors: Dannie M. Hendrix and Orval Holcomb

ISBN: 978-1-61942-633-7
© 2012 Nova Science Publishers, Inc.

*Chapter 7*

# THE BEHAVIORS OF CONSCIOUS AND UNCONSCIOUS MEMORY: EVIDENCE FROM RESEARCH ON DISSOCIATION OF MEMORIES WITHIN A TEST

## *Chao-Ming Cheng*

Department of Psychology Fo Guang University
Department of Psychology National Taiwan University, Taiwan

## ABSTRACT

Conscious and unconscious forms of memory are explored based on results of the studies in which the two forms of memory within a test were separated by either the *process-dissociation* (for explicit tests) or the *metacognition-based dissociation* (for implicit tests) procedure.

The results across explicit and implicit tests suggest that conscious memory in a test is not only driven by the nature of the test but also driven conceptually, whereas its unconscious counterpart is driven strictly by the nature of the test itself.

Besides, the conscious memory benefits from a study condition to the extent that the memory driving process recapitulates the encoding process engaged in that study condition.

In contrast, its unconscious counterpart benefits to the extent that the cognitive environments, contents of preexisting association, or categorical structures at test and at study match to activate the same type of information (e.g., visual, lexical, or semantic) about a memory item.

**Keywords**: Processes of conscious and unconscious memory; Process-dissociation procedure; Metacognition-based dissociation procedure

A major focus of recent research on memory has been the distinction between two forms of human memory (e.g., Graf and Schacter, 1985; Schacter, 1987; Warrington and Weiskrantz, 1970). One form is *conscious memory*, which involves intentional retrieval or self-awareness of memory. The other is *unconscious memory*, which refers to the cognitive use of previous experiences without involving self-awareness of memory. Historically, a widely used method to illuminate these two forms of memory has been to compare differences in performance between explicit and implicit tests (i.e., the task-dissociation method). Explicit tests such as recall and recognition are assumed to tap conscious memory. Implicit tests such as word-stem completion and word identification, in which participants are not instructed to make reference to studied words, are thought to reflect unconscious memory.

It has been shown that the memories measured by these two types of test differ from each other in their sensitivity to experimental variables such as *level-of-processing* (LoP) and *self-generation* (e.g., Challis, Velichkovsky, and Craik, 1996; Jacoby, 1983; Winnick and Daniel, 1970). For example, Winnick and Daniel reported that compared with reading study words, generating study words increased free recall but decreased memory in implicit word identification. Challis et al. found that the variation in LoP produced positive effects on memory in a variety of explicit tests but no effect on memory in implicit tests.

However, while a number of studies agree that the manipulations of LoP and self-generation produce a positive effect on explicit performance, the two variables do not produce consistent effects on implicit performance across and within studies (e.g., Brown and Mitchell, 1994; Challis and Brodbeck, 1992; Challis et al., 1996). For example, despite initial evidence that LoP produces no effect on memory in implicit tests (e.g., Challis et al., 1996; Graf, Mandler, and Hayden, 1982; Jacoby, 1983), more recent studies have shown a positive effect (or a tendency of positive effects) of LoP in implicit tests (e.g., Hamann, 1996; for reviews, see Brown and Mitchell, 1994; Challis and Brodbeck, 1992). Also, as compared to shallow processing, self-generation decreased memory (e.g., Blaxton, 1989; MacLeod and Masson, 1997; Smith and Branscombe, 1988), increased memory (e.g., Gardiner, 1988, 1989; Gardiner, Dawson, and Sutton, 1989; Mulligan, 2002), or produced no effect on memory (e.g., Gardiner, 1988; MacLeod and Masson, 1997; Nicolas and Tardieu, 1996) in implicit tests.

A possible cause of this inconsistency is that implicit tests can be differently driven so that memories measured by various implicit tests are different from one another in their sensitivity to LoP and generation. Implicit word-fragment and word identification are data-driven; implicit word association and category-exemplar production are conceptually driven. Implicit word-stem and word-fragment completion not only are perceptually driven but lexically driven as well because either a word stem or a word fragment is to be completed with a word from potential word candidates that are lexically relevant to the stem or the fragment.

A second possible cause is that implicit tests do not provide a pure measure of unconscious memory. Rather, such tests involve both conscious and unconscious memories, at least for healthy persons. Evidence for this possibility is given by Mulligan, Guyer, and Beland (1999), who showed that LoP produced a positive effect on implicit category-exemplar production. They also showed that when participants claiming test awareness or intentional retrieval were excluded from analyses, the positive LoP effect was eliminated completely. These results suggest that effects of LoP in an implicit test involve an effect of LoP on conscious memory in the test. The involvement of conscious memory in implicit tests is also evidenced by neuropsychological studies contrasting implicit performance between amnesic patients and healthy controls (e.g., Hamann and Squire, 1996; Squire, Shimamura, and Graf, 1987; Warrington and Weiskantz, 1970) and between drug-induced amnesia and placebo controls (e.g., Arndt, Passannante, and Hirshman, 2004; Curran, Barrow, Weingartner, Lader, and Bernik, 1995; Hirshman, Passannante, and Arndt, 2001).

In this study, the mechanisms underlying conscious and unconscious memory are explored based on results of the studies in which the two forms of memory within a test were separated from each other by either the *process-dissociation* (Jacoby, 1991; 1998) or the *metacognition-based dissociation* (Cheng, Lin, and Tsai, 2008) *procedure*. Because such a dissociation procedure separates conscious from unconscious memory under the same study-test situation, the procedure is more appropriate than the task-dissociation procedure for assessing whether the two forms of memory measure different memory systems.

## THE PROCESS-DISSOCIATION PROCEDURE

Jacoby (1991, 1998; see also Jacoby, Toth, and Yonelinas, 1993) proposed that conscious and unconscious memory within a test can be separated from each other by contrasting performance between an *inclusion* and an *exclusion* condition. In a test of word-stem completion following an incidental study phase, the inclusion condition requires participants to use a stem as a cue to recall a studied word and to complete the stem with the recalled word; if they cannot do so, then they complete the stem with the first appropriate word that comes to mind. The exclusion condition also requires the participants to recall a studied word upon seeing a stem, but the stem is to be completed with a word other than the recalled word (for detailed instructions for the inclusion and exclusion conditions, see Jacoby, 1998). Given these two conditions, the percentage of completion with studied words in the inclusion condition, $I$, estimates *the probability of recalling a studied word*, $R$, plus the *probability that the studied word comes to mind automatically*, $A$, when there is a failure of recollection. Namely,

$$I = R + (1 - R)A. \tag{1}$$

The percentage of completion with studied words in the exclusion condition, $E$, estimates only $(1 - R)A$. Namely,

$$E = (1 - R)A. \tag{2}$$

The probability $A$ in Equations 1 and 2 is said to be *the probability of unconscious memory*, $U$, plus *the baseline probability of completion with a studied word, B* (i.e., $A = U + B$), without involving any memory effect. Equations 1 and 2 are formulated under the assumption that events responsible for $R$ and $A$ are independent of each other (i.e., *the independence assumption*). It is also assumed that $R$ is equal for Equations 1 and 2; so is $A$ (i.e., *the equality assumption*). Under these two assumptions, Equations 1 and 2 can then be legally derived from Equations 1 and 2 to estimate $R$ and $A$ as follows:

$$R = I - E, \tag{3}$$

and

$$A = \frac{E}{1 - R}. \hspace{4cm} (4)$$

## A User's Guide for the Process-Dissociation Procedure

Because Equations 3 and 4 are derived from Equations 1 and 2, Jacoby (1998) proposed a user's guide for proper use of the process-dissociation procedure without violating the equality and independence assumptions. For the test of stem completion, the user's guide requires participants to use a stem as a cue to *recall* a studied word in inclusion and exclusion conditions (i.e., *direct-retrieval* instructions). Such instructions will result in process dissociation and invariant automatic memory, namely, the manipulation of an experimental variable will produce a positive effect on $R$ but leave $A$ invariant with baseline performance being equal in inclusion and exclusion tests.

In contrast, when the participants are instructed to complete stems based on the criterion of *recognition* (*generate-recognize* instructions) to judge studied words, completions with "nonstudy" experimental words may occasionally be falsely recognized as "*studied*" and excluded. This exclusion will result in lower baseline performance in exclusion than in inclusion conditions. In addition, completions that come to mind automatically would also be more likely to be recognized as "*studied*" and excluded. Thus, consciously recognized completions will be a subset of those automatic completions, thereby violating the independence assumption. For these reasons, the use of recognition as the criterion to judge studied words will violate the two assumptions, resulting in a paradoxical dissociation and variance in automatic memory (i.e., an experimental variable produces a positive effect on $R$ but a reverse effect on $A$).

Jacoby (1998) tested the user's guide by assessing how *attention* and *study time* affected $R$ and $A$ in a word-stem completion test. As expected, when participants were instructed to use *recall* as the criterion to include and exclude studied words, the two experimental variables produced a positive effect on estimates of $R$ but left estimates of $A$ invariant. In contrast, when *recognition* was used instead as the criterion, the two variables produced a positive effect on the $R$ estimate but a reverse effect on the $A$ estimate, with baseline performance being lower in exclusion than in inclusion tests.

## Results of Previous Studies Using the Process-Dissociation Procedure

However, the results of other previous studies using the process-dissociation procedure (e.g., Bodner, Masson, and Caldwell, 2000; Jacoby et al., 1993; Toth, Reingold, and Jacoby, 1994) have shown that differences in response to an experimental variable between $R$ and $A$ are determined more by the characteristics of the experimental variable manipulated than by the criterion to judge studied words. Most of the experiments in these studies were conducted by requiring participants to use a mixed criterion to judge studied words: used *recall* as the criterion in an inclusion but *recognition* as the criterion in an exclusion condition. Toth et al. found that LoP produced a positive effect on the estimate of $R$ but left the estimate of $A$ invariant. However, compared with reading study words, generating study words increased the $R$ estimate but decreased the $A$ estimate, without showing unequal baseline performance for inclusion and exclusion tests.

Bodner et al. (2000) also found a similar pattern of results in a study instructing their participants to use the same mixed criterion to judge studied words in their experiments (except that in their Experiment 4) following three encoding tasks: *read, association,* and *self-generation.* In the read task, the participants simply read study words aloud. In the association task, the participants read each study word aloud and then reported aloud the first associated word that came to mind. In the generation task, the participants generated study words upon seeing generation cues and read the study words aloud. Bodner et al. found that the $R$ estimate was larger, but the $A$ estimate was smaller, under the association and self-generation than under the read task, without finding unequal baseline performance in inclusion and exclusion conditions. This pattern of results was also found in their Experiment 4 strictly using the direct-retrieval criterion to judge studied words.

The aforementioned results, therefore, did not fully support the prediction of Jacoby's (1998) user's guide. The present author argues that the user's guide needs to be further tested for its validity for at least two main reasons. First, to assess whether the use of the process-dissociation procedure should be constrained by the user's guide, it is necessary to assess whether Equations 3 and 4 for estimating $R$ and $A$ should be derived from Equations 1 and 2 and under the independence and equality assumptions. If Equations 3 and 4 can be derived by bypassing Equations 1 and 2 and the two assumptions, then the process-dissociation procedure can be properly used without necessarily using *recall* as a criterion to include and exclude studied words. Second, before the user's guide can be accepted as a general framework for predicting process versus paradoxical dissociation, the user's guide should be further tested in more study situations in which experimental variables other than *study time* and *attention* are varied.

## A GENERATION-RECOGNITION APPROACH TO CUED RECALL IN THE WORD-STEM COMPLETION TEST

In this section, it will be demonstrated that the $R$ expressed by Equation 3 and $A$ expressed by Equation 4 can be derived in terms of a generation-recognition model of cued recall, bypassing Equations 1 and 2 and the independence and equality assumptions. Anderson and Bower (1972), Kintsch (1968), and Watkins and Gardiner (1979) have proposed a two-factor theory of recall that recall requires a studied item to be generated and then recognized. This generation-recognition theory of recall will especially be appropriate for describing the recall cued by a word stem in a stem-completion test. That is, *the probability of conscious recall, C,* in a stem-completion test can be regarded as the product of (a) *the probability of generating a studied word as a completion, G,* and (b) *the probability of recognizing the completion as "studied", $R_g$.* $G$ can be estimated by *the percentage of completion with studied words in an inclusion condition, I,* in which participants are instructed to complete a stem using either direct-retrieval or generate-recognize instructions. Thus, $C$ can be expressed as follows:

$$C = GR_g = IR_g. \tag{5}$$

The generation–recognition theory of cued recall can also be extended to describe *the percentage of completion with studied words in a corresponding exclusion condition, E*, using the same criterion to judge a studied word. In that condition, $E$ estimates the probability of a studied word being generated as a completion but not recognized as *studied*. Namely,

$$E = G(1 - R_g) = I(1 - R_g) = I - IR_g \qquad (6)$$

It is immediate from Equations 5 and 6 that $C$ is estimated by

$$C = I - E. \qquad (7)$$

The $C$ expressed by Equation 7 is equal to the $R$ expressed by Equation 3; but the former was derived based on generation and recognition, bypassing Equations 1 and 2 and the independence and equality assumptions.

Next, given $I$ and the $C$ expressed by Equation 7, the corresponding *probability of automatic memory, A'*, can be expressed as

$$A' = \frac{I - C}{1 - C} = \frac{E}{1 - C} = \frac{E}{1 - R}. \qquad (8)$$

The $A'$ expressed by Equation 8 is equal to the $A$ expressed by Equation 4 because $C$ is equal to $R$. However, the $A'$ was not derived from Equations 1 and 2. Rather, it was derived based on the reasoning that the increase in observed percentage of correct responses from $C$ by automatic memory (i.e., *unconscious memory* plus *baseline performance*) in a test, $I - C$, cannot exceed the limit (maximal automatic memory) that remains to be increased from $C$ in the test, $1 - C$. Thus, it is more appropriate to estimate automatic memory in a test by the extent to which the observed automatic memory approaches its maximal limit in the test rather than by the observed automatic memory alone.

The derivations of Equations 7 and 8 suggest that participants instructed to use a *direct-retrieval* strategy to complete stems may in fact implicitly complete stems based on the processes of generation and recognition in word-stem completion. In other words, the process-dissociation procedure can be properly applied to the case in which a *generate-recognize* strategy is explicitly used to complete stems, as long as $R_g$ is equal in Equations 5 and 6. Keeping the same $R_g$ in these two equations can be achieved by consistently using the same strategy to include and exclude studied words.

## A Test of the User's Guide

Equations 7 and 8 suggest a need to reexamine if the sensitivity of conscious and unconscious memory within a test to experimental variables is independent of the criterion (*recall* and *recognition*) used to judge studied words. As mentioned, the user's guide has been empirically supported by Jacoby's (1998) findings mentioned above. However, the findings may have been specific to the version of *generate-recognize* instructions used in his 1998 study, which were characterized by two features. One was that the participants in his *inclusion* test were instructed to complete stems with a word as fast as possible, without worrying about whether the word was presented earlier or not. Because the *inclusion* test did not require the participants to complete stems by first making reference to either recall or recognition of studied words, it corresponded to a conventional implicit rather than a typical inclusion test. Conscious memory involved in the implicit test, if any, would, therefore, be lower than in a typical inclusion test and lower than to be excluded from a typical exclusion test, which would in turn be less than conscious memory to be excluded from his *exclusion* test because a word that seems at all familiar is excluded from the test.

The other feature was that the participants in his *exclusion* test were required to exclude words if they seemed at all familiar. This exclusion procedure would inevitably force the participants to complete stems with a rare or a low-frequency word that guarantees to be not familiar at all, thus decreasing the probability of completing a stem with an experimental word (either presented or not presented for study). As a result, automatic memory and baseline performance would be lower in the *exclusion* than in the *inclusion* test. For the reasons mentioned above, the equality and independence assumptions may have been violated due to the use of the version of *generate-recognize* instructions rather than due to the use of *recognition* as the criterion to include and exclude studied words.

For a proper comparison of recall and recognition as a criterion to judge studied words, Cheng and Huang (2011) conducted two series of experiments investigating performance on stem completion under two versions of instructions that are identical in all aspects except the criterion (*recall* versus *recognition*) used to judge studied words. The first series of experiments consisted of three experiments investigating effects of LoP on stem completion: *Experiments 1A, 1B, and 1C.* The method for the three experiments was the same except for that, in a test phase, participants in Experiment 1A were instructed to use *strict recall*, while those in Experiments 1B and 1C were instructed to use *strict recognition* and *familiarity*, respectively, as the criterion to complete stems in inclusion and exclusion conditions.

The second series of experiments consisted of two experiments investigating effects of self-generation and/or association on stem completion: *Experiments 2A and 2B.* Participants in Experiment 2A were instructed to use strict recall, while those in Experiments 2B were instructed to use strict recognition, as the criterion to complete stems in inclusion and exclusion conditions.

*Method.* To mimic an English word-stem completion test following the presentation of study words with each word consisting of two morphemes and its first morpheme serving as a stem for completion (see Bodner et al, 2000; Toth et al., 1994), the experimental stimuli used in each experiment of the Cheng and H study were two-character Chinese words [i.e., each word consisted of two characters such as 地毯 (carpet)]. The "character" (e.g., 地 of 地毯) in visual form is the unit of writing in Chinese. Linguistically, it is more equivalent to an English free morpheme than to an English word. Like a written English word that may consist of a single morpheme or a combination of several morphemes for symbolizing a meaning, a written Chinese word may consist of a single or several separate characters for communicating a meaning (see Cheng and Yang, 1989). According to this orthographic structure of Chinese words, the first constituent character of a two-character word in Chinese corresponds to a stem in an English word for completion. The experimental stimuli were Chinese two-character words and word stems created from these words. The word stems were created by replacing the second constituent character of each experimental word by a dash (for example, the stem for the experimental word 地毯 is 地__). Participants were native speakers of Chinese mandarin who were tested individually. The experiment was conducted in two phases: study and stem-completion test. In each of the first series of experiments, one of two study blocks was presented for each participant to rate character complexity (shallow processing task) by asking the participant, upon seeing a stimulus word on the monitor, to judge roughly whether the first constituent character was more complex than the second one with respect to number of strokes. The participant was to respond as quickly as possible by pressing one of the three response keys on the computer keyboard corresponding to three response alternatives: "yes", "no", and "about equal". The other study block was presented for rating pleasantness (deep processing task) of each word by asking the participant to press a response key corresponding to one of three alternatives: "pleasant", "unpleasant", and "neutral".

In each of the second series of experiments, one study block was presented for simple reading or complexity rating by asking the participant either to read aloud or to judge the complexity of each study word exposed on the computer monitor. Another study block was presented for association by asking the participant to read each study word aloud and then report aloud the first associated word that came to mind. The third study block presented English words for translation by asking the participant to verbally translate each English word into a two-character Chinese word. *Results.* Compared with the results of previous studies (e.g., Jacoby, 1998; Jacoby et al., 1993; Toth et al., 1994), the present results show relatively low inclusion and exclusion scores and baseline performance. A possible reason for this outcome is that each Chinese character serving as a stem has a large number of two-character word completions. For example, the stems used in Experiment 1A had the number of completions ranging from 8 to 40 two-character words with a mean of 18 words, with the stems originated from the word whose frequency of occurrence ranked from the second to the 15th in a word group sharing the first constituent character. This large number of potential completions would decrease baseline performance and, hence, inclusion and exclusion scores. On the other hand, English stems used in previous studies had a relatively small number of completions under a certain restriction criterion. For example, the stems used by Jacoby (1998) had the number of five-letter word completions ranging from two to nine words. The results across Experiments 1A, 1B, and 1C consistently showed that LoP produced a positive effect on estimates of $R$ but left estimates of $A$ invariant, regardless of the criterion (*recall, recognition,* or *familiarity*) used to include and exclude studied words. The results across Experiments 2A and 2B consistently showed that association and generation produced a positive effect on estimates of $R$ but a reverse effect on estimates of $A$, independent of the criterion used to include and exclude studied words.

## THE METACOGNITION-BASED DISSOCIATION PROCEDURE

The process-dissociation procedure and its variants (e.g., Banks, Chen, and Prull, 1999; Richardson-Klavehn and Gardiner, 1995) estimate conscious and unconscious memory within a test by requiring participants to perform the inclusion and exclusion tests making reference to recollection of studied words. As a result, the two forms of memory are estimated from explicit rather than from implicit tests. A standard explicit test is regarded as conceptually driven because performance on the test draws on information at a deep level; the situations using such a test following a study phase are, therefore, relatively limited for investigating conscious and unconscious memory. On the other hand, various implicit tests can be differently driven so that memories measured by these tests may be different from one another in their sensitivity to experimental variables. Thus, the use of different implicit tests following different stimulus encodings can provide different study-test situations for investigating conscious and unconscious memory. According to this analysis, research investigating conscious and unconscious memory in implicit tests is not redundant to that in explicit tests.

Cheng et al. (2008) proposed a method to separate conscious and unconscious memory contributions to an implicit test. The method is illustrated below in the context of implicit word-stem completion.

It begins by administering an incidental learning of words in which an experimental variable such as LoP is varied, followed by a traditional implicit test of word-stem completion in which stems originating from experimental words are presented to participants for completion with the first word that comes to mind.

In general, the conscious component of memory in the test can be based on either recollection or recognition of studied words which involves self-awareness of the words as *studied* at the time of test, whereas its unconscious component does not involve participants' self-awareness of memory at test.

The method separating these two components of memory is, therefore, based on participants' metacognitive monitoring of studied words at test and, hence, termed as a *metacognition-based dissociation* (MBD) procedure.

Because the implicit test requires participants to perform the test without making any reference to either recall or recognition of studied words at the time of test, the MBD procedure requires the participants to judge studied words immediately after the test from among the words that had been used to complete stems. They judge a response word as *studied* only when they are quite sure the word had been presented for rating in the study phase.

Because the test stage is immediately followed by a memory-judgment stage without introducing any distraction task or lengthy instructions for the memory-judgment task, the participants at the judgment stage are supposed to be able to judge what they recalled or recognized at the test stage.

In other words, the MBD procedure would introduce a minimal, if any, lapse of memory in the interval between the two stages. This argument was empirically verified by participants being able to discriminate between studied and "nonstudy" experimental words (Cheng et al., 2008).

Performance on a test condition can be denoted by $P(i,j)$ which represents either the percentage of completion with experimental words (either presented for study or not presented for study) ($i = 1$) or that with other words ($i = 0$), with the words being judged as either *studied* ($j = 1$) or *not studied* ($j = 0$). For example, $P(1,1)$ denotes the percentage of completed experimental words that were judged as *studied*; $P(1,0)$ denotes that of completed experimental words judged as *not studied*.

**Table 1. Sources (and Probabilities) for Completion of a Stem with a Studied Word at the Testing Stage and the Probability of Judging an Experimental Word (Either Presented for Study or Not Presented for Study) as "Studied" or as "Not Studied" at the Memory-Judgment Stage Based on Each Source, as Prescribed by the MBD Procedure**

| Source at the testing stage and its probability | The probability of judging an experimental word as *studied* or as *not studied* at the memory judgment stage based on each source |
|---|---|
| Conscious memory ($C$) | $C$ (for a *studied* judgment based on conscious memory) |
| Unconscious memory, when there is a failure of conscious memory, $[(1 - C)U]$ | $(1 - C)Ug$ (for a *studied* judgment based on unconscious memory and the guessing rate in favor of a *studied* judgment, $g$) |
| | $(1 - C)U(1 - g)$ (for a *not-studied* judgment based on unconscious memory and $1 - g$) |
| Baseline performance, when there is a failure of both conscious and unconscious memories, $[(1 - C)(1 - U)B]$ | $(1 - C)(1 - U)B_1$ (for a *studied* judgment based on judgment-induced recognition) |
| | $(1 - C)(1 - U)B_2g = (1 - C)(1 - U)(B - B_1)g$ (for a *studied* judgment based on baseline performance without leading to judgment-induced recognition and $g$) |
| | $(1 - C)(1 - U)B_2(1 - g) = (1 - C)(1 - U)(B - B_1)(1 - g)$ (for a *not-studied* judgment based on baseline performance without leading to judgment-induced recognition and $1 - g$) |

$P(1,1) = C + (1 - C)(1 - U)B_1 + [(1 - C)U + (1 - C)(1 - U)B_2]g$.

$P(1,0) = [(1 - C)U + (1 - C)(1 - U)B_2](1 - g)$.

$P_o = P(1,1) + P(1,0) = C + (1 - C)U + (1 - C)(1 - U)B$,

where $B = B_1 + B_2$

Table 1 shows that, the MBD procedure identifies two types of conscious memory contributing to $P(1,1)$ following a study condition. One is conscious memory contributing to performance at the time of test. The probability of this type of conscious memory is denoted by $C$. The other type of conscious memory is based on completion with studied words without involving conscious and unconscious memory at the time of test, but later the studied words are recognized as *studied* at the time of making memory judgments. This type of recognition memory (termed *judgment-induced recognition*) would be attributed to part of baseline performance in a traditional implicit test in the case in which participants are not required to make post-test memory judgments. Given that *the probability of baseline performance* is $B$, *the probability of judgment-induced recognition* should be a part of $B$, $B_1$.

The probability of unconscious memory, $U$, is estimated by the percentage of memory without involving participants' self-awareness of memory at both the test and the memory-judgment stages. Guessing occurs at the judgment stage when completion with studied words is either based on unconscious memory or based on the part of baseline performance without leading to judgment-induced recognition, $B_2$, where $B_2$ is equal to $B - B_1$.

## P(1,1) under a Study Condition

$P(1,1)$ under a study condition estimates $C$, $B_1$ (when there is a failure of conscious and unconscious memory during the test), and the guessing rate in favor of a *studied* judgment, $g$ (when the completion with studied words is either based on unconscious memory or based on $B_2$ under that condition) (see Table 1). Namely,

$$P(1,1) = C + (1-C)(1-U)B_1 + [(1-C]U + (1-C)(1-U)B_2]g. \qquad (9)$$

The guessing rate $g$ in Equation 9 is estimated by the rate of falsely judging "nonstudy" experimental words as *studied*, namely, the ratio of $P_n(1,1)/[P_n(1,1) + P_n(1,0)]$, where the $P_n(1,1)$ and $P_n(1,0)$ denote the percentage of completed "nonstudy" experimental words that were judged as *studied* and as *not studied*, respectively.

## P(1,0) under a Study Condition

$P(1,0)$ (i.e., the percentage of completed studied words judged as *not studied*) following a study condition estimates $U$ and $B_2$ under that condition without guessing the completed studied words as *studied*. Namely,

$$P(1,0) = [(1-C)U + (1-C)(1-U)B_2](1-g). \qquad (10)$$

Table 1 also shows that, the sum of $P(1,1)$ and $P(1,0)$ in a study condition, $P_o$, is

$$P_o = C + (1-C)U + (1-C)(1-U)B. \qquad (11)$$

Events responsible for $C$, $U$, and $B$ may be regarded as independent of one another because the probability of intersection of two or three of the events for $C$, $U$, and $B$ is expressed in Equation 11 as the product of the probabilities of individual events.

## Estimates of C and U in a Study Condition

Let $P'(1,1)$ and $P'(1,0)$ be $P(1,1)$ and $P(1,0)$ after correction for guessing under a study condition, respectively. $P'(1,1)$ is, therefore, obtained by subtracting the component involving $g$, $[(1-C)U + (1-C)(1-U)B_2]g$, from $P(1,1)$ expressed by Equation 9, namely,

$$P'(1,1) = P(1,1) - [(1-C)U + (1-C)(1-U)B_2]g = C + (1-C)(1-U)B_1.$$

Because the component of $[(1-C)U + (1-C)(1-U)B_2]$ is equal to $P(1,0)/(1-g)$ (see Equation 10) and $g$ is equal to $P_n(1,1)/[P_n(1,1) + P_n(1,0)]$, where the $P_n(1,1)$ and $P_n(1,0)$ are the $P(1,1)$ and $P(1,0)$ scores for "nonstudy" experimental words, respectively. The component of $[(1-C)U + (1-C)(1-U)B_2]g$ is equal to $P(1,0)g/(1-g) = P(1,0) P_n(1,1)/ P_n(1,0)$. Thus,

$$P'(1,1) = P(1,1) - \frac{P(1,0)P_n(1,1)}{P_n(1,0)} = C + (1-C)(1-U)B_1. \tag{12}$$

$P'(1,0)$ is the $P(1,0)$ of Equation 10 divided by $(1-g)$, namely,

$$P'(1,0) = \frac{P(1,0)}{1-g} = \frac{P(1,0)[P_n(1,1)+P_n(1,0)]}{P_n(1,0)} = (1-C)U + (1-C)(1-U)B_2. \tag{13}$$

Solving $C$ and $(1-C)U$ as unknowns from Equations 12 and 13, one obtains

$$C = P'(1,1) - \frac{B_1(1-P_o)}{1-B}, \tag{14}$$

and

$$U(1-C) = P'(1,0) - \frac{B_2(1-P_o)}{1-B}. \tag{15}$$

Equations 14 and 15 were derived to estimate the conscious and unconscious components of memory in a traditional implicit test, respectively. The probability of $B_1$ (judgment-induced recognition) in Equation 14 is estimated based on the finding that the percentage of conscious memory as a function of the depth of processing study words in implicit tests (e.g., Hamann and Squire, 1996; Mulligan et al., 1999; Squire et al., 1987) is the same as in explicit tests (e.g., Challis et al., 1996; Hyde and Jenkins, 1969, 1973; Toth et al., 1994). As mentioned previously, Mulligan et al. showed that effects of LoP on memory in an implicit test were in fact contributed mainly by a positive effect of LoP on conscious memory involved in the test. Squire et al. and Hamann and Squire showed that compared with amnesic patients, normal participants exhibited a positive LoP effect on implicit word completion. This effect was explained as a positive LoP effect on conscious memory in the test. Such an effect of LoP parallels that in an explicit test. Thus, it is reasonable to assume that the proportion of judgment-induced recognition memory (a type of conscious memory) in the memory-judgment test (an explicit test), $B_1/B$, is equal to the proportion of conscious memory at test (an implicit test), $C/P_o$. That is, $B_1/B$ is equal to $C/P_o$ (i.e., $B_1 = BC/P_o$). Given $B_1$, $B_2$ in Equation 15 is equal to $B$ minus $BC/P_o$ [i.e., $B(1-C/P_o)$]. Given that $B_1$ is equal to $BC/P_o$ and $B_2$ is equal to $B(1-C/P_o)$, Equation 14 becomes

$$C = P'(1,1) - \frac{BC(1-P_o)}{(1-B)P_o} = \frac{P'(1,1)(1-B)P_o}{(1-B)P_o + B(1-P_o)}. \tag{16}$$

**Table 2. Mean Percentages of Completion with Experimental Words (Studied and "Nonstudy"), Po, With the Words Being Either Judged as Studied, P'(1,1), or as Not Studied, P'(1,0), After Correction for Guessing, and Mean Estimates of C and U in Experiment 1: the Implicit Stem-Completion Test (Cheng et al., 2008)**

| | Experimental condition | | | |
| --- | --- | --- | --- | --- |
| | Study | | | "Nonstudy" |
| | Shallow | Deep | Semantic generation | |
| | Response measure | | | |
| $P_o$ | 27.0(12.3[b]) | 31.9(15.2) | 24.4(9.6) | 12.1(6.9) |
| $P'(1,1)$[a] | 10.3(10.4) | 20.3(11.0) | 19.7(9.7) | 0.4(3.7) |
| $P'(1,0)$ | 16.7(13.2) | 11.7(8.3) | 4.8(6.2) | 11.7(6.9) |
| | Estimate | | | |
| Conscious memory ($C$) $[C = \frac{P'(1,1)(1-B)P_o}{(1-B)P_o + B(1-P_o)}.]$ | 7.5(7.3) | 15.7(9.6) | 13.8(6.3) | -,- |
| Judgment-induced recognition memory involved in $P'(1,1)$, $B_1$ $[B_1 = \frac{BC(1-P_o)}{(1-B)P_o}.]$ | 2.7(2.5) | 4.6(2.7) | 5.9(2.8) | -,- |
| Automatic memory ($A$) $[A = \frac{P'(1,0)}{1-C}.]$ | 18.1(11. | 13.9(8.5) | 5.6(4.5) | -,- |
| Baseline performance without leading to judgment-induced recognition, $B_2$ $[B_2 = \frac{B(1-P_o)(P_o-C)}{(1-B)(1-C)P_o}.]$ | 7.8(5.2) | 5.6(5.5) | 5.2(5.1) | -,- |
| Unconscious memory ($U$) $[U = \frac{P'(1,0)}{1-C} - \frac{B(1-P_o)(P_o-C)}{(1-B)(1-C)P_o}.]$ | 10.5(10. | 8.5(7.0) | 0.5(4.5) | -,- |

[a]$P(1,j)$ stands for the percentage of association with experimental words (either for study or "nonstudy"), with the words being either judged as *studied* ($j = 1$) or not judged as *not studied* ($j = 0$).

[b]Values in parentheses are standard deviations.

$$U = \frac{P'(1,0)}{1-C} - \frac{B(1-P_o)(P_o-C)}{(1-B)(1-C)P_o}. \tag{17}$$

The proportion of $P'(1,0)/(1 - C)$ in Equation 17 is termed *automatic memory* in this study, which equals to $U$ plus $[B(1 - P_o)(P_o - C)]/[(1 - B)(1 - C)P_o]$ (i.e., the baseline performance without leading to judgment-induced recognition).

The component of judgment-induced recognition involved in $P'(1,1)$ following a study condition is expressed by $[BC(1 - P_o)]/[(1 - B)P_o]$ in Equation 16.

Equation 15 becomes

**Table 3. Mean Percentages of Completion with Experimental Words (Studied and "No"), Po, With the Words Being Either Judged as Studied, P'(1,1), or as Not Studied, P'(1,0), After Correction for Guessing, and Mean Estimates of C and U in Experiment 2: the Implicit Word-Association Test (Cheng et al., 2008 )**

| | Experimental condition | | | |
| | Study | | | "Nonstudy" |
| | Shallow | Deep | Semantic generation | |
| | Response measure | | | |
| $P_0$ | 8.3(5.1[b]) | 15.0(10.2) | 15.0(8.3) | 5.3(2.9) |
| $P'(1,1)$[a] | 3.0(3.8) | 8.1(9.5) | 11.8(7.9) | 0.0(1.2) |
| $P'(1,0)$ | 5.3(6.1) | 6.9(9.2) | 3.2(5.2) | 5.3(3.4) |
| | Estimate | | | |
| Conscious memory (C) $[C = \frac{P'(1,1)(1 - B)P_o}{(1 - B)P_o + B(1 - P_o)}]$ | 1.9(3.2) | 6.1(7.3) | 8.9(9.4) | -,- |
| Judgment-induced recognition memory involved in $P'(1,1)$, $B_1$ $[B_1 = \frac{BC(1 - P_o)}{(1 - B)P_o}]$ | 1.2(1.2) | 1.9(2.2) | 2.8(2.8) | -,- |
| Automatic memory (A) $[A = \frac{P'(1,0)}{1 - C}]$ | 5.4(11.8) | 7.3(8.2) | 3.5(5.2) | -,- |
| Baseline performance without leading to judgment-induced recognition, $B_2$ $[B_2 = \frac{B(1 - P_o)(P_o - C)}{(1 - B)(1 - C)P_o}]$ | 3.2(5.2) | 3.0(6.3) | 2.1(5.8) | -,- |
| Unconscious memory (U) $[U = \frac{P'(1,0)}{1 - C} - \frac{B(1 - P_o)(P_o - C)}{(1 - B)(1 - C)P_o}]$ | 2.1(6.7) | 4.1(5.6) | 1.5(3.4) | -,- |

[a]$P(1,j)$ stands for the percentage of association with experimental words (either for study or "nonstudy"), with the words being either judged as *studied* ($j = 1$) or not judged as *not studied* ($j = 0$).

[b]Values in parentheses are standard deviations.

## The Usefulness of the MBD Procedure

The MBD procedure illustrated above in the task of implicit stem completion can equally apply to other implicit tests such as word identification and word association, without any modification. It should be noted, however, that the procedure was developed to separate the two forms of memory so that they can be adequately assessed, without claiming that the procedure is able to separate these two forms to a perfect degree. The procedure can be justified if the two forms of memory estimated by the procedure are different from each other in their sensitivity to experimental variables. Generation produced a reverse effect on this estimate in implicit stem completion and word identification but no effect on this estimate in word association.

## Results of Studies Using the Metacognition-Based Dissociation Procedure

**Table 4. Mean Percentages of Completion with Experimental Words (Studied and "Nnonstudy"), Po, With the Words Being Either Judged as Studied, P(1,1), or as Not Studied, P(1,0), After Correction for Guessing, and Mean Estimates of C and U in Experiment 3B: the Implicit Word-Identification Test (Cheng et al., 2008 )**

| | | Experimental condition | |
| --- | --- | --- | --- |
| | | Study | "Nonstudy" |
| | | Shallow | Semantic generation | |
| | Response measure | | | |
| $P_0$ | | 43.0(19.0) | 42.7(20.4) | 31.5(17.3) |
| $P'(1,1)$[a] | | 17.0(14.3) | 33.5(20.1) | 4.0(6.9) |
| $P'(1,0)$ | | 26.0(16.3) | 9.2(9.7) | 27.5(16.8) |
| | Estimate | | | |
| Conscious memory (C) | | 10.6(9.2) | 20.7(13.8) | -,- |
| $[C = \frac{P'(1,1)(1-B)P_o}{(1-B)P_o + B(1-P_o)}.]$ | | | | |
| Judgment-induced recognition memory involved in $P'(1,1)$, $B_1$ | | 6.4(5.7) | 12.8(6.2) | -,- |
| $[B_1 = \frac{BC(1-P_o)}{(1-B)P_o}.]$ | | | | |
| Automatic memory (A) | | 29.1(20.6) | 11.6(11.8) | -,- |
| $[A = \frac{P'(1,0)}{1-C}.]$ | | | | |
| Baseline performance without leading to judgment-induced recognition, $B_2$ | | 22.1(18.5) | 17.4(10.3) | -,- |
| $[B_2 = \frac{B(1-P_o)(P_o-C)}{(1-B)(1-C)P_o}.]$ | | | | |
| Unconscious memory (U) | | 7.3(8.9) | −5.2(6.5) | -,- |
| $[U = \frac{P'(1,0)}{1-C} - \frac{B(1-P_o)(P_o-C)}{(1-B)(1-C)P_o}.]$ | | | | |

[a]$P'(1,j)$ stands for the mean percentage of experimental words (either for study or not for study) correctly identified, with the words being either judged as *studied* (*j* = 1) or as *not studied* (*j* = 0), after correction for guessing.
[b]Values in parentheses are standard deviations.

Using the metacognition-based dissociation procedure, Cheng et al. (2008) investigated how LoP and self-generation of Chinese words (translating from English) affected conscious and unconscious memory of the words with three implicit tests: *word association, word identification,* and *word-stem completion.*

Tables 2, 3, and 4 showed that both LoP and generation consistently produced a positive effect on the estimate of $C$ (see Equation 16) across the three implicit tests. On the other hand, LoP produced a reverse effect on the estimate of $U$ (see Equation 17) in word identification but no effect on this estimate in implicit stem completion and word association.

**Table 5. Effects of Stimulus Encoding on Estimates of Conscious Memory in Explicit and Implicit Tests, Measured by the R Expressed by Equation 3 and the C Expressed by Equation 16, Respectively**

| Test in which conscious memory was estimated | Study condition | | | |
|---|---|---|---|---|
| | Shallow/read | Deep | Association | Generation |
| Explicit stem-completion test (strict recall as a criterion) | | | | |
| Bodner et al. (2000), Experiment 4 | + | -,- | ++ | ++ |
| Cheng & Huang (2011), | | | | |
| Experiment 1A | +[a] | ++[b] | -,- | -,- |
| Experiment 2A | + | -,- | ++ | ++ |
| Explicit stem-completion test (strict recognition as a criterion) | | | | |
| Cheng & Huang (2011), | | | | |
| Experiment 1B | + | ++ | -,- | -,- |
| Experiment 1C | + | ++ | -,- | -,- |
| Experiment 2B | + | -,- | -,- | ++ |
| Explicit stem-completion test (mixed criterion) | | | | |
| Toth et al. (1994), Experiment 1 | + | ++ | -,- | -,- |
| Experiment 2 | + | -,- | -,- | ++ |
| Bodner et al. (2000), Experiment 1 | + | -,- | ++ | ++ |
| Experiment 2 | + | -,- | ++ | ++ |
| Experiment 3 | + | -,- | ++ | ++ |
| Implicit stem-completion test | | | | |
| Cheng et al. (2008) | + | ++ | -,- | ++ |
| Implicit word-association test | | | | |
| Cheng et al. (2008) | 0[c] | + | -,- | + |
| Implicit word-identification test | | | | |
| Cheng et al. (2008) | + | ++ | -,- | ++ |

[a] The "+" sign stands for a positive effect of either perceptual- or conceptual-encoding in a study condition on the estimate of conscious memory in a test.

[b] The "++" sign stands for an effect indicated by the "+" sign with the effect being larger than its counterpart in a shallow condition.

[c] The "0" sign stands for a non-significant effect of a study condition on the estimate of conscious memory in a test.

Generation produced a reverse effect on this estimate in implicit stem completion and word identification but no effect on this estimate in word association.

# LEVEL OF ANALYSIS FOR ASSESSING CONSCIOUS AND UNCONSCIOUS MEMORY

Contemporary explanatory frameworks based on differential influences of a variable on conscious and unconscious memory do not provide an adequate account of conscious and unconscious memory.

**Table 6. Effects of Stimulus Encoding on Estimates of Unconscious Memory in Explicit and Implicit Tests, Measured by the A Expressed by Equation 4 and the U Expressed by Equation 17, Respectively**

| Test in which unconscious memory was estimated | Study condition | | | |
|---|---|---|---|---|
| | Shallow | Deep | Association | Generation |
| Explicit stem-completion test (strict direct-retrieval strategy) | | | | |
| Bodner et al. (2000), Experiment 4 | + | -,- | 0 | 0 |
| Cheng & Huang (2011), | | | | |
| Experiment 1A | +[a] | + | -,- | -,- |
| Experiment 2A | + | -,- | 0[b] | −[c] |
| Explicit stem-completion test (strict generate-recognize strategy) | | | | |
| Cheng & Huang (2011), | | | | |
| Experiment 1B | + | + | -,- | -,- |
| Experiment 1C | + | + | -,- | -,- |
| Experiment 2B | + | -,- | -,- | − |
| Explicit stem-completion test (mixed criterion) | | | | |
| Toth et al. (1994), Experiment 1 | + | + | -,- | -,- |
| Experiment 2 | + | -,- | -,- | 0 |
| Bodner et al. (2000), Experiment 1 | + | -,- | − | − |
| Experiment 2 | + | -,- | 0 | 0 |
| Experiment 3 | + | -,- | − | 0 |
| Implicit stem-completion test | | | | |
| Cheng et al. (2008) | + | + | -,- | 0 |
| Implicit word-association test | | | | |
| Cheng et al. (2008) | 0 | 0 | -,- | 0 |
| Implicit word-identification test | | | | |
| Cheng et al. (2008) | + | 0 | -,- | 0 |

[a]The "+" sign stands for a positive priming effect of either perceptual- or conceptual-encoding in a study condition on the estimate of unconscious memory in a test.

[b]The "0" sign stands for a non-significant effect of a study condition on the estimate of unconscious memory in a test.

[c]The "−" sign stands for a repetition-inhibition effect of a study condition on the estimate of unconscious memory in a test (evidenced by the estimate of unconscious memory under the study condition being lower than baseline performance).

For example, compared with a shallow condition, generation producing a positive effect on conscious memory in a stem-completion test can be caused by at least two different patterns of encoding effects on conscious memory: (a) a nonsignificant effect of the shallow and a positive effect of the generation condition, and (b) a positive effect of the shallow and generation conditions, with the effect being larger following the generation than following the shallow condition. The two patterns of encoding effects may suggest two different ways in which conscious memory operates in a test. Likewise, a reverse effect of generation on unconscious memory can result at least from four possible patterns of priming effects on unconscious memory: (a) a positive priming effect of shallow and generation conditions, with the effect being larger under the shallow than under the generation condition, (b) a positive priming effect of the shallow and a nonsignificant effect of the generation condition, (c) a positive priming effect of the shallow and a repetition-inhibition effect of the generation condition (i.e., unconscious memory under the generation condition is lower than baseline performance), (d) a nonsignificant effect of the shallow and a repetition-inhibition effect of the generation condition. These four patterns of encoding effects may suggest four different ways in which unconscious memory operates in a test. The combination of these patterns of effects on conscious and unconscious memory can make a total of eight alternatives of how conscious and unconscious memory operate in response to the variation in self-generation.

## SUMMARY OF RESEARCH FINDINGS

The aforementioned analysis suggests that, for a better understanding of the influences of an experimental variable on conscious and unconscious memory, it is necessary to specify the type of information activated by each encoding condition, the type of information required by each test, and how encoding and retrieval processes interact. The results of the studies reviewed above (Bodner et al., 2000; Cheng et al., 2008; Cheng and Huang, 2011; Toth et al., 1994) showed a positive effect of LoP, association, and generation on conscious memory, independent of the study, the version of instructions to judge studied words, and test in which conscious memory was investigated.

The effect was caused by a positive encoding effect of shallow, deep, association, and generation conditions, with the effect being larger following deep, association, and generation than following shallow conditions.

However, the effect of LoP and generation on conscious memory in the Cheng et al. (2008) implicit test of word association was caused by a positive effect of deep and generation conditions and a nonsignificant effect of shallow conditions on conscious memory. These encoding effects on conscious memory are summarized in Table 5. In contrast, LoP, association, and generation produced either a reverse or no effect on unconscious memory. LoP produced a reverse effect on unconscious memory in the Cheng et al. (2008) implicit word-identification test but no effect on unconscious memory in the explicit and implicit stem completion and implicit word association. The reverse LoP effect was caused by a priming effect of shallow and a nonsignficant effect of deep conditions on unconscious memory. The nonsignificant LoP effect was caused by a positive priming effect of shallow and deep conditions in explicit and implicit stem completion but caused by a nonsignificant priming of shallow and deep conditions on unconscious memory.

Association and generation produced a reverse effect of unconscious memory in all tests except Cheng et al.'s (2008) implicit word-association in which generation produced no effect, due to a nonsignificant effect of shallow and generation on unconscious memory. The reverse effect of association and generation was caused by a positive priming effect of shallow conditions and either a nonsignificant priming or a repetition-inhibition effect of generation on unconscious memory (evidenced by the estimate of automatic memory under a condition being smaller than its corresponding baseline score). These effects are summarized in Table 6.

## IMPLICATIONS OF THE RESULTS IN TABLE 5 FOR THE PROCESS OF CONSCIOUS MEMORY

To accommodate the results in Table 5, it is proposed that conscious memory in a test is not only driven by the nature of the test but also driven conceptually. Besides, conscious memory benefits from a study condition to the extent that the driving process of conscious memory recapitulates the encoding process engaged in that study condition.

### Conscious Memory in Stem Completion

As mentioned, a word-stem completion test is perceptually and lexically driven. conscious memory in the test is, therefore, perceptually, lexically, and conceptually driven and will benefit from perceptual processing in shallow, deep, and association conditions and from conceptual processing in deep, association, and generation conditions.

As a result, each of the shallow, deep, association, and generation conditions produces a positive effect on conscious memory. The perceptual encoding in shallow and both perceptual and conceptual encodings in deep and association conditions predict a positive LoP and association effect on conscious memory.

If conceptual encoding produces larger effects than does perceptual encoding for the retrieval of conscious memory, then there will also be a positive effect of generation on conscious memory. These predictions are supported by the results shown in Table 5.

### Conscious Memory in Implicit Word Identification

Conscious memory in an implicit word-identification test is visually and conceptually driven so that it benefits from visual encoding in shallow, deep, and association conditions and from conceptual encoding in deep, association, and self-generation conditions, resulting in a positive effect of LoP, association, and self-generation with a positive effect of shallow conditions on conscious memory.

## Conscious Memory in Implicit Word Association

Conscious memory in an implicit word-association test is conceptually driven so that conscious memory in the test does not benefit from perceptual encoding in shallow, deep, and association conditions but benefits from conceptual encoding in deep, association, and self-generation conditions, which will result in a positive effect of LoP, association, and self-generation on conscious memory in this test without showing a positive effect of shallow conditions on conscious memory.

# IMPLICATIONS OF THE RESULTS IN TABLE 6
# FOR THE PROCESS OF UNCONSCIOUS MEMORY

The results in Table 6 are taken to support the view that unconscious memory in a test is strictly driven by the nature of the test itself, and unconscious memory benefits from a study condition to the extent that the cognitive environments, contents of preexisting association, or categorical structures at test and at study match to activate the same type of information (e.g., visual, lexical, or semantic) about a memory item.

## Unconscious Memory in Stem Completion

The mechanism underlying unconscious memory in stem completion (either explicit or implicit tests) is illustrated as follows:

If a visual stem such as *cru__* originated from the study word *crust* is presented and to be completed with a five-letter word, then the stem is to trigger a word from a set of potential word candidates which are perceptually and lexically relevant to the stem such as the set of *crude$_p$*, *crumb$_p$*, *crump$_p$*, *crust$_p$*, and *crush$_p$* (a word with a subscript $p$ represents a perceptual copy of the word). The perceptual encoding of *crust* in shallow conditions, *crust$_p$* and perceptual and conceptual encodings of *crust* in deep conditions, *crust$_p$*/*crust$_c$* ( a word with a subscript $c$ represents a conceptual copy of the word), can allow a copy of *crust$_p$* to be included in and selected with a top priority from the set of potential word candidates, resulting in a positive priming effect of shallow and deep conditions on unconscious memory in the stem-completion test.

In contrast, in a generation condition in which *crust* is generated by a cue, the cue is perceptually and conceptually encoded, *cue$_p$*/*cue$_c$* and the word is conceptually encoded, *crust$_c$*, without simultaneously being perceptually encoded. Under this condition, *crust* is encoded in a complex cognitive environment, *cue$_p$*/*cue$_c$*/*crust$_c$*, which will not allow a copy of *crust$_p$* to be selected with a top priority from the set of potential word candidates, resulting in a probability of completion with *crust* being about equal to baseline probability under the generation condition. Alternatively, it is likely that *crust* encoded in the cognitive environment of *cue$_p$*/*cue$_c$*/*crust$_c$* will not allow a copy of *crust$_p$* to be included in the set of potential word candidates. As a result, the probability of completing *cru* with *crust* under the generation condition would be lower than baseline performance, resulting in a repetition-inhibition effect of this condition on unconscious memory.

In an association condition in which the study word *crust* is visually presented for association by asking participants to read the word aloud and then reported aloud the first associated word that comes to mind (see Bodner et al., 2000; Cheng et al., 2008), *crust* is perceptually encoded and the associated word is perceptually and conceptually encoded. Thus, *crust* is encoded in the complex cognitive environment, $crust_p/word_c/word_p$. In this case, perceptual information about the study word is overridden by that about the associated word and, therefore, *crust* encoded in this condition would not allow a copy of $crust_p$ to be included in or selected with a top priority, resulting in either a repetition-inhibition or a null effect of association on unconscious memory.

## Unconscious Memory in Implicit Word Identification

Unconscious memory in an implicit word-identification test is data-driven. In this test, a word is to be identified from a set of potential visual words sharing the same set of visual features detected through the visual presentation of *crust*. A complexity rating of *crust* in shallow conditions involves visual or graphemic encoding as well as other aspects of perceptual encoding of *crust*. This visual encoding can allow a copy of *crust* in a visual form to be included in and selected with a top priority from the set of potential visual words, resulting in a priming effect of shallow conditions on unconscious memory of *crust*. On the other hand, deep processing of *crust* involves perceptual and conceptual encoding of *crust*, $crust_p/crust_c$, and generation of *crust* involves its conceptual processing in $cue_p/cue_c/crust_c$. These two encoding conditions would not allow a visual copy of *crust* to be selected from a top priority from the set of potential words sharing the same visual features, resulting in the absence of an effect of deep and generation on unconscious memory in the test and, hence, a reverse effect of deep and generation on unconscious memory. Such results are evident in Cheng et al. (2008).

## Unconscious Memory in Implicit Word Association

If a cue word is presented for an implicit conceptual test (e.g., word association or categorical instance production) (normally, the cue for this test is not physically originated from a studied word), unconscious memory in such a test will benefit to the extent that either preexisting word-association systems or categorical structures at test and at study match to activate the same information about a memory item. This process is supported by the finding of a conceptual repetition effect and no conceptual repetition effect on memory in conceptually-driven tests for amnesic or drug-induced amnesic participants (e.g., Arndt et al., 2004; Keane, Gabriell, Monti, Fleischman, Cantor, and Noland, 1997; Shimamura and Squire, 1984). According to this view, unconscious memory in the implicit word-association test used in the Cheng et al. (2008) study should not benefit from the shallow condition because the perceptual encoding did not activate the preexisting word association that was necessary for the word-association test. It is also expected that there should be no repetition effect on unconscious memory under the pleasantness rating of study words and generating Chinese study words through English-Chinese translation because both conditions fail to activate the preexisting association necessary for the word-association test.

# CONCLUSIONS

Based on evidence from the studies on dissociation of memories within a test, the present study identifies conscious memory in a test as not only being driven by the nature of the test but also being driven conceptually. Such a conceptual processing without being driven by the test is regarded as participants' intention to retrieve memory information at a deep level. On the other hand, a process that is strictly driven by the test can be regarded as unconscious because it can be executed without involving participants' intentional retrieval.

The present study also finds that conscious memory benefits to the extent that the driving process of conscious memory recapitulates the encoding process engaged in that study condition. Thus, an item retrieved at test may be labeled with a time and a spatial tag of study and, hence, a self-awareness of memory, as a result of recapitulating the encoding process. On the other hand, unconscious memory benefits to the extent that the cognitive environments, preexisting associations, or categorical structures at test and at study match to activate the same type of information (e.g., visual, lexical, or semantic) about a memory item. Such a matching process can occur without involving self-awareness of memory.

Finally, although it is important to look at how conscious and unconscious memories differ, it is also important to focus on their common elements. According to the metacognitive approach to human cognition proposed by Nelson (1996), the human cognitive system consists of two levels. One is *object level*, at which cognitions concern objects and events of the external world, without involving self-awareness of cognitive activities. The second is *meta-level*, at which cognitions concern cognitions at the object level and, therefore, involve self-awareness of cognitive activities. Conscious and unconscious memories correspond to memories at the meta-level and object level, respectively. The two forms of memory, therefore, should be linked together by some common operations between the two.

# ACKNOWLEDGMENT

This research was supported by Grants 93-2752-H-002-004-PAE and 93-2752-H-002-005-PAE to the author from the National Science Council of Republic of China. Correspondence concerning this article should be addressed to Chao-Ming Cheng, Department of Psychology, Fo Guang University, 160, Linwei Road, Jiaosi, Yi-Lan County 25247, Taiwan (e-mail: cmcheng@ntu.edu.tw).

# REFERENCES

Anderson, J. R., and Bower, G. H. (1972). Recognition and retrieval processes in free recall. *Psychological Review, 79*, 97-123.

Arndt, J., Passannante, A., and Hirshman, E. (2004). The effect of midazolam on implicit and explicit memory in category exemplar production and category cued recall. *Memory, 12*, 158-173.

Banks, W. P., Chen, Y.-P., and Prull, M. W. (1999). Memory and awareness. In B. H. Challis and B. M. Velichkovsky (Eds.), *Stratification in cognition and consciousness* (pp. 129-172). Amsterdam/Philadelphia: John Benjamins.

Blaxton, T. A. (1989). Investigating dissociations among memory measures: Support for a transfer-appropriate processing framework. *Journal of Experimental Psychology: Learning, Memory, and Cognition, 15*, 657-668.

Bodner, G. E., Masson, M. E. J., and Caldwell, J. L. (2000). Evidence for a generate-recognize model of episodic on word-stem completion. *Journal of Experimental Psychology: Learning, Memory, and Cognition, 26*, 267-293.

Brown, A. S., and Mitchell, D. B. (1994). Levels of processing in implicit memory: A reevaluation. *Memory and Cognition, 22*, 533-541.

Challis, B. H., and Brodbeck, D. R. (1992). Level of processing affects priming in word-fragment completion. *Journal of Experimental Psychology: Learning, Memory, and Cognition, 18*, 595-607.

Challis, B. H., Velichkovsky, B. M., and Craik, F. I. M. (1996). Levels-of-processing effects on a variety of memory tasks: New findings and theoretical implications. *Consciousness and Cognition, 5*, 142-164.

Cheng, C-M., and Huang, C.-L. (2011). Processes of Conscious and Unconscious Memory: Evidence From Current Research on Dissociation of Memories Within a Test. *American Journal of Psychology*, in press.

Cheng, C-M., and Yang, M. J. (1989). Lateralization in the visual perception of Chinese characters and words. *Brain and Language, 36*, 669-689.

Cheng, C-M., Lin, W-Y., and Tsai, C-S. (2008). Conscious and unconscious forms of memory in different implicit tests. *Cognitive Systems Research, 9*, 213-328.

Curran, H. V., Barrow, S., Weingartner, H., Lader, M., and Bernik, H. (1995). Encoding, remembering and awareness in iorazepam-induced amnesia. *Psychopharmacology, 122*, 187-193.

Gardiner, J. M. (1988). Generation and priming effects in word-fragment completion. *Journal of Experimental Psychology: Learning, Memory, and Cognition, 14*, 495-501.

Gardiner, J. M. (1989). A generation effect in memory without awareness. *British Journal of Psychology, 80*, 163-168.

Gardiner, J. M., Dawson, A. J., and Sutton, E. A. (1989). Specificity and generality of enhanced priming effects for self-generated study items. *American Journal of Psychology, 102*, 295-305.

Graf, P., Mandler, G., and Hayden, P. E. (1982). Simulating amnesic symptoms in normal subjects. *Science, 218*, 1243. -1244.

Graf, P., and Schacter, D. L. (1985). Implicit and explicit memory for new associations in normal and amnesic subjects. *Journal of Experimental Psychology: Learning, Memory, and Cognition, 11,* 501-518.

Hamann, S. B. (1996). Level-of-processing effects in conceptually driven implicit tasks. *Journal of Experimental Psychology: Learning, Memory, and Cognition, 16*, 970-977.

Hamann, S. B., and Squire, L. R. (1996). Level-of-processing effects in word-completion priming: A neuropsychological study. *Journal of Experimental Psychology: Learning, Memory, and Cognition, 22,* 933-947.

Hirshman, E., Passannante, A., and Arndt, J. (2001). Midazolam amnesia and conceptual processing in implicit memory. *Journal of Experimental Psychology: General, 130*, 453-460.

Hyde, T. S., and Jenkins, J. J. (1969). The differential effects of incidental tasks on the organization of recall of a list of highly associated words. *Journal of Experimental Psychology, 82*, 472-481.

Jacoby, L. L. (1983). Perceptual enhancement: Persistence effects of an experience. *Journal of Experimental Psychology: Learning, Memory, and Cognition, 9*, 21-38.

Jacoby, L. L. (1991). A process dissociation framework: Separating automatic from intentional uses of memory. *Journal of Memory and Language, 30*, 513-541.

Jacoby, L. L. (1998). Invariance in automatic influences of memory: Toward a user's guide for the process-dissociation procedure. *Journal of Experimental Psychology: Learning, Memory, and Cognition. 24*, 3-26.

Jacoby, L. L., Toth, J. P., and Yonelinas, A. P. (1993). Separating conscious and unconscious influences of memory: Measuring recollection. *Journal of Experimental Psychology: General, 122*, 139-154.

Keane, M. M., Gabriell, J. D. E., Monti, L. A., Fleischman, D. A., Cantor, J. M., and Noland, J. S. (1997). Intact and impaired conceptual memory processes in amnesia. *Neuropsychology, 11*, 59-69.

Kintsch, W. (1968). Recognition and free recall of organized lists. *Journal of Experimental Psychology, 78*, 481-487.

MacLeod, C. M., and Masson, M. E. J. (1997). Priming patterns are different in masked word identification and word fragment completion. *Journal of Memory and Language, 36*, 461-483.

Mulligan, N. W. (2002). The effects of generation on conceptual implicit memory. *Journal of Memory and Language, 47*, 327-342.

Mulligan, N. W., Guyer, P. S., and Beland, A. (1999). The effects of levels-of-processing and organization on conceptual implicit memory in the category exemplar production test. *Memory and Cognition, 27,* 633-647.

Nelson, T. O. (1996). Consciousness and metacognition. *American Psychologist, 51,* 102-116.

Nicolas, S., and Tardieu, H. (1996). The generation effects in a word-stem completion tasks: The influence of conceptual processes. *European Journal of Cognitive Psychology, 8,* 405-424.

Richardson-Klavehn, A., and Gardiner, J. M. (1995). Retrieval volition and memory awareness in stem completion: An empirical analysis. *Psychological Research, 57,* 166-178.

Schacter, D. L. (1987). Implicit memory: History and current status. *Journal of Experimental Psychology: Learning, Memory, and Cognition, 13*, 501-518.

Shimamura, A. P., and Squire, L. R. (1984). Paired-associate learning and priming effects in amnesia: A neuropsychological study. *Journal of Experimental Psychology: General, 113*, 556-570.

Smith, E. R., and Branscombe, N. R. (1988). Category accessibility as implicit memory. *Journal of Experimental Social Psychology, 24*, 490-504.

Squire, L. R., and Shimamura, A. P., and Graf, P. (1987). Strength and duration of priming effects in normal subjects and amnesic patients. *Neuropsychologia, 25*, 195-210.

Toth, J. P., Reingold, E. M., and Jacoby, L. L. (1994). Toward a redefinition of implicit memory: Process dissociations following elaborative processing and self-generation. *Journal of Experimental Psychology: Learning, Memory, and Cognition, 20*, 290-303.

Warrington, E. K., and Weiskantz, L. (1970). Amnesic syndrome: Consolidation or retrieval? *Nature, 228,* 629-630.

Watkins, M. J., and Gardiner, J. M. (1979). An appreciation of generate-recognise theory of recall. *Journal of Verbal Learning and Verbal Behavior, 18*, 687-704.

Winnick, W. A., and Daniel, S. A. (1970). Two kinds of response priming in tachistoscopic word recognition. *Journal of Experimental Psychology, 84*, 74-81.

In: Psychology of Memory         ISBN: 978-1-61942-633-7
Editors: Dannie M. Hendrix and Orval Holcomb     © 2012 Nova Science Publishers, Inc.

*Chapter 8*

# MOTIVATIONAL INFLUENCES ARE IMPORTANT FOR UNDERSTANDING PROSPECTIVE MEMORY PERFORMANCE IN CHILDREN

## *Suzanna L. Penningroth[1], Karen Bartsch[1] and Ethan A. McMahan[2]*

[1] Department of Psychology, University of Wyoming, US
[2] Department of Psychology, Western Oregon University, US

## SUMMARY

Prospective memory refers to remembering to perform a delayed intention such as returning a library book. In this chapter, we focus on the role of motivation in prospective memory in children. We suggest two theses, specifically that motivation improves prospective memory performance in children and that it is particularly influential for younger children. A review of past research reveals support for both theses although research on motivation, and its relationship to age, in children's prospective memory is sparse. We report the results of a study of younger (age 7-8 years) and older (age 10-11 years) children in which parents were asked to complete diary reports for two weeks, describing their children's real-life prospective memory tasks on school days. We chose a naturalistic design because little is known about real prospective memory tasks children have and variables that affect their performance. Our results provide support for both of the central theses of this chapter. That is, prospective memory performance was better for tasks regarded as more important, and older children outperformed younger children on low importance tasks but not on high importance tasks. We conclude that motivational variables need to be considered in theoretical models of prospective memory in childhood, and we propose extending one motivational-cognitive model of prospective memory to explain prospective memory in children.

# INTRODUCTION

This chapter concerns the development of prospective memory (i.e., memory for performing planned intentions) in children. As children get older, they are no longer just directed by adults to immediately perform tasks, but in addition, they are expected to remember to perform tasks on their own. For example, a 6-year-old might be asked to remember to bring home a sweater that has been left at school. An 11-year-old might be expected to wait for her father to pick her up after school instead of taking the usual bus home. A child's success in remembering to perform these everyday prospective memory tasks will depend on multiple factors (e.g., Kvavilashvili, Kyle, & Messer, 2008), but we contend that an important factor is motivation to perform the task.

This chapter is organized around two central theses. First, we suggest that motivation is a critical element in prospective memory performance in children. Specifically, increased motivation improves prospective memory performance in children. Second, we suggest that motivation may be especially important for younger children and that younger children can sometimes remember to perform prospective memory tasks just as well as older children if the task is important to them. We will review the extant literature relevant to these claims and present new supporting evidence from a study of parent reports of prospective memory in school-age children. We limit our focus to the topic of prospective memory in children through age 12 (about 5th or 6th grade in the U.S.) and do not address prospective memory performance or development in adolescence or young adulthood.

# THESIS #1: MOTIVATION (E.G., TASK IMPORTANCE OR GOAL-RELATEDNESS) IMPROVES PROSPECTIVE MEMORY PERFORMANCE IN CHILDREN

The idea that motivational factors play a central role in children's prospective memory is suggested in two aspects of the extant prospective memory literature. First, there are many studies showing that motivation improves prospective memory in adults. We summarize this research in the next section. Second, there is a small but convincing set of findings supporting the more specific conclusion that motivation improves prospective memory in children. These findings, along with some that raise questions about this thesis, are summarized and evaluated following the next section.

## Research Has Shown that Higher Task Motivation Improves Prospective Memory Performance in General

Researchers from both social psychology and cognitive psychology have theorized that motivation is pivotal in remembering to perform prospective memory tasks (e.g., Kruglanski, et al. 2002; McDaniel & Einstein, 2000; Meacham, 1982; Sheeran, Webb, & Gollwitzer, 2005; Winograd, 1988). Many studies have shown that prospective memory tasks that are regarded as more important are remembered better (e.g., Kliegel, Martin, McDaniel, & Einstein, 2004; Kvavilashvili, 1987; Marsh, Hicks, & Landau, 1998; Meacham & Singer,

1977). For example, in one naturalistic study, participants who first listed their upcoming real-life prospective memory tasks, and later reported on whether they remembered them, reported higher forgetting rates for tasks they had rated as lower in importance (Marsh et al., 1998). Possible reasons for links between task importance and improved performance include an increased use of memory strategies (Einstein & McDaniel, 1990; Penningroth, 2005), performance benefits specifically for social and prosocial tasks (i.e., tasks that benefit others; Altgassen, Kliegel, Brandimonte, & Filippello, 2010; Brandimonte, Ferrante, Bianco, & Villani, 2010; Penningroth, Scott, & Freuen, 2011), and an increased allocation of attentional resources when monitoring for performance cues (Kliegel et al., 2004).

### A Motivational-Cognitive Model of Prospective Memory

Results showing motivational effects on prospective memory in adults have inspired a motivational-cognitive model of prospective memory (Penningroth & Scott, 2007). This working model summarizes effects of motivation on prospective memory and has spurred new research related to the model (see Figure 1). This model draws on contemporary research on goal frameworks (e.g., Kruglanski et al., 2002) to understand prospective memory. Accordingly, goals are seen as knowledge structures with associative links to prospective memories. For example, a college student might have the goal of getting accepted into a Ph.D. program in psychology. Specific prospective memory tasks such as mailing an application would be related to this goal. The model equates perceived task importance with goal-relatedness. Prospective memory tasks that are related to goals (are more important) should reap specific benefits in processing.

Studies showing task importance effects on prospective memory in adults have supported this model, including some of the hypothesized links or mechanisms (e.g., Kliegel et al., 2004; Sheeran et al., 2005). With regard to children, Marcovitch, Boseovski, and Knapp (2007) recently provided evidence that keeping a goal activated in memory seems to be important for remembering to do related actions. These researchers tested the ability of 4- and 5- year olds to sort cards correctly after the sorting rule changed (e.g., bunnies go in this box now, not red things). Children were more likely to sort the cards correctly if the goal was kept activated in memory (through more frequent experiencing of "conflict" trials where the child had to actually apply the new rule). Thus, these results provide some basis for extending the motivational-cognitive model of prospective memory to children. It appears that for both adults and children, an activated goal increases remembering of goal-relevant actions. More research is still needed, of course, both to test proposed mechanisms in the model and to test the ecological validity of the model.

Studies showing task importance effects on prospective memory in adults have supported this model, including some of the hypothesized links or mechanisms (e.g., Kliegel et al., 2004; Sheeran et al., 2005). With regard to children, Marcovitch, Boseovski, and Knapp (2007) recently provided evidence that keeping a goal activated in memory seems to be important for remembering to do related actions. These researchers tested the ability of 4- and 5- year olds to sort cards correctly after the sorting rule changed (e.g., bunnies go in this box now, not red things). Children were more likely to sort the cards correctly if the goal was kept activated in memory (through more frequent experiencing of "conflict" trials where the child had to actually apply the new rule). Thus, these results provide some basis for extending the motivational-cognitive model of prospective memory to children. It appears that for both adults and children, an activated goal increases remembering of goal-relevant actions. More research is still needed, of course, both to test proposed mechanisms in the model and to test the ecological validity of the model.

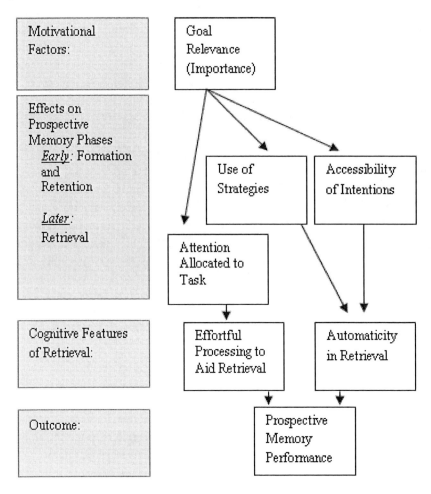

Figure 1. A goal-based motivational-cognitive model of prospective memory. Adapted from "A motivational-cognitive model of prospective memory: The influence of goal relevance," by S. L. Penningroth and W. D. Scott, 2007, in F. Columbus (Ed.), Psychology of motivation, (pp. 115 – 128). Copyright 2007 by Nova Science Publishers, Inc.

## Evidence that Higher Task Importance Improves Children's Performance on Prospective Memory Tasks

Several studies have demonstrated that children can improve their performance on prospective memory tasks when the tasks are considered to be important. Somerville, Wellman, and Cultice (1983) enlisted preschoolers' caretakers (mothers) to examine prospective memory in 2-, 3-, and 4-year old children. Each caretaker asked the child to remind him or her to do something at a specific time in the future, thus targeting unique, non-recurring events that could systematically differ with regard to the child's level of interest (e.g., buying candy at the store versus bringing in the washing) and the length of time involved before reminding was to occur (e.g., a few minutes versus from evening to the next morning). Toddlers usually (in 73% of opportunities) reminded their caretakers when tasks involved high interest and short delays, with even 2-year-olds succeeding 80% of the time. In contrast, reminding for low-interest tasks was infrequent.

Recently, McCauley and colleagues have demonstrated better prospective memory performance for children in a high incentive condition relative to a lower incentive condition (McCauley, McDaniel, Pedroza, Chapman, & Levin, 2009; McCauley et al., 2010; McCauley et al., 2011). In three studies, these researchers examined the effectiveness of monetary incentives for improving prospective memory in children with moderate tbi (traumatic brain injury), severe tbi, and no tbi. The samples contained children aged 6-19 (McCauley et al., 2009), 7-13 (McCauley et al., 2010), or 7-16 (McCauley et al., 2011). The prospective memory task was always to verbally remind the experimenter to give the child three points (to be exchanged for money) whenever the experimenter said "Let's try something different" during the course of administering a test battery. Motivation was manipulated within participants such that the child earned a dollar (U.S. currency) for each point in the high motivation condition and earned a penny for each point in the low motivation condition. Results showed that the more important task was remembered more often. Also, this result was replicated across all three studies for children with no tbi or with moderate tbi. However, for children with severe tbi, incentives only improved prospective memory when the prospective memory assessment took place at least one year after the injury (McCauley et al., 2009). In the prospective memory assessments done soon after a severe tbi event or within three months of a severe tbi event, incentives did not significantly improve performance (McCauley et al., 2010, 2011).

## Evidence that Does Not Support the Claim that Higher Task Importance Improves Children's Performance on Prospective Memory Tasks

Although task importance has been shown in some studies, as reported above, to affect children's prospective memory performance, several studies have failed to find such an effect. Guajardo and Best (2000) examined prospective memory performance in preschoolers (ages 3 and 5) by using computerized tasks. In the context of memorizing simple pictures for recall, the children had the prospective memory task of pressing the spacebar whenever they saw the target picture (a house or a duck). In the high incentive group, children received a small reward (e.g., goldfish crackers or pennies, as chosen by the child) after each correct prospective memory response. In the low incentive group, children received no rewards for prospective memory performance. Results showed no effect of incentive for the computer task. However, as noted in Kvavilashvili et al.'s (2008) review, the ongoing task (memorizing pictures for recall) was more difficult for the 3-year-olds than the 5-year-olds, and may have masked any motivational effects on the computer task used to assess prospective memory performance. In addition, Guajardo and Best observed that more 3-year-olds remembered to request a sticker (presumably a rewarding event) than remembered to close the door (presumably a less rewarding event), leading the authors to conclude that there was mixed evidence for the effectiveness of incentives in this preschool-aged sample.

Kliegel, Brandenberger, and Aberle (2010) also examined the effect of task importance on preschoolers' prospective memory performance. Specifically, 3- and 5-year-olds' prospective memory was tested in lab tasks that were designed to be as naturalistic as possible. Task motivation was manipulated by using two different prospective memory tasks, both embedded in a standardized test battery that served as the ongoing task. High task motivation was instilled by asking children to remind the experimenter to give them a gift from a "magic box" when the next task was done. Low task motivation was instilled by asking children to remind the experimenter to record their name when the next task was done. Results showed no main effect of motivation, but they revealed an age group by motivation interaction. This interaction is discussed in detail below with respect to our second thesis, that younger children can show high levels of prospective memory performance for important tasks.

In a laboratory study that included a group of 7-10 year olds, Ward, Shum, McKinley, Baker-Tweney, and Wallace (2005) found no advantage to prospective memory performance when the importance of the prospective memory task was stressed. The ongoing task in this study was a lexical decision task performed on a computer. That is, participants saw strings of letters on the screen and, using a response box, pressed a green key if the string was a word or a red key if the string was not a word. The prospective memory task entailed pressing a new key on the response box whenever the letter string being judged contained any letters in italics. The experimenter manipulated the importance of the prospective memory task (within-participants) through differences in the instructions. However, a close examination of the instructions suggests that the low importance instructions might have actually carried a bigger motivational impact than intended. The high importance instructions stressed the importance of both the prospective memory task (spotting letters in italics) and the ongoing task (the lexical decision task). The low importance instructions were intended to minimize the importance of the prospective memory task by referring to performance as doing a favor for the experimenter. However, recent research has shown that tasks perceived to help others are considered more important (Penningroth et al., 2011) and performed more often than other tasks (e.g., Brandimonte et al., 2010; Penningroth et al., 2011). In fact, Altgassen et al. (2010) found that adding a phrase about doing the experimenter a favor by remembering to perform the prospective memory task improved task performance significantly (at least for older adults). Therefore, the null effects of task importance reported by Ward et al. (2005) need to be replicated with different instructions before it can be concluded that task importance has no effect on performance.

In summary, a review of research in adult populations strongly supports our first thesis in this chapter, namely, that task importance should be very important for children's prospective memory success. A review of research with children provides more support, albeit somewhat mixed, for this claim. Clearly, there is a need for more research on this question.

## Thesis #2: Motivation can Moderate Age Group effects in Prospective Memory Performance: Younger Children can Remember just as Well as Older Children if the Task is Important to Them

We would guess that, if queried, most parents and caregivers would be able to recount an instance when their preschool- or school-aged child had shown a truly amazing ability to remember to perform an action. These surprising memory feats might even cause a parent to reflect on his or her child's memory abilities, perhaps viewing this latest accomplishment as something the parent would not have imagined possible. When these phenomenal prospective memory feats occur, they seem to often involve remembering to do things for a highly desirable reward (e.g., getting a special dessert after remembering to do a chore) or remembering to do things in order to do a highly enjoyable activity (e.g., getting up early to go fishing on Saturday). Are such informal impressions supported by research findings? When comparing children of different ages, do age-related effects on performance disappear for high importance tasks? Although research on prospective memory in children has not been as plentiful as research on prospective memory in adults, a few studies have examined age-group differences in performance and possible moderating variables.

Overall, in the extant reported research, age-related effects on children's prospective memory performance have not been consistently found. As noted in a recent review of prospective memory in childhood (Kvavilashvili et al., 2008), some studies have found increasing age-related prospective memory performance, but when the proper controls were included (e.g., equating ongoing task difficulty across age groups), age-related effects were either small or moderated by other variables. Kvavilashvili et al. noted that several moderating variables were likely, including task motivation, but no studies showing an interaction of task motivation and age on prospective memory performance in children had yet been published.

What evidence supports the claim that younger children can remember prospectively as well as older children under high motivation conditions? One of the seminal studies of prospective memory performance in children (Somerville et al., 1983, described earlier) has been described in various sources as showing an interaction of motivation level and age (e.g., Kliegel et al., 2010), but it should be noted that although high motivation was more effective for the youngest group (2-year-olds, when compared to 3- and 4-year-olds), the interaction was not statistically significant, probably due in part to the small sample size (only 10 children per age group). However, the interaction pattern was later replicated in statistically significant results by Kliegel et al. (2010), as described below. We also note that Somerville et al. (1983) used a naturalistic design that afforded high ecological validity to their findings. Preschoolers were simply asked to remind their caregivers to do tasks that would not seem out of the ordinary or artificial in the context of their everyday lives.

Clear evidence for the thesis that younger children can remember prospectively if highly motivated comes from the recent study by Kliegel et al. (2010) described earlier. In that study, performance showed an interaction between task importance and age group. Specifically, 3-year-olds performed as well as 5-year-olds on the high motivation task (remembering to ask for a prize). However, the younger children showed worse prospective remembering than the older children when it came to the low motivation task. Importantly, these researchers equated ongoing-task difficulty for the two age groups so that differences in the prospective memory task were not confounded by the younger children having a tougher set of tasks overall. Therefore, the differential motivation effect was revealed.

# SUMMARY OF PAST RESEARCH FINDINGS

We have shown that past research findings support two conclusions concerning motivational influences on prospective memory in children. First, motivation plays an important role in their prospective memory performance. Second, motivation can moderate age-related differences in prospective memory performance such that higher task importance derived from, say, incentives can boost performance in younger children especially. However, both contentions would be strengthened by additional evidence from direct tests of the effect of motivational influences in prospective memory in children. Moreover, an examination of this issue in the context of children's everyday activities is needed. Most past studies on motivation and prospective memory in children claim to have used naturalistic or pseudo-naturalistic tasks, yet the tasks were typically assigned by an experimenter in a laboratory setting. These lab studies have the advantage of achieving high levels of control in isolating key variables, but the controlled setting entails the usual tradeoff in ecological validity. In a specific examination of whether context matters, Ceci and Bronfenbrenner (1985) found different levels of motivation for tasks performed in the child's home versus a lab. Only Somerville et al. (1983) directly assessed children's prospective memory for everyday tasks to be done outside of the lab and as part of children's real lives. The need for more research of this sort prompted us to conduct a diary study of parent reports of prospective memory in school-aged children. The remainder of this chapter is devoted to describing this study.

# THE CURRENT STUDY

Our goals were to provide evidence from a naturalistic study regarding the contentions that 1) motivation has an appreciable effect on prospective memory performance in children, and 2) high task motivation can especially improve the performance of younger children. Toward these ends, we employed an approach not previously used to investigate prospective memory in children, namely, a diary study on parents' reports of their children's behaviors and experiences. More specifically, parents completed structured diary forms in which they reported their child's real prospective memory tasks on school days, along with importance ratings and remembering rates for the tasks. We also interviewed parents prior to their completion of the diary reports. While a parent's perspective is clearly limited, there is evidence to suggest that it can provide valuable information about children's capabilities (e.g., Kliegel & Jager, 2007; Miller, Manhal, & Mee, 1991). We restricted the scope of the investigation to elementary school-age children, on the assumption that their structured school days might provide a common structure for prospective memory activities as well as one that is of particular interest to parents and teachers. Our sample consisted of parents of first- and second-graders and fourth- and fifth-graders (aged 7-8 and 10-11 years) in the western United States. Here we will focus on the parts of the collected data concerned with children's performance of non-routine prospective memory tasks. We defined non-routine prospective memory tasks as those tasks that do not occur on a daily basis (e.g., taking a permission slip to school, remembering to get picked up after school at an odd place or time).

## Hypotheses

1) We predicted that prospective memory performance, as reported by parents, would be better for tasks rated high in importance compared to those rated low in importance (as indicated through parent reports of children's perceptions).
2) We predicted that task importance would interact with age, with younger children (grades 1 and 2) performing as well as older children (grades 4 and 5) on memory for high importance tasks but worse for low importance tasks.
3) We predicted that older children would do better than younger children in remembering to perform tasks. Although age-related improvement in prospective memory performance has not been found with complete consistency in past research, some research has accorded with this plausible claim and our comparison involved children who differed in age by two to four years.

## METHOD

### Participants

Parents of children in first- or second-grade and/or children in fourth- or fifth-grade were recruited through advertisements placed at schools and community centers in a small town in the western United States. Thirty-seven parents, including 36 mothers and 1 father, were recruited to participate. Together, they provided reports on a total of 46 children (28 younger, 39% female, and 18 older, 50% female). The sample was 96% Caucasian and 4% African American. Reports on multiple children in the same household were always collected at different time points. That is, parents never completed diary reports for more than one child at a time.

### Design and Materials

Our aim was to determine how age (younger or older) and task importance affected children's remembering to perform real-life tasks. We interviewed children's parents on these matters and also asked parents to complete a two-week diary study on their child's prospective memory activities, so we had two sources of data to inspect.

In the diary observations (described in detail below), parents reported on children's daily tasks-to-be-remembered, the child's perception of the importance of those tasks, and whether or not the child remembered to do the tasks. Parents rated how important each task was to the child on a 1-5 scale (1 = not at all important, 5 = very important). Tasks were later dichotomized into low importance tasks (ratings of 1-3) and high importance tasks (ratings of 4-5). The main dependent variable was the proportion of prospective memory tasks the child remembered to perform, as recorded in the diary report data. That is, for each prospective memory task parents listed in the diary, the parent checked whether the child remembered, forgot, or "other" (e.g., task was cancelled). Very few tasks fell in the "other" category, so performance on individual tasks was essentially scored as remembered or forgotten.

In addition to this information on child performance from the diary study, we interviewed parents before they initiated the diary observations. Specifically, we asked parents to report three non-routine prospective memory tasks their child had had in the past. Parents then completed the same ratings for these reported tasks (e.g., perceived importance for the child and whether the task was remembered or forgotten). However, many parents did not list a second or third task (not listed for 9% and 35%, respectively), and so we decided to only examine the first task listed (and related ratings) so that the entire sample was represented. These reports provided us with data for a secondary analysis pertinent to our hypotheses.

## Procedure

Parents were first interviewed about their child in an hour-long session and then they engaged in a two-week period of recording their observations of their child in a diary.

### Initial Interview to Explain the Diary Task

A graduate or undergraduate research assistant first interviewed the parent in a session lasting 45 minutes to one hour, providing general information about the study and instructing the parent to complete several forms that requested demographic information, information about past events in which the child remembered or failed to remember tasks (as mentioned above), and information relevant to other measures not reported here. Parents were told that the study concerned their child's performance on non-routine memory tasks and required that parents keep a diary of the child's memory performance for such tasks over a two-week period. Non-routine memory tasks were defined as those tasks that do not occur on a daily basis (e.g., bringing money to school for a special ice-cream party). Parents were shown a copy of the diary forms (in a booklet form) and went through a "training form" to practice completing the diary forms by filling in information about three prospective memory tasks the child had on the most recent school day in the past. Each of the daily diary forms allowed parents to report up to three tasks their child was supposed to complete that day. For each task, the parent described what the task was and then stated when the task was to be performed. The form used an open-response format for these questions. Task importance was assessed with the rating scale described above.

Parents were told that they should not provide their children with special tasks for the study but that they should simply observe their child's performance on any naturally occurring non-routine memory tasks and record information about those tasks on the provided diary forms. As such, the number of responses recorded for each child varied, depending on the number of tasks the child was actually expected to complete during the two-week period. Parents were asked to complete each daily form during the evening or night, or if that was not possible, as soon as possible on the following morning.

### Diary Period

The diary phase consisted of a two-week period following the initial interview, always starting on a Monday (and always on a day when school was in session.) Parents were required to fill out one diary form per weekday for this two-week period. This yielded ten diary forms per child. Parents chose one of two formats for completing the diary forms: a hard-copy version (provided by the experimenter at the initial interview) or an electronic version. Parents were instructed to complete and keep each hard copy form until the end of the two-week diary period and then return all the completed forms. The electronic versions of the diary were sent via email to the parent every weekday during the two-week diary period. Parents were instructed to fill out the forms electronically and, once completed, to send the forms back via email to the researcher every day. All parents, regardless of diary format, received a daily reminder to complete the diary (they chose the reminder delivery format: texting, phone call, or email). Forty-six out of 47 diaries were completed and submitted. All analyses are based on this sample of 46.

## Coding of Open-Ended Responses

Recall that, in order to discover what kinds of prospective memory tasks children had in their everyday lives, we asked parents to list their children's real prospective memory tasks when reporting them for both the diary forms and the survey item during the initial interview. We had also asked when the tasks were to be performed. We needed to develop a coding scheme for these various tasks that would allow us to describe them, but there is little precedent in the literature for such coding, other than schemes developed for adult tasks (e.g., Meacham & Kushner, 1980).

**Table 1. Categories for task descriptions and expected completion times**

|  | Category Name | Examples |
|---|---|---|
| Task descriptions |  |  |
|  | 1. Bring to or take from school | Take lunch money to school |
|  | 2. Bring to or take from non-school | Give note to friend |
|  | 3. Chore | Take the trash out |
|  | 4. Appointments/meetings | Meet babysitter at 3:00 |
|  | 5. Practice, clubs, or lessons | Violin lessons |
|  | 6. Tell/ask/call/remind someone | Call mom at work after school |
|  | 7. Medicine/safety | Take medicine for sore throat |
|  | 8. Homework or individual practice | Read book |
|  | 9. Pack/prepare/get ready | Pack for ski trip tomorrow |
|  | 10. Personal care/hygiene | Take shower after breakfast |
|  | 11. Act appropriately/manners | Don't touch other kids |
|  | 12. Transportation/go somewhere | Get picked up from band |
|  | 13. Other | Buy shoes at store |
| Expected completion times | 1. Before school | In the morning, before school |
|  | 2. At school | At the end of the school day |
|  | 3. After school | After school |
|  | 4. Evening | After dinner |
|  | 5. Today, anytime | Today |
|  | 6. Tomorrow/later | Tomorrow |
|  | 7. Other | Sometime this week |

These schemes included categories such as "write, mail something" and "take something somewhere" which were too general for our purposes and failed to capture the typical tasks of school-aged children. Therefore, we developed a new coding scheme, drawing on published schemes used for adult tasks, but also using a bottom-up approach such that categories were determined after scrutinizing the types of responses elicited. The coding schemes we developed are shown in Table 1. We ended up with 13 categories for types of prospective memory tasks and 7 categories for expected completion times. Two independent raters initially coded a subset of the data to determine inter-rater reliability. Inter-rater reliability was sufficiently high for categorization of task description (92%) and expected time of task completion (98%), and so each rater then categorized half of the remaining data. When we examined the full set of ratings, three categories for types of tasks showed almost no occurrences ("medicine/safety," "personal care/hygiene," and "acting appropriately"), and so we combined those few instances into the "other" category, leaving 10 final categories for task type. Similarly, three categories for expected completion time showed almost no occurrences ("today," "tomorrow," and "other") and these categories were dropped.

# RESULTS

## Diary Data

Before examining reported performance rates for prospective memory tasks, we inspected the general patterns of task types commonly reported for these school-aged children. To do this, we calculated the percent of the sample that showed any occurrence of each of the 10 task type categories. For example, a child was counted as showing a "chore" task type if a task from that task category ever appeared in the diary reports, whether it was one time or 30 times. We were pleased with the number of tasks parents actually recorded. With a maximum of 30 tasks possible, the mean number recorded was 13.8 (range = 4 – 29). Also, the average number of tasks recorded did not differ by child age group ($F < 1.0$). We found that parents were most likely to report that their child had tasks that involved "bringing things to or from school" which was a task for 89% of the children. Examples of tasks reported for this category were "Take saxophone to school" and "Bring home specific book for a book report." This type of task was by far the most common across the sample; a McNemar test using the binomial distribution showed a significant difference between this task type and the next most common type, "chore" ($N = 46$, exact $p = .001$), which was reported for 57% of the sample. Other task types were fairly uniformly represented, occurring for 37-54% of the children. After "chore," the next most common task types were "other" (54% of the sample), "tell/ask/call/remind someone" (48% of the sample), and "transportation" (46% of the sample). Importantly, we also tested for differences between younger and older children. If younger children had different types of tasks than older children, this might complicate our analysis of age group and motivation effects on performance. However, chi-square tests conducted on each of the 10 task type categories showed no age-group differences for specific types of tasks (all $X^2$s < 1.8).

Similarly, we inspected the general patterns for expected completion times. To do this, for each of the 46 children, we calculated the mean percentage of tasks for each expected completion time category. We then calculated overall means for each of the four completion time categories. Results showed that mean occurrences for the four completion time categories differed significantly, $F(3, 42) = 7.92$, $p$ (two-tailed) < .001, $\eta_p^2 = .361$. The highest percentage of tasks were supposed to be performed "after school" ($M$ = 37%), with less commonly reported times reported for "before school" ($M$ = 22%), "in the evening" ($M$ = 17%), and "at school" ($M$ = 16%). Post-hoc comparisons showed that "after school" tasks were more common than each of the other three time periods ($t$'s > 2.9). We did not assess when the tasks were first assigned, and so for any specific task, we do not know whether the child was expected to remember the task for several minutes (e.g., if a teacher assigned a task at the end of the day or a parent assigned a task as the child arrived home from school) or for many hours (e.g., if a parent assigned a task in the morning that was to be completed after school, such as picking up a younger sibling to walk him or her home). However, qualitative analysis of the diary data suggests that for many tasks, children were expected to remember the task for several hours and often for the length of the school day (e.g,. "Wait for friends after school to loan them costumes"). Importantly, there was no interaction between age group and expected completion time, $F(3, 42) = 0.94$, $p$ (two-tailed) = .431, indicating that these expectations for when tasks were to be completed applied to younger and older children equally. Our overall evaluation of this completion time data prompts two remarks. First, these data from real-life prospective memory tasks show much longer delay intervals than are seen in laboratory investigations of prospective memory in children. Therefore, the results reported below also offer an extension of past findings, showing that they apply to tasks with longer delays, and to tasks that are more ecologically valid in general. Second, our failure to detect an age-group difference on expected completion times (i.e., the null finding for the interaction of age group and completion time category) means that even children as young as 7 and 8 years old are regularly expected to remember to do things over a fairly long delay.

### Percentage of Diary Tasks Performed

Our first prediction was that children would best remember to perform tasks they regarded as important. Data for four children were excluded from our analysis on the diary data pertinent to this topic because their tasks were rated as either all high or all low in importance, rendering a within-child comparison on this variable impossible. For the remaining 42 children, the results supported our hypothesis. That is, more important tasks were remembered more often ($M$ = 86.3%; $SD$ = 18.0) than less important tasks ($M$ = 49.6%; $SD$ = 30.6), $F(1, 40) = 31.92$, $p$ (two-tailed) < .001, $n^2_p$ = .444.

We had also predicted that the influence of task importance would depend on the age of the child, such that younger children might remember high importance tasks as well as older children but would remember low importance tasks less often. We conducted two sets of planned comparisons to compare younger to older children, using one-tailed significance tests corresponding to our a priori predictions. Data from two children were excluded from this analysis because either no low importance tasks or no high importance tasks were reported. Results based on the remaining 44 children supported the second hypothesis (see Figure 2). That is, for less important tasks, older children remembered a higher percentage of their tasks ($M$ = 61.2%; $SD$ = 25.6) than younger children ($M$ = 43.1%; $SD$ = 31.6), $t(42) = 1.89$, $p$ (one-tailed) = .033, $n^2_p$ = .078. For tasks of higher importance, there was no age-group difference, $t(42) = 0.97$, $p$ (one-tailed) = .169, $n^2_p$ = .022. Table 2 lists examples of tasks parents reported for their children, grouped by age group and task importance level.

Finally, we also predicted, somewhat tentatively in view of mixed past reports, higher rates of remembering for older children than younger children. In fact, the diary data results showed that the overall remembering rates did not differ for younger and older children, $t(44)$

= 0.57, $p$ (two-tailed) = .571, $\eta_p^2$= .007, with both groups remembering about three-fourths of the tasks (younger $M$ = 72.3%, SD = 14.6; older $M$ = 75.1%, $SD$ = 18.6). Recall that our earlier analysis of task type categories and expected completion times showed the same patterns for younger and older children. Therefore, the similar overall rates of remembering for these two age groups is likely not due to older children having vastly different types of tasks or longer delays until performance. Of course, to rule out these possibilities more definitely, a more controlled study would need to be conducted, for example, a study that assigns the same tasks, preferably "naturalistic" tasks, to different age-groups of school-age children (as was done for a preschool aged sample in Somerville et al., 1983).

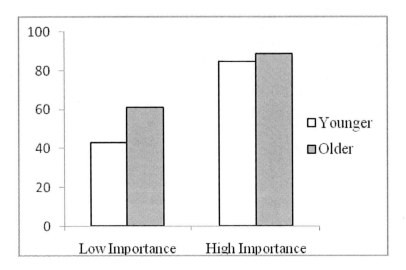

Figure 2. Reported performance of children's prospective memory tasks (mean % remembered) from parent diaries, by child age group and task importance level.

## Table 2. Examples of real prospective memory tasks parents reported for their children, by age-group and task importance level, from diary reports

| Task Importance | Younger group (age 7-8) | Older group (age 10-11) |
|---|---|---|
| Low | Clean room after school | Give me permission slip |
| | Take money for school pictures and give to teacher | Pick up sister from class and take to chorus practice |
| | Empty food from plate and not feed it to dog | Bring home spelling words |
| High | Pajama day at school | Remember tap shoes |
| | Take the book to "show and tell" at school | Pack for school ski trip for next day |
| | Remember glasses for shooting sports (4-H) | Remember to bring home script for play |

## Data from the Survey Item on any Non-Routine Task from the Past

Recall that we had a secondary interest in testing whether our predictions would be supported not only in the diary reports but also in the survey data concerning a real prospective memory event collected during the parent interview. Our first hypothesis was again that greater importance would be associated with improved performance. However, the dependent variable for performance on this measure was categorical (the child either had remembered or forgotten to do the task), and so to maintain as much statistical power as possible we used the continuous measure of task importance (the 1-5 ratings) rather than the dichotomized (categorical) version of this variable. The point-biserial correlation between rated task importance and performance was significant, $r_{pb}$ = .33, $p$ (two-tailed) = .026, indicating that past prospective memory tasks that were more important to the child (according to the parent) were more likely to be remembered and performed. This finding replicated the pattern revealed by the diary data.

Our second prediction, as before, was for a moderating effect of task importance on age-related improvements on performance. Again, to test this hypothesis with as much statistical power as possible, we used the continuous measure of task importance. Therefore, we were interested in whether younger children (compared to older children) showed a stronger correlation between task importance rating and performance ("remembered" vs. "forgot"). The results provided some support for this prediction. The point-biserial correlation between task importance and performance was significant for the younger group ($r_{pb}$ = .38, $p$ (two-tailed) = .048) but not the older group ($r_{pb}$ = .21, $p$ (two-tailed) = .403). However, when these two correlations were compared using Fisher's z-test, they were not found to be significantly different ($z$ = .56). We conclude that for this one-item index of prospective memory performance for one task from the recent past, both age groups best remembered more important tasks, but the correlation was only reliable for the younger children. This pattern replicated the pattern we found for the diary data.

Our third hypothesis was that older children, more than younger children, would remember to do the tasks, according to parent reports. For this one-item measure of remembering a past task, remembering was more likely for older children (94.4% of this group remembered) than younger children (64.3% remembered), $X^2$ = 5.48, $p$ (two-tailed) = .019. This result differs from the results from our primary data source, the diary data, which revealed no age-group difference in overall remembering rates. In comparing the two measures used to assess performance, we consider the diary measure to be the more reliable measure because performance rates were based on many observations (almost 14 on average) whereas the survey item measure was based on only one observation (for an argument against using binary measures (i.e., "success" vs. "failure") in prospective memory performance, see Graf & Uttl, 2001). We also consider the survey item to be an inferior measure of performance (compared to the diary measure) because in answering the survey item, parents relied on their retrospective memory for an event that might have occurred days or even weeks before. In contrast, the daily diary assessments minimized memory distortions that are known to increase for more distal events (e.g., da Costa & Baddeley, 1991).

## DISCUSSION

In the study reported here, our main goal was to examine evidence from real-life prospective memory tasks in children in order to evaluate two theses: 1) that motivation influences whether children remember to perform prospective memory tasks, and 2), that being highly motivated is especially important for younger children, potentially raising their performance to a level comparable to that older children. Our approach was to have parents report on their children's real prospective memory experiences in a daily diary over a two-week period. This technique has not, to our knowledge, been used in this field and has the advantage of tapping real-life experience, albeit indirectly through the eyes of a parent. We also directly asked parents about their child's prospective memory in an interview session, thus obtaining a secondary measure.

We found, as we expected, that higher task motivation (operationalized here as tasks viewed by children, according to their parents, as more important) was associated with better remembering of prospective memory tasks. This effect was observed in both the diary data and the interview data, and we suspect that when tasks are important to the child, the associated motivation causes higher rates of remembering to perform tasks. Of course, with our correlational design, we cannot rule out an opposite causal direction or the influence of an unmeasured third variable. However, in defense of our interpretation, we note that task importance effects on performance have also been demonstrated in many previous studies in which there was an experimental manipulation of task importance (e.g., Kliegel et al., 2004; Kvavilashvili, 1987; Marsh et al., 1998; Meacham & Singer, 1977), including several studies that demonstrated the effect in children (e.g., McCauley 2009, 2010, 2011; Somerville et al., 1983). Our findings converge with these and verify that the effect is detectable even in real-life events.

How does the importance with which tasks are viewed boost prospective memory performance in children? The present study did not address underlying mechanisms. However, the motivational-cognitive model of prospective memory described earlier in the chapter (see Figure 1) does propose such specific mechanisms. Our findings provide additional support for the central tenant of the model, that motivation (as relates to task importance or goal relevance) improves remembering to perform prospective memory tasks. Our results extend this claim, and therefore the model's application, to naturalistic prospective memory situations and also accord with results from other recent studies of children that have demonstrated performance boosts from task importance or goal activation (E.g., Marcovitch et al., 2007; McCauley et al., 2009, 2010, 2011). Together, these data justify extending the motivational-cognitive model of prospective memory to children, a prospect that offers opportunities for further testing of this model. For instance, the apparent decrease in the task importance factor between early and middle childhood requires attention as does the link between task importance and greater use of memory strategies.

Also as expected, we found that when it came to remembering tasks considered to be highly important (e.g., "Sleepover on Friday night"), children in first or second grade got the job done just as well as children in fourth or fifth grade. Younger children showed worse memory performance than older children when it came to less important tasks (e.g., "Get water bottle at school - to wash"). This pattern was replicated in parents' reports and in the single recalled prospective memory event during an interview. It seems that younger school-aged children are capable of very good prospective memory performance in their daily lives, and are in fact capable of performance on par with children two to four years older, when they consider the tasks to be meaningful. Therefore, we offer these results as new evidence in support of the second thesis put forth in this chapter, that motivation can affect whether younger children exhibit worse prospective memory performance than older children, and age-group differences can disappear for high importance tasks.

Our third prediction was for better overall prospective memory performance for older children than younger children although this effect had not been consistently found in the past. Parents' diary reports showed that the overall prospective memory performance rates did not differ for younger and older children. Analysis of the secondary measure of performance, from a survey item on a past prospective memory task, showed a higher reported performance rate for older children. However, the diary measure is the more reliable of the two measures (e.g., see Graf & Uttl, 2001). Therefore, we conclude that there was more evidence to suggest equivalent general performance rates for the age groups we studied. Having said that, it should also be noted that we do not interpret these findings to mean that there is no development of prospective memory performance in the age range studied (i.e., age seven through eleven). Instead, we acknowledge that performance differences for these two age groups may be revealed under certain circumstances and not others. In fact, the moderating effect of task importance on age effects exemplifies this possibility. Future research is needed to discover other factors (e.g., attributes of the task or the children) that moderate age-related improvements in prospective memory performance in children.

## Limitations

In addition to the limitations in our investigation that have already been described, there were several others. First, we relied on parents' reports of their children's real prospective memory behaviors and experiences. However, we attempted to minimize some of the usual shortcomings associated with this type of data collection method (e.g., biased retrospective reporting of events) by using structured diary forms completed nightly and also providing daily reminders for parents. In instructing parents, we also emphasized the need for objective, accurate reporting. For example, parents were instructed that we were interested in measuring real-life memory for intentions in children, no matter how inaccurate, and they were told to try to avoid biased reporting, for example not "enhancing" reports of their child's performance rates. Second, the naturalistic design we chose meant that we had less control over extraneous variables than would be the case in a controlled lab study. While we acknowledge this limitation, we would argue that this approach was necessary for our study's purposes, and the benefits gained by measuring real-life prospective memory tasks in children's lives outweighed these limitations. Additionally, we note that the two key performance findings from the current study (the main effect of importance and the interaction of importance and age-group) have also been found in controlled laboratory studies (e.g., Kliegel et al., 2010; Somerville et al., 1983).

# CONCLUSIONS

In conclusion, in this chapter we have presented two theses related to children's prospective memory performance (i.e., remembering to perform tasks such as turning in a homework assignment or taking a book to school for "show and tell"). The first thesis was that motivation is important in children's prospective performance, with enhanced motivation leading to enhanced prospective memory. The second thesis was that the level of motivation for a prospective memory task can affect whether age-group differences are seen in performance. Specifically, for important or valued tasks, younger children can sometimes show prospective memory abilities that are equivalent to those of older children. In reviewing extant evidence relevant to each of these theses, we concluded that both claims have empirical support although there has not been as much evidence supporting the second thesis. In the latter part of this chapter, we presented findings from a new study that generated parent reports of children's prospective memory activities in everyday life. Our results offered further support, from real prospective memory events, for the claim that task importance boosts performance in general and especially for younger children.

# REFERENCES

Altgassen, M., Kliegel, M., Brandimonte, M., & Filippello, P. (2010). Are older adults more social than younger adults? Social importance increases older adults' prospective memory performance. *Aging, Neuropsychology, and Cognition, 17*, 312 – 328.

Brandimonte, M. A., Ferrante, D., Bianco, C., & Villani, M. G. (2010). Memory for pro-social intentions: When competing motives collide. *Cognition, 114*, 436-441.

Ceci, S. J., & Bronfenbrenner, U. (1985). 'Don't forget to take the cupcakes out of the oven': Prospective memory, strategic time-monitoring, and context. *Child Development, 56*, 152-164

da Costa P. A., & Baddeley, A. D. (1991). Where did you park your car? Analysis of a naturalistic long-term recency effect. *European Journal of Cognitive Psychology, 3*, 297 - 313.

Einstein, G. O., & McDaniel, M. A. (1990). Normal aging and prospective memory. *Journal of Experimental Psychology: Learning, Memory, and Cognition, 16*, 717 – 726.

Graf, P., & Uttl, B. (2001). Prospective memory: A new focus of research. *Consciousness and Cognition, 10*, 437 – 450.

Guajardo., N. R., & Best, D. L. (2000). Do preschoolers remember what to do? Incentive and external cues in prospective memory. *Cognitive Development, 15*, 75 – 97.

Kliegel, M., Brandenberger, M., & Aberle, I. (2010). Effect of motivational incentives on prospective memory performance in preschoolers. *European Journal of Developmental Psychology, 7*, 223 – 232.

Kliegel, M., & Jager, T. (2007). The effects of age and cue-action reminders on event-based prospective memory performance in preschoolers. *Cognitive Development, 22*, 33 - 46.

Kliegel, M., Martin, M., McDaniel, M. A., & Einstein, G. O. (2004). Importance effects on performance in event-based prospective memory tasks. *Memory, 12*, 553 – 561.

Kruglanski, A. W., Shah, J. Y., Fishbach, A., Friedman, R., Chun, W. Y., & Sleeth-Keppler, D. (2002). A theory of goal systems. In M. P. Zanna (Ed.), *Advances in experimental social psychology* (Vol. 34, pp. 331-378). New York: Academic Press.

Kvavilashvili, L. (1987). Remembering intention as a distinct form of memory. *British Journal of Psychology, 78,* 507 – 518.

Kvavilashvili, L., Kyle, F. E., & Messer, D. J. (2008). The development of prospective memory in children: Methodological issues, empirical findings, and future directions. In M. Kliegel, M. A. McDaniel, & G. O. Einstein (Eds.), *Prospective memory: Cognitive, neuroscience, developmental, and applied perspectives* (pp. 115 – 140). Mahwah, NJ: Lawrence Erlbaum Associates.

Marcovitch,S., Boseovski, J. J., & Knapp, R. J. (2007). Use it or lose it: examining preschoolers' difficulty in maintaining and executing a goal. *Developmental Science, 10,* 559 – 564.

Marsh, R. L., Hicks, J. L., & Landau, J. D. (1998). An investigation of everyday prospective memory. *Memory & Cognition, 26,* 633 – 643.

McCauley, S. R., McDaniel, M. A., Pedroza, C., Chapman, S. B., & Levin, H. S. (2009). Incentive effects on event-based prospective memory performance in children and adolescents with traumatic brain injury. *Neuropsychology, 23,* 201 – 209.

McCauley, S. R., Pedroza, C., Chapman, S. B., Cook, L. G., Hotz, G., Vásquez, A. C., & Levin, H. S. (2010). Event-based prospective memory performance during subacute recovery following moderate to severe traumatic brain injury in children: Effects of monetary incentives. *Journal of the International Neuropsychological Society, 16,* 335 – 341.

McCauley, S. R., Pedroza, C., Chapman, S. B., Cook, L. G., Vásquez, A. C., & Levin, H. S. (2011). Monetary incentive effects on event-based prospective memory three months after traumatic brain injury in children. *Journal of Clinical and Experimental Neuropsychology, 33,* 639 – 646.

McDaniel, M. A., & Einstein, G. O. (2000). Strategic and automatic processes in prospective memory retrieval: A multiprocess framework. *Applied Cognitive Psychology, 14,* S127 - S144.

Meacham, J. A. (1982). A note on remembering to execute planned actions. *Journal of Applied Developmental Psychology, 3,* 121 – 133.

Meacham, J. A., & Kushner, S. (1980). Anxiety, prospective remembering, and performance of planned actions. *The Journal of General Psychology, 103,* 203-209.

Meacham, J. A., & Singer, J. (1977). Incentive effects in prospective remembering. *The Journal of Psychology, 97,* 191 – 197.

Miller, S. A., Manhal, M., & Mee, L. L. (1991). Parental beliefs, parental accuracy, and children's cognitive performance: A search for causal relations. *Developmental Psychology, 27,* 267 – 276.

Penningroth, S. L. (2005, July). *Strategy differences for remembering important and less important real-life intentions.* Paper presented at the International Conference on Prospective Memory, Zurich, Switzerland.

Penningroth, S. L., & Scott, W. D. (2007). A motivational-cognitive model of prospective memory: The influence of goal relevance In F. Columbus (Ed.), *Psychology of motivation,* (pp. 115 – 128). Hauppauge, NY: Nova Science Publishers, Inc.

Penningroth, S. L., Scott, W. D., & Freuen, M. (2011). Social motivation in prospective memory: Higher importance ratings and reported performance rates for social tasks. *Canadian Journal of Experimental Psychology, 65*, 3 – 11.

Sheeran, P., Webb, T.L., & Gollwitzer, P. M. (2005). The interplay between goal intentions and implementation intentions. *Personality and Social Psychology Bulletin, 31*, 87–98.

Somerville, S. C., Wellman, H. M., & Cultice, J. C. (1983). Young children's deliberate reminding. *The Journal of Genetic Psychology, 143*, 87 – 96.

Ward, H., Shum, D., McKinlay, L., Baker-Tweney, S., & Wallace, G. (2005). Development of prospective memory: Tasks based on the prefrontal-lob model. *Child Neuropsychology, 11*, 527 – 549.

Winograd, E. (1988). Some observations on prospective remembering. In M. M. Gruneberg, P. E. Morris, & R. N. Sykes (Eds.), *Practical aspects of memory: Current research and issues, Vol. 1: Memory in everyday life* (pp. 348 – 353). Oxford, England: John Wiley & Sons.

In: Psychology of Memory
Editors: Dannie M. Hendrix and Orval Holcomb

ISBN: 978-1-61942-633-7
© 2012 Nova Science Publishers, Inc.

*Chapter 9*

# MEASUREMENT OF PROSPECTIVE MEMORY: IMPORTANCE OF DELAY AND CONTINUOUS MEASURES

## *Bob Uttl*[*], *Joanna McDouall and Carrie A. Leonard*

Psychology Department, Mount Royal University, Canada

## ABSTRACT

The research on prospective memory (ProM) has generated many controversies (Uttl, 2005a, 2008, 2011). Many of these controversies can be traced to conceptual and methodological issues including a failure to distinguish between ProM proper vs. vigilance/monitoring; use of poor, unreliable, and inefficient measurement methods (i.e., binary success/failure measures); ceiling effects; low sample sizes; and low statistical power. In this chapter, we examine the following questions: Does the delay between ProM instructions and the appearance of the first cue decrease performance on ProM tasks as predicted from the theoretical distinction between ProM proper and vigilance/monitoring? Does the instruction to ongoing task delay reduce ProM performance? Does larger numbers of ProM cues convert ostensibly ProM proper task into vigilance/monitoring task? Is the instruction to ongoing task (IO) delay more important than the ongoing task start to the appearance of the first cue (OC) delay? The results of three studies (two quantitative reviews of previous literature and one experimental study) indicate that delays decrease ProM performance and are important for flushing the previously formed plan from examinees' consciousness, that larger numbers of ProM cues convert ProM tasks to vigilance/monitoring tasks, and that the IO delay appears to be more or at least as important as the OC delay. Our third study also indicates that the continuous measures of ProM are superior to the binary measures of ProM in widespread use; the continuous measures are more efficient, reliable, valid, and less likely affected by ceiling effects. The binary success/fail measures of ProM should be abandoned in favor of the continuous measures of ProM and, to measure ProM proper

---

[*] Correspondence concerning this article should be addressed to Bob Uttl, Department of Psychology, Mount Royal University, 4825 Mount Royal Gate SW, Calgary, AB, T3E 6K6, Canada. Email: buttl@mtroyal.ca or uttlbob@gmail.com

rather than vigilance/monitoring, researchers should include IO and OC delays to flush the previously formed plan from consciousness.

## INTRODUCTION

Prospective memory (ProM) is the ability to become aware of a previously formed plan at the right time and place (Brandimonte, Ferrante, Feresin, & Delbello, 2001; Graf & Uttl, 2001; Meacham & Leiman, 1982; Uttl, 2005a, 2008). For example, becoming aware that you previously made a plan to return borrowed money to Fred as you see Fred coming towards you in the hall or becoming aware that in the morning you made a plan to buy groceries as you are coming upon a supermarket on your way home from work. This latter typical situation is illustrated in Figure 1. We make a plan to get groceries en route home from work and then engage in various unrelated activities. The function of ProM is to bring this plan back to awareness at the right time and place in response to the ProM cue (e.g., supermarket) on our way home. However, as illustrated in Figure 1, success on the task – whether or not we bring all the groceries back home – depends not only on ProM but also on retrospective memory (RetM). Three outcomes are possible. We may become aware of the plan (ProM success), recall all the grocery items we planned to buy (RetM success), and succeed on the task. However, we may also fail the task for two different reasons: we may not become aware of the plan (ProM failure) and/or we may fail to recall all grocery items we planned to buy (RetM failure). Thus, to assess the contribution of ProM alone, it is critical to minimize the influence of the RetM component, for example, by minimizing demands on RetM and redefining success on the task as becoming aware of the previously made plan at the right time and place, rather than bringing home all the groceries (Graf & Uttl, 2001).

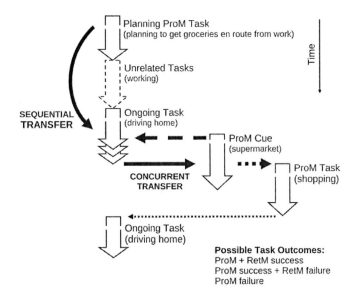

Figure 1. A typical situation requiring ProM proper. We make a plan to get groceries en route from work, engage in unrelated activities, and the ProM is responsible for bringing the plan back to consciousness at the right time and place, in response to the ProM cue (e.g., supermarket).

Graf and Uttl (2001) distinguished between different subdomains of ProM (cf. Harris, 1984): ProM proper (or episodic ProM), vigilance/monitoring, and habitual ProM. ProM proper brings back to awareness a previously formed plan at the right time and place; it "requires that we are aware of a plan of which meanwhile we have not been thinking, with the additional consciousness that we had made the plan earlier" (Graf & Uttl, 2001, p. 444). In contrast to ProM Proper, vigilance/monitoring scans the environment for cues to execute a plan that remains in consciousness and does not have to be brought back by the ProM cue. Lastly, habitual ProM brings back to awareness a previously formed plan at the right time and place and does so repeatedly whenever the appearance of the cue calls for plan execution. In contrast to vigilance/monitoring, however, with habitual ProM, the plan leaves consciousness between successive appearances of the ProM cues. As Table 1 illustrates, these subdomains parallel subdomains of retrospective (RetM) memory: short-term memory, long-term memory, and semantic memory. Researchers also distinguish between event-cued and time-cued ProM (Graf & Uttl, 2001; Harris, 1984; Uttl, 2005a, 2008). In event-cued ProM, the ProM cue is an event, for example, encountering Fred or noticing a supermarket. In time-cued ProM, the ProM cue is a specific time, for example, having a meeting at 11:00AM.

### Table 1. Subdomains of prospective and retrospective memory

| RetM | ProM |
|---|---|
| **Short-term memory**<br>Looking up and dialling phone number | **Vigilance/monitoring**<br>Preventing a bathtub from overflowing |
| **Long-term memory**<br>Encoding and recollecting previous events | **ProM Proper/Episodic ProM**<br>Buying groceries en route home |
| **Semantic memory**<br>Knowing facts, things, and procedures | **Habitual ProM**<br>Taking same medication every evening |

Reviewing the literature on ProM and aging, Uttl (2005a, 2008, 2011) has noted that ProM research is plagued by a number of conceptual and methodological problems including the failure to distinguish between vigilance/monitoring and ProM proper, widespread ceiling effects, low sample sizes, and low statistical power. Although most researchers endorse the distinction between ProM proper and vigilance/monitoring (Brandimonte et al., 2001; Graf & Uttl, 2001; Marsh, Hicks, Hancock, & Munsayac, 2002; McDaniel, Guynn, Einstein, & Breneiser, 2004; Shapiro & Krishnan, 1999; Uttl, 2005a, 2008), Uttl (2008) noted that only a few published studies explicitly state whether each study was concerned with vigilance/monitoring or ProM proper. One must carefully examine the method section to determine if a particular study investigated vigilance/monitoring or ProM proper, that is, whether it included a delay between ProM instructions and the ongoing task start and/or the first ProM cue. Researchers who include a delay between ProM instructions and the start of the ongoing task typically do so to ensure that the plan leaves participants' consciousness and that the ProM task measures episodic ProM rather than vigilance/monitoring. To illustrate, Marsh et al. (2002) explain: "this task was merely a distractor task placed between the prospective memory instruction and the onset of the rating [ongoing] task so that the prospective tasks did not become a vigilance task" (p. 304).

Surprisingly, a recent review of the delay effects on ProM performance (Martin, Brown, & Hicks, 2011) concluded that the effects of a delay between ProM instructions and the appearance of the ProM cue were "varied", suggesting that about half of the previous studies showed no delay effects (Brandimonte & Passolunghi, 1994; Einstein, Holland, McDaniel, & Guynn, 1992; Guajardo & Best, 2000; Guynn, McDaniel, & Einstein, 1998; Kvavilashvili, 1998; Nigro & Cicogna, 2000), another half showed declines (Loftus, 1971; Meacham & Leiman, 1982; Meier, Zimmermann, & Perrig, 2006; Scullin & McDaniel, 2010), and one study showed improvements in ProM performance (Hicks, Marsh, & Russell, 2000). However, Martin et al. (2011) focused only on whether or not the previous studies showed *statistically significant* differences due to delay manipulations and did not consider a possible lack of statistical power in many of these studies as a potential explanation for the null findings. Accordingly, a systematic quantitative review of previous research may yet find that a delay does decrease performance, consistent with the notion that ProM proper requires retrieval of the previously made plan whereas vigilance/monitoring does not.

Uttl (2005a, 2008) has also noted that almost without exception, ProM has been investigated using binary success/failure measures that are inefficient, unreliable, and often limited by ceiling or floor effects, causing many null findings. Indeed, the lack of reliability of binary success/failure measures has been lamented in the ProM literature for quite some time (Graf & Uttl, 2001; Kelemen, Weinberg, Alford, Mulvey, & Kaeochinda, 2006; Schmidt, Berg, & Deelman, 2001). In an attempt to resolve this measurement issue, Kelemen et al. (2006) studied the differences in the reliability of ProM tasks using 6 vs. 30 cues and found that the tasks with 30 cues were more reliable than the tasks with 6 cues. In turn, they suggested that the problem of low reliability has a straightforward solution: to increase the number of ProM cues and reduce performance levels in order to avoid ceiling effects (Uttl, 2005b). However, increasing the number of ProM cues may convert ostensibly ProM proper tasks to vigilance/monitoring tasks if the plan does not leave consciousness following the participant's response to the first ProM cue. Kelemen et al. (2006) examined this possibility and analyzed performance across the successive 6-item cue blocks in his 30 cue ProM task. Finding no monotonic increase in performance across the blocks, he concluded that the nature of the task was unchanged and continued to measure episodic ProM. Unfortunately, this conclusion is unwarranted in light of pervasive ceiling effects in Kelemen et al.'s data – performance in all five 6-item blocks was at the ceiling (the mean performance on the very first block was .89 and performance ranged from .85 to .92 across the five cue blocks). In turn, these severe ceiling effects made it nearly impossible to find monotonic increases in performance across the successive blocks statistically significant (Uttl, 2005b, 2008).

An alternative approach to increasing the reliability of ProM assessment as well as avoiding ceiling effects is to develop continuous measures of ProM. In 1999, we (Uttl & Graf, 1999) developed the first continuous measure of ProM proper based on a simple idea. Our approach employs ProM cues (pictures) whose intrusiveness (i.e., size) increases over time and the dependent variable is the cue size when a participant responds to it. Specifically, participants are shown a ProM cue – a picture of a helicopter or a teddy bear – and are told to stop whatever they are doing when they notice the ProM cue anytime and anywhere in the experiment. Participants are engaged in a series of attention-demanding tasks – sorting cards displayed on a computer monitor by pressing either left or right arrow keys. While sorting the cards, pictures of common objects appear in various sizes in the four quadrants of the screen and one picture is replaced with each key press. The ProM cue appears at random among these pictures. If a participant fails to notice the ProM cue, it appears again a few trials later, but this time in a larger size. The cue grows larger across trials until the participant detects it or until the maximum size is reached. In a series of experiments, we demonstrated that this method provides a valid and reliable index of ProM proper in both young and older adults (Graf, Uttl, & Dixon, 2002; Uttl, 2006). Extending this work, Uttl (2006) also developed an auditory continuous index of ProM: A ProM cue (sound) increases in intrusiveness (loudness) over time to the point of being impossible to ignore. As with the visual index, the auditory index of ProM proper also has high reliability and high validity in both young and older adults. Most recently, Uttl and Kibreab (2011) developed the first paper-and-pencil continuous measure of ProM proper. The ProM cue appeared in increasingly intrusive visual form (e.g., in bold, in capitals) and increasingly intrusive spatial location (e.g., at the end or beginning of an unrelated questionnaire). The reliability of two assessments was respectable at 0.71, generally much higher than the reliability of binary measures of ProM.

In this chapter, we report the results of three studies. The first one examines the effects of delay between ProM instructions and the appearance of the first ProM cue using a quantitative review of previous research. The second study, also relying on a quantitative review of the previous research, examines whether the instruction to ongoing task delay (IO delay) reduces performance and whether increasing the number of ProM cues would increase performance in ostensibly episodic ProM tasks. The third study investigates experimentally whether IO and the ongoing task start to the first cue appearance delay (OC delay) influences performance on ProM tasks.

## STUDY 1

The main objective of this study was to systematically review the literature on the effects of delay on ProM performance. Summarizing the previous literature on the effects of delay, Martin, Brown, and Hicks (2011) recently concluded that "the delay between intention formation and the opportunity for retrieval either negatively affects PM or has no effect." (p. 48). Unfortunately, Martin et al.'s review focused on whether the previous studies reported *statistically significant* delay effects and did not attempt to quantitatively synthesize the literature. Because the vast majority of studies of ProM are likely underpowered (Uttl, 2005a, 2008, 2011), the conclusion that delay has no effect on ProM performance may be an artifact of low statistical power.

## METHOD

### Sample of Studies

We searched for studies in several steps: First, the PsycLIT database was searched from the earliest available date to the end of July 2011 for the following terms: "prospective memory" and "memory for intentions". These two searches were combined with OR operator and then combined using AND operator with a search for all articles with "delay" as a keyword. Second, the references in several key studies (Martin, Brown, & Hicks, 2011) on the effects of delays on ProM were examined for potentially relevant articles. Third, the references in all relevant articles and book chapters, retrieved by any methods were examined for potentially relevant articles. Finally, a full text search of all potentially relevant articles was examined for studies that reported effects of delay on ProM.

Several studies that included ProM performance in different delay conditions were excluded because different ProM tasks were used in different delay conditions (Guajardo & Best, 2000; West, 1988), several ProM tasks were overlapping and/or participants were instructed for a second ProM task shortly before they were to act on the first ProM task (Cicogna, Nigro, Occhionero, & Esposito, 2005; Stone, Dismukes, & Remington, 2001). We also excluded a study by Guynn, McDaniel, and Einstein (1998); although Guynn et al. (1998) studied effects of delay on ProM and concluded that the delay did not affect ProM performance, they failed to report relevant performance data (e.g., condition means).

## RESULTS AND DISCUSSION

Table 2 shows delay effects contrasts including authors, year of publication, experiment, participants, number of participants per condition, condition, length of short delay (i.e., shortest reported), length of long delay (i.e., longest reported), mean performance in the short delay condition, mean performance in the long delay condition, delay effect, and notes. The delay effects contrasts are organized by task setting (lab, naturalistic) and ProM cue type (event cue, time cue).

Several aspects of the data shown in Table 2 are notable. First, most previous studies have investigated delay effects on event-cued ProM in laboratory settings and only a few studies have investigated effects of delay on time-cued ProM and/or ProM in naturalistic settings. Second, previous studies have used a wide variety of delay manipulations. Third, participants in most previous studies were undergraduate students, although a few studies were done with secondary school students, children, and older adults. Fourth, a substantial number of conditions suffer from either ceiling or floor effects (see Uttl, 2005a, 2008, 2011, for a discussion of this problem in studies of ProM and aging). Fifth, most of the studies used a very small number of participants and thus lacked enough statistical power to find even large delay effects (Uttl, 2005a, 2008). Notably, studies that used large samples found delay effects statistically significant (Loftus, 1971; Uttl & Kibreab, 2011). Finally, previous studies are heterogeneous in terms of many other design features including the number of ProM cues, type of ongoing task, and the type of delay manipulation. To illustrate, in some studies delay was manipulated by changing the instructions to ongoing task start delay (IO delay) by changing the ongoing task start to the first ProM cue appearance delay (OC delay), or both.

Figure 2 shows performance in the long delay condition as a function of performance in the short delay condition, by ProM cue type (event cue, time cue) and setting (lab, naturalistic) with the size of bubbles dependent on the study size (i.e., number of participants in each condition). To the extent to which the bubbles lie below the diagonal, delay manipulation decreased ProM performance. This figure highlights that in the vast majority of studies/conditions, performance was lower in the longer vs. shorter delay conditions. Only a small number of studies/conditions found improved performance with longer delays and most of them were reported in one article by Hicks and his colleagues (2000).

# Table 2. Summary of delay contrasts

| Study | Exp. | Participants | n | Condition Laboratory/ Event Cued | Short Delay (min) | Long Delay (min) | $M_{short}$ | $M_{long}$ | Effect | Note |
|---|---|---|---|---|---|---|---|---|---|---|
| **Single Cue** | | | | | | | | | | |
| Loftus (1971) | 1 | students+ | 50 | cue | 1 | 5 | 0.74 | 0.64 | - | |
| Loftus (1971) | 1 | students+ | 50 | no cue | 1 | 5 | 0.62 | 0.44 | - | |
| Nigro & Cicogna (2000) | 1 | students | 42 | | 10 | 20160 | 0.57 | 0.43 | - | |
| Nigro et al. (2002) | 1 | children | 20 | event cued | 5 | 10 | **0.90** | 0.70 | - | |
| Graf et al. (2002) | 1 | students | 18 | b&w cue | 6 | 20 | **0.84** | 0.54 | - | |
| Graf et al. (2002) | 1 | students | 18 | color cue | 6 | 20 | **0.90** | 0.74 | - | |
| Meier et al. (2006) | 2 | students | 40 | general | 5 | 45 | 0.55 | 0.30 | - | |
| Meier et al. (2006) | 2 | students | 40 | specific | 5 | 45 | 0.65 | 0.53 | - | |
| **Multiple Cues** | | | | | | | | | | |
| Einstein et al. (1992) | 1 | students | 12 | young/1 word | 15 | 30 | 0.58 | 0.42 | - | |
| Einstein et al. (1992) | 1 | students | 12 | young/4 words | 15 | 30 | 0.58 | 0.47 | - | |
| Einstein et al. (1992) | 1 | old adults | 12 | old/1 word | 15 | 30 | 0.53 | 0.61 | - | |
| Einstein et al. (1992) | 1 | old adults | 12 | old/4 words | 15 | 30 | **0.19** | **0.11** | - | |
| Brandimonte et al. (1994) | 1 | students | 16 | fam/non-dist. | 0 | 3 | 0.54 | 0.23 | - | |
| Brandimonte et al. (1994) | 1 | students | 16 | fam/dist. | 0 | 3 | 0.64 | 0.33 | - | |
| Brandimonte et al. (1994) | 1 | students | 16 | unfam/dist. | 0 | 3 | **0.98** | 0.51 | - | |
| Brandimonte et al. (1994) | 1 | students | 16 | unfam/non-dist. | 0 | 3 | 0.66 | 0.49 | - | |
| Brandimonte et al. (1994) | 3 | students* | 10 | information | 0 | 3 | 0.60 | **0.16** | - | |
| Brandimonte et al. (1994) | 3 | students* | 10 | no information | 0 | 3 | 0.60 | 0.25 | - | |
| Brandimonte et al. (1994) | 4 | students* | 10 | related activity | 0 | 3 | 0.73 | **0.10** | - | |
| Brandimonte et al. (1994) | 4 | students* | 10 | unrel. Activity | 0 | 3 | 0.73 | 0.19 | - | |
| Brandimonte et al. (1994) | 5 | students* | 10 | practice | 0 | 3 | 0.71 | 0.19 | - | |
| Brandimonte et al. (1994) | 5 | students* | 10 | unfilled delay | 0 | 3 | 0.71 | 0.56 | - | |
| Brandimonte et al. (1994) | 5 | students* | 10 | artic, suppression | 0 | 3 | 0.71 | 0.71 | = | |
| Brandimonte et al. (1994) | 5 | students* | 10 | motor suppression | 0 | 3 | 0.71 | **0.20** | - | |
| Kvavilashvili (1998) | 2 | students | 20 | no information | 0 | 5 | 0.75 | 0.73 | - | |
| Kvavilashvili (1998) | 2 | students | 20 | information | 0 | 5 | 0.85 | 0.73 | - | |
| Hicks et al. (2000) | 1a | students | 15 | pleasantness rating | 2.5 | 15 | **0.18** | 0.32 | + | a |
| Hicks et al. (2000) | 1a | students | 15 | syllable counting | 2.5 | 15 | **0.20** | 0.39 | + | a |
| Hicks et al. (2000) | 1b | students | 12 | pleasantness rating | 2.5 | 15 | 0.38 | 0.63 | + | a |
| Hicks et al. (2000) | 1b | students | 12 | syllable counting | 2.5 | 15 | 0.44 | 0.60 | + | a |
| Hicks et al. (2000) | 3 | students | 24 | one task | 2.5 | 15 | 0.52 | 0.66 | + | a |

## Table 2. (Continued)

| Study | Exp. | Participants | n | Condition | Short Delay (min) | Long Delay (min) | $M_{short}$ | $M_{long}$ | Effect | Note |
|---|---|---|---|---|---|---|---|---|---|---|
| Hicks et al. (2000) | 3 | students | 24 | five tasks | 2.5 | 15 | 0.59 | 0.79 | + | a |
| Jinquan et al. (2003) | 1 | | 61 | | 0 | 57 | 0.63 | 0.40 | - | |
| Scullin & McDaniel (2010) | 1 | students | 24 | morning | 20 | 720 | 0.48 | **0.17** | - | |
| Scullin & McDaniel (2010) | 1 | students | 24 | evening | 20 | 720 | 0.47 | 0.37 | - | |
| Martin et al. (2011) | 1 | students | 31 | short filler | 3 | 18 | **0.18** | **0.15** | - | a |
| Martin et al. (2011) | 1 | students | 31 | long filler | 3 | 18 | 0.36 | **0.12** | - | a |
| Martin et al. (2011) | 1 | students | 31 | short ongoing | 3 | 18 | **0.18** | 0.36 | + | a |
| Martin et al. (2011) | 1 | students | 31 | long ongoing | 3 | 18 | **0.15** | **0.12** | - | a |
| **Single Cue** | | | | **Laboratory/Time-Cued** | | | | | | |
| Nigro et al (2002) | 1 | children | 20 | time cued | 5 | 10 | 0.55 | **0.05** | - | |
| **Single Cue** | | | | **Naturalistic/Event-Cued** | | | | | | |
| Somerville et al. (1983) | 1 | 2 years old | 10 | 2 years old/high interest | 3 | 360 | **0.80** | 0.50 | - | |
| Somerville et al. (1983) | 1 | 3 years old | 10 | 3 years old/high interest | 3 | 360 | 0.60 | 0.50 | - | |
| Study | Exp. | Participants | n | Condition | Short Delay (min) | Long Delay (min) | $M_{short}$ | $M_{long}$ | Effect | Note |
| Somerville et al. (1983) | 1 | 4 years old | 10 | 4 years old/high interest | 3 | 360 | **0.80** | 0.60 | - | |
| Somerville et al. (1983) | 1 | 2 years old | 10 | 2 years old/low interest | 3 | 360 | **0.20** | **0.00** | - | |
| Somerville et al. (1983) | 1 | 3 years old | 10 | 3 years old/low interest | 3 | 360 | 0.30 | **0.20** | - | |
| Somerville et al. (1983) | 1 | 4 years old | 10 | 4 years old/low interest | 3 | 360 | **0.20** | 0.30 | + | |
| **Single Cue** | | | | **Naturalistic/Time-Cued** | | | | | | |
| Meacham & Leiman (1982) | 1 | students | 7 | eight cards/tag | 2880 | 8640 | **1.00** | **1.00** | = | |
| Meacham & Leiman (1982) | 1 | students | 7 | eight cards/no tag | 2880 | 8640 | **0.83** | 0.67 | - | |
| Meacham & Leiman (1982) | 1 | students | 7 | four cards/tag | 2880 | 14400 | **1.00** | 0.71 | - | |
| Meacham & Leiman (1982) | 1 | students | 7 | four cads/no tag | 2880 | 14400 | **0.86** | **1.00** | + | |
| Meacham & Leiman (1982) | 2 | students | 7 | long interval/no tag | 2880 | 14400 | **1.00** | **1.00** | = | |
| Meacham & Leiman (1982) | 2 | students | 7 | long interval/tag | 2880 | 14400 | 0.87 | 0.62 | - | |
| Meacham & Leiman (1982) | 2 | students | 7 | short interval/tag | 2880 | 8640 | **1.00** | 0.57 | - | |
| Meacham & Leiman (1982) | 2 | students | 7 | short interval/no tag | 2880 | 8640 | **1.00** | **0.86** | - | |

| Study | Exp. | Participants | n | Condition | Short Delay (min) | Long Delay (min) | $M_{short}$ | $M_{long}$ | Effect | Note |
|---|---|---|---|---|---|---|---|---|---|---|
| Meacham & Leiman (1982) | 2 | students | 7 | delayed short interval/no tag | 25920 | 31680 | **0.86** | **0.86** | = | |
| Meacham & Leiman (1982) | 2 | students | 7 | delayed short interval/no tag | 25920 | 31680 | 0.57 | 0.71 | + | |
| Meacham & Leiman (1982) | 2 | students | 7 | short interval/no tag/first date | 2880 | 20160 | **1.00** | **0.86** | - | |
| Meacham & Leiman (1982) | 2 | students | 7 | short interval/tag/first date | 2880 | 20160 | **0.94** | 0.57 | - | |
| Uttl & Kibreab (2011) | 1 | students | 240 | email | 4320 | 10080 | 0.35 | 0.25 | - | |

Note. Students+: sample included non-students; students*: secondary school students; Effect: - decline; = equal, + increase; a: ProM instructions included information about during which task ProM cues would occur. Means printed in bold are afflicted by severe ceiling or floor effects.

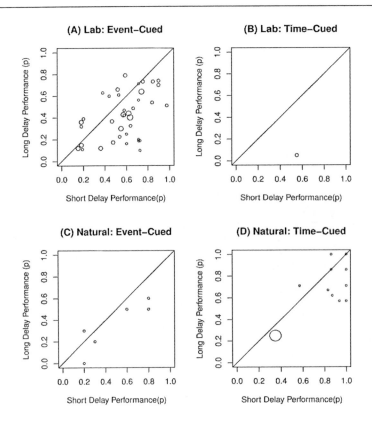

Figure 2. Performance in long delay conditions as a function of performance in short delay conditions for event-cued and time-cued ProM assessed in laboratory settings (Panels A and B) and for event-cued and time-cued ProM assessed in naturalistic settings (Panels C and D). The bubble sizes indicate the study/condition sizes.

For the only condition with sufficient data to conduct meaningful inferential analysis (event cued ProM assessed in laboratory settings), a sign test indicated that delay decreased ProM performance with 29 declines, 8 improvements, and 1 tie, $p < .001$.

This robust meta-analysis indicates that, like with retrospective memory, the delay between ProM instructions and start of the ongoing task (IO Delay) and/or delay between start of the ongoing task and the appearance of the first cue (OC Delay) decreases ProM performance, at least for event cued ProM assessed in laboratory conditions. The review also highlights that previous studies focusing on the effects of delay on ProM performance have been seriously underpowered and too often limited by ceiling and floor effects. In turn, they have failed to find the effects of delay statistically significant.

## STUDY 2

In reviewing the literature on ProM and aging, Uttl (2005a, 2008) noted that many studies of ProM did not include any delay between instructions and ongoing task start (IO delay) and most likely in this case studied vigilance/monitoring rather than ProM proper. In contrast, other researchers typically included a 5 to 15 minute IO delay to ensure that the ProM plan left participants' consciousness. Accordingly, if an IO delay reduces performance, we should see lower performance in studies with an IO delay than in studies without an IO delay.

Moreover, in an attempt to increase the reliability of ProM measures, many investigators have presented participants with multiple cues (i.e., the same cue presented, for example, 8 times throughout the duration of the ongoing task) rather than with just a single ProM cue (Kelemen et al., 2006; Uttl, 2005a, 2008). However, this strategy is likely to convert an ostensibly ProM proper task to a measure of vigilance/monitoring as a participant may effortfully monitor for ProM cues once they detect the first one. If so, ProM performance should be high in studies without an IO delay regardless of the number of ProM cues. In contrast, in studies with an IO delay, performance should be low in single ProM cue studies and should increase in studies with a greater number of ProM cues. We examined these predictions with an archival study of ProM performance means reported in previous studies of ProM. We searched for studies of ProM that used normal healthy adults, extracted various condition means, and for each extracted mean, we recorded the IO delay and the number of ProM cues associated with that mean.

# METHOD

## Sample of Studies

We searched for studies in several steps: First, the PsycLIT database was searched from the earliest available date to the end of July 2011 for the following terms: "prospective memory" and "memory for intentions" and these two searches were combined with OR operator. Second, we hand searched all retrieved articles for studies reporting performance on ProM with normal (healthy) younger adults (i.e., we excluded aging studies, studies of neuropsychological disorders, etc.). For each eligible study, we extracted all reported condition performance means and, for each extracted mean, we recorded the IO delay length and the number of ProM cues presented during the ongoing task. Here, we report preliminary results based on an analysis of the first 589 condition means extracted from 63 eligible ProM articles.

# RESULTS AND DISCUSSION

The number of ProM cues used to assess ProM in various studies and conditions ranged from 1 to 128, with 70% of the means based on 10 or fewer cues. Accordingly, we limited our analyses to studies and conditions with up to 30 ProM cues. Thirty or fewer cues were used in 82% of all studies and conditions.

Figure 3 shows ProM performance as a function of the number of cues for all data (Panel A), means from conditions with no IO delay (Panel B), and means from conditions with IO delay (Panel C). As expected, for studies with no IO delay, ProM performance was very high in studies with a single ProM cue and dropped off slightly in studies with more than one cue. In contrast, for studies with an IO delay, ProM performance was very low in single cue studies and rapidly increased in studies with multiple ProM cues, with increases reduced for studies with more than nine cues. These observations were confirmed using multiple regression analyses. For studies with no IO delay, neither linear nor quadratic trend coefficients reached significance, $t(134) = -1.62$, $p = .108$, and $t(134) = 1.36$, $p = .177$, respectively (multiple $R^2 = 0.02$). For studies with IO delay, both linear and quadratic trend coefficients were significant, $t(440) = 7.63$, $p < .001$, and $t(440) = -5.35$, $p < .001$, respectively (multiple $R^2 = .16$).

These preliminary findings are consistent with the prediction that an IO delay can flush the plan from one's consciousness. Without an IO delay, the plan remains in consciousness at the start of the ongoing task, participants monitor for ProM cues, and performance on even the first few cues is very high. In contrast, an IO delay is capable of flushing the plan from one's consciousness; it then has to be brought back in response to a ProM cue, and performance on the very first cue is low. Moreover, performance increases as the task includes more and more ProM cues, consistent with the notion that once a participant responds to a ProM cue, he or she is reminded of the plan, the plan remains in consciousness during a relatively short inter-cue interval, and the task is converted to a vigilance/monitoring task for all subsequent ProM cues.

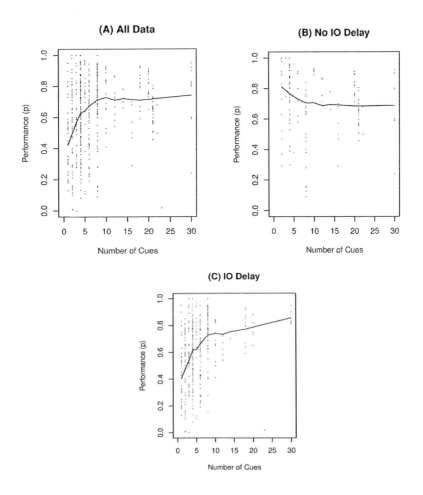

Figure 3. Mean performance on ProM tasks as a function of a number of ProM cues for all data, conditions with no IO delay, and conditions with IO delay.

# STUDY 3

In combination, the two studies above suggest that the delay between ProM instructions and the first ProM cue reduces ProM performance. The second study strongly suggests that an IO delay can flush the plan from one's consciousness but that the use of multiple cues helps to maintain the plan in consciousness and converts a task to vigilance/monitoring rather than ProM.

The main objective of the third study was to investigate experimentally the effect of both IO and OC delay on ProM performance. The second objective was to develop a new continuous measure of ProM and to examine the effects of IO and OC delays using this new continuous measure. We developed a new continuous measure of ProM patterned after the measures developed by Uttl and his colleagues (Graf et al., 2002; Uttl, 2006; Uttl & Kibreab, 2011). For the present study, participants were instructed to circle any and all occurrences of a ProM cue while working through various questionnaires. The ProM cue appeared 11 times in an increasingly intrusive font size. The first ProM cue circled was used as an index of ProM ability. To examine the test-retest reliability of this new measure, each participant completed two assessments within a single test session.

# METHOD

## Participants and Design

Participants were 278 undergraduate students who participated for course credit (67% women, 33% men). The first language of the majority of participants was English (92%).

The design had two between subjects factors: Instruction to Ongoing Task Delay (IO Delay) (No IO Delay, IO Delay) and Ongoing Task to the first ProM Cue Delay (OC Delay) (No OC Delay, OC Delay). Participants were randomly assigned to the four conditions: 67 were assigned to No IO/No OC Delay, 71 were assigned to No IO/OC Delay, 74 were assigned to IO/No OC Delay, and 66 were assigned to IO/OC Delay.

## Procedure

Participants were tested in small groups, in a single session lasting 120 minutes, as part of a larger study. They were tested in a small classroom, seated widely separated. After providing written consent and basic demographic information, they completed the set of tasks listed in Table 3. The table shows the order of the tasks as well as approximate time required to complete each task. In this paper, we report only the effect of IO and OC delays on ProM performance and test-retest reliability of the new continuous ProM measures.

For the first ProM assessement, we embedded 11 ProM cues within the 300-item IPIP NEO PI-R personality inventory (www.ipip.ori.org) designed to measure NEO PI-R factors and facets and added 19 fillers (from IPIP personality item database) to ensure that each page of this 23 page instrument (including the instruction page) had 15 personality items. For the second ProM assessment, we embedded 11 ProM cues within the 240 NEO PI-R (Costa &

McCrae, 1992) and added 79 fillers (also selected from IPIP personality item database). The ProM cue became progressively larger and more intrusive on each successive page (the smallest cue size was 12 pts and the largest cue size was 28 pts). If an examinee detected the very first cue, he or she obtained a score of 1; if the examinee detected the last cue, he or she obtained a score of 11; and if the examinee did not detect any cues, he or she obtained a score of 12. Figure 4 shows the sequence of ProM cue sizes.

### Table 3. Experiment 3: Sequence of tasks

| Assessment Instrument | Approximate Time (min) |
|---|---|
| Demographics (age, sex, first language) | 1 |
| Math verification | 4 |
| Cancel H | 3 |
| Verbal Learning Test (Uttl, 2006) | 10 |
| Cancel Arrows | 3 |
| ProM Instructions 1 (ProM cue: "close") | 1 |
| Words/A40 in 5 min IO Delay condition only | 7 |
| ProM Assessment #1 (IPIP NEO PI-R) (0 vs. 15 min OC Delay) | 35 |
| Words/A40 in 0 min IO Delay condition only | (7) |
| Words/B40 | 7 |
| ProM Instructions 2 (ProM cue: "above") | 1 |
| SILS Vocabulary in 5 min IO Delay condition only | 7 |
| ProM Assessment #2 (NEO PI-R) (0 vs. 15 min OC Delay) | 35 |
| SILS Vocabulary: 0 min IO Delay condition only | (7) |
| Total | 114 |

Note. Times in parentheses are not counted in total because the assessment is given only once, either before or after ProM assessment.

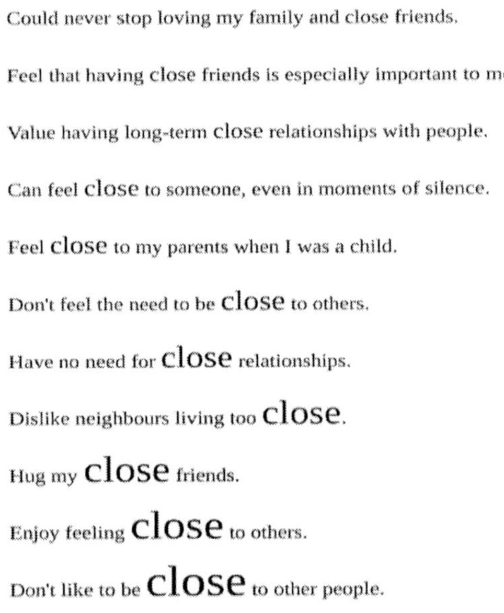

Could never stop loving my family and close friends.

Feel that having close friends is especially important to me.

Value having long-term close relationships with people.

Can feel close to someone, even in moments of silence.

Feel close to my parents when I was a child.

Don't feel the need to be close to others.

Have no need for close relationships.

Dislike neighbours living too close.

Hug my close friends.

Enjoy feeling close to others.

Don't like to be close to other people.

Figure 4. Study 3: ProM cue size sequence (1st Assessment). ProM cue became progressively large and more intrusive on each successive page (the smallest cue size was 12 pts and the largest cue size was 28 pts).

The ProM instructions for the first assessment were as follows:

> We want to examine your ability to do something in future. Thus, if you encounter the word *close* at any point during this experiment, please circle it. You will not be reminded again but it is important that you circle any and all occurrences of the word *close*. Please copy the following sentence below in your hand writing so that we are sure you did not miss these instructions: "I am to circle all occurrences of the word *close*."

Following the ProM instructions, participants either proceeded directly to the IPIP NEO PI-R modified as described above (No IO Delay condition) or they first completed a 40-item multiple choice word knowledge test Words/A40 (Uttl, 2006) for about 7 minutes (IO Delay condition). The IPIP NEO PI-R presented participants with brief instructions on the first page followed by actual IPIP items on pages 2 to 23. In the No OC Delay condition, the first cue appeared on the second page, immediately after the IPIP instruction page. In the OC Delay condition, the first cue appeared on the 13th page, or about 15 minutes later.

The second ProM instruction and assessment was identical with the following exceptions: (1) the ProM cue word was "above", and (2) NEO PI-R (modified) was used instead of IPIP NEO PI-R.

## RESULTS AND DISCUSSION

Figure 5 shows the size of the first detected ProM cue on the first ProM assessment by IO and OC Delays, with error bars indicating 95% confidence intervals on the individual means. Participants in the only no delay condition were able to detect smaller ProM cues (performance was at the ceiling) than participants in the delayed conditions. Two planned tests revealed that both IO and OC delays reduced ProM performance relative to the No IO/No OC Delay condition, $t(139) = 3.01$, $p < .003$, and $t(136) = 2.53$, $p = .012$, respectively. Thus, consistent with both ProM proper vs. vigilance/monitoring requiring retrieval of the previously formed plan and quantitative summaries of the previous research, performance was worse (participants required larger ProM cues) in all conditions with delay between ProM instructions and the appearance of the first cue.

Moreover, consistent with prior research findings (Graf et al., 2002; Uttl, 2006; Uttl & Kibreab, 2011), ProM performance improved on the second ($M = 2.18$, $SD = 1.24$) vs. first ProM ($M = 2.82$, $SD = 1.81$) assessment, $t(275) = 6.90$, $p < .001$. Although the performance on the second ProM assessment was limited by ceiling effects, the test-retest reliability (correlations between the first and second assessment) ranged from .49 in the No IO/No OC Delay condition (the most limited by ceiling effects) to .62 in the IO/OC Delay condition (the least limited by ceiling effects). Using the Spearman-Brown prediction formula, the reliability of the average of the two assessments is expected to be .77, very respectable. In contrast, the test-retest reliability for binary success/failure measure (i.e., whether or not participants responded to the very first cue) ranged from .07 to .35. Thus, these new continuous paper-and-pencil measures of ProM have favorable characteristics and distributions, are more reliable, and are likely to be more useful for assessment of individual differences in ProM than widely used binary success/failure measures.

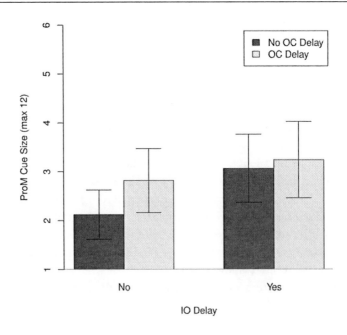

Figure 5. Study 3: ProM cue size required for ProM response by IO delay and OC delay. The bars indicate 95% Confidence Intervals for condition means.

## CONCLUSION

The first study, a quantitative review of the previous literature on the delay effects in ProM, revealed that the delays between ProM instruction and the appearance of the first ProM cue decreased ProM performance, at least for event-cued ProM assessed in the laboratory. The second study, also a quantitative analysis of the previously published data, revealed that (1) the IO delay substantially decreased performance on the first few cues and (2) that ProM performance in the studies with an IO delay increases monotonically with the number of ProM cues used to assess ProM, strongly suggesting that the nature of the task changed from assessment of ProM proper to assessment of vigilance/monitoring. These findings are consistent with the prediction that multiple cues help maintain the intention in consciousness and convert a nominally ProM proper task to a vigilance/monitoring task (Graf & Uttl, 2001; Uttl, 2005a, 2008). Finally, the third experimental study with continuous measures of ProM found that both the IO and OC delays decrease ProM performance, as expected from the theoretical distinction between ProM proper and vigilance/monitoring (Brandimonte et al., 2001; Graf & Uttl, 2001; Uttl, 2008). Moreover, the 7-minute IO delay seems to be more detrimental to ProM performance than the 15-minute OC delay, contrary to recent claims by Martin et al. (2011). Critically, the third study also demonstrated that continuous measures of ProM are far more reliable than binary success/failure measures and that the average of the two assessments displays sufficient reliability for measurement of individual differences in ProM in individual difference studies (Graf et al., 2002; Uttl, 2005a, 2008; Uttl & Kibreab, 2011).

Our findings suggest that researchers who wish to investigate ProM proper rather than vigilance/monitoring are best advised to include IO and/or OC delays to flush the plan from participants' consciousness. They also strongly suggest that increasing the number of ProM cues in an attempt to increase the reliability of ProM measures is an ill-advised strategy. Figure 3 Panel 3 highlights that in studies with multiple cues performance increases rapidly for each successive cue, reaching ceiling-limited performance by the third cue in many studies. We believe that a productive strategy is to employ continuous measures of ProM such as the one used in our third study or in our previous studies. The newly developed, easily administered paper-and-pencil continuous measure of ProM used in our third study has favorable psychometric properties when compared to binary success/failure measure.

## ACKNOWLEDGMENTS

We thank Amy L. Siegenthaler and Alain Morin for careful reading and comments on the manuscript. This research was supported by NSERC Discovery Grant to Bob Uttl.

## REFERENCES

Brandimonte, M. A., & Passolunghi, M. C. (1994). The effect of cuefamiliarity, cue-distinctiveness, and retention interval on prospective remembering. *Q. J. Exp. Psychol. A*, *47*(3), 565-587.

Brandimonte, M., Ferrante, D., Feresin, C., & Delbello, R. (2001). Dissociating prospective memory from vigilance processes. *Psicologica*, *22*(1), 97-113.

Cicogna, P., Nigro, G., Occhionero, M., & Esposito, M. (2005). Time-based prospective remembering: Interference and facilitation in a dual task. *Journal of Cognitive Psychology*, *17*(2), 221-240.

Costa, P. T., & McCrae, R. R. (1992). *Revised NEO Personality inventory (NEO PI-R) and NEO five-factor inventory (NEO-FFI): Professional manual*. Odessa, FL: Psychological Assessment Resources.

Einstein, G., Holland, L., McDaniel, M., & Guynn, M. (1992). Age-related deficits in prospective memory: The influence of task complexity. *Psychology and Aging*, *7*(3), 471-478.

Graf, P., & Uttl, B. (2001). Prospective memory: A new focus for research. *Consciousness Cognition*, *10*, 437-450.

Graf, P., Uttl, B., & Dixon, R. A. (2002). Prospective and Retrospective Memory in Adulthood. *In: Graf P, Ohta N., eds. Lifespan Development of Human Memory* (pp. 255-282). London: The MIT Press.

Guajardo, N., & Best, D. (2000). Do preschoolers remember what to do? Incentive and external cues in prospective memory. *Cognitive Development*, *15*(1), 75-97.

Guynn, M., McDaniel, M., & Einstein, G. (1998). Prospective memory: When reminders fail. *Memory & Cognition*, *26*(2), 287-298.

Harris, J. E. (1984). Remembering to do things: A forgotten topic. *In: Haris JE, Morris PE, eds. Everyday memory: Actions and absentmindedness* (pp. 71-92). London: Academic Press.

Hicks, J L, Marsh, R. L., & Russell, E. J. (2000). The properties of retention intervals and their affect on retaining prospective memories. *Journal of Experimental Psychology. Learning, Memory, and Cognition, 26*(5), 1160-1169.

Kelemen, W., Weinberg, W., Alford, H., Mulvey, E., & Kaeochinda, K. (2006). Improving the reliability of event-based laboratory tests of prospective memory. *Psychonomic Bulletin & Review, 13*(6), 1028-1032.

Kvavilashvili, L. (1998). Remembering intentions: Testing a new method of investigation. *Applied Cognitive Psychology, 12*(6), 533-554.

Loftus, E. F. (1971a). Memory for intentions: The effect of presence of a cue and interpolated activity. *Psychonomic Science, 23*(4), 315-316.

Marsh, R., Hicks, J., Hancock, T., & Munsayac, K. (2002). Investigating the output monitoring component of event-based prospective memory performance. *Memory & Cognition, 30*(2), 302-311.

Martin, B. A., Brown, N. L., & Hicks, J. L. (2011). Ongoing task delays affect prospective memory more powerfully than filler task delays. *Canadian Journal of Experimental Psychology = Revue Canadienne De Psychologie Expérimentale, 65*(1), 48-56.

McDaniel, M., Guynn, M., Einstein, G., & Breneiser, J. (2004). Cue-focused and reflexive-ssociative processes in prospective memory retrieval. *Journal of Experimental Psychology, 30*(3), 605-614.

Meacham, J. A., & Leiman, B. (1982). Remembering to perform future actions. *Memory observed: Remembering in natural contexts* (pp. 327-336). San Francisco, CA, US: Freeman.

Meier, B., Zimmermann, T., & Perrig, W. (2006). Retrieval experience in prospective memory: Strategic monitoring and spontaneous retrieval. *Memory, 14*(7), 872-889.

Nigro, G., & Cicogna, P. (2000). Does delay affect prospective memory performance? *European Psychologist, 5*(3), 228-233.

Schmidt, I., Berg, I., & Deelman, B. (2001). Prospective memory training in older adults. *Educational Gerontology, 27*(6), 455-478.

Scullin, M. K., & McDaniel, M. A. (2010). Remembering to execute a goal: sleep on it! *Psychological Science, 21*(7), 1028-1035.

Shapiro, S., & Krishnan, H. (1999). Consumer memory for intentions: A prospective memory perspective. *Journal of Experimental Psychology, 5*(2), 169-189.

Stone, M., Dismukes, K., & Remington, R. (2001). Prospective memory in dynamic environments: Effects of load, delay, and phonological rehearsal. *Memory, 9*(3), 165-176.

Uttl, B. (2005a). Age-Related Changes in Event-Cued Prospective Memory Proper. *In: Ohta N, MacLeod CM, Uttl B, eds. Dynamic Cognitive Processes* (pp. 273-303). Tokyo: Springer.

Uttl, B. (2005b). Measurement of Individual Differences: Lessons from Memory Assessment in Research and Clinical Practice. *Psychological Science, 16*, 460-467.

Uttl, B. (2006). Age-related changes in event-cued visual and auditory prospective memory proper. *Aging, Neuropsychology, and Cognition, 13*(2), 141-172.

Uttl, B. (2008). Transparent meta-analysis of prospective memory and aging. *PLoS ONE, 3*(2), e1568.

Uttl, B. (2011). Transparent meta-analysis: does aging spare prospective memory with focal vs. non-focal cues? *PloS One, 6*(2), e16618.

Uttl, B., & Graf, P. (1999, November). Pro- and retro-spective memory. Los Angeles, CA: Psychonomic Society.

Uttl, B., & Kibreab, M. (2011). Self-report measures of prospective memory are reliable but not valid. *Canadian Journal of Experimental Psychology = Revue Canadienne De Psychologie Expérimentale, 65*(1), 57-68.

West, R. L. (1988). Prospective memory and aging. *In: Gruneberg MM, Morris PE, Sykes RN, eds. Practical aspects of memory: Current research and issues, Vol. 1: Memory in everyday life.* (pp. 119-125). New York: John Wiley & Sons.

# INDEX

## F

## G

## T

## U